COOL GRAY
CITY OF LOVE

BY THE SAME AUTHOR

Shadow Knights: The Secret War Against Hitler

COOL GRAY CITY OF LOVE

49 VIEWS OF SAN FRANCISCO

GARY KAMIYA

BLOOMSBURY

NEW YORK · LONDON · NEW DELHI · SYDNEY

Published by Bloomsbury USA, New York

All papers used by Bloomsbury USA are natural, recyclable products made from
wood grown in well-managed forests. The manufacturing processes conform to the
environmental regulations of the country of origin.

LIBRARY OF CONGRESS CATALOGING-IN-PUBLICATION DATA

Kamiya, Gary.
Cool Gray City of Love : 49 Views of San Francisco /
Gary Kamiya. —1st U.S. edition.
pages cm
Includes bibliographical references.
ISBN 978-1-60819-960-0 (hc : alk. paper) 1. San Francisco (Calif.)—
Guidebooks.   2. Walking—California—San Francisco—Guidebooks.
3. Historic sites—California—San Francisco—Guidebooks.   I. Title.
F869.S33K35 2013
917.94'6104—dc23
2013014527

First U.S. Edition 2013

1 3 5 7 9 10 8 6 4 2

Typeset by Westchester Book Group
Printed and bound in the U.S.A. by Thomson-Shore, Inc., Dexter, Michigan

TO JONATHAN ALFORD,
FOR A LIFETIME OF FRIENDSHIP

AND TO MY CHILDREN, ZACHARY AND CELESTE

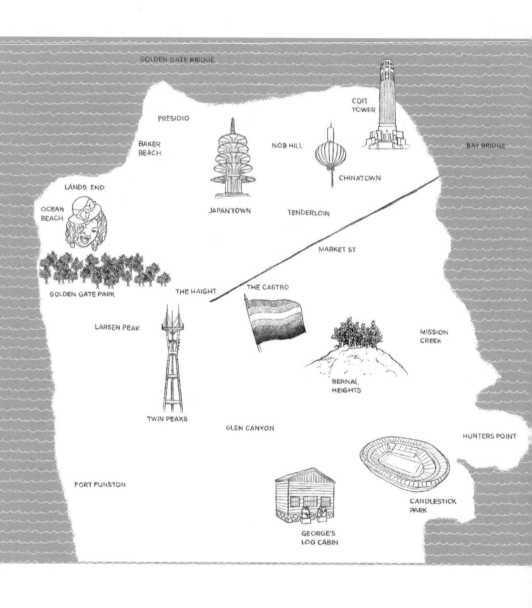

CONTENTS

PREFACE

This book begins and ends with walking. Its spirit is ambulatory—the product of the countless explorations I have made across San Francisco on foot. I began those wanderings more than 40 years ago, but only in the past 2 years have they assumed the obsessive form that has led my friends to hide when I come calling, chirpily announcing another thrill-packed excursion to the Outer Mission.

Blame it on titanium. For most of the past two decades, my knees were so shot that I could not walk without pain. You learn to work around chronic pain, but you lose certain things you are not even aware of. One of them is whims. A whimless city is a diminished city, a city whose mysteries are kept under lock and key, a city that repeats itself like a scratched record. After I had my knees replaced, San Francisco became endless and enticing. Like an iron-jointed butterfly, I began flitting around town—at first aimlessly, then systematically. And so it was that one fall day, after dropping off my daughter at her high school a block from that endearingly city-soaked rectangle of green called the Panhandle, I decided to finally learn Golden Gate Park.

I should have known the great park better. I'd been going there forever. But every time I got off the beaten trail, I got lost. The problem was that I'd never tried to learn it in a systematic way. Golden Gate Park is so big—at 1,017 acres, it's 20 percent larger than Central Park, and much more overgrown and opaque—that if you don't approach it methodically, you'll just keep forgetting whatever you learned. So I divided it up into rough grids and started exploring.

It took about 20 days, walking an hour or two a day with my dog, to cover just about every part of the park. It was glorious and addictive, making new discoveries every day. I savored the mingled pleasure of the mapmaker and the outlaw. I was Tom Sawyer *and* Huck Finn—one part of me greedily storing up information, the other blissfully absorbing experiences that had not yet blazed trails through the forest of my neurons. I discovered that systematic flitting, if not the secret to human happiness, is a pretty good start.

My park voyage turned out to be a dry run, an experiment on a bite-size part of San Francisco. For I had so much fun that when I was done, I decided to do the same thing with the rest of the city. I set out to "do the Knowledge" for San Francisco.

"Doing the Knowledge" is an expression used by London taxi drivers. To get a license, hacks must learn every single street in that vast metropolis— and as anyone who has ever looked at the endless map-book *London A to Z* knows, that is a feat that would tax even Funes the Memorious, the character in the Borges story who never forgets anything. Preparing for the test is called "doing the Knowledge."

I figured it wouldn't be that hard. Compared with London, San Francisco is a one-horse town. Plus, I already had a head start, having been a taxi driver here for years. So I set out to do the Knowledge (walking and rolling version) for San Francisco—to explore as many hills, streets, inlets, trails, vacant lots, and beaches as I could in the entire city. I left some out, for reasons of logistics, personal safety, and utter boredom, but I was pretty thorough. If you divide the city into 1,000 approximately quarter-mile-square grids, I can honestly say I have set foot or bike tire on every one of them.

I undertook this somewhat demented odyssey, in part, to do research for what was to become this book—but only in part. I knew that very little of what I discovered would ever make it into print. I was not planning to write a guidebook, and even if I had been, it seemed highly doubtful that there would be a large market for a tome offering detailed instructions on how to slip between the two houses at the end of Valletta Court (was Thomas Pynchon involved in naming the SF streets?), skirt someone's backyard, make your way through a dense thicket of blackberry bushes, push past a bright yellow Bailey acacia, clamber over some dead trees, and climb up the craggy face of an obscure hill on O'Shaughnessy Hollow.

So what drove me to go on those countless 8 A.M. walks was not just a search for material I could use. It was the same impulse that drove me to master the park: Curiosity. Passion. The desire to discover the unknown. To make my little world bigger and deeper. Thoreau described it in his essay "Walking": "An absolutely new prospect is a great happiness, and I can still get this any afternoon. Two or three hours' walking will carry me to as strange a country as I expect ever to see."

I can't deny that there was a childish, game-like element to my quest. Like all games, it involved a kind of miniaturization, a shrinking of the world. To be interesting, my little universe had to have borders. I made the arbitrary decision that the 46 square miles bounded by Ocean Beach on the west, the waterfront on the north and east, and Daly City on the south were sacred space. Everything inside those lines was interesting by definition.

"Man's maturity," Nietzsche wrote, "consists of regaining the seriousness one had when a child at play." And it was child's play for me, the whole peculiar odyssey. It was my version of Blind Travel, the game played by Hugh Lofting's Dr. Dolittle: When the good doctor wanted to go on a voyage but wasn't sure where, he closed his eyes, opened his atlas to a random page, and made a mark with a pencil. Wherever the pencil landed, he had to go. My world atlas was a tattered old Thomas Brothers map of San Francisco, and I didn't choose my spots quite that blindly, but the selection process was similar. It was almost absurd how euphoric I felt as I tramped merrily through remote parks, across hidden trails, and through vacant lots, planting my little invisible flags like some two-bit Cabrillo. Best of all, I realized that I could play this game forever. If I went to a different place in the city every day, at the end of a year I could start again and it would all feel new—an urban explorer's version of Kierkegaard's "rotation method." I felt so giddy I began to be a little embarrassed. This was not grown-up behavior. John Calvin did not wander the streets of Geneva with a blissed-out grin on his face.

I was starting to write myself off as one of those inexplicably beaming homeless kooks you see stumbling down Market Street when I remembered an explorer who was even happier than me: John Muir. The legendary naturalist walked into the Sierra Nevada one day, and that was it. He was permanently stoned on some kind of divine speedball ever after.

I had found my role model. If stumbling around in a happy daze was good enough for John Muir, it was good enough for me. I never tried to wipe the smile off my face again.

Actually, I needn't have worried about being too euphoric. Life being what it is, the smile tended to vanish of its own accord. On all too many days, San Francisco became just a dull backdrop to my duller mind.

On those days, I sometimes found it useful to remind myself of what happened to the Spanish after they discovered California in 1542. For more than two hundred years after that, as their explorers sailed up and down the coast, dreaming of a safe harbor, they kept missing that narrow, fog-shrouded break in the coastal mountains that we now call the Golden Gate.

That story is a parable that applies to all of us, whether we live in San Francisco or Sheffield, Perugia or Paris, New York or New Delhi. The real treasures are right under our noses.

This book is a voyage to a beautiful land I discovered long ago. And one that I am seeing for the first time today.

INTRODUCTION

In the 1820s, the Japanese artist Katsushika Hokusai began working on a series of woodblock prints titled "36 Views of Mt. Fuji." Hokusai depicted the great mountain from a variety of perspectives—from the sea, across the plains, with pilgrims in the foreground, through a screen of trees. Sometimes the mountain dominates the composition; at other times it is barely visible. People appear in some prints; others simply portray the mountain itself, in all its stark grandeur.

Hokusai's magnificent series was extremely influential in the West. It had a particularly powerful impact on the French painter Henri Rivière, who in 1898 began work on a series of lithographs titled "36 Views of the Eiffel Tower." Just as Hokusai did with Mount Fuji, Rivière portrayed the mighty steel tower—the highest structure in the world when it was completed in 1899—from many different viewpoints, at different times of day and night, and in different weather. Sometimes it is a tiny smudge on the horizon you have to strain your eyes to see.

Rivière published *Thirty-six Views of the Eiffel Tower* as a book in 1902. In his prologue to the book, the critic Arsène Alexandre extolled it as a record "to describe the daunting beauty of Paris . . . to those carefree, ungrateful Parisians who are forever forgetting it. To make this album a memento of beauty for those who live now and a testimonial for all those who will follow."

In the spirit of Hokusai and Rivière, this book is a series of 49 portraits of San Francisco. Like them, I approach my subject from many different perspectives: from the shark-haunted islands 28 miles off its coast, and the teeming tenements of Chinatown; from the dreamlike summit of Russian Hill, and the mad depths of the Tenderloin; from the patrician mansions of Nob Hill, and the windswept dunes of Larsen Peak.

Like Rivière's portraits of Paris, this book attempts to capture the "daunting beauty" of San Francisco. I feel no qualms about emphasizing her appearance. San Francisco's beauty may be only skin-deep, but it is the most enduring thing about her. People come and go, but the land and water and sky remain. As Joseph Brodsky wrote in *Watermark*, his exquisite little book on Venice, "Surfaces—which is what the eye registers first—are often more telling than their contents, which are provisional by definition, except, of course, in the afterlife." Every writer always describes, or creates, the city that is closest to his or her heart. And my San Francisco is first and foremost a *place*—a jagged peninsula that faces one of the most dramatic straits on earth, a 46-square-mile cornucopia of sea cliffs and hidden beaches and deep canyons and flowing streams and hills, always hills.

But of course San Francisco is more than its terrain. It is a vast human hive with a long human history. From the first San Franciscans, who hunted enormous beasts at what is now the bottom of the bay, to the Keystone Kops–like explorations that finally led the Spanish to the shores of the bay, the lost-boy Yerba Buena years, the collective lunacy of the Gold Rush, the catastrophic earthquake and fire, the muscular port city years, the poignant last-stop intensity of World War II, the uncanny eruptions of the Beats and the hippies, the tragedy and triumph of the AIDS crisis, to the dot-com delirium and beyond, San Francisco's history is as extraordinary as her landscape. Her story, like every city's, is a mixture of the inspiring and the dismal, the noble and the disgraceful, the sublime and the ridiculous. I have not shied away from her dark side. My intention has been to paint as complete and unvarnished a portrait of San Francisco as I can.

A few words should be said about this book's structure. It is not a strictly chronological tale. There is a historical through-line here, but it is constantly interrupted and intersected. Space trumps time. A chapter on the first San Franciscans is followed by one on the Filbert Steps. The dark farce of the Bear Flag Revolt is succeeded by the story of an eccentric San Francisco geologist and the feisty woman he inspired. This kaleidoscopic approach is an attempt to capture the visceral, spatial experience of moving through the city while simultaneously relating her history and my own journey. By crisscrossing space and time, I hope to bring both dimensions to life, stripping away the shroud of familiarity that can make both historical narratives and descriptive writing feel formulaic. But it's not a scientific approach. Much as I'd like to see myself as the creator of a revolutionary new Cubist School of Spatial

History, the truth is, I'm just a humble bartender, trying to mix the perfect San Francisco cocktail.

For there is nothing neutral or dispassionate about this book. I fell in love with San Francisco as a child when I first saw her rising up like a fairy-tale castle at the end of a rainbow bridge, and half a century later I still find her miraculous. As I walk her streets, the only thing that keeps me from stopping on every block and throwing my hands in the air in amazement are the old Jacob Marley chains we all clank around in, chains forged not so much by sin as by the weight of the weary world. But San Francisco, like the ghosts who visit Scrooge, always offers me another chance. In San Francisco, it is always Christmas morning.

That sense that redemption is attainable simply by opening one's eyes is found in the poem that gave this book its title. For years, I played in a weekly basketball game in Alice Marble Park on top of Russian Hill. Just below the court, on a gravel path overlooking a (strikingly Hokusai-like) view of Mount Tamalpais, there stood a forlorn plinth bearing a bronze plaque on which was inscribed the following:

Tho the dark be cold and blind
Yet her sea-fog's touch is kind,
And her mightier caress
Is joy and the pain thereof;
And great is thy tenderness,
O cool, grey city of love!

Those words are the last lines of a poem titled "The Cool, Grey City of Love," written in 1920 by George Sterling. Now largely forgotten, Sterling in his day was the leading light of San Francisco's artistic rebels, whose more talented friends, including Jack London and Ambrose Bierce, loved him because he embodied the bohemian ideal. The poem is purple in places, but still powerful, and Sterling's fierce, melancholy passion for his city—not just that of a lover but of a patriot, as if San Francisco were a medieval city-state—shines through it. When he called San Francisco the "city of love," Sterling was thinking of the gentle saint after whom the city was named. Today the phrase evokes the hippies and the Summer of Love. But Sterling's almost elegiac use of the word (he was an alcoholic who committed suicide six years after he wrote the poem) adds a deeply personal dimension to it, as if San Francisco were the mother or lover he never had.

Although I do not personify San Francisco quite that explicitly, anyone who loves a city inevitably comes to think of it as a true companion, a faithful friend who grows old with us. But a beloved city is more than that. It is a mirror; it is a universe; it is a home. This book is a love letter to the place in the world that means the world to me—my city, San Francisco.

CHAPTER 1

THE OUTER LIMITS

The Farallon Islands,
30 miles west of the Golden Gate Bridge

For almost 50 years, an amusement park called Playland at the Beach stood just off the Great Highway. I used to go there as a kid. It was a gaudy, decrepit place, filled with clanking roller coasters, shrieking children, unnerving carnies, and every conceivable variety of fried food. Playland was vulgar, vaguely sad, and magnificent—a greasy Garden of Earthly Delights marking the place where America ran out of land. When the sun went down and night swept in off the Pacific, Playland became a foolish illuminated wonderland, its innumerable lightbulbs creating a magic circle within which hormone-addled teenagers could whirl rapidly through space and tired smiling dads could buy their daughters teddy bears.

Beyond that illuminated circle, the darkness waited. If you were to leave Playland and cross the Great Highway, by the time you walked halfway across the wide sands of Ocean Beach, the night would have taken over, and the sound of the surf would drown out the shrieks from the rickety Alpine Racer. If you waded into the ocean and began to swim, the lights of Playland would flicker behind you like birthday candles for a long time, until the dark miles blew them out. When you cleared the cliffs at Lands End, the red lights atop the towers of the Golden Gate Bridge, a last faint link with the human world, would come into view. Then they, too, would disappear, and you would be alone in the cold, slapping Pacific. For more than two thousand miles between here and Hawaii, there would be nowhere you could stand up—with one vicious exception. For if you kept swimming, after many hours you would hear the unexpected sound of waves crashing on rocks. And suddenly a grim citadel, a mountain in the middle of the ocean, would loom up before you.

Twenty-eight miles from the end of the continent, you would have come upon the most forbidding piece of real estate to be found within the borders of any major city in the world: the Farallon Islands.

The face-off between Playland at the Beach and the Farallones is the ultimate San Francisco dissonance. For if Playland represents humanity's invincible drive to conquer nature by deep-frying it and serving it on a stick, the Farallones are the exact opposite—they are absolutely resistant to domestication. This city specializes in such collisions.

From the safety of the continent, the Farallones look dreamlike and mysterious, guardians of a distant West as mythical as Tolkien's Grey Havens. But for the mariners who have come to grief on them, the only myth they conjure up is that of the Clashing Rocks, those ferociously mobile islands that specialized in destroying passing Greek ships.

The Farallones have sent many ships to the bottom of the sea. The most potentially catastrophic incident took place one fog-shrouded morning in 1944, when a Liberty ship bearing 1,300 Navy men returning from the Pacific theater inadvertently entered the creepily named "silent zone," a dead auditory area where the sound of the island's foghorn was blocked by a massive granite peak. The ship smashed into a reef and quickly foundered. Men who had survived Guadalcanal and Midway bobbed in the turbulent seas, in danger of drowning just a few hours outside the Golden Gate. When the SOS came in, a motley fleet of vessels raced at top speed out of San Francisco harbor. It was the city's biggest nautical rescue mission since the 1906 fire, when a flotilla of ships picked up thousands of people as flames raged toward them on the northern waterfront. All the sailors were saved.

But not every Farallon shipwreck has had such a happy ending. The seas around the islands are treacherous. On April 14, 2012, five experienced crewmen on a racing yacht were killed when a huge wave swamped their boat, hurling them into the water and smashing their boat on the rocks.

The ominousness of the Farallones may have inspired a myth even older than that of the Clashing Rocks. The central coast Indians who inhabited this part of California for thousands of years believed that when people died, their spirit would travel across the sea to a place called the Island of the Dead. Some of them thought that this was a happy place. But others had a less sanguine vision. The self-taught ethnographer Stephen Powers wrote of a Pomo tribe, "They say it is an island in the bitter, salt sea, an island naked, barren, and desolate, covered only with brine-splattered stones, and with glistening salt, which crunches under the tread, and swept with cursed winds and blinding acrid sea-spray. On this abhorred island bad Indians are condemned to live forever, spending an eternity in breaking stones one upon the other, with no food but broken stones and no drink but choking brine."

Whether this nightmarish myth was inspired by the Farallones is unknown. The tule boats used by the central coast Indians weren't capable of sailing that far in the open ocean, so the vision couldn't have been based on firsthand experience. Perhaps the myth originated in ancient stories told by the Bay Area's first inhabitants, who lived here when it was possible to walk to the Farallones. If the Pomos did use the islands as a model for their hell, a later divine followed in their footsteps: A U.S. Navy chaplain said, "God has done less for it and with it than any other place."

But the Farallones are only barren and desolate from a human perspective. For the myriad other living things that swarm all over and around them, they're like Times Square on New Year's Eve.

First, there are the birds. There are enough birds on the Farallones to give Alfred Hitchcock nightmares. The islands are the largest seabird breeding colony in the contiguous United States. More than 300,000 birds of 13 species are found there, including the tufted puffin, the Cassin's auklet, the ashy storm-petrel, and the pelagic cormorant.

Then there are the mammals. The islands are a haul-out and breeding site for five species of seals and sea lions, including the jaw-droppingly huge northern elephant seal, whose males can weigh 5,500 pounds. Humpback, gray, and blue whales, the largest animals on the planet, feed in these krill-rich waters during the so-called upwelling season, when the California Current forces nutrient-rich cold water from the ocean floor to the surface. The upwelling makes the waters just outside the Golden Gate among the most productive marine habitats in the world.

The Farallones' most lethal visitors arrive in the fall: 30 to 100 great white sharks, killing machines that can weigh 5,000 pounds and that wreak havoc on the seals and sea lions (and, when the sharks venture near Stinson Beach or Tomales Bay, an occasional swimmer or surfer. There are more shark attacks along the central California coast than anywhere in the world). But these monsters are mere minnows compared with the killer whales, which can weigh up to 20,000 pounds, that drop in from time to time. In 1997, a killer whale killed a great white shark off the Farallones, the Super Bowl of species conflict on planet Earth.

The islands are a Federal Wilderness and National Wildlife Refuge, which means visitors are forbidden. The only inhabited island is Southeast Farallon Island, where, since 1968, a few intrepid scientists and naturalists from the Point Reyes Bird Observatory have been monitoring and studying the wildlife.

However, their remarkable wildlife is not the only noteworthy thing about the Farallones. In a region marked by extraordinary geology, they may be the most bizarre anomaly of all. For they are just passing through.

Eighty to 110 million years ago, during the Mesozoic era—the age of dinosaurs—the granite rocks that compose the islands were formed when two of the planet's seven major tectonic plates, the Pacific Plate and the North American Plate, collided with each other. This collision took place 300 miles south of where the islands are now, in the southern part of the Sierra Nevada range. They and the other rocks that make up what's known as the Salinian Complex, including Point Reyes and Montara Mountain, were separated from the rest of the Sierra, which sits on the North American Plate, by the motion of the San Andreas Fault, then taken for a ride on the neighboring Pacific Plate, which is inexorably moving north at the dizzying rate of 1.6 inches a year. It took perhaps 20 million years for the Farallones to travel to their current location. In another 10 million years they will have migrated to somewhere off the coast of Oregon, giving the denizens of that sensitive state another excuse to whine about being overrun by vulgar arrivistes from California.

So, rather than the Clashing Rocks, it would be more apt to compare the Farallones with the subject of another Greek myth, the Wandering Rocks. Rootless cosmopolitans that have installed themselves temporarily on the horizon, they are the perfect outer limit—a moving one—for this city of runaways.

Actually, until recently, the Farallones were not islands at all. During the last glacial period, which ended 12,500 years ago, sea levels were much lower than they are today, and the Farallones were a ridge of peaks just east of the continental shelf. The first San Franciscans, who arrived some 13,000 years ago, could have walked out there.

After the waters rose, Spanish explorers used the Farallones as landmarks. Boston traders hunted seals on the islands in the early 19th century, followed by a colony of Russians. But it was the Gold Rush that gave the Farallones their strange, short moment in the sun. Some of the men who poured into San Francisco realized that the profits to be made from mining for gold were puny in comparison with those that could be made by "mining the miners." Any scarce commodity, including food, could be sold for obscene profits. In San Francisco, eggs were rare and pricey. In 1849, there were an estimated 300,000 common murres nesting on the Farallones. The murre lays eggs almost twice as big as a chicken egg, and equally tasty. Some shrewd entrepreneurs quickly realized that there was gold in them thar guano-befouled cliffs.

In 1851, six men landed on the Farallones, declared themselves owners by right of possession, formed a stock company, and began gathering eggs and selling them in San Francisco. Their success inspired others who paid no attention to their claims of ownership. The enmity between rival eggers grew to staggering proportions, culminating in the heartbreaking "Egg War" of 1863, during which two men were shot dead. Eventually the U.S. government, which ran the lighthouse on the main island, banned egging altogether.

The Farallones have been inhabited off and on ever since the Gold Rush. In 1897, they even briefly had their own public school, whose first and only principal, the wonderfully named Miss Daisy Doud, brought a flock of homing pigeons with her so that she could communicate with the mainland.

The school lasted only two years but the islands still belong to San Francisco.

I had wanted to visit the Farallones ever since I set eyes on them, and I finally took a boat tour out there one May morning with my sister. Our boat headed up the spectacular Marin coast to near Bolinas, then turned southwest for the 20-mile haul to the islands.

As the land disappeared behind us, I realized that in almost half a century of living in the Bay Area, I had never been this far outside the Golden Gate. A flock of surf scoters appeared next to the boat, blasting from the top of one wave to the next, at once ungainly and graceful, like self-propelled rocks barreling through the waves. I had never seen these birds before.

The Pacific was a whole different animal from the bay. There was nothing human-size about it. It was green and moving and dangerous, and it was going to stay like that all the way to Japan.

The sea was choppy, and I began to feel a little woozy. The boat barreled on through mile after mile of churning water. Finally the captain announced that we were approaching the Farallones.

They rose up out of the ocean like a hallucination in shit-covered granite. Even though I knew they were there, there was still something shocking, almost obscene, about that first sight. They were not like the islands in the Aegean, which feel like stepping-stones strewn by friendly gods. These were more like mines. Early visitors called the Farallones "the Devil's Teeth," and the name is a calumny on Satan's dentist. The hills were massive: Tower Hill on Southeast Farallon Island is 348 feet high, only 28 feet lower than Nob Hill. The island looked like a rubble-strewn quarry in the middle of the ocean: jagged cliffs running down to a brown, dirty, talus-strewn tableland, with a few old buildings scattered around. I don't know what I thought the Farallones would look like, but it wasn't like the spine of Baja California.

But the next moment the brown talus was forgotten. As we approached Fisherman's Bay on the island's northeast side, three gray whales suddenly appeared a few hundred yards ahead of us, blowing white plumes in the air. The naturalist on the boat told us they had been hanging around for a while, which was unusual: Most of the whales in the vicinity were transients. We had only a few brief glimpses of parts of their long, sinuous bodies slicing through the water, but to see one of these great beings in its home was a benediction, as if it had extended its fluke in fellowship.

After the whales moved off, I looked up at Tower Hill. It took me a moment to realize that the black dots covering that massive brown monolith were common murres. It was more birds than I had ever seen in one place. When we sailed downwind of the island, the smell of the guano was intense.

Great Arch Rock came into view, a stunning formation so huge it can be seen on clear days from Point Reyes. Its monumental scale made it look like a magic portal into the Jurassic: You half expected to see a tyrannosaurus stalk through it. Now that we had left the scarred brown hillside behind, the island's savage beauty emerged. The waves surged and crashed on the rocks. Sea lions and seals were hauled out. The salt air was clean and cool.

Before heading back, we followed three humpbacks as they relentlessly fed and surfaced and dived to feed again, their mighty flukes waving in the air as they went down. When we turned for home, a brown albatross—another bird I had never seen before—suddenly whipped across our bow.

It was a warm, hazy day, and it took a long time for the two towers of the Golden Gate Bridge to appear. As we drew nearer, the complex topography of the peninsula and the city announced itself, unfolding south to north: Point San Pedro, Montara Mountain, Mount San Bruno, Mount Davidson, Mount Sutro. The long expanse of Ocean Beach stretched out in the foreground.

It was oddly unimpressive, this approach from the west. It had none of the drama that greets you when you come over the Bay Bridge at dusk and see the city rising up against its hills like an electric Atlantis, all turrets and pennants and twinkling lights, a Joseph Stella vision of a stained-glass city. This was a flat and exposed and sandy coast with some lumpy hills behind it. It was not San Francisco's good profile.

But as soon as we passed the mighty cliffs at Lands End, the dumpy matron became flashing-eyed Cleopatra again. We were back in the land of high geographical cheekbones. We sailed past Mile Rock, then under the impossibly high bridge and past Fort Point. Now that we were in the bay, it felt like we had come back from outer space. Sailboats sailed cheerfully past, the Marina Green sparkled, bicyclists wheeled along, Coit Tower smiled at us. Everything was as colorful and gay as a Raoul Dufy painting.

We pulled into a slip on the west side of Fort Mason and walked off the boat onto solid ground.

Maybe it was the lingering seasickness, maybe it was the endlessness of the ocean, but I felt quite happy to be walking *east*. Away from the ocean. Toward downtown.

Before I had visited the Farallones, I had pictured them as the essential San Francisco. I imagined that they were the city stripped of superfluity, the city with its clothes off. But at this moment they didn't feel as much to me like the city with its clothes off as like the city with its *skin* off. They were skeletal, the granite embodiment of King Lear howling in the storm— naked, terrifying, crazy.

San Francisco grew up around the bay, not the ocean. Its nucleus was a shallow curved cove in what is now the Financial District. Its most famous hills and neighborhoods—North Beach, Telegraph Hill, Nob Hill, Russian Hill—look out over the bay, not the Pacific. There are practical reasons for this. There was no reason for the city to start at the ocean. The best anchorage was at Yerba Buena, on the bay. The famous hills were close to that anchorage. And the west was a desert of sand dunes, whipped by the northwesterly wind that blows constantly down the California coast. This city ended up concentrated in the east simply because it followed the lay of the land.

San Franciscans are drawn to the sea—at least to its edge. We are not like the Balinese, who live on an island but turn inward because they are afraid of the ocean. To picnic at Baker Beach or surf at Ocean Beach or walk at Fort Funston, to look out toward the horizon from Larsen Peak or the Cliff House, is an essential part of life here.

Yet that trip to the Farallones, 28 miles out into the Pacific, made me realize just how enormous the ocean is, and what an infinitesimally small fraction of it we experience here. Even someone who lives on 48th Avenue, the last street before the beach, is still only looking at the ocean from terra firma. And if we could take in more of the ocean, would we even want to?

In *Moby-Dick*, Melville describes how the little cabin boy Pip, abandoned in the open ocean, is driven mad by its "heartless immensity." That heartless immensity had shaken me, too. But as I walked toward North Beach, my Gothic mood began to lift, like a finger of fog on the bay burning off in the morning sun. I remembered the lazy whale, at peace in its vast swimming pool, and the sea lions sunning themselves on rocks made of the same granite as my beloved Sierra. The ocean was vast, but it was not infinite. And hadn't Melville himself opened his book by describing how all human beings are drawn to water—and especially drawn to the ocean, where life began? We are all forever running away to sea.

And so, as I wander through my city, I am glad that the Farallones are part of it. I am glad that they stand on the horizon, mighty stone doors at the beginning of the long, long west. Warm sun caressing them in summer. Majestic sharks cruising through their waters in fall. Icy winds blowing through their crags in winter. Flocks of crying seabirds returning to them in spring. While we flit through the corridors of this fragile palace we have built to keep out the cold, it is good to know that they are out there, in darkness and in light, facing the unknowable world.

CHAPTER 2

ADVENTURES IN THE SKIN TRADE

Turk and Taylor Streets

I n the universe of San Francisco, the Tenderloin is the black hole, the six-block-by-six-block area where the city's urban matter is most intensely concentrated. It is the only part of San Francisco that remains untamed, its last human wilderness. Without the Tenderloin and its radioactive core of junkies, drunks, transvestites, dealers, thugs, madmen, hustlers, derelicts, prostitutes, and lowlifes, this overpriced, increasingly homogenous burg would feel like one of those motel bathrooms that are "sani-sealed for your protection."

The Tenderloin is the creepy Mr. Hyde (which happens to be the name of a street running through it) to the rest of San Francisco's respectable Dr. Jekyll (who, appropriately, goes unhonored). And this evil twin isn't hidden away in some asylum on the outskirts of town. The Tenderloin is surrounded by Union Square, Nob Hill, the Civic Center, and the gentrifying mid-Market district. It's about as central as you can get.

This is weird. Many cities used to have "bad" neighborhoods in the heart of downtown, zones of misrule where the primal human urges—to get laid, to get high, and to get money—were allowed to bloom furtively in the night. But most of them are gone now, victims of gentrification. New York's Times Square feels like Disneyland, Vancouver's Gastown has been tamed, Boston's Combat Zone was rendered hors de combat years ago. And of those that remain, none take up 36 square blocks of prime real estate in the middle of one of the most expensive cities in the world.

Union Square is the center of San Francisco's downtown, the quintessential public space of Any Corporate City, 2013. An invisible capitalist force field (in the beginning was the Logo, and the Logo was with God, and the Logo was God) emanates down from the airline- and Midori-touting billboards looming over it. But you only have to walk a couple of blocks from the square's bustling southwest corner at Geary and Powell to find yourself in a lurid demimonde populated by characters out of a Denis Johnson novel.

All of which is to say that the Tenderloin is a large turd—often a literal one—floating in the crystal punchbowl that is San Francisco. So why is it still here?

Because the city wants it to be here.

For decades, the Tenderloin has been carefully protected by the city and various nonprofit organizations. It's not that these officials, social workers, homeless advocates, and low-cost housing activists want to maintain a zone of crime and filth in the heart of San Francisco; it's simply an inescapable consequence of their laudable commitment to defend society's most vulnerable members. The problem is that by saving the baby, you also save the bathwater. No one has figured out a way to help the "deserving poor," to use the condescending 19th-century parlance, without also helping the creepy, kooky, and dangerous poor. The result is, in effect, a protected urban wildlife zone, a Bottle City of Squalor.

But the Tenderloin is more than that. It is also a memorial to a rich and vanished era—what geographer Richard Walker has called "the high tide of dense urbanism." For it was here, in the neighborhood's unique collection of single-room occupancy (SRO) hotels and apartment houses, that the great army that once made up the blood and guts and sinew of American cities lived. Tens of thousands of clerks and salesmen and stenographers and hoboes and longshoremen and cops and dressmakers and carpenters and factory workers inhabited these cheap but decent rooming houses. Most of them were single. Many of them were women. They were drawn to the city because they could find work here. As Paul Groth writes in *Living Downtown: The History of Residential Hotels in the United States*, for these newcomers, inexpensive rooming houses offered freedom, anonymity, and sexual liberation—all in the heart of the city.

What is remarkable about the Tenderloin is that it has remained physically unchanged for more than 80 years. It is a time capsule. The same progressive forces that have kept out "progress," and inadvertently created a Museum of Depravity, have also created a Museum of the Lost City, a vanished world memorialized in the neighborhood's extraordinary collection of residential hotels. There are hundreds of these historic SROs in the Tenderloin, the largest number in the world. The SROs are the reason that in 2008 the Uptown Tenderloin was placed on the National Register of Historic Places, the 24th San Francisco neighborhood to be so listed. All of these three- to seven-story brick and masonry buildings were built between 1906 and the Great Depression. Almost all of them are essentially unchanged, right down to their blade signs. These once-elegant buildings have fallen on very hard times, but they still conjure up the romance and mystery of the Naked City, with its 8 million stories. They are the ultimate urban hives.

In an uncanny way, the Museum of Depravity helps bring the Museum of the Lost City to life. If all of those rooming houses were occupied by employees of Twitter—and that day may be coming—the ghostly romance of the Tenderloin's past would not feel quite as rich and strange.

The very first time I set foot in the Tenderloin was when I was a 17-year-old student at Berkeley High School. I went with my friend Ben, a black guy who smoked Kools and read Heidegger, over to the big city from Berkeley to meet up with a pal of his for some reason I have forgotten. We went into an old apartment building, took the elevator up, and walked into a studio apartment that looked out over downtown. It was the first time I had ever been in *an apartment.* I dimly remember that it was airy and spacious— there are a lot of beautiful rooms in those old buildings—but my memory is somewhat cloudy because his friend pulled out a water pipe (another first) and we proceeded to get stoned. This was an appropriate introduction to the Tenderloin: A longhaired half-Japanese dude and two black guys interrupting their vague urban mission to puff away on a water pipe (unless that *was* the mission). The die was cast. Most of my subsequent experiences in the Tenderloin have involved some kind of sin.

I got to know the Tenderloin during the seven years I was a taxi driver in San Francisco. Sin and taxi driving go together like gin and tonic, and the Tenderloin was the smudged highball glass where they mixed. The 'Loin was ground zero for sex, the sub-basement of the lower chakras. Sex radiated out of its innumerable windows and filthy sidewalks, from Frenchy's K&T bookstore (the name Frenchy a subtle tip-off as to the types of books it carried) to the gaudy, teetering whores on Geary Street, from the bottom-of-the-barrel all-night Mini Adult Theatre on the lunar corner of Golden Gate and Jones (admission $2, no charge for an attempted blow job by the drunken homeless guy who just sat down next to you) to the scary Last Exit to Brooklyn drag queens on Larkin, from the gay male hustlers hanging outside the Peter Pan bar on Mason near Market (an intersection delicately known as "the Meat Rack") to Jim and Artie Mitchell's upscale flesh joint on O'Farrell Street.

There was a major cross-dressing and transgender scene in the TL, catered to by unnerving bars like the Black Rose. One night at about 2 A.M., I picked up a 30ish straight man on O'Farrell. He was pretty drunk. He was a nice guy who seemed completely freaked out. He started babbling as soon as he sat down. "Oh my God," he said, "the weirdest thing just happened to me. I picked up this girl and she turned out not to be a girl." He had gone drunkenly through with the sexual encounter anyway and now he needed to exorcise the whole bizarre incident. I tried to reassure him that he would be OK, but he was as jangled and jumpy as if he had just poured 10 cups of espresso into his id.

The Tenderloin was often involved in these libidinous journeys, either as a starting point or a destination. Two Japanese salarymen once asked me to take them to something that sounded like "hlibod sho." I had no idea what they were talking about. They had to repeat it twice until I realized they were saying "ribald show." I felt like calling up the editors of the *OED* and reporting the first conversational use of the word "ribald" since 1911. I took them to the Mitchell Brothers.

Say what you will about Japanese businessmen, they are not self-conscious about sex. Indeed, for some of them, it appeared that having a naked woman shove her ass in their faces was a tourist activity to be checked off the to-do list, on a par with visiting the Legion of Honor or Golden Gate Park. During a trip to a slightly sleazier fleshpot than the Mitchell Brothers—the New Century on Larkin, if memory serves—I was surprised to suddenly hear a piercing whistle. I looked away from the gyrating woman on the pole to observe 10 or 15 Japanese men getting up and moving methodically toward the exit, heading back to the tour bus. It was the finest display of organized horniness I'd ever seen.

I myself was a master of disorganized horniness. I once met a lunatic stripper who worked at one of the 'Loin's legendary strip clubs, the Chez Paree on Mason, famous for its neon sign of a long female leg, bent and ready to kick the can-can. I met this woman on the beach at Aquatic Park and took her the next day to Lake Anza in Berkeley. Unfortunately, her spectacular body turned out to be accompanied by a schizophrenic brain. We were sitting on our towels, talking about this and that, when she suddenly and suspiciously asked me if I was gay. Apparently, trying to make innocuous first-date conversation was a bad move. Later we did manage to get in a little groping in the back seat of my stepmom's 1962 VW bug. It was pretty hot, but in the middle of it, she suddenly pulled a hairbrush out of her purse and began utilizing it in a way for which it was not designed. That would have been all right—in fact, it would have been all right to an unparalleled degree—except for the fact that (1) it felt like she had suddenly gone into her Chez Paree routine, and (2) I couldn't convince her to come back to my apartment. When I dropped her off at her apartment, she told me to come by the Chez Paree after 2 A.M., when she got off work. I did, and waited for half an hour, but the only person who came out was a large, violent-looking bouncer who told me to get lost. Hairbrush woman, in the extremely unlikely event that you are reading this, where did I go wrong?

In addition to being haunted by such crackpot Circes, the Tenderloin also featured—and still does—more than its share of young males whose approach to life is summed up by the line delivered by the blackmailing George Sanders character in *Rebecca*: "I'd like to have your advice on how to live comfortably without working hard." Two of these worthies, one a tattooed white guy who had long hair of the non-hippie kind and one an ominous-looking Latino blood, hailed me on Taylor and Eddy one night. I was a fairly new driver, and it was a slow night, so when they said they wanted to go to the airport, I agreed. Tilt! Taxi commandment number one: Do not pick up scary dudes in the Tenderloin who look like they just got out of the joint and say they want to go to the airport even though they have no luggage! Taxi commandment number two: If one of these scary dudes gets in the front seat and one gets in the back, directly behind you so you cannot observe the gun he is pulling out, immediately defecate in your pants, exit the vehicle, and run screaming down the street!

Unfortunately, I failed to follow either of these easy rules. Instead, I drove down Sixth Street and got on the freeway. After a minute or two, I felt the unpleasant sensation of a gun barrel pushing up against the back of my head. I was informed by the muscle-y San Jose speed freak white dude in the front seat that this was a stickup. They made me drive around while they looked for a remote place. They got kind of chummy as we rolled along. Blood in the back seat said, "Hey, you drive pretty good. You ever think about a life of crime?" Laugh? I thought I'd die!

Finally they told me to exit at Colma and had me drive into the vast city of the dead, where Wyatt Earp is buried in a cemetery called Hills of Eternity. I did not like this at all. They told me to get out of the car. I jumped out and sprinted down the road, screaming "Help!" while waiting for the bullets to rip into my back. But the only sound was the engine roaring as they drove off at top speed.

The S.F. police soon came and picked me up. This turned out to be almost as arduous an ordeal as the robbery and kidnapping, because as we headed back to the city, they suddenly got a radio call about some heavy crime that had just gone down in the Geneva Towers, the scariest projects in town before they were blown up in 1998. They took off at 90 miles an hour toward Visitacion Valley. As we approached the terrifying high-rises, the cop riding shotgun actually pulled out, yes, a shotgun, and stuck it out the window. When the radio said the suspect was a black male, the driver sneered, "Oh, yeah, that's a big fucking surprise." They were total macho cowboys, but considering they were working the Geneva Towers beat during the crack-crazed 1980s, which would have to qualify as one of the worst jobs in the history of the world, I had to cut them a little slack. They finally dropped me off at the Yellow Cab lot. The next day the cab turned up hidden in an old railway cutting at the base of Potrero Hill, just a few blocks away.

"If you were to throw a ball a thousand feet into the air from here," Peter Field told me as we stood on the corner of O'Farrell and Mason, "wherever it landed, the chances are it would hit a building that was once involved in some kind of illegal activity."

Field probably knows more about the Tenderloin than anyone else. A social worker who worked in the neighborhood for 12 years—he himself slept on the streets for a while when he first came to town—he evinces the no-bullshit kindness of a man who has been exposed to the darkest side of humanity yet hasn't given up hope. Field is obsessed with the Tenderloin's history. He has spent hundreds of hours poring over city directories and Sanborn insurance maps, the sources that allow sleuths to follow the convoluted trails of people and businesses through the vanished urban landscape. I came upon some pieces he'd written about the TL online and called him up. He gives a walking tour of the neighborhood twice a year through City Guides, a nonprofit organization whose volunteer guides lead tours all over town. I had just missed his tour, but he offered to take me around. His normal tour lasts about two and a half hours. We spent six and a half hours walking about six blocks.

I met Field at the dead center of San Francisco, the Powell Street cable car turnaround at Eddy Street. It was a hot June Sunday, and thousands of tourists and locals were swarming the streets. But they soon faded into the background as Field drew me into a lost world—of lonely merchant sailors in sad rooms, old people eating in white-tablecloth cafeterias, thousands of excited men on Ellis waiting for a boxer to emerge from a weigh-in, evil pimps drugging girls, French restaurants with discreet upstairs rooms, Miles Davis riffing with Wynton Kelly at the Black Hawk, military shore patrols and San Francisco's finest scouring the streets together looking for AWOL sailors, homeless kids selling their bodies on the corner of Geary and Polk, hoboes returning to the same shabby hotels for decades. By the end of the six and a half hours, it felt as if I had just watched a time-lapse film of the neighborhood's entire long, rich life.

Like most of old San Francisco, the Tenderloin was once a wasteland of sand dunes and scrub brush. Its first white inhabitant was a viticulturist named Henry Gerke, who in 1847 built a two-story building at Eddy and Mason (the streets did not yet exist), near a large spring-fed pond that stood where the Flood Building is today. The isolated area was known as St. Ann's Valley. It was only three-fourths of a mile to the center of town, the old Spanish plaza, which had been renamed Portsmouth Square after the American conquest of California in 1846, but the dunes were so high and deep that it was a long hike to get there. A saloon called St. Ann's Rest opened in the 1850s, catering to travelers on their way to old Mission Dolores. But there were few inhabitants until 1860, when the Market Street Railway opened, its path cleared by "steam paddies"—steam-powered excavating machines that were so named because they could supposedly do the work of 20 Irishmen. By 1866, the former wasteland was completely developed. It was a typical San Francisco neighborhood of homes and small businesses, with a few mansions scattered here and there.

The event most responsible for turning the Tenderloin into what Field called "San Francisco's premier entertainment and vice district" took place in 1878, when an entrepreneur named Lucky Baldwin built the opulent Baldwin Hotel at Powell and Market. The first-class hostelry, which competed with the famous Palace Hotel a few blocks east, included a theater. Other theaters and music halls followed, along with office buildings. "This brought new customers into the neighborhood," Field said. "Rich rancher Johnnies, rich town Johnnies, office workers." Following the law of supply and demand, in 1884 the neighborhood's first "parlor house"—a genteel brothel—opened at 223 Ellis, presided over by a Miss Ines Leonard of Virginia City. Others soon followed. By the 1890s, the Tenderloin had been transformed from a stolid middle-class neighborhood into a jumping district of theaters, hotels, parlor houses, restaurants (many of which doubled as brothels or places of assignation), and gambling joints.

As we spoke, a young guy with a scar on his face lurched up and demanded to know what we were talking about. When we wouldn't tell him, he punished us by releasing a toxic cloud of Royal Gate vodka fumes in our faces. "The court said I was not allowed to own a pencil or anything to write with. Do you know why?" he asked. Receiving no answer, he stumbled off.

Sex was a prime Tenderloin draw, just as it was for San Francisco's more famous red-light district, the Barbary Coast near the waterfront on Pacific. But the two fleshpots were completely different. "The Tenderloin was more refined than the Barbary Coast," Field said. "The Barbary Coast attracted sailors and some upper-class men going slumming. But the Tenderloin attracted all classes. You could go out to dinner, go to the theater, and then maybe stop in at a parlor house." The semi-respectable nature of the neighborhood was solidified when it became the center of San Francisco's fraternal societies—the Odd Fellows, Masons, Elks, and so on. "These societies would have their monthly or yearly meetings here, and the men would want to have a good time," Field said. "They'd wander around the neighborhood, go to the bars and parlor houses. The newspapers of the time are filled with stories about men who lost their fraternal diamond stickpins in the neighborhood."

We walked up to the corner of Ellis and Powell. East on Ellis, where a parking lot now stands, was a saloon and betting parlor owned by Harry Corbett, the brother of "Gentleman Jim" Corbett, the former heavyweight champion of the world. "This was the center of betting parlors in San Francisco," Field said. "Corbett became a boxing promoter and had his own set of scales on a Turkish rug. When you made it as a boxer, you weighed in on his scales. Ellis Street would be crowded with men waiting to get a look at their heroes. Men like Bob Fitzsimmons and Sailor Sharkey." The joint was raided repeatedly by the police. After 1906, it was rebuilt as a "French restaurant" with private rooms upstairs—a San Francisco tradition. The purpose of these rooms was made clear by the discreet behavior of the waiters, who were trained not to enter the rooms unless summoned.

The great earthquake and fire of 1906 destroyed the Tenderloin, along with all of downtown San Francisco. The postquake reconstruction was responsible for the Tenderloin's unique architectural character. Its buildings had mostly been one- or two-story wooden houses and small hotels. The new buildings were higher, three to seven stories, made of brick or masonry, and they had many more units, mostly studios. Into this densely built-up, compact area, close to offices and factories and restaurants and bars, poured the 1920s and 1930s equivalent of the young people who today work as baristas or retail clerks and live in the Mission District (or maybe, mutatis mutandis, those who work at the Home Depot and live in San Leandro)—clerks and salesmen and barbers and firemen. Starting in the 1920s, as Paul Groth notes, women began to move to the rooming houses in large numbers. (Until salaries for stenographers rose in the 1920s, women did not make enough money to be able to live alone.) For the sheltered young American men and women who found themselves bumping into each other in the hall on the way to the bathroom, the Tenderloin and similar cheap downtown neighborhoods offered the chance to break free of Victorian small-town sexual codes.

The sinful side of the neighborhood flourished openly until it was forced into hiding by the U.S. military, which was alarmed by sky-high rates of venereal disease among soldiers, and by Prohibition. Sin City prospered even in hiding, but a double whammy set it on the road to decline. "The big hotels in the southeast Tenderloin were banking on being part of a theater district, but after the quake, most of the theaters moved north, to Geary and O'Farrell," Field said. "The hotels had to readjust their sights to a lower class of tenants. Then the Depression hit and caused upkeep and maintenance on the buildings to go down."

Despite the neighborhood's decline, it was still clinging to respectability. By the 1930s, the typical Tenderloin resident in one of the SROs was a transient worker, a hobo, or a step up from a hobo—someone who worked seasonally harvesting crops or in manufacturing. There were also a lot of merchant seamen. Bums had not yet appeared. Some seasonal farmworkers returned to the same rooming houses for 50 years.

"When World War II came, the TL prospered again with all the military around," Field went on. "But after the war, it slumped again. It briefly picked up again during the Korean War—in the 1940s and 1950s you have military shore patrols cruising through the area side by side with regular police."

Horny G.I.s were keeping the Tenderloin on life support, but in the 1950s a number of things happened that sent it into a death spiral. Swing music played by big bands had drawn crowds into TL clubs: when the big band era ended, those clubs lost most of their audience. Bebop, the more harmonically advanced jazz that succeeded swing, was not nearly as popular. And the rise of folk music drew away still more paying customers. The last jazz club in the Tenderloin, the legendary Black Hawk at Turk and Hyde—where Miles Davis recorded two classic albums in April 1961—went out of business in 1963. At the same time, the remaining theaters in the area, which had switched to showing movies instead of live shows, began to go downhill, becoming grindhouses.

Meanwhile, the neighborhood's population was getting older and poorer. "The residents were aging and retired seniors living on limited means," Field said. The big cafeterias where the people of the Tenderloin used to eat, Clinton's and Compton's—which in their heyday had table service—also began their final descent. When SROs were razed in other San Francisco neighborhoods in the early 1960s, their poor residents had nowhere to go except to the Tenderloin. "In the 1930s, the papers started calling this a 'seedy neighborhood,'" Field said. "By the 1950s it was a 'very seedy neighborhood.' By the 1960s it was 'a central city neighborhood.'"

The cultural upheavals of the 1960s sent runaways flooding into the Tenderloin. These boys and girls, the lost souls of the Flower Generation, hung out on street corners, doing drugs and prostituting themselves. The few working-class residents of the Tenderloin moved out as manufacturing jobs left the city. The housing stock deteriorated further. Then thousands of social outcasts flooded in during the 1960s and 1970s as prisoners were released from overcrowded jails and the mentally ill were deinstitutionalized. "These people became a customer base for drug dealers, hustlers, and street criminals," Field said. In the 1980s the Tenderloin became increasingly black. The first homeless in the neighborhood were mentioned in the *Tenderloin Times* in 1984. "The eighties are when the Tenderloin actually becomes dangerous," Field said. "When I started to work here."

We turned down Taylor Street and approached the corner of Turk. A half-dozen people were milling around in front of a doorway. "This is the Tenderloin's own private jail," Field said. I looked more closely at the crowd. It was mostly young Latino men. One guy was wearing a Steeler's jersey and gesticulating. They gave off a familiar sense of confused desperation mingled with bravado. "To get in there, you have to show ID, have a reason to be there, and go through all kinds of security," he said. "It's run by a company that contracts with the state of California to house parolees, people on probation, awaiting trial. It's cheaper for the state to keep them here."

As we spoke, a young Latino guy a few feet away was talking on a cell phone. I paid no attention, but Field had street ears. "Did you hear what that guy just said? 'Do you think he recognized me?' That's typical of the conversations you'll hear on this corner."

An ominous Indian-looking guy dressed all in black swaggered past us on Taylor, exuding a major don't-fuck-with-me vibe. Field had street eyes too. "Did you see that?" Field said under his breath, pointing at the guy's leg. A knife at least 10 inches long was tightly strapped against his thigh. "Uh, I don't think that's legal," I said. "Yeah. Well, maybe no one will notice," Field said drily. "It kind of goes with his outfit."

I asked Field what he thought was going to happen to the neighborhood. "The Tenderloin is the last battleground," he said. "For nonprofit housing outfits and social services, this is Fort Apache. It's Custer's Last Stand. Historically, poor people and improving neighborhoods don't mix. Either the poor people move out or the neighborhood collapses. The Tenderloin is a case of the irresistible force meeting the immovable object. As a historian, I'm curious to see if the Tenderloin can resist the forces that always win out in cities."

An example of the irresistible force was the impending gentrification, green-lighted by Mayor Ed Lee, of the blighted mid–Market Street area. Spearheading the assault on this legendarily bleak and intractable stretch was Twitter, which in June 2012 moved 800 employees into a building between 9th and 10th Streets. Though mid-Market is on the Tenderloin's borders, the move was a portent. It struck me as ironic that a social media company, specializing in creating disembodied "communities," might simultaneously destroy and revitalize the neighborhood that had once been a dense nexus of city life.

The immovable object, the thing keeping the Tenderloin from being gentrified, is a combination of city policy and nonprofit housing entities, both dedicated to providing extremely low-cost housing in the heart of San Francisco. If it were not for these factors, the Tenderloin would probably look like any other revitalized downtown neighborhood, a high-priced 2013 version of Jane Jacobs's urbanist utopia.

The city made two crucial decisions, Field said. In 1981 it passed a law forbidding owners from demolishing SROs or converting them into tourist rentals unless they replaced the converted units or paid a fee into a fund for affordable housing. Then in 1985 it imposed height limits on new buildings in the Tenderloin, preventing Manhattanization. These decisions, combined with its active enforcement of rent laws—in particular, those preventing eviction of existing tenants—and its purchase of some SRO buildings, have helped keep market forces out of the Tenderloin.

Just as significant, nonprofits like the Tenderloin Neighborhood Development Corporation and the Tenderloin Housing Clinic have purchased or leased many SRO hotels in the neighborhood, providing subsidized housing and social services for people who meet their criteria—those who are poor, disabled, have substance abuse problems, etc. Field said their rent is typically one-third of their monthly income, which means a lot of people living in the Tenderloin are paying less than $200 a month rent. (The median asking rent in San Francisco in December 2012 was $3,100, making it the most expensive U.S. city in which to rent.)

As we stood on the corner, a young black guy stumbled up to us. "What are you doing?" he demanded, pointing to my notebook. "We're just talking," Field said. "No, no," the guy said. "You come down here to *my* neighborhood, you gotta . . ." "Look, my friend, it's my neighborhood too," Field said. "It belongs to all of us." When he told the guy he had worked here for 12 years and had himself briefly slept on the streets when he first arrived, the guy's jive bluster deflated like a pricked balloon. He seemed abashed and didn't know what to say. We both shook his hand and he wandered off.

Field was deeply conflicted about what he wanted to see happen in the Tenderloin. "As a social worker, I want to do everything in my power to protect these people from the landlords who would throw them out," he said. "They're evil motherfuckers. But as a San Franciscan, as a guy who likes to walk, I want all this stuff cleaned up." He was sick of the crime, the prostitution ("as a social worker, I see absolutely no redeeming value in it"), the filth, the drugs.

"When I give my tours," Field went on, "I ask how many people live in the Tenderloin. More and more people say they do. They're in their 30s and 40s. They've been living here a few years. They're invested in the neighborhood. OK, they go off to work and they relax. When they come home, they get tense. How long will this go on? And then there are all the Southeast Asians with kids who have moved into the neighborhood. How long will they put up with this?"

In the end, Field came down on the side of letting the Tenderloin be. "I've got my dark glasses on so you can't see me blushing," he said. "But God help me, I do see it as romantic."

The tour was over, and I said goodbye to Field. I was glad that he had been my Virgil on this tour of San Francisco's Purgatory. His ambivalence about the Tenderloin mirrored my own. Like him, I found it appalling and fascinating and consummately strange. And like him, I could not imagine San Francisco without it.

I went down Mason, turned on Turk, and headed toward the setting sun. People were milling around in front of a defunct old porno arcade. It was still warm, but a cool wind was kicking in from the west. I looked up at the rows of hotels and apartments, once-elegant buildings where countless ordinary working people had lived. All those vanished lives seemed to have sunk into their shabby lobbies and blank windows. In a city without memory, they were still here. There was a sadness about them as they stood there in the harsh slanting rays of the late-afternoon sun, but it was a good sadness, like the peeled apple that falls from the father's hand at the end of Ozu's *Late Spring*. A sadness to keep.

CHAPTER 3

THE ALCATRAZ TRIANGLE

Harding Rock, submerged between
Alcatraz and Angel Island, San Francisco Bay

Beneath the waters of San Francisco Bay, slightly to the north and west of Alcatraz Island, lie three large submerged rock formations called Harding, Arch, and Shag Rocks. During the 19th century, at low tide Arch Rock used to appear above the bay like the eye of a needle, attracting daredevils who would try to row through it. This pastime was abandoned after two young men were killed when their rowboat was smashed against the arch by a heavy swell. "The forty-niner cannot recall the day when this picturesque menace to navigation was not anathematized by the sailor man," noted the *Portland New Age* in 1900. Arch Rock was saved for a while by "the sentimental opposition of a few veteran Californians who hated to see their odd-looking old friend disappear forever," but the rock was dynamited in 1901.

The fact that there was a Gold Rush–era aquatic thrill ride in the middle of the bay is an odd footnote to San Francisco history. But Arch and its fellow spires have a much older and infinitely stranger history. For among these towering rocks, thousands of years before the bay existed, the first San Franciscans engaged in life-and-death struggles with some of the most stupendous creatures ever to walk the earth.

Human beings probably arrived in San Francisco around 13,000 years ago, some 2,000 to 4,000 years after their ancestors left Siberia. (Just when humans left Asia for North America, and how they got here, is a subject that occasions nasty footnoted brawls between archaeologists, geneticists, and linguists.) But these earliest San Franciscans, so-called Paleo-Indians, left no traces. The oldest skeleton found in the city is that of a female, unearthed during excavation for the Civic Center BART station in 1969, dating to about 5,000 years ago. Human beings are known to have been present in what is now San Francisco from 6,000 years ago, and present twice that long in the greater Bay Area.

The Paleo-Indians arrived during the geological epoch known as the Pleistocene, which started about 2.5 million years ago and ended 11,700 years ago, roughly coinciding with the end of the last glacial period. The middle and late Pleistocene was the age of the enormous beasts known as Rancholabrean megafauna, after the famous Rancho La Brea tar pits that yielded a treasure trove of prehistoric fossils. Which meant that the biped newcomers to North America arrived just in time to witness the curtain call of a pageant of wildlife so extraordinary that archaeologist E. Breck Parkman calls it "one of the greatest natural phenomena of all time."

These awe-inspiring creatures moved across a landscape so different from today's that it would have been scarcely recognizable. To begin with, there was no bay. There had been one 120,000 years earlier, during the previous warm, or "interglacial," period, when the melting polar ice caps released vast quantities of water into the sea. And the bay had come and gone several other times in the million years before that, like a bathtub filled and emptied by a capricious god playing with a tap. (We ourselves have now become that capricious god, and are filling the planet's bathtub quite quickly.) But when the first humans arrived in San Francisco, the last glacial period was not yet over, and the sea level was 300 feet lower than it is now. The bay was a valley, dubbed the Franciscan Valley by archaeologists.

A mighty river ran through the Golden Gate, thundering in waterfalls and cascades, its relentless force carving out Angel Island from Tiburon. This vanished river flowed through a coastal prairie, the Farallones Plain, that extended all the way to the Farallon Islands, 28 miles away, where it emptied into the sea.

Much of the terrain was covered with scrub brush, although groves of live oak, California buckeye, and bay laurel trees grew in a rectangle running from the southern border halfway through central San Francisco, with isolated stands elsewhere. Juniper, pine, birch, poplar, and salix trees ringed prairie grasslands, bogs, and freshwater ponds in the low-lying terrain in the eastern part of the city. Huge sand dunes, carried down from the Sierra by vast rivers and deposited at the coastline, had begun to cover the western part of the city, blown by the wind. Streams ran down from the central peaks, Twin Peaks and Mount Davidson and Mount Sutro, and from springs in the Presidio and north of the Civic Center, draining into the bay in curling streams and estuaries. Mission Creek ran all the way from the bay to the Mission District, surrounded by tidal flats and swamps.

But the strangeness of this landscape would have paled in comparison to the animals that inhabited it. A Paleo-Indian who climbed to the top of Telegraph Hill would have witnessed a procession that would make the Serengeti look like a petting zoo. Across the wide grassy plain now covered by the bay roamed vast herds of enormous beasts. Huge Columbian mammoths rumbled along next to gigantic mastodons. Hundreds of giant bison, weighing two tons and standing more than eight feet high, headed through the Golden Gate on their seasonal migration, next to the roaring river. Herds of the Western horse and its larger cousin the Giant Horse trotted past. Western camels, antelopes, deer, elk, and possibly moose made their way across the plain. Tapirs and ground sloths the size of oxen lurked in nearby forests and woodlands.

These grazing herd animals were stalked by the most terrifying mammalian killing machines ever to walk the earth. At the top of the food chain stood the American lion and the short-faced bear. The American lion, which probably had come fairly recently across the land bridge known as Beringia—where it had terrorized the people crossing to Alaska—could weigh as much as 750 pounds, 25 percent larger than the modern African lion. It had a larger brain than any other lion and, at its peak, had the widest range of any wild land mammal species. Parkman estimates that there were 800 of these lethal animals prowling the Bay Area.

Even more frightening was the short-faced bear. Standing 13 feet tall and weighing one ton (25 percent larger than the grizzly), the short-faced bear was the largest and most powerful carnivore ever to live in North America. Able to run an astonishing 40 miles an hour for up to a mile and more rapacious than modern bears, it was the most feared predator of them all. An estimated 450 short-faced bears inhabited the Bay Area.

As if those ferocious beasts weren't enough to give an ungulate—or a feeble biped—indigestion, they were joined by saber-toothed cats, grizzly (brown) bears, dire wolves, scimitar cats, coyotes, and even jaguars, which existed as far north as San Francisco until the 1820s. If an animal was wounded, giant condors with 12-foot wingspans sailed overhead, waiting to pounce.

Together, hunters and hunted made up a bestiary of staggering size and diversity. Parkman estimates that the Bay Area was home to 227,000 bison, 35,000 horses, 7,000 camels, 1,450 mastodons, 725 Columbian mammoths, 450 saber-toothed cats, and 400 dire wolves. And many of these mighty animals would have gone past Arch, Harding, and Shag Rocks.

Parkman calls the area occupied by these rocks, between the Golden Gate, Alcatraz Island, and Angel Island, the "Alcatraz triangle." The Alcatraz triangle was on the migratory path that led from the Franciscan Valley to the Farallones Plain. The three lofty pinnacles—Harding, the tallest, was more than 300 feet high before its top, like Arch's, was dynamited as a hazard to navigation—would have provided the first San Franciscans with a perfect ambush site.

The hunters would have gone after the smaller, less ferocious animals like the bison, the horses, and the tapirs. But desperation could have led them to take on even dangerous behemoths like the Columbian mammoth. Working in small groups, they would have leaped out, surrounded their prey, and tried to spear it in its underbelly or throat. If they succeeded in wounding it, they would follow it until it collapsed from loss of blood or infection. It would have been extremely dangerous work. But a successful hunt could feed their band for weeks.

Whether humans killed off the megafauna, or climactic changes brought about by the end of the last glacial period did them in, or both, the magnificent creatures that had flourished for more than 240,000 years (some for much longer) suddenly died off. In just 1,500 years, most of them vanished forever.

Remains of these extinct Rancholabrean megafauna have been found all over the Bay Area, but few in San Francisco. In 1993, however, paleontologists made an astonishing discovery. They unearthed the 25,000-year-old skeletons of three Columbian mammoths and one giant bison on the southeast corner of Pacific and Columbus—549–559 Pacific, to be precise. The skeletons were found in what had been a shallow, muddy freshwater pond or bog at the base of Telegraph Hill, surrounded by a prairie grassland and a variety of deciduous trees.

This is one of the city's sacred blocks, in the heart of the old Barbary Coast, across the street from City Lights, Francis Ford Coppola's flatiron Sentinel Building, and fabled Beat-era bars like Vesuvio, Spec's, and Tosca. It is fitting that this archaeological find was made here, if only because certain denizens of those bars are becoming increasingly difficult to distinguish from 25,000-year-old mammoths.

Once the big game disappeared, which they did by 10,000 B.C.E., the San Francisco peninsula had little to offer the few people—there were no more than several thousand total—living in California. Exposed to the prevailing westerly winds, San Francisco was colder than the surrounding areas, had less game, and less seed-bearing grasses and other edible plants. There were modest numbers of live oaks and buckeyes, but California Indians did not make acorns their staple food until 2500 B.C.E. Most critically, San Francisco had no marshes or mudflats. Those muddy, murky areas at the edge of land and water would later generate a cornucopia of shellfish, shallow-water fish, and waterfowl. But the bay did not yet exist.

Then, around 9000 B.C.E., the great glaciers started melting, and the sea levels began to inexorably rise. At a rate of three-quarters of an inch a year, or more than 100 horizontal feet in some areas, sea levels rose quickly enough that the change was noticeable to anyone camped permanently or temporarily along San Francisco's coast. The shoreline moved eastward, turning the Farallon peaks into islands. The bay began to fill—a process that continued for 3,000 years. As the sea poured in, the Golden Gate turned into a wide channel. Within a generation, ancestral homelands and hunting and fishing areas vanished beneath the water. When sea level rise slowed to

0.001 inch a year, by 4000 B.C.E., extensive marshes began to appear at the edges of the bay—a perfect environment for mollusks, fish, and birds. By 2500 B.C.E., the Bay Area had been completely transformed: It was now a superrich food environment, with oysters, clams, mussels, fish, and waterfowl easily available.

Before this time, it's unlikely that more than a few people lived permanently on San Francisco Bay. They probably came to the great estuary to collect shellfish or ducks, then moved on to warmer and more food-rich places in a migratory pattern common to hunter-gatherers. But when word got out that a vast free shellfish restaurant had opened its doors off Hunters Point, and Mission Bay, and Ellis Landing in Richmond, and West Berkeley, more and more people began to settle permanently or semi-permanently on the bay. Most of them chose the East Bay, but a few chose the cold, windy, hilly, sandy peninsula on the west side.

We don't fully understand why. Trading probably played a role: San Francisco Indians engaged in three-way trade with the people living in the North Bay, who had access to coveted obsidian, and with those in the East Bay, with whom they could trade coastal shells. For whatever reason, a few people ended up on the tip of the peninsula, discovered they could gather enough food to survive, and either kept coming back or never left. By the time the Great Pyramid of Giza was built, a few hundred people had settled in San Francisco. They and their successors, following a way of life that remained largely unchanged, lived here for the next 4,000 or 5,000 years. It is one of the great success stories in the history of the human race.

CHAPTER 4

STAIRWAY TO HEAVEN

The Filbert Steps, between
Telegraph Hill Place and Sansome Street

S an Francisco is filled with steps and staircases, shortcuts and obscure passages. These walkways constitute a kind of alternative and secret grid, a human-size way of moving through the city. There is something playful and gratuitous about steps. Walking on them makes a journey less purposeful and more like a game of hide and seek. They turn grown-ups into kids, and the city into a giant backyard. A delicious, slightly illicit quality hangs over stairways; walking on them has a faint whiff of climbing over the neighbor's fence, an essential tactic in reclaiming one's city and one's soul. They blur the sharp boundary between public and private space that makes urban life alienating. They offer an escape from the abstract machinery of the city.

Many cities have memorable stairs. Lisbon, a gorgeous white seaport that resembles San Francisco in many ways (right down to having suffered a catastrophic earthquake), has its share. Paris, in its flat river valley, doesn't have a lot of stairs, but the few that it does are world-class: The old steps that run up to Sacré Coeur evoke the lost yellow-white-and-black world of Utrillo. Pittsburgh claims to have 712 stairways, even more than San Francisco does. (One could compare this with Birmingham, England's idiotic boast that it has "more miles of canals than Venice," a claim that avoids addressing the issue of quality, but Pittsburgh is a lovely and underrated city.) Hong Kong has its mighty escalator system climbing up Victoria Peak, which sort of counts. Every Italian hill town, from Perugia to Erice, has divine stairs. So does Guanajuato in Mexico. Rio has some wonderful steps. The list could go on indefinitely.

But none of these cities have stairways that possess the extraordinary variety and beauty of those in San Francisco. According to Adah Bakalinsky, author of the delightful little book *Stairway Walks in San Francisco*, there are more than 600 of them. Because San Francisco is so hilly, stairs are found all over town, from the Richmond District to the Bayview. And each one of them has a different flavor.

There are the long, exposed, steep stairs that go up from 16th Avenue and Moraga to Golden Gate Heights, the city's great western balcony. There are the gaunt ones on the north slope of Hunters Point. There are the stately ones that go up to tiered Alta Plaza, ominously reminiscent of ceremonial steps leading to an Aztec sacrificial site. There are virtually unknown ones like the overgrown, uneven passageway—as much a trail as a set of steps—that emerges onto 19th Street from Kite Hill, as unexpected as the wardrobe that opens onto Narnia. There are the superb Vulcan Steps on Twin Peaks and the formal, *Last Year at Marienbad*–like Pacheco Stairway in Forest Hill and the verdant Green Street steps on Russian Hill and the wondrous Pemberton Steps on Twin Peaks. But the most sublime of them all are the Filbert Steps.

What makes the Filbert Steps so beautiful is the way they mediate between and harmonize the human world and the natural one. That harmony is epitomized by the gardens that surround them, which must be among the most stunning gardens on any public passageway in the world. From those lush gardens you have a tree-filtered view to the wharves of the Embarcadero and the bustling bay. Standing on these old, worn, wooden steps, next to some of the oldest houses in the city, you can almost hear the footsteps of a wandering 49er, or a 1930s longshoreman walking home from the docks. The two little wooden lanes that intersect the steps, Darrell Place and Napier Lane, are hideaways so magical there should be a permanent rainbow pointing at them. And this oasis is located in the most dramatic location in San Francisco, on the sheer, quarried eastern face of Telegraph Hill, which rises improbably up in the city's extreme northeastern corner.

The Filbert Steps made a memorable appearance in the 1947 film noir *Dark Passage*, when escaped con Humphrey Bogart, his face bandaged after plastic surgery, walks up them to Lauren Bacall's apartment on Montgomery Street.

It was a fitting scene, because the steps connect wildly disparate realities. Just seconds after you leave their dreamlike confines, you emerge on Sansome Street next to Levi Plaza, amid landscaped grounds and modern office buildings. You're back on the grid. You feel like you've just climbed down a rope ladder that drops from a tree house to Times Square.

The Filbert Steps run between Coit Tower and the waterfront, but they take you to the best destination of all: nowhere. On those worn steps, surrounded by fuchsia and redwood and magnolia and cypress and roses, the city fades away. You and this verdant dell are all that's left, a green thought in a green shade.

CHAPTER 5

THE HARBOR
AT THE END
OF THE WORLD

Mouth of Drakes Bay, Point Reyes National Seashore

S ome historical events are so strange, so incongruous, so haunting, that they feel like dreams. Usually, the locations where those events took place are unremarkable, but every now and then their appearance is as otherworldly as their history. Drakes Bay is one of those places. For the two beleaguered sea captains who missed San Francisco Bay and put in there in the 16th century, Drakes Bay was a harbor at the end of the world. And that's exactly what it still looks like.

Drakes Bay and the surrounding Point Reyes peninsula are a world apart. That isn't just a figure of speech: Point Reyes sits on a different tectonic plate than the rest of North America. The silence that hangs over its drowned bays and enigmatic inlets is the cosmic, indifferent silence of the high mountains. At once toylike and eternal, this landscape is the perfect setting for an apparition from another universe. You don't even have to half-close your eyes to imagine a galleon sailing in below its white cliffs. It's like a stage set designed by God.

The two galleons that sailed into Drakes Bay came within 30 miles of the future city of San Francisco, but they had absolutely nothing to do with its history. They might as well have been hallucinations, tunnels through space-time that immediately collapsed. Which makes them perfect emblems for the city.

For most of its history, San Francisco was the Rosencrantz and Guildenstern of cities. It could not even manage to get itself discovered. Until it made its grand entrance onto the world stage with the Gold Rush, it was a meaningless bystander in a grand drama, a two-bit courier carrying self-defeating messages, not even worthy of being killed onstage. Its entire early history is one of futility—missed opportunities, blind alleys, roads that led nowhere, farcical mistakes, and enormous events that it had nothing to do with.

For a San Franciscan, there is something perversely satisfying about this dubious genealogy. If you can't be at the center of the universe, better to be an unknown asteroid whirling through some distant galaxy. Plus, it suits San Francisco's character more.

Blame it on Pangaea. When the primordial supercontinent broke up and left the continents in their present configuration, the west coast of North America ended up being terrestrial Pluto. During the great Age of Exploration, California was harder to get to from Europe than almost anywhere on earth. To reach it, explorers had to either sail across two mighty oceans or cross a vast continent filled with towering mountain ranges, waterless deserts, and hostile Indians.

From the 15th century until well into the 18th, the west coast of North America was the great unknown, a blank spot on maps, thought to be part of Asia or a mythical Strait of Anian leading to the riches of the East. When Christopher Columbus discovered the New World, it was by mistake: He was trying to find a sea route to the East Indies. He never knew what he had found.

In 1513 Vasco Núñez de Balboa waded into the Pacific off Panama and claimed it and all of its islands for the king of Spain, becoming the first

European to reach the great western ocean, which he called the "South Sea." Seven years later, Ferdinand Magellan sailed into the Pacific through the straits at the bottom of South America that bear his name. But the South Sea's northern extent remained unknown, as did almost all of the west coast of the New World.

This ignorance is reflected in contemporary maps. A 1508 map by Johannes Ruysch depicts South America as the New World, with Asia in the place where North America actually is. Seventy-five years later, the "northern mystery" was still a mystery. Indeed, some cartographic depictions of this blind spot in the world seem to have been simply made up. One of Ignazio Danti's two famous hemispheric "Mappamondos" (world maps) in the Vatican loggia, executed in 1583, shows a long, narrow peninsula, inexplicably in the shape of a huge "V," connecting the west coast of North America with China. A 1600 map by cartographer Gabriel Tatton depicts California running almost due west and virtually touching China (although the trustworthiness of that depiction is somewhat undercut by a note admitting that the land "was yet to be discovered.") Cosmographers—a wonderful, sadly extinct profession—argued about what lay in the northern stretches of the South Sea: A land mass connected to Europe? An open sea? Four great islands? California remained terra incognita.

The idea that California was an island, which largely derived from the peninsular shape of Baja California, proved particularly hard to kill. Even after an intrepid Jesuit Father named Eusebio Kino led overland expeditions over the top of the Sea of Cortez in the early 1700s, the myth persisted. Maps depicting California as an island appeared as late as the 1750s, despite King Ferdinand VI of Spain's 1747 edict—a leading candidate for the title of Most Hilarious Royal Decree of All Time—that "California is not an island." (In a disgraceful act of lèse-majesté, Ferdinand's pronouncement has been ignored by the editors of the *New York Times* and other East Coast publications, who continue to obsessively run any story depicting California—in particular, Northern California—as an island of wild-eyed utopian dingbats given to hedonistic, slightly stupid practices. Which is not to say that Northern Californians do not frequently provide them with ammunition. The *Times* recently seized with relish upon a story about how George Lucas's wealthy Marin County neighbors rejected his proposal to build another state-of-the-art film facility in their bucolic vicinity, leading

Lucas to change plans and instead propose—suck on this, rich white people!—a low-income housing development. The horrified neighbors began squabbling among themselves. One anonymous woman said the atmosphere was "sheer terror" and—this is what really must have made the *Times* editors drool—compared the situation to "Syria.")

The endurance of the irrational belief that California was an island highlights another reason, besides its remoteness, that it remained undiscovered for so long: It was shrouded in myths. Those myths originated in a wildly popular chivalric potboiler called *Las sergas de Esplandián* (*The Exploits of Esplandian*), written by Garcia Odoñez de Montalvo and published in 1510 as a sequel to *Amadis of Gaul*, the most successful printed work in the early 1500s in Spain. These fantastical romances, featuring addictive yarns about noble Christian knights battling evil giants and hot Amazon warrior queens, were the comic books, bodice-rippers, and raised-type-silver-and-purple-cover airport thrillers of their day. They were so popular that there was actually an attempt to ban them.

The very word "California" comes from Montalvo's wild page-turner—a fact that may have somehow made its way into the state's Hollywood-laden DNA. In *Las sergas*, the brave and chaste hero woos and wins an Amazon queen named Calafia, who is fighting with pagan forces besieging Constantinople. In the course of his quest, Esplandian is told an enthralling story about Queen Calafia's island homeland: "Know, then, that on the right hand of the Indies there is an island called California, very close to the side of the Terrestrial Paradise, and it was peopled by black women, without any man among them, for they lived in the fashion of Amazons. They were of strong and hardy bodies, of ardent courage and great force. Their island was the strongest in all the world, with its steep cliffs and rocky shores. Their arms were all of gold, and so was the harness of the wild beasts which they tamed and rode. For, in the whole island, there was no metal but gold."

The Amazon legend found in *Las sergas* inspired the first explorations of Baja California and was "confirmed" by reports from soldiers who told Hernán Cortéz that while exploring the northern coast of Mexico they had heard of an "island of women" and spoken to "the lords of a province named Ciguatan, who strongly affirmed that there was an island populated entirely by women 10 days' journey away . . . very rich in pearls and gold." Tales of the opulent "Seven Cities," another medieval legend, circulated widely, becoming mixed up with the stories about California and other fabulous places like *La Gran Quivira*, where even the kitchen utensils were made of gold. (The word "Quivira" appears on the abovementioned map by Danti.) The most peculiar story was about a king called El Dorado ("the gilded one"), a kind of ur-Goldfinger who was supposedly painted with gold dust every morning and washed off every evening.

But subsequent expeditions to Baja California in search of the fabulous island kingdom were disastrous. Cortéz's final, inglorious expedition ended with more than half of his men dead of famine and disease, and the survivors cursing his name and the land he had discovered. When later explorers bestowed the name "California" upon the barren peninsula, they may have done so in bitter mockery: The godforsaken coast they encountered bore no resemblance to the gold-filled "earthly paradise" described by Montalvo.

(To the cavalcade of futility that is California's Hispanic history, we must fast-forward 300 years to attach a final "Kick Me" sign. James Marshall discovered gold in California on January 24, 1848. On February 2, 1848, former Spanish colony Mexico signed the Treaty of Guadalupe Hidalgo, ceding California to the United States. The heirs of the conquistadores had unknowingly owned the real El Dorado for nine days.)

The first European to set foot on the soil of what is now California was a former crossbowman and companion of Cortéz's named Juan Rodríguez Cabrillo. Considering the genocidal impact the "civilized" races would later have on California's native inhabitants, it is appropriate that Cabrillo as a boy had taken part in a hideous massacre of Indians in Cuba and, during the siege of Mexico City, caulked ships with pitch made from the rendered fat of slain Indians. (These facts do not appear in any of the standard accounts of the discovery of California.)

Cabrillo's mission was to find the mythical Strait of Anian—the supposed passage between the Atlantic and Pacific Oceans that would allow Spanish ships to sail directly to the East Indies. He set sail from Navidad in New Spain (Mexico) on June 27, 1542. After three months at sea, Cabrillo discovered "a port, closed and very good," which he called San Miguel— now known as San Diego. On September 28, 1542, he landed and formally took possession of Alta California. (Alta, or "upper" California, was the name the Spanish gave to the area that was to become the American state. Arid Baja, or "lower" California, was a Spanish possession and remains a

Mexican one.) Cabrillo followed the prescribed ritual: He claimed the land in the name of the king of Castile, placed his hand threateningly on his sword while saying he was prepared to defend it, cut down some plants and tore up grass, moved stones around, and splashed water from the sea onto the land. According to accepted tradition, this symbolic mumbo jumbo conferred upon Spain eternal ownership of the land. Alta California would remain first in Spain's hands, then in those of its former colony Mexico, for more than 300 years.

Soon after this, the captain suffered one of those ordinary mishaps that often proved fatal in the days before antibiotics. While on San Miguel Island, Cabrillo heard that his men needed help in a battle with local Indians. Jumping out of a rowboat, Cabrillo broke his arm or leg slipping on a rocky ledge. He continued to sail north, making it as far as a cape near Fort Ross, 90 miles north of San Francisco, before turning back. He discovered Drakes Bay but did not put in there. Like every other explorer for the next 234 years, he missed the Golden Gate, either because his course took him too far out to sea, or because of fog, or because the opening was obscured by the East Bay hills and Angel Island. Meanwhile, Cabrillo's wound had become gangrenous. While wintering in the Channel Islands near Santa Barbara, the old conquistador died on January 3, 1543.

Cabrillo had discovered California. But the discovery had almost no effect on history. No one followed up on it. Cabrillo's voyage had been a failure. He had not found the Strait of Anian, or any passage to the riches of the East, or the fabulous cities of gold and silver. His expedition did perhaps leave one tangible legacy: a small rock. In 1901, on a small Channel Island, someone stumbled upon a rock bearing the initials "J.R.C." If that stone—which now sits in the anthropology museum at the University of California, Berkeley—is indeed Cabrillo's gravestone, it is the oldest European artifact in California.

Cabrillo's voyage was followed by one of the most storied and romantic chapters in Spain's entire imperial saga: the Manila galleon. And once again, San Francisco remained just outside the frame of this Technicolor epic.

The Manila galleon carried spices and goods from the Philippines to Acapulco. Their northerly route followed the trade winds across the Pacific to Cape Mendocino in Northern California, then south past the Farallon Islands and on to Mexico. It was a brutal journey, the longest regular voyage in the world, and the most dreaded, but for those who braved it, the rewards were great: A single voyage could make a captain comfortable for life, and ordinary seamen could make more money than on any other trip. Starting in 1565, and continuing for an astonishing 250 years, the great treasure galleons would sail past the Farallones, one each year. But they never saw the Golden Gate.

In 1579, a Manila galleon named the *Nuestra Señora de la Concepción* played a key role in the oddest of all the peculiar episodes that make up San Francisco's long non-history: the mysterious visit of Sir Francis Drake.

The celebrated English privateer had left Plymouth in 1577 in his flagship, the eighty-foot *Pelican*, which he later renamed the *Golden Hind*. Drake took her through the stormy Strait of Magellan, emerging into the Pacific like a wolf in a sheepfold. The Spanish ships sailing up and down the coast of South and Central America were unprepared for this hostile interloper into their ocean (until the 17th century, the Pacific was called "the Spanish lake"), and Drake found the pickings rich. He captured several ships and sacked Spanish towns before coming upon the *Concepción*, the biggest prize of his career, on her way to Manila. After a short fight, Drake seized 80 pounds of gold, 26 tons of silver, 13 chests of silver coins, and jewels—a haul worth twice as much as Queen Elizabeth's tax income for the year.

Drake sailed north, searching for—what else?—the Strait of Anian. Unable to find it but not wanting to sail back south where Spanish warships would be searching for him, he looked for a place on the northern Pacific coast to refit his ship and take on supplies, before heading west toward the Moluccas and home. He landed somewhere near San Francisco. The exact location of his landing remains controversial—his own journal is lost, and his chaplain's record was deemed unreliable by Drake himself. But most scholars believe, and the federal government now concurs, that the great mariner sailed into Drakes Bay, guided the *Golden Hind* over the shallows into Drakes Estero, and careened his ship in a shallow cove about a mile inside the mouth of the estuary.

Drake remained in the cove for three weeks, repairing his ship and meeting the friendly Miwok Indians who came down to the shore to stare at the great wooden ship that had suddenly glided into their unchanging world. It was the first encounter between northern California Indians and white men. When the hull was shipshape, Drake left a "plate of brasse" inlaid with a sixpence that claimed "Nova Albion" for England. (He named the harbor New England because the white cliffs of Drakes Bay reminded him of the white cliffs of Dover.) Then he sailed off into the Pacific, passing the Farallon Islands (which he named the Ilands of St. James) but missing the Golden Gate. In 1580, more than two and a half years after he had left Plymouth, Drake returned to a hero's welcome. He was the second man to circumnavigate the globe.

The appearance of an Elizabethan mariner in Point Reyes was like a deus ex machina conjured up by one of the less intelligent gods on Mount Olympus. This contact with the Age of Shakespeare had no effect on San Francisco's subsequent history whatsoever, except to leave an embarrassing boo-boo on the legacy of a famous professor.

There is no physical evidence that Drake visited Point Reyes. But an inscribed brass plate found in 1936, supposedly the one left by Drake, was pronounced genuine by the eminent U.C. Berkeley historian Herbert Bolton, who excitedly exclaimed, "One of the world's long-lost historical treasures apparently has been found." Bolton's view was initially confirmed by metal-lurgical testing. Although many were immediately skeptical—debates raged about such arcane matters as whether the letter "J" existed in the English alphabet during Drake's lifetime—the plate was generally considered gen-uine until 1977, when exhaustive analysis revealed it to be a fake. The mo-tive for the hoax has never been established—no one made any money off it—although it has been suggested that it was an elaborate student prank at Bolton's expense, whose perpetrators were too embarrassed to admit what they had done after their esteemed professor was taken in.

With the infamous "Calaveras skull," which allegedly proved that hu-mans, mastodons, and elephants coexisted in California during the Plio-cene epoch that ended about 2 million years ago—and also snookered an august academic—the "plate of brasse" is California's most famous fraud.

The Drake episode was weird enough. But 16 years later, another cap-tain, sailing under the flag of Spain, landed in the same toy harbor. The adventure he had in California was even more epic than Drake's, but in the end just as pointless.

In 1590, the scurvy problem that had always plagued the Manila galle-ons had become intolerable. By the time the big-bellied ships got near California, the bodies of dead crewmen were invariably being tossed into the sea. Moreover, Spain was increasingly worried about the raids of Drake and another feared (and less chivalrous) English pirate, Thomas Cavendish. New Spain's new viceroy decided that it was essential to find a way station on the California coast where the crew of the Manila galleon could regain its health, and pick up word of English pirates and possibly an armed escort.

A Portuguese mariner named Sebastián Cermeño was chosen to head the voyage of discovery. Cermeño sailed from Acapulco on March 21, 1594, to Manila, where he changed ships to a smaller, 200-ton ship named the *San Agustín*. With the ship fully laden with Chinese porcelain and silks, Cermeño sailed for California, reaching the coast several months later. After an abortive attempt to enter Trinity Bay, he sailed south and anchored in Drakes Bay.

A week later, disaster struck. While almost the entire crew was ashore, a rare southeast storm blew up, driving the *San Agustín* onto the rocks. Helplessly, the crew watched as their ship—it might as well have been their space shuttle—was battered in the pounding surf. The ship and everything in it was lost, and several men were killed. Fortunately, the Spanish had a small open dugout with sweeps and one or two sails called a *viroco*. Cermeño packed all 70 members of the crew and a dog into the tiny launch and headed for Mexico. In one of the epic feats in the annals of seamanship, they made it, although the unfortunate dog was devoured skin and all.

Cermeño's voyage, like Cabrillo's and Drake's, had no effect whatsoever on California history. A few years later, Spain sent another captain, Sebastián Vizcaíno, on a similar voyage. In 1602 Vizcaíno discovered the harbor of Monterey, which he praised effusively. But in an appropriately deflating end to the whole saga, the viceroy argued that if Spain did establish a port in Monterey, it would actually attract the English, who would simply take it over. The viceroy's letter was the opening strategic salvo in a long game of chess over California that would eventually involve Spain, England, France, Russia, and finally a country whose first settlers would not land in Jamestown, on the other side of the continent, for five more years—the United States.

Vizcaíno's voyage was the last attempt to explore California during the Age of Discovery. In one of those strange discontinuities of history, the west coast of North America simply vanished again. For a few moments three or four spotlights had probed the darkness, illuminating fugitive glimpses of an unknown world. Then the spotlights flickered out and the darkness fell again, not to be lifted for 167 years. When San Francisco was finally discovered, it was not by sea at all, but by land.

Marx said that history repeats itself first as tragedy, then as farce. But San Francisco reversed his dictum. It started out as farce. For the native people, whose unchanging existence was spared for almost two centuries by the European failure to find the Golden Gate, the tragedy would come later.

CHAPTER 6

THE CANYON

Glen Canyon

Every great city is like a memorable cassoulet, containing secret ingredients that give it a unique flavor. One of San Francisco's secret ingredients is its Mystery Hills.

Because I am obsessed with horizons, I have tried to explore all the hills that you can see from San Francisco, from the 50-odd ones in the city itself to the dozens that surround it, some of them 40 miles or more away. But it is a vast undertaking, and I've barely started. And even after I've climbed a hill, I often don't recognize it later. The landscape here is so complicated that little pieces of hills, both inside and outside the city, are constantly coming into view. There are so many hills, the relationships between them are so convoluted and the views of them so fragmented, that no matter how long you've lived here, half the time you're not sure what you're looking at. For example, I know that from the summit of Nob Hill at Sacramento and Jones, the long ridge eight miles to the south that appears behind Bernal Heights and drops down to Highway 101, is the eastern end of Mount San

Bruno. But I am not sure what the higher rounded ridge behind it is. I think it's Sweeney Ridge, the bay discovery site, but I'm not positive—even though I've hiked to the top of Sweeney Ridge twice. Even more irritatingly elusive is a piece of a big hill in the southeastern part of town that keeps popping into view. Is it the ridge in McClaren Park, Hunters Point, Silver Terrace, or Bay View? And what about the most distant mountain of all, somewhere way up north in Napa—is that part of the Mayacamas? The list is endless.

These Mystery Hills—does any other city contain so many unknown vistas?—make San Francisco feel permanently enigmatic, like one of those surreal backgrounds in George Herriman's *Krazy Kat* cartoons in which new mountains and objects appear in every panel. I sometimes suspect that the hills are gaslighting me—getting up in the middle of the night and moving furtively around.

In this cryptic landscape, the most surprising site of all is Glen Canyon. Glen Canyon is not only the most peculiar geographical anomaly in San Francisco—a concave feature in a convex city—it is also the least known. In any other city, a deep, wild, rocky canyon with a creek flowing through it, in almost the exact geographical center of town, would be celebrated far and wide. But even most San Franciscans have never set foot in Glen Canyon. In a city of Mystery Hills, it is the Mystery Gorge.

Glen Canyon is literally a tear in the city's fabric. It runs directly south of towering Twin Peaks and east of the city's highest point, Mount David-son. Its ancient chert boulders were formed by the same chthonic forces that lifted up those 900-foot hills, and the little stream that trickles through it is a reminder of the river that scoured it out. Glen Canyon was formerly called "Little Switzerland," but it feels more like a weird combination of Scotland and the Wild West. Its steeply sloping sides, verdant riparian strip, and long views to the southern mountains give it the feeling of a highlands valley; its massive red boulders, sparse trees, and parched beauty recall a canyon in Utah.

Aside from the Farallones and Lands End, Glen Canyon is the wildest and most unspoiled part of San Francisco. To hike through this deep notch surrounded by the highest hills in the city is to experience San Francisco's primordial landscape in its most dramatic form. Owls nest in its eucalyptus trees, raptors circle above it, and two or three coyotes live in the dense willow thickets along the creek. An area that still shelters coyotes is a nut that man has not yet completely cracked.

By rights, Glen Canyon should have been developed or filled or otherwise ruined decades ago. It's economically useless, and it takes up 70 acres of land in the heart of the city. If it had been a wetland and not a narrow, rocky gorge with a 350-foot drop, it would be home to a Costco today. It's only here because it was too big to fill in.

But that landscape was almost ruined. Glen Canyon's history is a microcosm of San Francisco's evolving attitude toward nature—from primordial innocence to man's-dominion-over-nature callousness to patriotic triumphalism to wrongheaded rationalism to citizen activism and enlightened ecological stewardship.

The native Californians were drawn to Glen Canyon because of Islais Creek. The creek, which over millennia carved out the canyon and still trickles through it for a mile, was once one of the few major streams in San Francisco, pouring down from Twin Peaks on its way to the bay four miles away. During the Mexican period, when the canyon was part of a vast land grant called Rancho San Miguel, cattle were grazed on it. But Glen Canyon's bucolic existence came to an end after the American conquest. In a development so egregious that it seems like an allegory of man profaning nature, the first dynamite factory in the United States opened in what was then called Rock Canyon in 1868. (The fact that dynamite was invented by Alfred Nobel, a lifelong pacifist who established the prize that bears his name so that he would not be remembered as "the merchant of death," makes the allegory even stranger.) After an explosion killed the factory's chemist and his teamster, the plant was moved into the remote sand dunes of the Richmond District.

In 1889 the estate of railroad tycoon Charles Crocker bought Glen Canyon from philanthropist and former mayor Adolph Sutro. In 1898, the Crocker estate, the largest landowner in the city, opened a pleasure garden and zoo in the canyon, hoping to use Little Switzerland to lure buyers to its development in nearby Glen Park. One of the attractions of the pleasure garden was a replica of Morro Castle, the citadel in Santiago, Cuba, that American troops had conquered just months before during the Spanish-American War, the fateful intervention that marked the rise of the United

States as an imperialist power (and was bitterly denounced by an old San Francisco newspaperman named Mark Twain).

After complaints about rowdy behavior in the canyon, the city bought it in 1922 and turned it into a park. The peaceful canyon seemed finally to have escaped the depredations of industrialism, jingoism, and other all-American by-products. But in 1958, the hyperrationalist postwar planners who saw the unfettered use of the automobile as America's salvation decided that the best use for Glen Canyon would be to install a "Crosstown Freeway" that would go through the canyon, tunnel under Twin Peaks, and emerge near Seventh Avenue to join up with—what else?—another freeway. Facing widespread resistance from citizens—a movement that would become known as the Freeway Revolt—a city official impatiently said, "Someone is always hurt by construction of a freeway. It comes back to the basic question facing the city: Does San Francisco want freeways, or not?" The residents of Glen Park did not, and their resistance, spearheaded by housewives, saved the canyon.

But it was too late to save Islais Creek. Starting in the 1920s, the expanding city had begun relentlessly covering its three miles of meandering, gentle, green-fringed chaos. Today the creek runs down to an old Works Progress Administration–built recreation center at the southern end of the canyon, then vanishes into a culvert leading to underground pipes. The water doesn't appear aboveground again until it flows into the bay north of Hunters Point, three miles away.

Islais Creek is lost, but San Francisco has come a long way from the days when it wanted to turn the canyon into a freeway. For today, Glen Canyon is not only a park; it is also a designated natural area, which means that the city is devoted to preserving it in its original state.

The Natural Areas Program, created in 1997, is a unique part of the San Francisco Recreation and Parks Department. It takes care of 31 natural oases throughout the city, with a total of 1,100 acres. A tiny staff of nine, along with thousands of volunteers, labor in these scattered places to preserve and restore as much of the city's native flora and fauna as possible. The seeds of the program were sown in 1977, when voters—after rejecting it twice—approved a city proposition that created the Open Space Fund. The city used the fund to acquire a number of open spaces, including some of the most magical places in town, like Tank Hill, Kite Hill, and Billy Goat

Hill. At first, acquisition was the most important part of the program, but over time, maintenance became more important. Eventually that led to the Natural Areas Program.

"We have about a quarter of the Rec and Park land and 1 percent of their budget," said Kirra Swenerton, who has worked for the Natural Areas Program for three and a half years. "We started our program in tandem with the volunteer program. We couldn't do it without them on our budget. All kinds of people volunteer—people between jobs, docents, seniors, students, and of course, neighbors. Glen Canyon has one of the most active neighborhood groups."

I first met Swenerton when I was wandering through Palou and Phelps Park, a tiny, little-known, unspoiled hillside in the gritty Bayview District where she was gathering seeds from a native plant called goldfields. A month later I met her high up on the stunning eastern slope of Glen Canyon, below Berkeley Way. Using water from a tank on a pickup truck, she, a couple of co-workers, and some volunteers were watering native plants they had planted on the hillside near one of the enormous boulders that dot the canyon. The volunteers included a retired businessman who lived in the neighborhood and two young hipster-ish guys who lived in the Haight, who said they loved nature and just wanted to work outdoors. Pulling up invasive plants nearby was an Asian high school student who had taken a summer job with the program.

Swenerton said the Natural Areas Program does "restoration ecology"—restoring natural areas to their original state, within the limits of feasibility and without unduly impacting other uses. One might think that in environmentally conscious San Francisco, a city department tasked with this greener-than-green mission would receive unanimous public approval. But anyone who thought that wouldn't know San Francisco. When it comes to left-wing NIMBYism, self-righteous argumentativeness, and just plain selfishness and ignorance, San Francisco is a serious threat to unseat the reigning world champion, my hometown of Berkeley. And the Natural Areas Program has implacable foes.

"Some people think we're Sierra Pacific [a huge logging company] because we cut trees," said Swenerton's colleague Dylan Hayes, who has worked in the program for eight years. "They get angry because we want to cut some of the eucalyptus trees on Mount Davidson, for example. Well, these are introduced, nonnative trees, and they're threatening habitats needed by endangered species. Our purpose is to preserve the most species for the most people for the longest time. And you have to make decisions to save things."

"Look, our plan is not to get rid of all the eucalyptus—far from it," Swenerton said. "We try to strike a balance. Natural spaces are a map of the human history of the world. European grasses came with the Spanish. Fennel may have originally come from a garden. Other plants come from the grazing era. Only a tiny percentage are aggressive. Like this wild radish." She pointed down to a purple plant growing on the hillside. "It's beautiful, but it's invasive. These are the ones we try to get rid of." Fortunately, Swenerton said, there are no controversies over the Natural Area Program's actions in Glen Canyon.

I left the workers on the hill to fight the good fight against wild radishes and ignorant NIMBYism and followed a winding trail down the canyon toward Islais Creek. I stopped at a spectacular chert outcropping whose intricate red patterns looked like a Max Ernst painting. Birds sang and insects buzzed in the noon sun. Farther up the canyon, a network of trails meandered on the steep slopes, past huge boulders that had been sitting there from time immemorial. I wandered down to the willow-fringed creek. The water, just a trickle, gleamed next to a muddy trail, from which a gnarly-rooted old tree grew. I walked out of the dense canopy and back into the sun. Looking down the canyon, past towering rock formations, Mount San Bruno loomed, five miles away. A hawk hovered silently overhead. I was in a steep canyon in the middle of the city. There was no one around.

CHAPTER 7

THE TEMPLE

The Palace of Fine Arts, Lyon and Bay Streets

T he beauty of the Palace of Fine Arts is inseparable from its strangeness. A vast, purposeless rotunda supported by mighty Corinthian columns and surrounded by a mysterious, vaguely ruinlike colonnade, it looms above its tranquil lagoon like one of those illogical, pseudo-classical structures that appear in the backgrounds of baroque paintings. The Palace is so familiar that it is easy to forget that it is a folly. And like the other members of that peculiar architectural genre, it is a mood enhancer, as much a drug as it is a building.

The Palace of Fine Arts is the only on-site survivor of one of the most delirious miniature cities ever created, the joyously ephemeral Panama-Pacific International Exposition of 1915 that announced the rebirth of San Francisco from the 1906 catastrophe. Magnificent courts—the Court of the Universe, the Court of Abundance, and the Court of Four Seasons—adjoined a pleasure strip called "The Zone," which featured enormous models of the Grand Canyon, Yellowstone, and, in a more modest vein, the Creation. The crown jewel—literally—of the fair was the Tower of Jewels, a 435-foot structure decorated with 102,000 cut-glass "novagems" that at night turned into a vast, glittering diadem. Not until Burning Man—which started on Baker Beach, just around the seafront corner from the fair's site—would the world see another fake city so dazzlingly psychedelic.

The Palace was so beloved that a movement to preserve it started while the Exposition was still going on. It was saved, but it had not been built to last, and in 1965 it was completely rebuilt. It is appropriate that the Palace is the last building on the site of the last of the great world expositions. For it is a shrine to absence, a tribute to a vanished world, a concrete manifestation of things unseen.

The Palace's architect, Bernard Maybeck, was charged with creating a building that would serve as a kind of decompression chamber for fairgoers, a mind-calming passageway between the crowded and chaotic fairgrounds and the paintings and sculpture housed in a hall behind the Palace. Maybeck drew his inspiration from the 18th-century Italian artist Giovanni Piranesi's atmospheric etchings of Rome, in particular his etching of the collapsing, overgrown ruin of the Temple of Minerva Medica. He was also deeply influenced by *Isle of the Dead*, the eerily evocative painting of a surreal funerary island by the 19th-century Swiss symbolist painter Arnold Böcklin.

Both works captured the emotion that Maybeck was searching for, a feeling he called "modified melancholy" or "a sentiment in a minor key." But as Maybeck noted in the fascinating little book he published about creating the Palace, Böcklin's painting was too sad to serve as an "art gallery frontispiece," just as a Greek temple set on a wild island surrounded by stormy seas and mighty cliffs would be too terrifying and uncanny. Maybeck's solution was to place his Greek temple (the Greeks did not have domes, but for the visionary Maybeck that fact was irrelevant) on "the face of a placid lake, surrounded by high trees and lit up by a glorious full moon." This temple, he wrote, "would recall the days when your mother pressed you to her bosom and your final sob was hushed by a protecting spirit hovering over you, warm and large." It would achieve a "transition from sadness to content."

As they wander around the Palace and its lagoon—for its magnificent setting is an inseparable part of it—some may feel the sense of a protecting maternal spirit. The Palace has never had that particular effect on me. But it could, because it offers every other effect.

For Maybeck achieved his goal. He created a building so mysteriously evocative, so perfectly balanced between nature and artifice, reflection and joy, sadness and content, that it is like a giant mood ring. Its appearance depends not only on what time of day you see it but on what emotions you bring to it. The associations it evokes are infinite: a granite peninsula in a High Sierra lake; the endless vegetation-tangled ruins in Termessos, Turkey; the altar of a kindly god, who left it as a gift after a brief visit here.

Who are those mysterious downward-looking women atop the colonnade, their faces turned away? Are they symbols of mourning? Or symbols of searching? Do they sum up the entire building, an impossible, Orpheus-like attempt to bring back the dead? Are they embodiments of time itself, which disappears even as we try to seize it?

Maybeck never explained. But in a way, perhaps he did. After noting that "the artist began his work a long time ago in a nebulous haze of whys," Maybeck wrote that he must work for a long time before he realizes that he is not aiming at an object, but at "a portrayal of the life that is behind the visible."

The life that is behind the visible: Maybeck's words recall those of another great Romantic, a young poet who in the face of his own impending death used an ancient urn to celebrate the eternal spirit of art:

Heard melodies are sweet, but those unheard
Are sweeter; therefore, ye soft pipes, play on . . .

Like Keats's "Ode on a Grecian Urn," Bernard Maybeck's Palace of Fine Arts is an elegy so profound that it takes its own place in the pantheon it extols. Like the urn, and the poem about the urn, it says to all those who stand before it,

"Beauty is truth, truth beauty,"—that is all
Ye know on earth, and all ye need to know.

CHAPTER 8

THE LONG MARCH

Mountain Lake, near Lake Street and 12th Avenue

After Sebastián Vizcaíno discovered Monterey in 1602, Spain lost all interest in Alta California for more than 150 years. What led Madrid to settle its neglected possession, oddly enough, was fear of the Russians—the first in a long history of bogus Red Scares that would culminate in the duck-and-cover cold war drills I was forced to take part in as a grade school student in Berkeley in 1960.

Russia was nosing around the west coast of North America. Its explorers had ventured across the Bering Strait in 1743 and begun hunting sea otters in the Aleutian Islands. When they brought their catch to China, they discovered the million-hairs-per-square-inch pelts—sea otters have the densest fur in the world—fetched exorbitant prices. More traders followed, setting up villages in the Aleutians. In late 1767, the Spanish ambassador in St. Petersburg received (false) reports that Indians had killed three hundred Russian troops who had landed in California. The next year, King Charles III was tipped off that two Russian Navy ships had sailed on a secret exploratory mission expedition to Alaska. Alarmed, he decided that the old grass-throwing rites of possession were no longer sufficient and that Spain needed to take actual control of Alta California.

An expedition was dispatched from Mexico to settle the unknown land to the north. Made up of two land parties and two ships, it was led by a veteran soldier named Gaspar de Portolá and under the spiritual guidance of a deeply pious, self-flagellating Franciscan father named Junípero Serra. Serra was once anointed as the greatest Californian of them all: He was the first person from the state who was honored with a statue in the National Statuary Hall in Washington, D.C. Today, California no longer knows what to think of him.

The Sacred Expedition, as it was called, was plagued by mishaps. One of the ships dispatched to San Diego, the *San Carlos*, did not arrive for 110 days. It was a death ship: 24 of the men aboard had died, and the rest were too ravaged by the dread scurvy to lower a boat. After Portolá and Serra established a mission in San Diego—whose priest was soon to be butchered by enraged Indians—Portolá headed up the coast by land, leading 64 men so emaciated from starvation he described them as "skeletons." His goal was to establish a camp at Monterey, which Vizcaíno had hyperbolically described as "a fine harbor sheltered from all winds."

When Portolá's party reached a hill above Monterey, they looked down upon a long, unprotected beach pummeled by great swells from the Pacific. Convinced this open roadstead could not be that snug harbor, he ordered his party to keep heading north. Portolá later explained that the reason no one in his party recognized Monterey was that "we were all under hallucination," the first recorded example of what would become a familiar San Francisco excuse.

Portolá pushed on, stopping to camp near a stream at present-day Linda Mar in Pacifica. Linda Mar, which is just north of a famously sheer stretch of coastal cliffs called Devil's Slide, is one of those slightly seedy and forlorn places that dot the central California coast, a collision of nature at its grandest and humanity at its most banal. It's the last beach enclave in the southern part of Pacifica, an endearingly unglamorous California beach town with a white trash element mixed into its middle-class population. When somebody did a study of drug use among Bay Area high school students some years ago, they had to go to Pacifica to find a big enough cohort of white students to measure their drug use. The weirdest place in the vicinity is Rockaway Beach, a bizarre "village"-like development, as fake as the one in *The Prisoner*, that seems to have been designed for naughty assignations between retirees and bikers. A few confused tourists stroll around its stage-set-like architecture, while foaming waves break on the jagged golden cliffs behind. For connoisseurs of the half-assed sublime, Rockaway Beach is a case of Château d'Yquem.

Portolá sent a scouting party north to look for Point Reyes, which he believed to be a great harbor. That party, led by Sergeant José Francisco Ortega, walked to the top of a nearby mountain—probably San Bruno Mountain—where they saw a vast body of water. They had discovered San Francisco Bay. A few days later the entire party saw the "grandiose estero" from the top of nearby Sweeney Ridge. By a weird coincidence, the plaque (more or less arbitrarily) marking the discovery site is just a few yards away from a decaying Nike missile guidance station—crumbling testimony to a later Red Scare.

Unfortunately, no one understood the significance of what they had discovered. Portolá and his men were desperately looking for Monterey and were not sure whether it or Point Reyes lay ahead. (Just to add to the Key-stone Kops quality of the whole thing, the suitable-for-bathtub-toys inlet at Point Reyes was called "San Francisco.") After they discovered there was no way to cross the estuary, they decided in discouragement to return to San Diego. On the way back, they again failed to recognize Monterey. Reduced to eating a mule a day ("What misery!" wrote Portolá), they staggered back to San Diego "smelling frightfully of mule meat," only to face the caustic tongue of Father Serra, who said, "You come from Rome without having seen the Pope."

So far, so stupid, but the comedy of errors had just begun. Believing that the bay was a great river running out of the heart of the continent, the Spanish kept up a futile search for the "port and great river of San Francisco" for years. When a high-strung captain named Fernando Rivera finally set foot on San Francisco soil in 1774, he dismissed it as a worthless site.

In 1775, the *San Carlos*, the same ship that had drifted into San Diego with most of its crew dead, became the first ship to sail through the Golden

Gate, under the command of Lieutenant Juan de Ayala. Ayala explored the bay for six weeks before departing for Monterey. In a foreshadowing footnote, Ayala's men named Mission Bay "Ensenada de los Llorones" ("Cove of the Weepers"), because they saw some Indians weeping on the beach.

(There is something creepy about the role this death ship plays in San Francisco's history. At the moment that California was born, the *San Carlos* delivered on her shores a dreadful cargo: Strong men cut down by a hideous disease that robbed them of their youth, turned them into emaciated ghosts, and slowly killed them. Later, the same ship was the first one to sail into San Francisco Bay. Two hundred years later, another terrible disease, with strikingly similar symptoms, swept through San Francisco. When I was a taxi driver, just before the AIDS epidemic, I used to regularly pick up gay men leaving a Mission District bathhouse, one of the major vectors for infection in the city. The bathhouse was on San Carlos Street.)

But the place where San Francisco's history officially begins is on the southern shore of a small body of water in the Richmond District called Mountain Lake. This is the site where, on March 27, 1776, Juan Bautista de Anza, who two years before had blazed an overland trail to California, camped on his first night in what is now San Francisco. He had just led 240 men, women, and children and 1,000 head of cattle 1,200 miles from the Sonoran presidio at Tubac, south of present-day Tucson, Arizona, to California. Crossing harsh deserts and snowy mountains and negotiating with suspicious Indian tribes, Anza had safely delivered the colonists who would permanently settle California to Monterey, then continued on to San Francisco. There he selected sites for the first buildings in the city, the presidio (military base) and the mission—the two indispensable instruments of Spanish colonizing. Only one member of the expedition, a woman who died in childbirth, did not make it to California. It was one of the epic treks in American history.

Anza recruited most of his colonists—soldiers, settlers, and their families—from the Mexican provinces of Sinaloa and Sonora, promising them rations for five years, supplies, and wages. The crown even provided ribbons for women's hair. Most of the colonists had been "submerged in poverty"; some had shady pasts. One was the mother of Juana Briones de Miranda, an illiterate woman who would escape an abusive husband to become one of the most remarkable figures in San Francisco's history. Another was an Apache. But a "free mulata" widow named Maria Arballo deserves special mention.

At a party to celebrate the arrival of some wayward members of the expedition, Arballo sang a few racy, teasing improvised songs called *glosas*. Some of her verbal barbs evidently struck the expedition's geographer and diarist, a Franciscan father named Pedro Font, in his soft posterior. Font was an excellent diarist, but he was also an insufferably self-righteous prig. After Arballo had, in Font's words, "brazenly sang some *glosas* that were not so nice," her male companion, apparently jealous of the applause, began beating her. When Anza came out of his tent and scolded the man, Font protested, "Let it be, sir, he is doing the right thing." But Anza replied, "No, Father, I must not allow these excesses in my presence." Font whined, "He was strict about this and not strict about the excesses of the party!—which went on until quite late."

A wild party, an outraged reactionary, a free-spirited woman and an enlightened leader—all the essential elements of the future San Francisco were there. But Maria Arballo deserves an honored place in California history just for irritating Font.

It was a long and difficult journey. As the party crossed the snowy mountains into California, the women cried "Ay!"—a plaintive wail of regret for the homeland they had left. In San Jose, the children cried because there was not enough to eat, which led the nearby hills to be named Lomas de las Lágrimas (Hills of Tears). But Anza, who could ride 50 or 60 miles a day fueled by only a cup of morning chocolate, guided them unerringly through the wilderness. When he said goodbye to the colonists in Monterey, they wept. He then gathered a smaller party, which he led to San Francisco. On his first night he camped at Mountain Lake because of its freshwater.

Mountain Lake is one of the stranger historical sites in San Francisco. It is hidden away at the end of a swanky dead-end street in the bland, pleasantly upscale Richmond District, two blocks away from bustling Clement Street. It's about the last place in the city you'd expect to find a 1,700-year-old freshwater lake. A beautiful little park fronts the lake, but its western side is profaned by Park Presidio Boulevard, the intrusive freeway that connects the western part of the city with the Golden Gate Bridge. The eight-foot-deep lake is polluted and only a couple of hundred yards wide. It used to be bigger and deeper before the freeway was built and eucalyptus trees encroached on it and shrank it. The lake drains out of a pipe on the west side and runs through culverts into the Lobos Valley, a short, wild stretch of sand and tangled brush hiding the only remaining significant free-flowing stream in the city, Lobos Creek, which empties into the Pacific at Baker Beach.

After leaving Mountain Lake and exploring the beaches to the west, Anza rode north, to the great gap in the Coastal Range. Font stood on the edge of a cliff overlooking the Golden Gate and marveled at what he saw: "The port of San Francisco . . . is a marvel of nature, and might well be called the harbor of harbors . . . And I think if it could be well settled like Europe there would not be anything more beautiful in all the world." Anza selected a site for a military base nearby, then headed south. A map drawn by Font suggests that Anza may have ridden to the top of Russian and Nob Hills on his way, Font's cryptic dotted line, like the markings on a pirate's treasure map, giving the downtown hills a tantalizing hypothetical cameo in the city's founding odyssey. In a warmer, more protected site a few miles away, Anza's party found "a handsome year-round stream of extremely fine water" surrounded by chamomiles and violets. Because it was the Friday of Sorrows, they named the stream the Arroyo de los Dolores and chose it as the site of the original mission.

That same day, Anza left the narrow peninsula that ended at the Golden Gate, never to return. He had brought Northern California its first colonists and prepared the way for the city to come. On June 27, just eight days before other colonists on the far side of the continent declared their independence from England, Anza's lieutenant, José Moraga, arrived in San Francisco with a small party of soldiers, settlers, and servants from Monterey. On September 17—the anniversary of the stigmata of St. Francis—Father Palou said Mass and blessed the presidio. Then Moraga took formal possession in the name of the king, accompanied by a blast of muskets and cannon fire from the *San Carlos*.

Two hundred and thirty-four years after Cabrillo sailed past the Golden Gate, the world had finally found San Francisco.

CHAPTER 9

THE BORROWED CITY

Filbert and Kearny Streets

Observations about San Francisco's weather tend to be variations on Mark Twain's supposed quip, "The coldest winter I ever spent was summer in San Francisco." (Twain never actually said this, although he did write a funny piece about a freezing early-morning trip to the Cliff House.) The wind also comes in for its share of abuse, while those of a poetic bent throw in a few references to the fog. The general sense is that San Francisco's weather is a subset of "California weather," a kind of inferior, cooler version of Los Angeles's.

Such complaints have a long historical pedigree. In 1539, the Spanish explorer Francisco Ulloa irritably called the prevailing northwest wind "the king of all that coast." In 1850, novelist Eliza Farnham declaimed, "San Francisco, I believe, has the most disagreeable climate and locality of any city on the globe." Farnham's distaste for the city's weather was so great that it led her to predict an early, comma-laden doom for anyone forced to endure it. "What sort of end the unfortunates, who spend their lives there, can expect under such circumstances, one does not easily foresee." Even so ardent a lover of San Francisco as the bohemian poet Charles Warren Stoddard described its weather as "invigorating as it is unscrupulous, having a peculiar charm which is seldom discovered until one is beyond its spell."

It cannot be denied that San Francisco's summers are a pale imitation of the real thing, or that the city was cursed by Aeolus. The cold gusts that swirled through Candlestick Park, the soon-to-be-demolished former home of the San Francisco Giants and 49ers, were the stuff of legend. Despised Los Angeles Dodgers first baseman Steve Garvey recalled, "I remember walking back to the tunnel after a one-run loss, and something whizzed by me. It was a gin bottle. I picked it up and saw it was half full. Right then, you knew you were at Candlestick. In New York they would have kept it full for more impact. At Candlestick, they had to drink half of it to keep warm."

San Francisco's climate will never please those who require a real summer, or need weather that falls into clearly defined categories. But the clichés about the city's weather completely miss the larger point. The truth is that San Francisco has the most *interesting* weather of any city I know. No other place that I've ever been has weather so complex, subtle, varied, and ephemeral—or so beautiful.

It may seem perverse to claim that San Francisco has uniquely varied weather. It's well known that this city, with its Mediterranean climate, does not have seasons in the normal sense of the word. It almost never snows, the last time the temperature hit zero was the last ice age, and it rarely gets above 80 for more than a few days at a time. It has only two observable seasons, wet and dry, and even the rainy season is hardly a monsoon. How is this monotonous round of eternal 50- to-70-degree days varied?

It's simple. San Francisco's weather features extreme variations within a relatively small range. The best analogy may be to good wine: All good wines are much more like each other than they are like rotgut jug red from Modesto, but the fine differences between them are precisely what connoisseurs appreciate. In the same way, a connoisseur of San Francisco's weather learns to enjoy every day's unique bouquet—for they are never exactly the same. San Francisco has sophisticated weather.

Not only is the weather here rarely the same two days in a row, but on any given day you can also experience a dozen different weathers, depending on what part of town you're in. This is because San Francisco is one of a handful of world cities—Halifax and Santiago are two of the others—that has microclimates. The city supposedly has seven microclimates, but the number is more or less arbitrary. The western parts of the city are foggier, windier, and cooler, and the eastern ones are warmer and clearer. The main barrier is Twin Peaks, which divides the city's weather as much as it does its inhabitants: "West of Twin Peaks" is political shorthand for conservative homeowners—and fog. East of Twin Peaks means liberal renters—and sun.

The difference between these microclimates can be dramatic. Every San Franciscan knows that if you live in the Mission and are going to a picnic at Ocean Beach or Golden Gate Park, you should be ready for a five-degree drop in temperature, plus the wind chill factor. But what is less widely known is that the weather here changes so quickly, and is so localized, that you can literally outrun it. Living in San Francisco gives a whole new meaning to the old saw "Everybody talks about the weather but nobody does anything about it."

One summer day I was visiting a friend who lives at Broderick and Eddy, on the western edge of the Western Addition. At 4 P.M. the fog rolled in over the Anza Vista hill and through the Geary Street gap and swallowed up his apartment. So I jumped on my bike and rode over to my house on Nob Hill, which was in bright sun. Two hours later, the fog had conquered Lafayette Park, routed resistance in Polk Gulch, and sent its advance scouts blowing in great gray streaks down Jackson Street. So I got back on my bike and zipped over to my office on Telegraph Hill, which was golden and toasty. An hour after that, Coit Tower, too, had fallen to the onrushing gray maelstrom. I drove over to have dinner with another pal who lives on Potrero Hill, two miles south and west. Her house was still in the sun.

And San Francisco's weather doesn't just change block to block; it changes foot to foot. Even the microclimates have microclimates. Mostly that's because of the wind. Any obstruction—a building, a hill, even a big tree—that blocks the wind has a dramatic impact. Since the wind almost invariably blows from the west, all you have to do to stay warm here (assuming the sun is shining) is to find the leeward side of a western wall and sit down. Five feet one way or the other can spell the difference between being able to sunbathe with your shirt off on any day of the year and wearing a sweater.

In his little book *Weather of the San Francisco Bay Region*, Harold Gilliam, whose writings on the natural world of San Francisco are unsurpassed, notes, "Probably no comparable area on earth displays as many varieties of weather simultaneously as the region around San Francisco Bay." As Gilliam eloquently describes, San Francisco's remarkable weather is caused by the ceaseless encounter between the sea and the land. This encounter is made possible—and uniquely dramatic—by the presence of the Golden Gate, the only breach in the Coast Range for its entire 600-mile length. "Through the funnel of the Golden Gate and San Francisco Bay, the immense aerial forces of sea and land wage a continuous war, and the tide of battle often flows back and forth with regularity," Gilliam writes. "The line between the two types of air masses, particularly in summer, may zigzag through the streets of San Francisco and extend in similar fashion across the entire region."

This swerving, ever-changing weather has a psychological and emotional impact on daily life here that is rarely mentioned but is incalculable. Cool and fresh, constantly cleansed by the sea, it is walking weather, thinking weather, *alert* weather. (I admit that the fact I have mostly lived in the warmer, eastern neighborhoods predisposes me to see the weather here as stimulating rather than frigid, and frisky rather than Gothic. While living at my father's house in Miraloma Park, near Glen Canyon, the first time I walked under a big line of eucalyptus trees, I got soaked to the skin, even though it wasn't raining. It took me a minute to realize that the leaves were dripping with condensation from the fog that had gathered on them overnight.)

The changeability of the weather, and the fact that several different kinds of weather often coexist at the same time, has a subtle effect on one's moods. Blue skies trigger a Pavlovian happiness response in us; gray skies are deeply associated with gloom. But when the sky is simultaneously sunny and overcast, as it so often is here, these instinctive associations short-circuit. This gives rise to new, nameless moods. It also encourages living in the moment. The knowledge that that gray sky at 2 P.M. may grow brighter and brighter until the fog burns off and the day ends up sunny, or dimmer and dimmer until darkness falls, is like having a Zen master standing behind you with a stick, ready to whack you if you don't pay attention to that glowing gray sky *right now*.

Above all, San Francisco's weather is a feast for the eyes. This is a city of famously clear light, but it is also one of a thousand exquisite shadings, of every possible combination of sun and clouds and warmth and coolness, mist and fog and wind and brightness and darkness. The San Francisco sky is a vast canvas, painted by the ever-changing sea. Those of us who live here take stupendous sights for granted because they happen so often: mighty banks of fog breaking like slow-motion waves over Twin Peaks, skies of cool translucent pearl clouded by evanescent washes of silvery mist, sunbeams landing on random spots in the city like the Annunciation in a medieval painting, winter mornings of such crystalline clarity that the whole city looks like an icicle-covered branch, the twin towers of the Golden Gate Bridge rising up above a billowing sea of thick white clouds.

But my favorite San Francisco weather moments are when two opposite types occupy the same space at the same time, leaving you in a strange physical and psychological never-never land. One example will have to stand for a thousand.

One summer afternoon I went down to Crissy Field. It was a pea soup. The fog there was so heavy that the entire bay was invisible. The diaphone foghorn on the bridge was blaring its dark two-toned warning. The sound reminded me, as it always does when the fog is especially heavy, of the haunting last scene in Eugene O'Neill's *Long Day's Journey into Night*, when the morphine-addicted mother descends the stairs. The foghorn that has kept the whole family up all night sounds in the distance. Lost in delusion, she is a child again, back in convent school. Then she speaks the play's shattering final lines. "Then in the spring something happened to me. Yes, I remember. I fell in love with James Tyrone and was so happy for a time." The foghorn sounds as she stares unseeing into the distance.

A little later I was in North Beach, walking up Filbert Street toward Coit Tower. The fog was burning off, but it still hung on the bay and covered the bridge, an impenetrable blanket. The foghorn sounded dully again. Because of some auditory trick, it was incredibly loud—it sounded like it was coming from the next block. Suddenly the clouds parted and the sky above cleared to a dazzling blue. And even as the sun shone down, something I had never seen before took place. A wild profusion of gentle water particles came blowing, tumbling, whirling through the air from the west. It was as if some mischievous kid up in the clouds was spraying a giant nozzle set on "mist."

I could see the particles dancing brilliantly in the sun. The foghorn blew louder than ever.

These are the kinds of things that happen when you live on a jagged peninsula at the end of the continent, under a torn-open sky, in a city that is only borrowed from the sea.

CHAPTER 10

THE LOST RIVER

Huffaker Park, Sixth and Channel Streets

San Francisco is famous for its natural beauty. But to call its beauty "natural" is slightly misleading. For aside from the cliffs at Lands End (which are actually covered with introduced trees), Glen Canyon, and a few other places, its beauty does not derive from nature in its pure state. The paradoxical truth is that before the city existed, its terrain was not particularly beautiful. Covered in sand dunes and with scant trees, it was a monotonous, even dreary landscape, largely devoid of color and contrast. Heretical as it is to say, much of San Francisco's terrain became more attractive when the city was built. San Francisco is the urban equivalent of an English garden, an artful blend of wildness and cultivation.

But there is one part of the city's primordial landscape that was breathtakingly beautiful, and whose loss was tragic: its vanished waters.

Compared with the East Bay or the Peninsula, San Francisco in, say, 1700 C.E. was fairly arid. It had no streams as large as Alameda Creek, which runs for 45 miles and drains 700 square miles, or 15-mile-long Butano

Creek in San Mateo County. But it had plenty of live water: four or five significant free-flowing streams, numerous springs, and more than a dozen lakes, at least 14 of them in what is now Golden Gate Park. And of all its aquatic features, the most magnificent was an estuary called Mission Bay.

This vast tidal cove, clearly visible in old bird's-eye illustrations of the city, took up much of what is now South of Market and ran deep into the Mission District. Fed by a meandering creek that wandered as far to the south and west as 20th Street and Florida, Mission Bay was surrounded by 260 gloriously squishy acres of salt marshes, mudflats, and serpentine streams. These nutrient-rich wetlands were home to an enormous bird population, including ducks, egrets, ospreys, seagulls, and herons, and supported a rich population of mussels and clams. Fish were abundant, as were small game. Not surprisingly, the native people, the Yelamu, were drawn to Mission Bay. (The 49ers had a saying that wherever there was freshwater, one would find Indian artifacts.) The Yelamu had a winter village on Mission Bay, near today's AT&T Park, and a summer village a few miles west on Mission Creek, near Mission Dolores. They could travel by boat between these villages on Mission Creek, a route still practical when the 49ers arrived.

Nancy Olmsted recounts the saga of this lost world in *Vanished Waters: A History of San Francisco's Mission Bay*. During the 19th century, the cove was home to San Francisco's shipbuilders and later the city's little-known whaling industry. A rope plant, an ironworks, and a sugar refinery stood on the cove's southern tip, Potrero Point, near present-day Third and 16th Streets. The thousands of Chinese immigrants that poured into the city disembarked at the Pacific Mail Steamship pier, near what is now First and Brannan.

But the waterways weren't only used for business. They were precious lungs for a city that had almost no parks. Long Bridge, the almost mile-long bridge that spanned three-quarters of the cove, was a favorite site for picnics and Sunday outings. Hunters wearing gum boots shot snipe in the marsh at Seventh and Mission. At the edges of the marshes, resorts like Russ's Gardens at Seventh and Harrison and the Willows at 17th and Mission, which pleasure-goers reached by going out the Mission plank road, offered outdoor dining and dancing.

But Mission Bay was as doomed as the more famous cove to its north, where the instant city first expanded. Flat downtown land was scarce, the hills and dunes blocked easy expansion, there was big money to be made in real estate, the omnipotent railroads needed space, and Mission Bay and its wetlands were in the way. As Philip J. Dreyfus notes in *Our Better Nature: Environment and the Making of San Francisco*, "San Franciscans seemed quite consumed by the concern that their city had been graced with too much water and too little earth." In 1852 a San Franciscan named David Hewes invented the "steam paddy," the steam shovel/railroad combination capable of moving 2,500 tons of sand a day. The enormous dunes that blocked Market and Mission Streets, some as high as 80 feet, were cleared away and dumped in marshes and wetlands. By 1874, Mission Creek above Ninth and Brannan was no longer classified as navigable. By 1889, most of Mission Bay had been filled in. By 1910 the job was finished.

Today, the entire majestic cove, its creek and its glorious marshes are gone. All that is left is a short stretch of Mission Creek, which opens onto the bay just south of the Giants' stadium, passes under two historic counterweighted bridges, and runs west four blocks to Seventh and Berry, where it abruptly ends at a wastewater pump just before the Caltrain tracks. The gigantic gray arch of the 280 freeway towers like a Brutalist amusement park ride above the western end of the creek, its mighty pylons walking across the stunted waterway.

I first came upon this unexpected stretch of water one night in the early 1970s. This whole part of town was part of what was once a vast world where the sidewalk ended. Near where AT&T Park now stands, there was a string of ancient warehouses, unchanged since the days of Harry Bridges. Nearby, a riotous old bar, appropriately named Bouncer's, catered to a bruising clientele, a Jack Daniel's–pounding mixture of bikers, rockers, and longshoremen. Management would have needed major bouncers, plural, to eighty-six any of these dudes. Vast empty fields stretched out to the south, the biggest open space in San Francisco. On the north side of the creek stood the sketchy San Francisco RV Park.

But this strangely truncated body of water was not just a surreal afterthought. A few people called it home. On the south side of the channel I was enchanted to discover the last thing I thought I'd see a few blocks from the train station: a motley collection of houseboats.

I wandered down along the less-than-perfumed banks of the creek, past the last houseboat, under the freeway. No one was around. A rotting board stretched out into the water. I walked onto it. After I had gone about six feet, it suddenly dipped into the water. Black water of unknown provenance ran toward my feet. Visions of one of those horror movies in which some hapless character falls into a maniac's bubbling vat and emerges as a skeleton raced through my head. I managed to get back to the bank.

Forty years later, those 20 houseboats are still berthed there, as they have been since 1960, when they were relocated from another one of the city's vanished streams, Islais Creek. Running along the bank a few feet away from them is a delightful little handmade-feeling park named Huffaker. Shiny new lawns and sidewalks installed by the city peter out into a stretch of grass and shrubbery as scruffy and well loved as a hobo's garden. A dusty collection of campers and old cars is parked nearby, having apparently been given some special dispensation from the authorities to remain forever.

But forever is running out. The University of California at San Francisco has built an imposing high-tech, high-rise complex just south of here, leaving only a few hundred square yards of unused land between it and the creek. Through this last no-man's-land, which is already fenced off, run two parallel chain-link fences, which meaninglessly delineate a *Twilight Zone*–like lane leading to Seventh Street. In early 2012 a few homeless people were camped out in this bizarre walkway; I saw a guy sleeping in a sleeping bag next to a shopping cart and, of all things, a double bass. The musical clochard and his brethren are gone now, probably forever.

For the pitiless laser beam of money has found Mission Creek. The north side has been transformed: A big cluster of expensive new condos rises up, with manicured walkways, a dog park, and a fancy kayak shed at the far end. It's only a matter of time before the laser turns to the south side and surgically excises the last patches of urban detritus, leaving the houseboats as a kind of floating museum of lost San Francisco funkiness.

In *Vanished Waters*, Olmsted quotes a houseboat resident, Sharon Skolnick, as saying, "It's an acquired taste to stick with an inlet that takes your house up six feet and then down six feet, twice in every 24 hours . . . that absorbs the effluvia of storm drains and simulates a sewer, and then two days later wins your heart back with a blue-lake duck."

The Mission Creek houseboats wouldn't be easy to live in—partly because of the smell, but more because of the surrealism. Mission Creek is deeply schizophrenic. It's simultaneously the most natural place in San

Francisco and the most artificial, the purest and the most polluted, the most bucolic and the most sterile. If you lived on the creek, you'd feel the tide rise and fall—and look up at a monstrous freeway towering overhead. You'd see sea lions outside your front door—and stare up at condos that look like they're in Legoland. And no matter how wonderful it would be to be rocked to sleep by the water, when you woke up, you'd still be living at Sixth and King, across from the train station.

And yet, you'd have to be a zombie not to fantasize about living there.

Some of the allure of Mission Creek is the idea of living on a houseboat. Having one's own little portable house is a delectable dream, like Mr. Toad's brief obsession with the canary-colored cart. But it's more than that. It's the water. Water in a city is irresistible. Even fountains are a magnet, as any visitor to Rome can attest. But natural, free-flowing water—that's pure magic.

There's not much of it left in San Francisco. There's the one-mile-long trickle of Islais Creek in Glen Canyon. The Presidio has Lobos Creek, the city's last major stream, and El Polin Spring, its largest. There's Yosemite Marsh, a small spring-fed pond in an obscure corner of McClaren Park, and the quasi-natural Chain of Lakes in Golden Gate Park, and a few others.

These places feel like shrines. The city recently daylighted the Tennessee Hollow Watershed in the Presidio, and San Franciscans would restore more of their city's lost waters if they could. The great paving-over, once seen as the pinnacle of progress, is now regarded as a tragedy.

San Francisco's vanished aquatic world is laid out in the elegaic "Creek and Watershed Map" published by the Oakland Museum. Here they are, in faint green lines: the waterfall that Anza saw tumbling near 18th Street and Castro; burbling Precita Creek, which cheerfully ran along the northern edge of Bernal Heights; the nameless little stream that ran down Sacramento Street and emptied into Yerba Buena cove. Other vanished waters, such as a spring that once bubbled at Washington and Powell, are too obscure to appear on the map.

The human fascination with water is atavistic. It's imprinted in our DNA. But for city dwellers, that fascination has a more poignant quality.

For cities are museums of time, and to live in them is to be haunted by the places they once were. The waterways that existed before the skyscrapers and freeways are a vanished world that beckons to us. When we catch glimpses of them, the city disappears. Its too-known streets dissolve into unfathomable terrain. It becomes innocent again. We want to unmake the city. To regain a lost paradise.

And perhaps we are also driven to unmake ourselves. To return to an earlier time in our own lives, one not yet marked off with streets and signs. To become again the children we once were, playing with a hose in the backyard. Back when happiness was easy, and water was everywhere.

CHAPTER 11

OUR LADY of SORROWS

Mission San Francisco de Asís, 17th and Dolores Streets

Mission Dolores is a riddle. Built in 1791, it is the oldest building in San Francisco, and one of the most beautiful. With its two-tiered colonnaded facade and four-foot-thick walls, the whitewashed adobe reposes on busy, palm tree–lined Dolores Street like a dignified old don, a white-haired survivor from a distant era. Its simple but majestic baroque interior, filled on a fall afternoon with golden light pouring in from the stained glass of the south window, evokes the monastic fervor and pious idealism of the Franciscans who journeyed to the end of the world to save souls. Indeed, Mission San Francisco de Asís—to give it its full title— seems to embody the entire Spanish era. To think of the church with anything but reverence while standing in its verdant little cemetery, where some of San Francisco's first citizens are buried, feels like a sacrilege against the very origins of the city.

But there is another way of looking at Mission Dolores. For also buried in its peaceful cemetery and the land outside it are some 5,000 local Indians who died during the half century that the mission carried out its appointed role. Most perished of measles, tuberculosis, venereal disease, and other illnesses brought by the Spanish. No one will ever know how many died of misery. The Indians living in San Francisco, the Yelamu, had the misfortune of living closest to the mission. They were wiped out. By the time the Americans took over, all of them except one old man and his son were dead, and their last descendant died in the 1920s. The other tribal groups that had lived on the peninsula were also devastated: Only one descendant of these groups, a sociology professor at California Lutheran University, is known to be alive. A people and a way of life that had existed in San Francisco for untold centuries had vanished forever.

So it's hard to know how to look at this small white building. Its beauty calls for gentle oblivion. But there is no statute of limitations on historical tragedy.

Strangely, the work that best evokes the uncanny quality of Mission Dolores, just as it captures the unresolved darkness of California's Spanish history, is a Hollywood movie about a completely different subject: Alfred Hitchcock's *Vertigo*. The scene when Kim Novak's Madeleine visits the mission cemetery and looks at the gravestone of Carlotta Valdes, the Hispanic ancestor who committed suicide and is haunting her, summons all the dark ambiguities that hang over the church on Dolores Street.

José Moraga, Juan Bautista de Anza's lieutenant, started building the first mission in the summer of 1776, after work on the presidio had gotten under way. The small structure was completed on October 9, to the blast of cannons, the ringing of bells, and the launching of fireworks. The noise terrified the local Indians, who ran away. "The day had been a joyful one for all," wrote Father Francisco Palou, who conducted the first Mass there. "Only the savages did not enjoy themselves on this happy day!"

Palou's words were inadvertently apt. The days when the "savages" would enjoy themselves were coming to an end.

Spain had evolved a unique three-headed approach—military, civil, and ecclesiastical—to its goal of turning Indians into Spaniards. The presidio, whose roots went back to the Roman *praesidium*, or frontier garrison, defended the area against hostile natives and served as the social and governmental center. The pueblo, or town (San Jose was the nearest one; San Francisco would not become a pueblo until much later) anchored the Spanish population.

The mission, by far the most important of the three, was responsible for "reducing"—i.e. converting and civilizing—the natives, who would provide manpower for the farming, cattle raising, and industry that would allow the entire colonial enterprise to be self-supporting. The 21 California missions, each about a day's ride from the next, were intended to be temporary: The converted Indians, known as neophytes, were supposed to be emancipated in 10 years, at which time they would assume the full responsibilities and rights of their Spanish-speaking "benefactors," who were known as *gente de razón* (people of reason).

In fact, that goal proved impossible to reach. The missionaries did succeed in converting thousands of Indians, teaching them the rudiments of Christianity, and putting them to work, but almost none of their charges ever became independent. By the time the missions were secularized in 1834, the entire system was already a shambles.

This was not surprising. As Malcolm Margolin, author of the classic *The Ohlone Way: Indian Life in the San Francisco–Monterey Bay Area*, points out, the Spanish "expected the Indians to desert everything they knew about life and to adapt overnight to a most peculiar and highly evolved European institution, the monastery—an institution under which, even at the height of its popularity, only a small number of Europeans themselves ever chose to live." People who had roamed freely through the hills and forests, who had a casual attitude toward sex and worked only when they needed to, were suddenly required to rise at dawn, say prayers, go off to work, attend religious classes, and sleep in segregated dormitories. Their entire universe, from their daily life to their spiritual beliefs, was simply erased. It was as psychotic a transformation as Pol Pot's Year Zero in Cambodia.

For the native people, the result was abject misery. Foreign visitor after foreign visitor commented on how sad the Indians looked. Otto von Kotzebue, leader of a Russian expedition that visited San Francisco in 1816, wrote of the Indians at Mission Dolores, "A deep melancholy always clouds their faces, and their eyes are constantly fixed on the ground." Another member of the expedition, artist Louis Choris, wrote, "I have never seen one laugh. I have never seen one look one in the face. They look as though they were interested in nothing." These are the same Indians whom earlier explorers had described as carefree and cheerful, who loved to dance, and whose incessant singing prevented the explorers from sleeping. They were, in effect, suffering from an incurable, culture-wide depression.

So-called gentiles—unconverted or "wild" Indians—came into the missions for a variety of reasons: awe at European technology, the presence of family members, and gifts given by the monks. Despite a prohibition against involuntary conversions, many Indians were brought into the church by force. As they lost their lands and ability to live, most Indians complied. But some did not. An Indian named Pomponio who lived at Mission Dolores in the 1820s escaped numerous times and killed those Indians sent to bring him back. When the commandant of San Francisco condemned him to death and shackled his legs with iron rings, Pomponio cut off his heels with a knife, squeezed his bloody feet through the rings, and fled.

Over the years, thousands of Indians tried to escape. In 1796, 200 of the 872 neophytes at Mission Dolores fled, a number so great that the governor convened an official investigation. Asked why the Indians had left, four soldiers stationed at the mission said it was the three *muchos*: too much work, too much punishment, and too much hunger. When some of the Indians were recaptured, six of them said they had run away because they had been whipped or beaten by one of the priests at the mission, Father Antonio Danti, who had already been upbraided by the governor for his cruel treatment of the Indians.

Serra's successor as president of the California missions, Fermín Francisco de Lasuén, replaced Danti with a kind priest named José María Fernández. Fernández arrived full of idealism, but he found that the two other priests at the mission treated their charges as harshly as Danti had. Appalled by their behavior, Fernández wrote an anguished letter to the governor, saying that the Indians had run away "due to the terrible suffering they experienced from punishments and work . . . I love the Indians very much and I will feel their misfortunes even more if they are to be treated like this. I repeat, I love them very much, because they have caused me great sorrow, very bad days, many sleepless nights, some tears, and ultimately my shattered health." The other priests retorted that Fernández was an impostor and a troublemaker. When the dispute became public, Fernández was recalled to Mexico City, a broken man. He was not the only priest whose mental and physical health was destroyed by his experience in California.

The punishments Fernández referred to, usually for disobedience, included whippings, shackles, and stocks. The most grotesque punishment was meted out to native women who had miscarried, and were thus assumed to be guilty of infanticide: Their heads were shaven, they were flogged for 15 straight days, they were shackled for three months, and as others taunted them, they were forced to carry a hideous red-painted wooden doll, known as a *monigote*, representing the dead child.

Sometimes priestly behavior tilted into sexual pathology. At Mission Santa Cruz, Father Ramón Olbes demanded that an infertile couple have sex in front of him to prove that they were incapable of having children. When they refused, Olbes insisted on inspecting the man's penis to see "whether or not it was in good order" and attempted to do the same with the woman's genitalia. When she refused and tried to bite him, Olbes ordered that she be chained, whipped, imprisoned, and forced to carry a *monigote*.

But such priests were the exceptions. Most of the monks who dedicated their lives to saving the souls of the "children of the wilderness" did not intend to harm them. As defenders of the missions have pointed out, the corporal punishments doled out to the Indians were standard practice in the Spanish culture of the time. Most missionaries were like Father Fernández: well-meaning, deeply devout men who believed they were doing God's work. They regarded the native people as their children, whom it was their holy duty to convert to the true faith. Many felt real affection for them and did their best to defend their charges from the soldiers, whose constant sexual misconduct led to constant conflicts with the church leaders, including Serra. At the fourth mission to be built, San Gabriel Archangel, a disgusted Serra reported that troops were lassoing women to rape them and that "even the boys who came to the mission were not safe from their baseness."

But none of the fathers' good intentions can alter the fact that their entire project, measured even by their own standards, was a complete failure. Fifty-four thousand Indians, most of them from the coastal regions between San Diego and San Francisco, were baptized in California in the mission period. But during that time, the native population in that area fell from 72,000 to 18,000. The biggest killer was disease. At Mission Dolores, a measles epidemic in 1806 killed 236 people in nine months. As the pioneering anthropologist Alfred Kroeber noted, "The brute upshot of missionization, in spite of its kindly flavor and humanitarian root, was only one thing: death."

Because of the cold weather and poor food, the death rate for Indians at Mission Dolores was the highest of any mission in the chain. Between 1800 and 1820, 200 replacement neophytes a year had to be brought in to keep the mission population at 1,000. Conditions were so bad that a hospital mission was opened at San Rafael in 1817. The Indian population at Mission Dolores peaked in 1825, with 1,252 people. By this time, most of the local Indians had come into the missions. Of those 1,252 people, only 190 were Ohlone speakers, and only 18 of those were Yelamu. Most of the rest had died.

By 1830, the decline of the native population meant that the mission population had dropped precipitously. There were only 13 Yelamu still alive—3 men and their wives and 6 children. By 1847, 14 years after the missions had been secularized, a census found only 34 Indians on the entire San Francisco peninsula.

In 1850, an Indian agent interviewed Pedro Alcantara, who was thought to be the last living Yelamu. Born in 1786 and baptized at Mission Dolores, Alcantara was Yelamu on his mother's side and Cotegen on his father's. He said, "I am very old . . . My people were once around me like the sands of the shore . . . many . . . many. They have all passed away. They have died like the grass . . . They have gone to the mountains. I do not complain, the antelope falls with the arrow. I had a son. I loved him. When the palefaces came he went away. I do not know where he is. I am a Christian Indian, I am all that is left of my people. I am alone."

In fact, Alcantara's son, Bernardino, had gone away only temporarily, possibly to the gold mines. Bernardino, in turn, had several children, one of whom, Marie Bernal Buffet, was tracked down by the *San Francisco Examiner* in 1922. The reporter found her dying in poverty in her little home in Millbrae. With her death, the last member of the Yelamu people passed from the earth.

Pedro Alcantara's lament was premature, but in the essentials the old man was right. His people, his culture, his world, had been destroyed, swallowed up by an unfathomable power whose symbolic center was the white adobe building with the three bells, the one that now stands peacefully on the edge of the Mission District.

I do not complain, the antelope falls with the arrow. Alcantara's words remain in the mind, like the fading overtones after the ringing of bells. The missions will always carry a bitter legacy. Those words cannot change that fact. But they can, perhaps, help us make peace with it. They can allow us to see that white church on Dolores Street without sentimentality but without rancor, as another ripple in the river, a blood-red pane in the vast stained-glass window of San Francisco.

CHAPTER 12

MAXIMUM CITY

Jackson and Hyde Streets

I live on Jackson Street, in northern Nob Hill, just below the corner where the cable cars on the Powell-Hyde line turn north onto Hyde. The cars rattle around that sharp curve with the tourists hanging on, head down the last block on Nob Hill, cross the saddle at Broadway, then clank along the top of Russian Hill, past the famous crooked street Lombard, over the crest of the hill, past the Norwegian Seaman's Church with its big anchor in the yard, and down the long 21-degree grade to the cable car turnaround near the northern waterfront, the gripmen leaning hard over their long levers.

The sweeping view of the bay you see looking down Hyde from the top of the hill, with Alcatraz straight ahead and Angel Island behind it, is one of the most spectacular in the city. It is also the one image of San Francisco that has probably been seen by more Americans than any other, thanks to a packaged food product of Armenian origin called Rice-A-Roni. TV commercials for Rice-A-Roni started running in 1958, and they have been on the air ever since—probably the most effective use of a city as branding in the history of American advertising. As a cable car drops over the hill, an insufferably catchy jingle ends with the phrase "Rice-A-Roni, the San Francisco treat!" and a final, chipper "*ding ding!*"

I sometimes wonder if any tourists on the Hyde Street line, as they look down at that stupendous view, find it polluted, or even replaced, by their memory of the Rice-A-Roni commercial. Roland Barthes compiled a whole list of such Invasion-of-the-Image-Snatchers moments in his book *Mythologies*. But you don't have to be a French semiotician to have experienced them. Every tourist has felt the letdown of being unable to see some world-historical monument because they're trapped inside a guidebook's description of it. I once spent two futile hours at the Colosseum, unable to make that vast arena become anything other than the visual appendage of some Cliff's Notes version of Roman history.

Like all fabled cities, San Francisco is in constant danger of disappearing into its own postcard. Critics have long accused San Francisco of being too touristy, too smug, too caught up in its own legend. But those are minor sins. A more serious charge was voiced by a New Yorker who once dismissively told a friend of mine (an ex–New Yorker herself), "Oh yeah, it's beautiful here—but it's not *real.*"

At bottom, her complaint was about money. The critique goes like this: San Francisco has become so expensive that it has lost its soul. It is an urban boutique, an overgrown version of Carmel or Santa Fe, a private playground for dot-com moguls and overpaid techies and investment bankers and businesspeople from Hong Kong. The cops and teachers and artists and barbers and clerks who gave it its sinews and muscle have been priced out, and what is left is a toy city, as impractical and overpriced as its cable cars.

There's some validity to this accusation. There's a reason San Francisco has the lowest percentage of children of any major U.S. city. But the reality is more complicated.

There's no denying that San Francisco is extremely expensive. In 2012, a two-bedroom apartment rented for an average of $2,364 a month, the highest price in the country. The average selling price of a single-family house in April 2012 was $1.24 million. Private high schools now cost $35,000 a year; private elementary schools cost $25,000. To buy a modest house and send two kids to private school here, a couple needs to make around $250,000 a year. In short, it's Manhattan West.

These prices have taken a toll. Money has a homogenizing effect. San Francisco feels less eccentric, and a lot less blue-collar, than it used to. And it has hardly any black people left. Despite its high crime rate, Oakland, the city's unglamorous sister across the bay, has a thriving black middle class and an infinitely more rich and mellow racial vibe.

But San Francisco is not a toy city—not yet, anyway. Despite the high cost of housing, plenty of young people and poor people and artists and working-class people still manage to live here. They live in rent-controlled apartments, or with roommates, or just scrape together the rent every month. It's harder than ever, and too many people are priced out. But it was never easy. When I moved here in 1971, rents were $250 a month, but there weren't any more jobs than there are now, and the ones there were paid $500 or $600 a month. The golden age when poets could pay $75 to live in a cottage on Telegraph Hill and eat spaghetti and red wine for 75 cents has been gone for 80 years, and it isn't coming back.

I personally think the city's low point, soul-wise, was during the nauseatingly named "go-go '80s," when young zombie business types escaped their containment zone in the Marina and shamelessly flaunted their suits and ties in North Beach. The Google, Twitter, and Zynga employees and graphic artist/baristas who have replaced those Reagan-era interlopers seem preferable to me, although it remains to be seen whether the second dot-com boom will bring in so much of what my schoolteacher pal Ed Lopez calls "air money" that the city becomes intolerable.

But arguments about whether a city has lost its soul are as subjective as arguments about whether a certain indie band has sold out. The only real way to evaluate a place is to get granular, to go through the streets building by building. The streets I know best are in my neighborhood, Nob Hill. Since Nob Hill is San Francisco's most famous neighborhood, a legendarily plutocratic address right in the center of town, it's a good place to test the toy-city thesis. And conveniently, the Hyde Street cable car line runs through it. So let's jump on and take an imaginary ride.

Before we board, it must be admitted that functionally, the cable cars *are* a toy—or more accurately, a Disneyland ride. They cost a tourist-gouging six bucks for a single trip—the most expensive local transit fare in the United States. But despite suffering the indignity of being used by the city as a de facto tourist tax, the cable cars are real. They were invented to haul people up and down San Francisco's hills, and they have been clanging up and down them since 1873. Moreover, they are still a viable means of transportation for San Franciscans. The two most popular lines, the north-south Powell-Hyde and Powell-Mason lines, carry almost exclusively tour-ists, but the east-west California Street line carries quite a few locals, people who live on Nob Hill or the southern edge of Pacific Heights and work in the Financial District. (A monthly pass makes these trips affordable.)

Our ride begins at one of the most touristy spots in town: the cable car turnaround at the foot of Hyde Street, at the west end of Fisherman's Wharf. Ignoring the buskers and the five-minute-sketch artists, we climb on. The gripman releases the brake, the old wooden car jerks forward, and we are pulled up the long, steep slope at nine and a half miles an hour. We come to the Rice-A-Roni vista at the top of the hill and go past crooked Lombard Street to Greenwich.

So far, so patrician. In the three minutes and six blocks we have traveled, we have traversed some of the priciest terrain in the country. Houses atop Russian Hill can sell for $13 million or more, and the rents are equally astro-nomical. (Although even up here, there are plenty of people in rent-controlled apartments.) But cities don't lose points because they have rich neighbor-hoods. They gain points when those rich neighborhoods are right next to poor ones, and both are right next to middle-class ones. And they hit the jackpot when multimillionaires live cheek-by-imported-*guanciale* from im-migrants who crush cans for a living. Which they do a few blocks away.

We roll along Hyde through the little restaurant-and-shop section of Russian Hill, cross Union, and drop down toward Broadway, the nebulous border between Nob and Russian Hills. This is still an expensive neighbor-hood, but it's more mixed. In another block, at Pacific, we have returned to Nob Hill and economic reality—Chinese families and working stiffs. The population of Nob Hill is at least half Chinese. We roll up to my corner, Jackson. A Latino jazz sax player and his singer wife live in the apartment building on the corner. Across from them, a sweet-faced Syrian man is struggling to keep his corner grocery going. He bought the store from a Chinese guy who called everybody "bra" and spent most of his time stand-ing outside, smoking cigarettes with a bunch of older Chinese men from the neighborhood, the world's most innocuous posse. The Chinese owner's wife is a waitress at a fancy dim sum restaurant downtown. The guy most often behind the counter now is a Yemeni man with a gold tooth who always jokes around with my daughter.

We climb up another block, then turn east on Washington, and head toward the summit of Nob Hill at Jones. On Jackson, where the Hyde Street car runs going the other way, my impecunious poet pal Tom lives in a literal garret. On the corner of Jackson and Leavenworth lives an elderly, bullet-headed Italian photographer who likes to ring a cable car bell that hangs in his window. He's been there forever. Up Jackson, the Chinese son of my former landlady has set up housekeeping with his young family in one of the buildings she owns. Another friend, a conceptual artist, lives in another of her buildings. The same motley cast of characters has been walking up and down Jackson Street for close to 30 years.

(Sometimes the character of a neighborhood is revealed in unexpected ways. In 2013, a Trader Joe's opened at California and Hyde, replacing a scary old 24-hour Cala Foods whose 3 A.M. clientele were legendarily unsavory. The grocery Mecca instantly provided a comprehensive portrait of Nob Hill's inhabitants: They are much younger, hipper, and more "San Francisco" than I had thought. Odd that a supermarket can permanently change one's sense of one's neighborhood.)

We cross Jones and drop down the steep grade, the buildings of downtown and the bay flashing in front of us. This identical view—all the buildings in it are still there—is depicted in a wonderful *Saturday Evening Post* cover that ran on September 29, 1945, six weeks after V-J Day. A bunch of sailors carrying their bags are running toward a cable car that is poised to drop downhill. The cable car is jammed with men, every one of them in uniform. Other sailors look down from the windows of apartment buildings on both sides of Washington, which have No Vacancy and Rooms to Let signs. The Bay Bridge and the Ferry Building glow in the sun in the distance. In the foreground a Chinese man with a basket of fruit on his head and a little Chinese kid, both wearing traditional clothes, gawk at the sailors. A young sailor leaning way outside the cable car looks back with a smile. The painting is corny as hell, and one of the most joyous images of San Francisco I know.

The two Chinese figures are a weird Orientalist touch. Except that they aren't. Because even on the windswept top of the hill, we're in a finger of Chinatown. And we're about to roll into it.

Going down Washington is like descending through an archaeological dig whose exposed strata reveal completely different cities. There's a spectacular new house on the very summit of the hill, and the first block is filled with classy, expensive apartments. But one block after you cross elegant Taylor Street, at Mason, decrepit tenements begin to appear. In the four blocks between Jones and Stockton (the cable car turns a block earlier, on Powell) you go from grand apartments and soaring vistas to filthy alleys and neon signs, from deserted streets to sidewalks so packed you shuffle along like you're on Nathan Road in Kowloon. It has to be one of the most dizzying four-block transitions in any city in the world.

Jane Jacobs nailed it 51 years ago in *The Death and Life of Great American Cities*. Cities are kept alive by heterogeneity—the juxtaposition of radically different things in a small space. Paris lost a piece of its soul forever when it bulldozed Les Halles. New York is still the king of glorious urbanism, but it took a heavy hit when Times Square was cleaned up. San Francisco's list of urban offenses is too long to count. But in its very heart, where its seven-by-seven-mile area gets compressed down to a little steep mile-by-mile square, everything essential to the city is jammed together, the rich and the poor, the sublime and the ridiculous, the ethereal and the raunchy. It's where the city's tectonic plates meet.

One of those fault lines runs through my block. In fact, it runs through my property. To explain this requires a brief real estate digression.

I've lived on Jackson Street for 29 years. For 16 of those years, I rented an apartment on Jackson between Jones and Leavenworth, two blocks from where I live now. It was a huge two-bedroom place with a panoramic view of the Golden Gate Bridge. The rent was low, and my kindly Chinese landlady didn't even raise it for years. Then, in 1999, I was strolling down Jackson past Hyde when I saw a small, run-down Edwardian house with a For Sale sign on it.

I was intrigued. This was my 'hood. There are very few single-family houses anywhere in the northeast heart of the city. My wife and I had been looking in a desultory way at houses, so we went to see it. It turned out that two buildings were for sale on the same deep, narrow lot—the house in front and a three-unit apartment behind it. A dozen or so potential buyers, mostly Chinese but with a few white people mixed in, wandered around checking it out.

The single-family house was, to put it mildly, not ready for its spread in *Martha Stewart Living*. It had been divided up into a bunch of locked-off rooms. The banister of the staircase leading upstairs had been covered over with plasterboard and a door framed in front of the stairs. There were about 15 Chinese people living in the house, including an old lady and a baby in the basement, an old couple in the front room, a young family of four in an ugly-linoleum-floored room next to the deeply yucky downstairs kitchen, and seven or eight more people living upstairs, where an even yuckier illegal kitchen had been installed. It looked like the joint hadn't been painted in 30 years.

The back building had even more tenants—about 20 in the three apartments—and was equally run-down. The whole deal wasn't nearly as squalid as another tenement we had looked at in the neighborhood, but it was definitely a Chinatown rooming house.

De facto rooming houses, many of which are nominally illegal, constitute the majority of apartments in Chinatown. Chinese landlords there generally rent to other Chinese, whom they pack into illegally divided houses or apartments with bedsheet partitions. The tenants live in incredibly crowded conditions, sharing kitchens and bathrooms in poorly maintained buildings, but entire families often pay only $400 or $500 a month rent. You could see the owners as slumlords, but you could also see them as providing a social service. And as I was about to find out, if you buy the building, you become your own private nonprofit housing agency.

This was at the height of the dot-com boom. People were throwing money hand over fist at anything that didn't move. Real estate, which has been a San Francisco obsession since city officials during the Gold Rush carved off the choicest lots in an orgy of self-dealing, was booming too. So you'd think that one of the only single-family houses on Nob Hill, a nice if trashed little 1908 Edwardian just off the cable car line, on a pleasantly residential, racially mixed street, with a yard, a rooftop view of the Golden Gate Bridge, and including an apartment house on the same lot, would have created a feeding frenzy—especially because the price was absurdly low.

But no one except us was interested. The reason was simple. The Chinese buyers were looking at the deal as a rental-income investment, and the numbers didn't work—the rents were much too low. The white buyers obviously had a different problem: They were going to buy it to live there, and they didn't want to have to deal with swarms of impoverished Chinese tenants. And if there were any dot-com moguls among them, they wanted to buy a place they could move right into.

I wasn't overjoyed by the prospect of becoming an involuntary slumlord, not to mention being locked in forever to collecting rents that were only four times more than the water bill, but I decided that it was worth putting up with it to buy a house. Besides, I'd been renting from a Chinese landlord for 16 years, so I was karmically due to reverse roles. So we made an offer $1,000 over the asking price—this at a time when bidding wars on shanties in the Mission District would routinely go up to $50,000 or more over asking. It was immediately accepted.

We've been living there ever since. Most of the tenants in the back building are still there. They're good people. We get along fine, observing the unspoken rule: They pay me almost nothing, and they don't bug me on landlord-related issues unless something fairly major goes wrong.

For years, one of my tenants was the grandfather of one of the extended families who live in the top apartment. They moved him in illegally and I was too hapless to do anything about it. My cousin nicknamed him the General because he stood as straight as a ramrod and had eyes like a hawk. It was impossible to say how old he was. He could have been 55 or 75. He spoke no English. Maybe he really was a general back in the Cultural Revolution, was accused of being a "capitalist roader," managed to escape, and ended up on Nob Hill. I have no idea.

The General spent his days collecting and selling cans and bottles at the local recycling center. This is a major Chinatown cottage industry. You'll see stooped old people walking down the street with a stick balanced over their shoulder and bags on either end. It's a sight you could have seen in Guangdong Province during the Tang Dynasty. I once watched an old woman sitting next to the sandlot of the playground on Hang Ah Alley, carefully pouring small measures of sand into cans to make them heavier.

The General wasn't that unscrupulous. I would hear him rummaging around down in the walkway that goes to the back building, shoving aluminum cans and bottles into black plastic garbage bags, and loading the bags onto a shopping cart. Then he'd head out to the closest recycling center to make a few bucks. He moved out a while ago, but his middle-aged daughter took over the enterprise. The edge of the walkway is still packed with bags of bottles and cans.

Across the street from our house is a brand-new three-unit modernist condo building that took more than a year to construct. It was one of those foundation-up jobs where they bring in structural steel with cranes. I took a tour of one of the units before it sold. The dishwasher was worth more than my car. The top unit had a rooftop hot tub with a panoramic view of the Golden Gate Bridge. It sold for $2.5 million. It's always empty. I've only seen the owner once.

So there we are, the three of us, the rich, the poor, and the downwardly mobile middle, within 100 feet of one another. Negative and positive charges. Creating the invisible electricity that keeps this screwed-up, heartless, unfathomable city running.

CHAPTER 13

OUTSIDE SANDS

Baker Beach

Baker Beach is the least celebrated great urban beach in the world. Most non–San Franciscans have never heard of it. When travel magazines put together their (admittedly moronic) 10-best-city-beaches lists, it is nowhere to be seen. In a superficial sense, this is understandable. Baker does not have the sweep of Ipanema or Copacabana, the golden sand of Waikiki, the exhilarating muscularity of Miami's South Beach or Tel Aviv's Gordon-Frishman, the surf of Sydney's Bondi. But it is every bit their peer. Because of its location just beyond the Golden Gate, Baker Beach faces the literal and symbolic gateway to a continent—and faces it from the *outside*. No other city beach in the world has such a location. It's as if Venice Beach were plunked down beyond the Statue of Liberty, between two sets of ancient cliffs through which the surging waters of an ocean and the tidal currents of a vast bay dueled.

The Golden Gate Bridge is such a symbol of finality, so associated with the end of the continent, that even San Franciscans tend to imagine it as standing at the extreme western edge of the city. The truth is that it hits the city a full two miles east of Point Lobos. Baker Beach, which occupies the gently curving center of that two-mile stretch, is a reminder that the most dramatic and spectacular part of the entire city lies *west* of the great bridge. For not only does the beach look back at the Golden Gate; it also faces the two mighty formations that guard it, the Marin Headlands and Lands End. This setting, between the towering cliffs to the west and the bridge, gives Baker Beach a feeling of being simultaneously detached from the city and nestled into its heart. It is more protected and comfortable than the city's longest beach, the exposed, windswept, west-facing Ocean Beach, and yet because it faces the Golden Gate and the channel cliffs, it is far more dramatic. Marvelous as it is, Ocean Beach could exist in any seaside city. Baker Beach could only be found in San Francisco.

Actually, the real reason this stunningly beautiful beach is so underappreciated is because San Francisco does not have a conventional beach culture. Los Angeles, Rio, Sydney, and the other legendary beach cities have a fully developed beach lifestyle. In Rio, I would stroll four downtown blocks to Ipanema wearing a Speedo through hordes of people, and each day that I walked to the sea, they looked straight ahead, not at me. The one time I tried that here, walking down Polk Street to Aquatic Park, I felt like some West Coast version of the Iranian Basij was about to beat me with sticks and force me to get dressed.

But this is San Francisco, after all, and Baker is as sybaritic as any of its more celebrated cousins. The northern part of the beach is filled on warm days with naked people, not all of whom embrace the nonlibidinous, carrot-juice-drinking, "varing no clothing iss only for vun's health!" approach to nudism. (Not that such people aren't around. Possibly the most jaw-dropping sight I have ever seen in San Francisco was an elderly, earnest-looking couple with walking sticks strolling briskly along next to the DiMaggio Playground in North Beach one warm summer afternoon—stark naked.) It is appropriate that this part of the beach dead-ends at an outcropping of serpentine, because I have witnessed quite a few snake-y dudes here, trying to convince various Eves to chomp on apples. If the fruit of that forbidden tree really did bring death into the world and all our woe, a significant part of that woe is contributed by the lame-ass voyeurs who sit high up on the bluffs with binoculars, scoping out the naked chicks below. Once, I actually saw a guy dressed in camouflage fatigues there, a disgrace to the proud military tradition of the Pacific Port of Embarkation.

The truly hard-core action, however, used to take place on the isolated and hard-to-get-to beaches north of Baker. In the venerable tradition of gay-cruising haunts in obscure locations, those beaches and the cliffs above them were a happy hunting ground for dozens of gay men. Hiking in that sublime stretch of lost coast was an adventure: You'd go past a bush and suddenly bump into a bearded guy in a plaid shirt just standing there like a flexed-up statue, ready for action. They were good furtive times while they lasted, but the lost coast was opened up when trails were put in. San Francisco cruising seems now to have returned to its time-honored haunt, Buena Vista Park. Or so at least one gleans from a Web site bearing the admirably straightforward name Cruising Gays City Hookup Guide. In the comments on Buena Vista Park, someone enthusiastically posted, "I just fucking love this park. It's like a game preserve of faggotry."

The *Satyricon*-like orgy on the adjoining sands may be over, but Baker Beach will always be associated with crazy revelry and hedonistic ritual. For it was here on the summer solstice in 1986 that a man named Larry Harvey and a friend built a wooden figure and set fire to it in front of 20 people. That fire grew to become Burning Man, the largest and most astonishing countercultural event in the world. It makes sense that it started here.

For years, I used to walk my dog at Baker Beach after dropping my daughter off at school, and I still come out here all the time, in sun, in clouds, in fog, in rain. No matter how many times you approach it from the road that winds along the edge of the cliffs in the Presidio, the view is breathtaking: a patch of white sand facing the sea, filtered by trees, framed by majestic rock formations, pounded by waves. In the early morning it is sometimes completely deserted. I am always astonished that this half-mile-long stretch of paradise exists in a big city. There are a dozen or so big houses on top of the cliff at the southern end, but other than that, it is completely unspoiled. Wondrous Lobos Creek enters the ocean here. Dolphins routinely cavort offshore. The big ships, still carrying their imperishable cargo of romance, sail past Mile Rock and disappear over the horizon. Others steam in, banged-up metal postcards from Liberia and Panama, getting longer and dirtier and more fascinating as they approach the Golden Gate.

The few houses aside, the beach looks almost exactly the same as it did on that spring day in 1776 when Anza and Font stood on its sands after riding over the dunes from Mountain Lake. The waves roll in and out as they did on that day, as they will do until this beach no longer exists. The one thing that is different looms up beyond the rocks to the north, a 746-foot-high reminder in International Orange that human beings, who have been here for such a short time, can sometimes create things that are as beautiful as the world itself.

CHAPTER 14

PLUTO ON THE PACIFIC

The Quadrangle, Moraga and Graham Streets,
the Presidio of San Francisco

The story of the Presidio's early years is a story of utter futility. No other time or place in the city's history is as pointless and woebegone. For half a century, a handful of illiterate soldiers, often lacking weapons or even uniforms, shivering in crude adobes so poorly built they would turn into mud pies with the first storm, stood pathetic guard at the fog-shrouded mouth of the Golden Gate, waiting for invasions that never came. The only time the Presidio fired its guns in anger, if you can call it that, was when its garrison fired a single shot at a mysterious ship that appeared offshore, refused to identify itself, and spent the night at anchor before sailing away. During the last 12 years of Spanish rule, the troops were never paid. When Mexico won independence from Spain in 1821, the news took more than a year to reach the Presidio. The Spanish outpost was so cut off from the world that it might as well have been called Pluto on the Pacific.

If possible, things got even worse during the 25 years that the Mexican flag waved over the crude quadrangle facing Angel Island. One year, the garrison was paid in cigarettes. Another year, all the troops seem to have simply disappeared.

Anza had originally selected a site for the Presidio on the heights above present-day Fort Point. Fort Point is the place where Madeleine jumps into the bay in *Vertigo*, and if the great captain had known the pathetic fate that awaited his fortress, he might have leaped into the water himself. When Anza's second-in-command, Lieutenant Moraga, arrived leading the "California *Mayflower*" party of 16 soldiers, two priests, seven colonists and assorted servants and *vaqueros*, he realized that the original site, although militarily logical, was too cold, windy, and far from water, so he relocated it to its present location a mile southeast. As was the Spanish custom, the outpost was laid out as a square quadrangle, 92 *varas* (a little less than a yard) per side. Construction commenced, and thunderous broadsides celebrated the Presidio's dedication on September 17, 1776—probably the most robust use of shot and shell in the fort's history.

The Presidio today is a lovely, shaggy space, run since 1996 by a unique U.S. government corporation called the Presidio Trust. The three-square-mile area was a U.S. Army base for 219 years, and it still has an odd, quaint feeling, halfway between military museum and overgrown park. Its barracks and fancy officers' houses have been taken over by a variety of nonprofits and commercial enterprises. *Star Wars* director George Lucas's company put in a state-of-the-art $300-million complex near the old Letterman Hospital. Some of the most wondrous spots in San Francisco, like El Polin Spring, are in the Presidio. But few tangible traces of the Spanish and Mexican eras remain. You have to pick up their scent in the air.

A stone monument on the gently sloping lawn that runs down to the bay marks the northwest corner of the old Presidio quadrangle. Almost nothing of it is left, although the present-day Officers' Club contains some adobe bricks that date to around 1815 (and are possibly as old as 1776). A parking lot covers most of the old enclosure. The desolation of the old Presidio cannot really be felt here. But on the obscure trails that wind through the sand dunes above El Polin Spring and peter out at Lover's Lane, the ancient footpath from the Presidio to Mission Dolores, it is not hard to imagine the loneliness of life 200 years ago, before there was a city or even a village.

The purpose of the Presidio was to wave the Spanish flag at the Golden Gate, warning off any foreign interlopers who harbored designs on the Great River and Harbor of San Francisco, and to assist the mission. For the Spanish crown, these were crucial objectives, but it was unable or unwilling to pay for them. It only funded two-thirds of Anza's initial request for 22,000 pesos, and the purse strings drew even tighter after that. After insurrectionists seized Spanish supply ships in 1810, the bankrupt crown stopped sending money altogether.

The Presidio had only a token garrison. For its first 20 years, 30 to 40 *soldados de cuera* (leather soldiers, so named because of their thick, arrow-stopping leather jackets) were officially enrolled, but only 10 to 20 were actually on duty. Two years after they arrived, half of this threadbare detachment still did not have muskets, pistols, swords, or lances. In the ultimate indignity, two-thirds of the leather soldiers did not even possess their trademark jackets.

These troops were technically Spanish, but as throughout California's Hispanic history, that term is misleading. Almost all were born in Mexico, and most of them were so-called *castas*, or people of mixed race. Over the centuries that it colonized the New World, Spain had developed a system of racial classification known as the *systema de castas*. The *systema de castas* was instituted in the early 1600s because the criollos, the colonial elite born in the Americas of unmixed or "pure" Spanish blood, wanted to be distinguished from people of mixed race. Since there was so much racial mixing, the crown formulated a bizarrely precise list of racial combinations:

Spanish and Indian: *mestizo*
Mestizo and Spanish woman: *castizo*
Castizo woman and Spaniard: *Spaniard*
Spanish woman and negro: *mulatto*
Spaniard and mulatto: *morisco*
Morisco woman and Spaniard: *albino*
Spaniard and albino: *torna atras*
Indio (Indian) and torno atras: *lobo*
Lobo and Indio woman: *zambaigo*
Zambaigo and Indio woman: *cambujo*

And so on. These classifications were never as rigid as the Anglo-American "one drop rule," according to which anyone with black ancestry, for example, was (and usually still is) identified as black. But although it allowed more mobility, it was still hierarchical: The Spaniards at the top enjoyed more privileges and status; the blacks and Indians at the bottom less.

Not surprisingly, Spanish-speaking people in the New World invariably changed their *casta* status "up." Negros became mulattos, mulattos became mestizos, and mestizos became Spaniards. By 1773, 49.3 percent of soldiers in Spain's frontier provinces were listed as *español*, even though a contemporary missionary said that almost none of them were of pure Spanish blood.

The soldiers at the Presidio also seized the opportunity to climb the racial ladder. In 1776, 39 percent of the Anza colonists were listed as *español*. By 1782 that had increased to 44 percent; by 1790 to 57 percent. Concomitantly, those who identified themselves as mulatto and indio decreased sharply. When ordered to identify the caste of soldiers and settlers, missionaries complained that it was impossible because they all claimed to be pure-blooded Spanish. Over time, the colonists dropped all racial classifications, preferring to identify themselves as *gente de razón* (people of reason—as distinguished from Indians), *hijos de pais* (sons of the country), or simply as *Californios*. Race mixing and identity shifting (or, in less politically correct terms, "passing") were thus inscribed in San Francisco from the start.

For these underequipped men and their families, the biggest challenge at first was just surviving. Housing was a nightmare: All the buildings they erected in 1778 had collapsed by 1780, with even the walls falling apart. Adobe was not the best choice of building material for a fog-shrouded place like the Presidio, and the adobe was of such poor quality that it started disintegrating with the first rains. In 1792 the comandante, Hermenegildo Sal, complained that his buildings kept falling down because his men lacked logs and construction skill.

The housing problem was never solved. When British captain Frederick William Beechey, commander of H.M.S. *Blossom,* visited the Presidio in 1826, he found one side of the quadrangle "broken down, and little better than a heap of rubbish and bones, on which jackals, dogs, and vultures were constantly preying." From a distance, he summed up the appearance of Spain's outpost as "a sickly column of smoke rising from some dilapidated walls."

The interiors of the buildings were equally primitive. When Captain George Vancouver visited in 1792 on the *Discovery*, the first non-Spanish ship to enter San Francisco Bay, he was shocked to discover that the commander's house not only lacked windows but did not even have a floor. He found himself standing on "native soil raised about three feet from its original level, without being boarded, paved, or even reduced to an even surface." And he noted: "The furniture consisted of a very sparing assortment of the most indispensable articles, of the rudest fashion, and of the meanest kind; and very ill accorded with the ideas we had conceived of the sumptuous manner in which the Spaniards live on this side of the globe."

Food was also in short supply, especially in the beginning. The soldiers were dependent on a yearly supply ship from San Blas, about 100 miles north of present-day Puerto Vallarta. After the Presidio was dedicated, it took 15 months for the first ship to arrive with the corn, beans, lentils, chickpeas, lard, brown sugar, and chili peppers that formed the basis of the enlisted men's mess. A soldier's typical meals were roast corn or cereal and milk for breakfast; cereal gruel or corn for lunch; and beans, cornmeal gruel, or *migas* (fried crumbs made of crushed corn) and roasted or stewed meat for dinner. Wine or brandy was not available for the rank and file.

This tedious and often scanty diet probably did not raise morale, and the sketchy military records show that several men got into trouble for fighting. A more serious problem arose in 1778, when thieves made off with 700 pesos' worth of supplies—equivalent to the comandante's salary. A soldier named Marcelo Pinto, another soldier, and two servants were accused and placed on trial at the Presidio. The wheels of justice in Alta California ground slowly: In 1782, four years later, Lieutenant Moraga was still waiting for a verdict. That same year, Pinto escaped but was soon recaptured; after an additional wait of a year and a half, he was sentenced to four years of labor on public works. After he was released, Pinto, who was from Sinaloa and had come with Anza on the California *Mayflower* expedition in 1776, found other ways to torment his superiors. When a soldier returned from duty one afternoon, he found Pinto hiding under a bed in his quarters, for reasons the man's wife presumably could explain. The exasperated comandante had to write to the governor to ask what to do with the exploding Pinto.

The officers at the Presidio were not all models of rectitude and competence, either. After the esteemed Moraga died in 1785, he was succeeded as comandante by one Diego González, who was so given to gambling, insubordination, and smuggling that he was placed under house arrest for three months and finally sent to Sonora. Another worthy leader named Lasso, who was "described by contemporaries as being careless and stupid," was inexplicably placed in charge of the Presidio's finances. Lasso proved incapable of roping in his budget, repeatedly losing large sums of money. After being relieved of his duties, he suffered possibly the most draconian wage garnishment of all time: His pay was cut to 25 cents a day for four years while he worked off his debt.

As a fortress, the Presidio was a joke. The fortress built on the Cantil Blanco in 1793, called the Castillo de San Joaquin, did not have enough cannons to repel even a puny invasion, and the ones it did have were more dangerous to their gunners than to whatever they were aimed at. During the festivities for a saint's feast day in 1792, a cannon exploded into 10 pieces, some of which flew as far as 125 yards. When the German-Russian navigator Otto von Kotzebue visited in 1824 and fired the customary salute, he claimed that a soldier from the Castillo came aboard to beg for powder so the fort could return the salute.

If all the underfed, underpaid, illiterate soldiers at the Presidio were doing was playing cards while waiting for the annual supply ship to come in, it might be possible to visualize the outpost as a kind of decrepit Bali Hai, a *Catch-22*–like hideaway. But as servants of the crown and the church, the soldiers had to do the dirty work of colonial policemen.

Indians were not required to join the church, but once they were baptized, they were no longer free to leave—a fact few of them understood. Since they were now Christians, the fathers were responsible for their salvation and saw it as their sacred duty to bring them back if they tried to escape and punish them to prevent future escapes. Because the conversion of heathens was the reason they were in California, the Spanish were under pressure to swell the numbers of neophytes by any legal means.

The Spanish troops also had a more immediate motivation to round up Indians. As archaeologist Barbara Voss notes in *The Archaeology of Ethnogenesis: Race and Sexuality in Colonial San Francisco*, the troops disliked manual labor and had come to rely on Indians to do it for them. Mission head Father Lasuén complained that the soldiers arrested Indians simply to use them as slaves.

For these reasons, the Spanish troops dealt increasingly harshly with native communities that sheltered fugitives, or that simply refused baptism. After 1800, pursuing runaway Indians became the major activity of the troops at the Presidio of San Francisco. These raids inevitably led the troops to trespass on native lands. When the Indians who possessed these lands fired on the foreigners, rightfully regarding them as invaders, the Spanish troops were considered to be fighting a just war under European law and custom and had the right to punish and capture the Indians at will. Many raids whose ostensible purpose was to capture a handful of *huidos*—runaways—thus ended up with Spanish troops killing numbers of Indians and capturing others who had never run away.

In July 1797, for example, soldiers from the Presidio fought with escapees from Mission San Jose and their allies. They captured 83 Christians and nine pagans. As was customary, the women and children were taken to the mission. Four Christian Indians and nine non-Christians were taken to the Presidio; they were sentenced to 2 to 12 months of hard labor in irons, placed on short rations and given 25 to 75 lashes. In October 1804, a punitive expedition was launched against a village refusing conversion. The women and children were turned over to missionaries. Thirty-two men were sentenced to labor at the Presidio at least through 1805.

Accompanied by numerous Indian auxiliaries, the Spanish troops ranged increasingly far in their quest to bring the savages to heel. By 1793, no native villages remained on the San Francisco peninsula, and virtually the entire Bay Area had been emptied by 1810.

After Mexican independence, little changed. The new government lacked funds to pay the troops, and the Presidio's population dwindled through attrition. When Kotzebue made a return visit to it, he said, "Everything was going on in the old, easy, careless way." By 1835, the comandante, Mariano Vallejo—who went on to become the most famous and influential Californio—decided that the Presidio was so decrepit that it was unsalvageable and relocated his troops to Sonoma. People from the new village of Yerba Buena, a cluster of shanties on the little cove on the sheltered eastern side of the peninsula, removed any useful building materials from the main garrison and the Castillo. In 1839, only three men were still nominally stationed at the Presidio, but they appear to have deserted, leaving it completely unmanned.

In 1843, a 19-year-old Bostonian named William Thomes recorded his impressions of the fort as his ship entered the bay: "As we drew near the presidio a Mexican flag was run up, in answer to our signal, and then the solitary soldier, who seemed to have charge, thinking that he had done his duty, pulled it down, put it away, lighted a cigarette, and went to sleep for the afternoon."

Thus ended the great Spanish imperial adventure that had started three and a half centuries earlier, when Columbus established the first city in the New World in Santo Domingo: a soldier slumbering in a deserted quadrangle, an empty flagpole rising above some decaying walls, the Castillo to the west collapsing slowly into the sea.

CHAPTER 15

THE CHRONICLER

San Francisco Chronicle Building, Fifth and Mission Streets

One Saturday afternoon in early 1997, I walked blearily out of my apartment on Nob Hill, chasing some carbonated sugar water after a night that had begun at a South of Market dive and ended seven hours later in North Beach. The *San Francisco Examiner* was lying on the doorstep. I glanced at the headline. "Herb Caen Dies," it read.

I stared at the paper for a moment. Then I looked slowly at the houses across the street, past the humming murmur of the cable car lines, up through the maze of telephone lines, into the cloud-torn gray sky. For a moment, the city's heart, too, seemed to have stopped beating. Then it came back to life, and it was changed.

It was not diminished: It was bigger. It was older, wiser, more haunted by history. It reached further back into the past, a past of neon jazz joints and starlets and big-nosed convertibles, glasses glowing in dark rooms, muscular men unloading cargo on the waterfront, white apartments rising up in the fog. The city had arranged itself around its chronicler, the way the forest rearranges itself around the empty place when one of the big trees falls.

It had always been his city, it struck me as I walked up Leavenworth Street, but it was only now that I really knew it.

Herb Caen was two things above all: He was a great newspaperman, and he was a great lover of San Francisco. What made him unique was the way he brought these two things together. He brought a deadline poetry to the life in the streets, the roistering and gossip and tragedy of 700,000 lives. His daily column was the city's agora, its Roman forum. The scoops, the sparkling one-liners, the praise and derision, and the endless dish he served up brought the city's people together, if only for 10 minutes over a cup of joe. But Caen was much more than the world's greatest gossip columnist: He was also a razor-sharp wit, a shrewd commentator on civic and national affairs, and an unabashed fan of his beloved city, whose set pieces celebrating San Francisco were way too good for a guy crashing daily deadlines. Think Walter Winchell crossed with Jon Stewart, with a little Anthony Lewis and Lawrence Durrell thrown in.

Here's Caen as three-dot man: "Long Gone: The day Frankie Flier drove his Cadillac into the parking lot at Seventh and Mission and with his lawyer started to cross the street to Federal Court. 'How long will you be gone?' the attendant asked after him. 'About five years,' answered Frankie, who a few minutes later pleaded guilty to a narcotics charge and was sentenced to—10 years."

Caen as fearless commentator: "The purpose of capital punishment [is] to set an Example. And if this is so, why isn't it done properly? Why isn't Caryl Chessman gassed in the middle of Union Square at high noon, so that thousands of people (plus millions of TV viewers) can witness the fate of wrongdoers and vow, then and there, never to step outside the law? But no, that would be an indecent spectacle, abhorrent to those who prefer to live by euphemisms. He must be done away with in a gloomy little room surrounded by a protective nest of walls, before the eyes of a few select witnesses—as though the act itself, the final demonstration of the majesty of the law, were some dark and dreadful thing. And a dark and dreadful thing it is."

And finally, Caen as bard of the town he found so fairy-tale-like that he christened it "Baghdad-by-the-Bay" (this was back in the innocent 1940s, when "Baghdad" evoked the Arabian Nights, not a war-ravaged monument to American folly): "San Francisco, the city born with the soul of a harridan, is more herself when the street lights flick up on her hills and in her valleys. The night becomes her. Suddenly there are implications of melodrama in the blackness of the Bay, splotched here and there by the amber reflections from the bridges. Sharply, you can hear the sighing of water among the rotting teeth of the piers that bite, like a row of jagged teeth, into the harbor. The cable slots sing more loudly among the quiet streets, and the fog drifts in and out of alleys, turning them into stage sets for a play that needs no actors. Only at night do you seem to get the old feeling—novelist Frank Norris always felt it—that 'anything can happen in San Francisco.'"

Caen was a living link to an almost mythical age, the fedora-hat era when a sweaty glamour hovered over the whole sidewalk-pounding enterprise of being a daily man. Writing a daily column is wiltingly hard work, but he did it with a panache and muscular zest that made the macho creed civilized. During my five years at the *Chronicle*'s great rival, the *Examiner*, where Caen was lured for a spell in the 1950s before returning to the *Chron* for good, I would sometimes see him parking his white Jaguar and strolling, with Jeeves-like insouciance, down Fifth Street, homburg jauntily on his head. The lesson of that supreme saunter was simple: You gotta enjoy it, all of it. Just knowing that he was there, pounding away in the same building as me on his old Royal, was as reassuring as a flask in the pocket or money in the bank. In an age when journalism has lost its style, its eccentricity, its balls, Caen was a Stoli-quaffing, nightclub-going, skirt-admiring anchor.

And then there was his humanity. Caen upheld the great democratic tradition of the American press—one fading as TV anchors and even elite print journalists occupy income brackets and sensibilities far removed from the people they're writing about. Caen hobnobbed with the wealthy and powerful, he enjoyed the good life, but he always retained a newsman's humility, a solidarity with the taxi drivers and waitresses and secretaries and dockworkers who made the city work. In a column after Pearl Harbor, he defended Japanese Americans. He stood up for the hippies (while poking fun at their follies). His early opposition to the Vietnam War, his opposition to all forms of bigotry, truly marked him as the apt chronicler for this most liberal of American cities. And he fought hard to save what was unique about San Francisco—opposing the freeways that were strangling it and the high-rises that were destroying its skyline.

There is something hilarious, and touching, and absolutely right about the fact that one of Caen's wives named San Francisco as a co-respondent in her divorce suit. She was the one he never left.

As the years went on, and the city moved further away from the enchanted, sparkling Baghdad-by-the-Bay era that he loved best, his tolerance acquired a pathos, an even greater emotional resonance: You knew that he was not entirely happy with what had happened to his city, but he refused to turn sour and bitter. He kept up with what was going on, could laugh at and appreciate the blue-haired punks on Folsom Street just as 40 years earlier he had laughed at and appreciated the hepcats in North Beach.

Duke Ellington, I think, once said that he stayed young by playing with young cats. Caen, old drummer that he was, kept swinging until the end. He taught a lot of us '60s kids who had erroneously thought that we had the market on tolerance—look at us now in our judgments and weep!—what that word really means. He taught us how to grow old.

Herb Caen said he wanted his gravestone to read "He never missed a deadline." That is a fine and fitting epitaph for a man who upheld the best traditions of his profession—and had a hell of a good time doing it. But his true memorial is larger.

It is all around the city, in every corner of this jumbled steep old treasure-hunt village running away from civilization and down to the sea, from the restless wind-blown waves at Ocean Beach to the rotting piers at Red's Java House, from the filthy numberless byways of Chinatown to the bleached stark vistas on Twin Peaks, from the lights in the big houses on the hills to the music in the little ones in the valleys. It comes alive and will always come alive every time anyone reaches far enough into imagination and tolerance to see the city as he did: whole and alive, intricate and majestic, a place in the heart at continent's end. As long as people love San Francisco, Herb Caen will live on.

Thanks, Herb. We'll see you around town.

CHAPTER 16

THE COUNTRY
IN THE CITY

35 Prospect Street, Bernal Heights

During three or four months in 1953 and 1954, a group of young Parisians undertook the weirdest series of city walks of all time. These adventurers—Guy Debord, Ivan Chtcheglov, and one or two others—wandered around Paris in a calculatedly illogical way, trying to short-circuit their received images of the city. Abandoning rational goals or destinations, they surrendered themselves to the terrain and to whatever adventures befell them. Debord said the purpose of these walks, which he called *dérives*, or creative drifts, was to "emotionally disorient" themselves and to "study the terrain." Chtcheglov wrote that "dériving" was so intense that doing it for a month was "really pushing it" and that the three- or four-month stint was "the extreme limit. It's a miracle it didn't kill us." The fact that he and his pals were constantly drunk may not have helped. Actually, three or four months may have exceeded the limit—Chtcheglov later went insane.

Being French, Debord—who is best known as the czar of the avant-garde movement known as Situationism—was required by law and the needs of future academics to claim that these wacked-out walks were part of a new science, which he dubbed "psychogeography." He defined psychogeography as "the study of the precise laws and specific effects of the geographical environment, consciously organized or not, on the emotions and behavior of individuals." When I first heard about psychogeography, it struck me as one of those Grand Theories that, to quote the philosopher John Searle's immortal words about Jacques Derrida, "give bullshit a bad name." But then I realized that when you got rid of the pretentious pseudoscience, the *dérive* was really not that different from what I was trying to do as I wandered around town. Its ultimate purpose was to rip off the veneer of routine, allowing the city to emerge in all its heartless, infinite splendor.

I wondered what Debord would have made of San Francisco. For Paris is mind-blowing in a very different way than San Francisco. Paris is drenched in history: The glories and horrors of mankind are memorialized on every corner. The strange juxtapositions revealed by the card shuffling of the *dérive* are human ones. San Francisco, by contrast, is all about the collision between man and the universe. It is on auto-*dérive*. Anarchic, blown-out, naked, it shuffles its own crazy deck. To walk its streets is to be constantly hurled into different worlds without even trying. As William Saroyan wrote, "This city has the temperament of genius. It is unpredictable. Any street is liable to leap upwards at any time . . . It is a city with no rules. Like nature itself it improvises as it goes along."

For these very reasons, I'm not sure that Debord would have gotten San Francisco. John Muir he was not: Deriding a surrealist experiment in aimless walking that took place outside a town, he wrote, "Wandering in open country is naturally depressing." Debord's love-hate fixation with the city as city, with the artificial and constructed, was driven by his Marxist-tinged ideology. His *dérives* were an attempt to escape the seamless web of capitalist domination he called "the Spectacle," but the escape could only take place by turning the Spectacle on itself. Nature was irrelevant; it left him cold.

But even though San Francisco's nature quotient is much higher than Paris's, it's still a city. The fallen world of late capitalism has many mansions. And leaving ideology aside, I like to think that Debord and his pals would have found San Francisco a fascinating challenge. As connoisseurs of terrain confronted with a city whose natural landscape trumps its man-made one, they would have been forced to expand their definition of urban space.

Of all the locations in San Francisco, I would have been most interested to know what these students of the "precise laws and specific effects of the geographical environment" would have made of Bernal Heights.

Bernal Heights is the city's trickiest psychogeographical conundrum. Its atmosphere is unmistakable, ineffable, and quintessentially San Francisco. Yet it is incredibly hard to describe.

More than any city I know, San Francisco is made up of discrete neighborhoods, each with its own unique aura. The main reason for this is its terrain. Its convoluted landscape defines San Francisco's neighborhoods, endowing each of them with a specific *terroir*. Many of them—Potrero Hill, West Portal, Cole Valley—almost feel like villages. These different atmospheres are more aesthetic and spatial than sociological: The days when the city's neighborhoods were ingrown ethnic enclaves are vanishing. Still, there's no shortage of neighborhood pride, as evidenced by the proliferation of hyperlocal newsletters, Web sites, and volunteer groups. A Sienna-style Palio here, with young bloods from North Beach and Ingleside and Potrero Hill and West Portal and the Sunset swaggering boisterously around town under medieval banners before staging a viciously contested bicycle race around Speedway Meadow, would be an instant success.

In this city of quasi-villages, sprawling Bernal Heights is the most village-like place of all. And it doesn't feel like just any village—it feels strangely *old*, like a Gold Rush town that was somehow lifted up and dropped down next to the freeway four miles southeast of downtown. It has the hand-tinted atmosphere of a 19th-century village in a Currier and Ives print. The place was originally an old cow pasture, and the sound of horses' hooves seems to have just faded in the distance. There are certain streets in Bernal that remind me of Angels Camp, the Mother Lode town where my mother's side of the family grew up. Angels still has an ancient set of decaying wooden chicken steps running down toward Main Street. If any neighborhood in San Francisco had chicken steps, it would be Bernal. In fact, I saw some chickens pecking in a yard over near the Rutledge Street Steps the other day.

Much of Bernal's enigmatic, quasi-rural atmosphere comes from the big round hill it occupies. The most isolated and dramatic of all of the city's

50-plus major hills (the exact number is a matter of theological disputation), its great bare top rises 433 feet above amiably bedraggled Mission Street, visible from all over town. With the possible exception of Twin Peaks, no other hill in San Francisco is so barren. The summit looks like it's right out of a Western, especially when you approach it from the old, arrow-straight streets that run into it from the south. A stark ridge of reddish chert looms up over those venerable streets, casting a weird, *Stagecoach*-like spell on the vicinity.

If the hill is the biggest reason Bernal feels like a 19th-century village, the second is its streets. Bernal's streets, especially on its eastern side, are a labyrinth, winding circuitously across the vast reaches of the hill. Peralta Avenue is the most interrupted and illogical street in the city, following what appears to be the logic of quantum mechanics as it suddenly appears again and again where it has no business being. And the streets on the northwest side of the hill, although straight, are equally eccentric, plotted on an odd off-center grid and approached by a strange diagonal street, Coso.

These irregular streets are old, and their houses are old. They are lined with Victorians of all shapes and sizes. The combination of the looming barren hill, the open ground, the eccentric streets, and the old wooden houses adds up to a disheveled 19th-century sublimity that is found nowhere else in town. Potrero Hill, which also has weirdly eclectic old architecture and fantastic views, comes closest to matching Bernal's atmosphere. But it is much smaller, it is less riddled by byways, and its streets are linear and wider. It only dissolves into mystery a few times. Bernal is permanently caught in a time warp.

In a wild, *dérive*-addled manifesto, Chtcheglov famously lamented the loss of a mythical "hacienda." No such building exists outside of Burning Man, but Bernal Heights—at whose foot an actual adobe hacienda once stood in the Spanish days—comes close.

The aura created by the hill and the streets would have given Chtcheglov and company plenty to jot down on their demented aesthetic spreadsheets. But what really would have overloaded their mental calculators is Bernal's peculiar motleyness. It's fitting that Bernal is home to a disproportionate number of writers and artists, for a sense of disorder and creative irregularity clings to it. There is more geographically induced entropy here, especially on the hill's steep and surreal eastern side, than anywhere else in town. The strangest of Bernal's many intriguing paths is a long little-known trail on city-owned freeway-fringe land off Mayflower Street and Holladay Avenue. This trail hugs the edge of the cliff 100 feet above the freeway, ending just below a dilapidated Dogpatch-y red house in a bizarre clump of prickly pear.

(It's an unavoidable fact that the most obscure and unused patches of ground in any city are close to freeways. In the 1980s I went on an expedition with a Situationist-inspired group called the Cacophony Society, in which our leader, John Law—who later played a role in creating Burning Man—set up a rigger's pulley over the 280 freeway on the east side of Potrero Hill, hoisted the attendees into the air, and swung us into one of those strange little concrete bunker-like spaces that were part of the structural reinforcement of the hill face. We sat there like a bunch of Futurist Tom Sawyers in a place no one had ever been, looking down at the cars roaring past at 65 miles an hour. Debord and Chtcheglov, eat your hearts out.)

The freeway trail is the weirdest, but Bernal Heights is riddled with peculiar byways. There are more staircases in Bernal Heights than anywhere else in San Francisco. There are also a disproportionate number of dirt paths, those humble byways that are more important to San Francisco's soul than all of its freeways and arterials put together. And there are big stretches of land too steep for anyone to use, and which neither the city nor anyone else has fenced off. Joy Street, one of the city's great undiscovered streets, faces one of these: a big hillside filled with anise plants and graced by a little bench from which the *flaneur* or *dériver* can gaze down at the freeway, the industrial stretches, and Bayview Hill.

These empty patches of ground are found all over San Francisco. In fact, one of my favorite ways to discover the city is to get onto high ground, look for a bare stretch of earth, and then head over there. When I find it, I walk onto it until I come to a sign telling me to stop. There usually aren't any. The comedy of the commons, not the tragedy, prevails in San Francisco. It's fitting that perhaps the most lovely common space in the entire city is in Bernal Heights, an obscure spot next to a marvelous community garden above Brewster and Costa. On this large, level lawn sits a round table and seven delightful chairs, free to all, tangible evidence that Hobbes was wrong.

When I moved to Bernal Heights in the early 1970s, one stretch of Brewster was completely unpaved. You'd go out walking past a huge Victorian house and a big eucalyptus tree and come to a dusty country lane, which petered out past a few ramshackle houses and decaying cars. It was not paved over until the 1990s. Today it is lined with sterile expensive buildings, but for me, that lost dirt lane is as permanent a part of San Francisco's eternal landscape as the cargo ship my dad once took me to watch being unloaded by crane at one of the piers north of the Ferry Building.

These are some of the things that make Bernal Heights feel the way it does. If Debord fed them into his psychogeographical algorithm, maybe he'd come up with the precise formula. But that formula would never capture all of my feelings about Bernal. For there is a variable that is impossible to control for, something that trumps the laws of location: time. Or, more precisely, felt time. Experience. Life.

I moved to Bernal in 1973. My cousin Jon and I were 20-year-old college dropouts and complete ne'er-do-wells. We took turns working clerical jobs for a temp service called Kelly Girl. The usual routine was for one of us to sign up and start working, while the other one leaned and loafed at his ease, observing a spear of summer grass. After four or five months, the job would end, and whoever was working would be laid off, which entitled him to begin collecting unemployment. At that point, the other one would sign up at Kelly Girl, and the whole cycle would begin again. It was not a pattern of behavior that would have brought joy to the heart of Ronald Reagan, governor of California at the time.

We actually felt quite middle-class. Before we became Kelly Girls, when we were both unemployed, we lived on potatoes and carrots with a few sausages thrown in, washing this serflike repast down with three-dollar-a-gallon Mountain Castle wine. Our Kelly Girl income allowed us to eat chicken and supplement the Mountain Castle with occasional fifths of Johnnie Walker. We had finished a house-sit on Pine Street and were looking for a place to rent. We saw an ad for a house on Prospect Street. It was an unusual deal, a lease-option to buy. We looked it up on the map and went over to Mission and Precita, where I made a call from the payphone at an old Rexall drugstore, which stocked liquor and paperback books. The house was a dilapidated 1886 Italianate Victorian on the steep slope of Prospect Street, on the northwest part of the hill, with a panoramic view of Twin Peaks and downtown and an overgrown backyard.

We decided to take it and drove down to South San Francisco to sign the papers. The terminally uptight middle-age realtor told us that the building was technically condemned but that the city would work with us on it. The rent was $250 a month, and the purchase price, if we decided to exercise the lease option, was $29,200. We moved in.

What is there to say, looking back from the moon of 40 years later, about being 20 years old and living in your first real place, the first place for which you paid rent? Music playing constantly. Johnnie Walker–fueled philosophical debates. Raucous parties. Long-gone girlfriends, long-gone friends. Throwing pork chop bones to the cats in the corner. Playing the guitar. Bowling. Eating at a cheap Mission Street joint called Palace Family Steak House. Looking out the window at the lights of Twin Peaks. Asking our parents for $5,000 to buy the place and being laughed at. Reading P. G. Wodehouse as a daily hangover cure. Wandering around San Francisco. Planning to read Nietzsche again and not doing it. Going to bed at 3 A.M. and waking up at noon for a year. Moving out.

In 2011, Jon and I found ourselves back in Bernal when he had a salsa gig at a bar on Mission Street called El Rio. Neither of us had walked through the old neighborhood in more than 30 years. We wandered around a little bit, marveling at what we remembered and what we had forgotten. Our old house was all fixed up and probably worth a million bucks. We bought a bottle of wine at a Mission Street liquor store and drank it while we ate dinner in the old Rexall drugstore, now a nouveau barbecue joint. Neither of us got drunk enough to start going on about how those had been the happiest days of our lives. But both of us knew that they were gone forever, and so were the two young, foolish, hopeful men we once had been. The hill was the only thing that was left.

At the time, that felt like a consolation. Right now, it doesn't. For a place can only summon up the past. What you do with those memories is up to you.

CHAPTER 17

HUCK'S HIDEAWAY

The Dick-Young Apartments, 823 Grant Avenue,
former site of William Richardson's lean-to

My favorite period in San Francisco's entire history takes place between 1835 and 1846. During those enchanted years, the village of Yerba Buena—the future San Francisco—was so tiny that almost every single person who lived there can be identified, so somnolescent that the slamming of a door was news, and so strangely, blissfully remote that its cast of resourceful oddballs, lucky veterans, and adventurous drunks seems to exist in a decrepit fairy tale, like the *paisanos* in John Steinbeck's *Tortilla Flat.* These were San Francisco's lost-boy years, when a band of merry souls—"a few romantics and dream-drugged escapists," in Bernard DeVoto's words—fleeted the time carelessly in their snug little hideaway west of the West.

Yerba Buena's first inhabitant, William Richardson, chose his house site above the cove on June 25, 1835. Five months later, halfway across the continent, a baby named Samuel Langhorn Clemens was born in what he later described as the "almost invisible hamlet" of Florida, Missouri. Mark Twain, who was to find his literary calling in San Francisco, created an unrivaled American paradise when he recollected his boyhood on the banks of a great river and the edge of civilization in *The Adventures of Huckleberry Finn*. At the end of Twain's masterpiece, Huck famously says, "I reckon I got to light out for the territory ahead of the rest." Huck wasn't talking about Yerba Buena, but he could have been. For the 11 years, seven months, and five days of its charmed existence, Yerba Buena was that territory. It was a place beyond the reach of the Aunt Sallies of the world.

In William Heath Davis's *Sixty Years in California*, one of the most delightful books about the city's earliest years, Davis recalls how in 1840 he spent a week on Goat Island (now Yerba Buena Island), cutting wood, reading, and fishing. It was a San Francisco version of Huck and Jim's stay on Jackson Island. Like their magical sojourn, Yerba Buena's first decade was a small miracle of racial harmony, an escape from American gravity. Also like theirs, it was not fated to last.

On August 2, 1822, the bedraggled "Spanish" soldiers at the Presidio, who did not even know that they had been subjects of Mexico for almost a year, fired a salute as the British whaler *Orion* sailed through the Golden Gate. The *Orion*, commanded by William Barney, sailed past the Presidio, weathered the northeast tip of the peninsula, and anchored in a cove off a vanished promontory called Clark's Point, near the present-day intersection of Broadway and Battery in the lee of Telegraph Hill. The ship, one of the first non-Russian vessels to enter San Francisco Bay, badly needed supplies. Her first mate, 27-year-old William Richardson, was sent ashore because he spoke Spanish.

Born in London, Richardson had gone to sea at the age of 12, starting as a cabin boy in the British merchant marine. He had seen the world. In the next 24 hours, he would reinvent his life.

Richardson rowed to the sandy beach, where he was greeted by a squad of soldiers who escorted him to the Presidio, three miles to the west. They rode through the wind-blown dunes, crossing between Nob and Russian Hills at the *puerto suelo* (low pass) at Pacific and Jones. Then they continued past the little lake at Gough and Greenwich and the old Indian village on the northern shore.

When Richardson arrived at the fort, he was greeted warmly by its co-mandante, Don Ignacio Martinez, who invited him to a fiesta he was hosting that very evening. Martinez introduced the young Englishman to his guests, a group of fellow officers and their wives, and began pouring *aguardiente* as the music began. Richardson found himself dancing with the co-mandante's eldest daughter, a 19-year-old named Maria Antonia Martinez with long black hair and flashing brown eyes. He himself was tall and slender and elegantly dressed in a braided coat and nankeen trousers.

Richardson did not know it, but Maria Antonia had fallen in love with him at first sight. As he had leaped off the boat, she had exclaimed to her friends, "Oh, que hombre tan hermosa el estranjero que desembarco del bote; el va hacer mi novio y yo voy hacer su esposa." ("Oh, what a handsome man that foreigner is who just got off the boat. He will be my bridegroom and I will be his wife.")

The guests danced the *jarabe*, the *jota*, the *contradanza*, and other Spanish dances. Richardson did an Irish jig, to the delight of the guests. The fiesta did not break up until dawn.

When Richardson returned to the ship, no doubt feeling like he had just visited a different and much superior planet, he found an enraged Captain Barney. Furious that his first mate had left the ship anchored all night in rough waters, envious that he had missed the party, or both, Barney severely reprimanded Richardson. What happened next is unclear, but Richardson apparently jumped ship and came ashore, where he explained his situation to Don Martinez. The comandante offered his hospitality. Smitten with Maria Antonia, Richardson decided to stay in California.

Romulus-and-Remus-like legends about the founding of cities are unreliable at best. But it cannot be a coincidence that one of the world's great cosmopolitan party towns was founded by a runaway who had just met a mixed-race hottie at an all-nighter.

Martinez advised Richardson to go to Monterey, the territory's capital, to get permission from the governor to stay. The governor granted Richardson permission, on condition that he teach the Californians navigation and carpentry, two of the many skills they sorely lacked. Richardson returned to live at the Presidio. He was the first foreigner to settle in the Bay Area. (In 1822 there were only eight English-speaking foreign residents in all of California, all of them sailors.)

Richardson converted to Catholicism, was baptized at Mission Dolores, and married Maria Antonia in 1825. He spent his honeymoon at a beautiful little harbor across the Golden Gate called Sausalito, becoming the first white man to fall in love with the Lugano-like splendors of that corner of the bay. Putting his seafaring skills to good use, he bought a 15-ton sloop and went into business transporting goods around the bay, piloting foreign ships and serving as a middleman between their captains and the Spanish-speaking ranchers. He became known as Captain Richardson.

Richardson had come at the right time. California was opening up to the world. Determined to keep its colonies completely tied to their mother country, Spain had forbidden foreign trade. But after Napoleon conquered Spain in 1808, Madrid's already-shaky grasp on Alta California grew even weaker. In 1821, Mexico won independence and opened the California ports to foreign trade.

Until the early 1830s, the missions dominated California's economic life. But it had long been clear that the fathers were never going to succeed in "civilizing" the neophytes, and the settlers coveted the vast lands the church was holding in trust for their charges. In 1833, over the bitter protests of the fathers, Mexico secularized the missions, taking the 10 million acres the church controlled and giving them to the neophytes and the settlers. The already-moribund mission system quickly collapsed—in many cases, literally. By 1846 many of the missions had fallen down, and there were only five priests left in California.

For the Indians, the decision proved disastrous. The neophytes were supposed to receive half of the church's holdings, but they ended up with nothing. Many became little more than slaves on the ranches they should have owned. For the *gente de razón*, however, secularization was a bonanza. And the biggest winners of the land jackpot were veterans.

Starting in 1833, Mexican governors approved about 800 petitions for land, totaling 13 million acres, mostly to retired soldiers, pueblo dwellers, and recent immigrants from Mexico. If they had become Mexican citizens and converted to Catholicism, foreigners—primarily Americans and British—could also apply for grants. The grants were easy to get, and they were vast. Most applicants received 10,000 to 20,000 acres, and a few received hundreds of thousands of acres. Former privates and sergeants who were neither as high-born nor as pure-blooded Spanish as they claimed to be suddenly found themselves the quasi-feudal heads of enormous estates. It was the world's most lucrative G.I. bill, and it opened what 19th-century historian Hubert Howe Bancroft dubbed the "California pastoral": the 25-year era of the 50-odd ranching families who, like the rest of the Spanish-speaking inhabitants of the territory, came to think of themselves not as Mexican citizens but as Californians—in Spanish, *Californios.*

Large tracts of San Francisco were deeded over to Mexican settlers, many of whose grandfathers had lived in grinding poverty. For example, a former soldier named José Bernal, whose impoverished grandfather had come with the Anza expedition, was given two enormous grants: the Rincón de las Salinas ("corner of the salt marshes"), including today's Excelsior, Crocker-Amazon, Outer Mission, and Bayview–Hunters Point; and the Potrero Viejo ("the old pasture"), today's Bernal Heights and Holly Park. Together these lands, granted in 1839 and 1840, made up the southeastern 15 percent of San Francisco. Bernal lived in an adobe way out in the country, at Duncan Street and San Jose Avenue. In 1846 José de Jesus Noe, a rancher and civil servant (he was Yerba Buena's last Mexican alcalde, a position, dating back to Moorish Spain, that combined the functions of mayor and judge) who had come from Mexico with an immigrant party in 1834, was granted the Rancho San Miguel, 4,444 acres constituting a huge chunk of south and central San Francisco, including Noe Valley, the Castro, Upper Market, Twin Peaks, West Portal, and St. Francis Wood. Other grants in San Francisco included the de Haro, Diaz, Bolton, and Ridley ranches.

San Francisco wasn't suitable for raising cattle, and none of these lands were ever ranched in more than a small way (although Richardson's future neighbor Jacob Leese grazed cattle on San Bruno Mountain, just south of the city). For a variety of reasons, most of the owners of these ranches failed to make any money from their land, or even to hold on to it for long. (After California became a state, the Californios were dispossessed of their vast holdings, thanks largely to unjust American laws that threw their land titles into question and forced them to sell off their ranches to pay for endless litigation.) But elsewhere in California, the great cattle ranches flourished—and became the backbone of the California pastoral. The ranchers—about a third of whom were foreign—used their seemingly endless lands to graze vast herds of cattle, which yielded two valuable commodities: hides and tallow. The Californios traded these for luxury goods brought by the Boston ships. Between 1826 and 1848, California exported more than 6 million hides and 700,000 tons of tallow. So universal was the use of hides for money that they became known as "California dollars." The era of the hide-and-tallow ships was immortalized in Richard Henry Dana's elegiac 1840 classic *Two Years Before the Mast*.

Richardson prospered thanks to the hide and tallow trade. He piloted the Boston ships into the cove he named Yerba Buena, or "good herb," after a fragrant mintlike herb that grew on the slopes of Loma Alta (Telegraph Hill) and in the sandy soil nearby. He also picked up hides and tallow from ranches around the bay and carried them back to the ships. To help him, he hired a team of Indians, who built a *temescal* (sweat lodge) near Montgomery and Sacramento, where a little stream flowed into the bay. As their ancestors had done for thousands of years, they would sit in the *temescal* until they were steaming hot, then run out and plunge into the cold water. It is one of the last carefree images we have of San Francisco's first inhabitants.

After seven years on the cove, Richardson moved his family south to Mission San Gabriel, where he befriended the governor of Alta California, José Figueroa. In 1834, he recommended that Figueroa establish a trading post and customhouse at Yerba Buena, and asked him to grant him a lot to build a house. That was the fateful year that the missions were secularized: The territorial assembly in Monterey had voted to make "San Francisco"— which included Yerba Buena and made up most of the peninsula as well as parts of the East Bay and Marin—a pueblo, or town, removing it from the jurisdiction of the mission. Eager to develop commerce in the barren northern reaches of Alta California, Figueroa appointed Richardson captain of the future town's harbor and granted him its first lot.

Richardson, his wife, and their three small children arrived on June 25, 1835. We know the exact date for a homely reason. When they reached the site of their new home, on a chaparral-covered rise a few hundred yards above the gently curving cove, Richardson's nine-year-old daughter, Mariana, asked if she could have a pony of her own. Richardson told her that if she was good, she could have a pony by Christmas, "just six months from today."

Richardson proceeded to erect Yerba Buena's first structure, a crude shelter made out of a ship's foresail stretched over four redwood posts. The tent stood on what is now Grant Avenue between Clay and Washington Streets in the teeming heart of Chinatown. A weather-beaten old metal plaque, hidden behind cheap T-shirts hanging on a rack at a tourist-trap shop and attached to a run-down apartment building at 823 Grant bearing the oddly hyphenated name the Dick-Young Apartments, announces: "The birthplace of a great city."

The Richardsons were the only people on the cove. Three miles away, next to Mission Dolores, there was a rural village where several extended Californio families lived. There were also a handful of people at the decaying Presidio, whose troops were being moved to Sonoma. A dauntless woman named Juana Briones and her family were the only other people not living at one of those two places: Briones, her husband Apolinario and their seven children inhabited a house on a little spring near what is now Lyon Street, just outside the Presidio. The only person the Richardsons saw regularly was a soldier named Candelario Miramontes, who had started an Irish potato garden on a level piece of land just below the Richardson's tent. That piece of land, soon to be known as "the Plaza," was renamed Portsmouth Square after the American conquest. It is San Francisco's historical ground zero.

The Richardsons had moved to a barren and inhospitable place. The terrain around the curving mile-long cove, now a concrete jungle of skyscrapers, was so different that it's impossible even to begin to visualize it. (One of the city's great secret views, looking down onto Aquatic Park from the lawn behind the Officers' Club on the bluff at Fort Mason, probably comes the closest to capturing the look of Yerba Buena cove, although in one-third scale.) Behind their tent was an unbroken stretch of low, thick brush, flattened by the wind and filled with quail. The beach, 100 feet wide and fronting today's Montgomery Street, was just two blocks from their tent, beneath a 10-foot bluff. At the base of a ravine that ran down Jackson Street, there was a swampy saltwater lagoon, the Laguna Salada, through which Richardson and his family had to wade to get to the anchorage at Clark's Point near the base of Telegraph Hill.

Sand dunes stretched in all directions. About 200 yards south of their tent was a big sand hill, running east-west along what is now Pine Street.

(In the 1840s, a colony of thieves, escaped convicts, and international desperadoes built a shantytown in a hidden hollow atop this hill, near the southwest corner of Bush and Sansome, from which they would descend at night in search of victims. The derivatives traders and investment bankers who now occupy this part of town have much better digs and work in broad daylight.) The incessant westerly winds whipped the sand into everything, although living in the lee of Nob Hill gave the Richardsons some protection.

The only sign of human habitation were two ancient trails. The first, which started a few hundred yards to the south of their tent, was a rough two-mile-long path covered with low-hanging trees that ran to decrepit Mission Dolores. To get to the even more decrepit Presidio meant ascending the *puerto suelo*, the 300-foot-high saddle between Nob and Russian Hills. In October, Richardson and Yerba Buena's first alcalde, a former Mexican officer named Francisco de Haro, laid out the grid of the future village. De Haro drew a proposed street in front of Richardson's house, which he called Calle de la Fundación, or Street of the Founding. This phantom street, the first in Yerba Buena, ran diagonally toward the *puerto suelo*. Eventually straightened and paved, it became Grant Avenue.

There was also a third trail, miles away across the sandy wastes, that connected Mission Dolores and the Presidio. Known as "the old Spanish trail," it zigzagged across the hills, following their lowest contours. Today, that trail—the lower Haight's version of the *puerto suelo*—lives on in a bike route called the Wiggle, on which hordes of cyclists zoom back and forth between the Mission, north of the Panhandle (NoPa), and other points northwest, in a hipster reincarnation of a trail once trod by priests, soldiers, and Indians.

There were no people living near the Richardsons, but there were lots of wild animals. One night when the family was inside the tent, a bear put his paw under the canvas, grabbed a screeching rooster, and made off with it. Richardson's son, Esteban (Steve), recalled looking down at the waterfront, along what is now Montgomery Street, and watching "bears, wolves and coyotes quarreling" over the fish that washed up on the shore. A true Californio, Steve started riding to Mission Dolores and ranches beyond it at the age of five or six, often passing bears and wolves "so close [he] could have thrown a lariat over them."

One story starkly illustrates their utter isolation. Richardson was away on a trip to Mission Santa Clara, leaving his family behind, when their fire went out. They had no matches and no neighbors. For two days, they had no fire to cook with, no heat, and no light at night. Finally, a soldier from the Presidio happened to pass by and made a fire.

CHAPTER 18

THE DEAD CITY

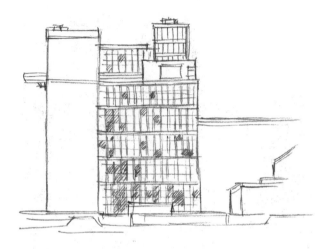

Building 253, Hunters Point Naval Shipyard

Many of my happiest moments have been spent in the weirdest, most obscure, often ugliest parts of San Francisco. Every explorer, even a two-bit one like me whose realm is only a seven-by-seven-mile square, lives for the moment of discovery. And just about the last places you can still discover in San Francisco are those nobody wants—vacant lots, abandoned buildings, unclassifiable patches of dirt filled with old tires and rusting cans and ripped-up girlie magazines and pieces of unknown machines. Wastelands.

But while part of the allure of wastelands is the joy of discovering them, their appeal is deeper. Cracked pavement and old mattresses and fading signs and broken springs and lost piers are the fallen leaves and branches in the great artificial jungle that is a city. Entropic, unclaimed, decaying, created by man but no longer under human control, they are a kind of second-order nature. No-man's-lands are evidence that a city is dying, which means that it is still alive, that it has not yet become an android. They are a healthy sign of defeat and decline. A city without wastelands is a city without soul.

The photographer Larry Sultan captured the weird allure of no-man's-lands in the ironically titled "Homeland," a stunning series of enormous staged compositions in which he placed Latino immigrants in suburban wastelands. By using as props people whose own exiled existence takes place in a twilight zone, Sultan heightened the surreal combination of nature and crumbling artifice that characterizes the strange locations where the sidewalk or the culvert or the mall or the ring road ends.

But urban wastelands are disappearing. Just as most people no longer have any personal experience of death, so, too, many cities are increasingly devoid of dead space. In the postindustrial age, the sterilizing power of ownership and money spreads further and further, a seamless facade, impossible to penetrate. Old cities had guts—factories and docks and train yards and produce markets. And like all guts, they produced organic waste, urban shit—weed-covered tracks and abandoned buildings and vacant lots. The new financial info-city, controlled by disembodied capital, every square inch leveraged for maximum profit, its workers pushing keys on computers or serving lattes, is gutless and shitless.

But there are still patches of human-made wilderness in San Francisco, places where a once-vital part of the city had a great fall and all the king's real estate developers have not been able to put it together again. Ground zero for these lost kingdoms is the old industrial shoreline, the complex and chaotic and polluted waterfront that runs between Mission Bay and Candlestick Park. Over the course of a week, I set out to explore it.

I made my first foray by bike. I rode south on Illinois Street, the yellow brick road that leads to a decaying Oz. The disorder and decline started as soon as I crossed Mariposa Street. Two enormous cranes on train tracks, covered with graffiti, appeared in a fenced-off lot on the east side of the street. They were almost identical to the 28-ton crane I failed to learn to operate at Newport News Shipbuilding and Drydock, the huge military shipyard where I worked after I dropped out of Yale. At the end of 20th Street was a foreboding complex of ancient brick factories and vast corrugated-iron warehouses. These dark satanic mills, complete with an old smokestack, looked like a stage set for a version of *On the Waterfront* filmed in Liverpool in 1885. You expected Johnny Friendly to be standing there, busting heads. All the buildings were locked up and had signs saying "Danger: No Trespassing" on them. An ancient wooden frame bore the faded words "Safety stories in pictures," along with the words "Stop," "Look," "Listen," and—weirdly—"Profit" in its four corners. This complex had been part of the massive Union Iron Works, started in 1849 to produce the drills, pumps, and other equipment needed for the mining industry. In 1908 it was bought by Bethlehem Steel, which also bought the dry docks at Hunters Point.

I rode down to the end of 20th Street and wound through some forlorn streets, past a big open gate that said "Do Not Enter." A decrepit parking lot faced the bay. Behind a chain-link fence fringed with anise plants was a long pier, running out to a boarded-up building 100 yards away. The pier had collapsed into the bay after 30 yards; its cement roadway was twisted and hanging down in the water, fringed with algae. Beyond the gap, the other section of the pier was also drooping down to the water but was still standing.

A five-minute ride south of the state-of-the-art AT&T Park and the million-dollar condos at Mission Bay, I had entered a netherworld of Dickensian factories, dead cranes, and collapsed piers. I rode on, crossing Islais Creek and rolling past the vast defunct Continental Grain plant. Its 10 enormous gray silos rose 100 feet into the air. It was the most visually stunning factory remaining in the city, a Futurist painter's wet dream. At the end of Amador Street, the road petered out at the entrance to a cement plant, next to a big pile of dirt. Three or four 20-foot-high pyramids of sand were scattered about near a trailer structure. No one was around. Past a low concrete barrier there was a little sign that said "Pier 94 Salt Marsh." I leaned my bike against a fence and walked onto the marsh.

Little sinuous inlets wove their way in from the bay. Sandpipers and gulls floated in the water. Looking north, I saw the Mark Hopkins Hotel atop Nob Hill through the legs of an enormous crane. A few steps to the south was a tiny pocket beach, about 30 by 15 feet, with very fine yellow sand. Immediately behind the tiny beach was a fence topped with razor wire. All four towers of the Bay Bridge were visible. A brisk wind blew. The mournful sound of a ship's horn sounded as a big container vessel approached Yerba Buena Island.

I rode on, heading for India Basin. This was one of the major coves on the bay's industrial shore, but I had never been here. The reason was simple: It was next to Hunters Point.

In the urban mythology of San Francisco, Hunters Point plays the role of Mordor. The public housing projects atop the Hunters Point ridge are among the most dangerous in the city, plagued by murderous drug-dealing gangs. Nobody walks around on the hill after dark unless they have to. And even in broad daylight, it's not a place you'd go out of your way to visit. When I was a taxi driver, most of the black drivers wouldn't pick up there.

Now I was approaching that mystery spot. My first view of India Basin, as I rode along Hunters Point Boulevard, was revelatory. I'll never forget it. It permanently altered my imaginative sense of the city. For that gentle cove embodied a lost world. I did not know anything about its history. But I knew with absolute certainty that native people had lived here, and working people, and that farms had been nearby, and that ships had been built and sailed in and out of this little harbor. I knew this in my gut simply because of how the cove looked. Geography was destiny here, and history, and poetry.

Later I found out it was all true, and more. In addition to shipyards and farms, San Francisco's Butchertown was located near here, after it was kicked out of the city proper. As late as the 1930s, cowboys—some of them Mexican Americans carrying on the tradition of the Californios who were the finest horsemen on earth—used to ride down Third Street.

I rode down to the waterfront park in the center of the cove. A few black men were sitting at a picnic table, smoking and laughing. Some Latino kids were playing in the playground. Out in the cove was what appeared to be a large abandoned houseboat, listing heavily to one side. The peaceful, protected atmosphere reminded me of another bayfront park, a lovely cove called China Camp in San Rafael, so named because of the Chinese shrimping camps that once stood there. It turned out there had been Chinese shrimping camps at India Basin as well.

I rode back up to the main street and headed south, below the projects. Some fancy new condos had just gone up, facing the water, rubbing shoulders with older buildings that had seen better days. Behind them, to the south, a series of bleak stairs ran down bare ground from some beige projects on the ridge. It was getting late. I turned around and went past a tiny shuttered-up Victorian house above the cove that looked like it hadn't changed in 140 years. Across the street was one of the most wonderful buildings in the city, a castlelike structure that in the 19th and early 20th century housed the Albion Brewery, whose owner made award-winning ale using water from springs that gushed out of the ground on the hill. I rode back around the industrial park, where huge sprinklers were washing trucks, up Illinois, across Mission Bay, and back into the familiar city.

A few days later I went back, this time with my car. I threw my bike in the back. I wanted to see everything, and I wasn't sure I could do it all by bike. Plus, I didn't really want to do the Tour de Hunters Point. I went back down Illinois, visited the salt marsh again, and drove out to India Basin. As I approached Middle Point, a street the taxi dispatcher used to call, I turned the wheel to the right and headed into the projects.

Mordor wasn't what I expected. There were a few run-down older buildings, but most of the housing was fairly new and well maintained. In fact, these were some of the better-looking projects in the city. The landscaping was good, too. There was no garbage on the street, no knots of ominous young dudes hanging around on corners. I drove around and around, reveling in finally being here, trying to cover every single block. I went past Dormitory Street, the name bearing witness to the reason these projects were here at all.

On the eve of World War II, the Navy took control of the huge shipyard to the east and began recruiting tens of thousands of workers. Many of them were blacks from Texas, Oklahoma, Arkansas, and Louisiana, eager to get decent-paying jobs and get out of the Jim Crow South. Between 1940 and 1943, 94,000 people migrated to San Francisco, the majority of them black. Blacks made up a third of the 18,000 workers at the Hunters Point Naval Shipyard.

Before World War II, there were virtually no black people in San Francisco. Its population of 634,536 was 94.5 percent white. (Mexican Americans and other Latinos were classified as white.) The Bayview–Hunters Point neighborhood had 14,011 people, 7 of whom were black. By the end of the war, 32,000 black people were living in the city. When they arrived, they had to find housing. Some moved into the Western Addition. But those who tried to find housing elsewhere, including in Hunters Point, ran up against landlords who would not rent to blacks, and restrictive covenants. Needing a place to house its workers, the Navy, along with federal and local housing authorities, seized Hunters Point Ridge and threw up 4,000 family apartments and 7,400 dormitories for single workers. Other wartime housing projects were built at Double Rock, Candlestick, Portola, and Potrero Hill. By all reports, the racially mixed housing projects were good places to live. (Jack Kerouac sang the praises of the similarly integrated Marin City projects in *On the Road*, saying they were "the only community in America where whites and Negroes lived together voluntarily.") After they were released from the camps, hundreds of Japanese Americans lived in the Hunters Point apartments, including a Kamiya family at 738 Northridge Road—Motojiro Kamiya, machinist; Sumiye Kamiya, housekeeper; and Wataru Kamiya, waiter.

I drove past Espanola Street, named after Espanola Jackson, one of the so-called Big Five—five indomitable community organizers, all black women, who for decades fought for integrated housing, social services, and affordable health care. Well-maintained town houses lined the streets. A few blocks away, an older Asian man was washing his car. A Latino family was unloading groceries. Two young black girls waited by a bus stop. It was hard to grasp that more murders per square foot took place up here than anywhere else in San Francisco.

I drove off the hill and through the surrounding streets, just cruising. At the top of a ridge, looking down on the vast shipyard, there was a big sign for Lennar Corporation. Lennar, in partnership with the city, was planning a $2 billion, 10,500-home development at Hunters Point and Candlestick Point. But Lennar had so far been unable to secure financing. Many Hunters Point residents charged that the scheme was just the latest attempt to kick black San Franciscans out of town.

I drove down to the shipyard, which the Navy closed in 1971. It's a Superfund cleanup site, filled with old chemicals and radioactive material. I had never been here. A bored guard at a little security booth waved me through.

The base was huge and silent and flat. Enormous buildings cast long de Chirico shadows in the late-afternoon sun. It was completely deserted. I parked my car near an odd wooden structure next to some railroad tracks— some kind of depot. As I got out of the car, a jackrabbit bounded away across the asphalt. I got on my bike and headed toward a big, green-windowed building I had noticed for years from Candlestick Point. A faded sign said "Building 253. Ordnance, electrical shops and electronics."

Building 253 turned out to be one of the most amazing buildings in the city, a stunning glass-walled monolith that could have been dreamed up by the design team of Willis Polk, Mondrian, and Le Corbusier, working under the direction of Uncle Sam. The two-colored green glass panes gave it a weirdly modernist look. A big crane thrust out near its top. I tried the door but it was locked. It was just as well: Later I learned that Building 253 was used to decontaminate ships on which the military had dropped hydrogen bombs during Operation Crossroads at Bikini Atoll in 1946.

Next to it, behind a fence, was a smaller frame building bearing a number of signs near its roof reading "Toilet." Near it was an ancient bus stop sign. Across from Building 253 was the cafeteria, where thousands of workers ate every day. I went down a little street and came upon an old office building that was starting to collapse. An open staircase led to the sagging roof. I tiptoed across it. In the distance, the signature structure of the shipyard loomed up, a monstrous 630-ton overhead traveling crane capable of lifting a million pounds.

Everything here was large and had once been strong. These 979 acres of filled and unfilled land contained six dry docks, 200 buildings, and 17 miles of railroad track. All of them were dedicated to turning out ships and turrets and guns and sights and explosives as quickly as possible.

It was the "Toilet" signs that did it. Maybe it was because I had worked in a military shipyard myself. Maybe it was the fact that I had just come from the ridge where so many of those workers once lived. Whatever it was, that silent and deserted place was suddenly filled with ghosts. I could see them clearly. They were coming out of the bathrooms and bustling into the electrical shop and pouring out of the cafeteria and lined up by the bus stop and welding in the dry dock. They were men and women, black and white and Hispanic. They were from New York and Texas and Louisiana and Ohio and every other state in the country. They moved past one another efficiently and easily. They were on the same team.

All that those black immigrants and their families needed when the war ended were decent places to live, decent jobs, a modicum of acceptance. They didn't get any of it, or not nearly enough of it. White San Francisco pretended they didn't exist and kept them segregated in de facto ghettos. There was little overt racism, but there was semi-intentional neglect, and it proved to be malignant.

In the 15 short years between 1945 and 1960, the die was cast. The young men who were born to those shipyard workers and grew up in the decaying housing on Middle Point or Hudson or Kiska Road, in an isolated, virtually all-black neighborhood that became even more cut off when the Bayshore Freeway was built in 1958, were angry and disaffected. And when the shipyard jobs began to dry up, things got worse.

In 1963, James Baldwin showed up in the Hunters Point projects with a TV crew to make a remarkably radical documentary, *Take This Hammer*, about "the San Francisco Americans pretend does not exist." The program features extensive interviews with a number of young black men. In 2012, Caroline Bins, a student at the U.C. Berkeley Graduate School of Journalism, tracked down several of the men who appear in the film for her own documentary, *Black San Francisco*. One of those men, James Lockett, had moved to Hunters Point from Oakland in 1959. "I turned to robbing to feed my family and the community," Lockett told me. "We couldn't get jobs. If you went downtown to look for work, they wanted skills, but there was no training. My mom was a single woman with four children. As we got older and hungrier, we decided we were going to eat like everyone else. We stole a quarter cow from James Allen's slaughterhouse and dragged it to the car. We fed about 30 families." Lockett said he felt no remorse. "What we did wasn't really crime as crime is today. It was survival."

The situation in Hunters Point was ready to ignite. "We had no income, that was the main thing," Lockett said. "There was corruption in the police department. And then we started seeing these busloads of Caucasians coming into Hunters Point to work in the shipyard, when we couldn't get work there. They had a store down there, G&E Liquors. We'd see them cashing these $200 and $300 checks. That was a lot of money in those days. Then we'd go home and eat these meatless dinners."

On September 27, 1966, a policeman shot a young black man who was running from a stolen car. He died in a ditch on Navy Road. Hunters Point exploded. Angry young men took to the streets, burning cars and smashing windows. The mayor called out the National Guard. Lines of guardsmen cleared Third Street and confronted hundreds of young black men who were farther up the hill.

What happened next could have been a tragedy on the scale of the Watts or Detroit riots, when dozens were killed. For the only time in San Francisco's history, an all-out firefight took place. "There were three levels—Third Street, uphill from that behind the school, and on top of the hill," Lockett said. "We started throwing rocks and bottles, but a lot of us had guns. When the National Guard began firing over our heads, we began firing back."

Miraculously, no one was killed in the shootout. The riots, which also took place in the Western Addition, lasted for four days.

The riots triggered an orgy of soul-searching, an invasion of social workers and bureaucrats and poverty pimps, grand promises, and large amounts of federal, state, and local money. Although some of the programs had an impact, it was too little, too late. The toothpaste was out of the tube. The same problems—widespread unemployment, poor schools, isolation, drug dealing, gangs, violence, the destruction of families and communities—have plagued Bayview–Hunters Point ever since. When real estate values soared in the district during the dot-com boom, thousands of black homeowners sold and moved out of the city. In 2010, there were only 48,000 black people in San Francisco—a drop of 22 percent in a decade. I wondered if the exodus would continue until there were as few blacks in the city as there had been before the war.

As I went past the derelict cranes on Illinois Street, it struck me that wastelands were not always what they seemed. The vast dead city of the shipyard was a wasteland, but it connected the visitor with a living and vital past, a past when blacks and whites worked together toward a common goal. Its buildings might be filled with radiation, but in a deeper sense they were as clean as the little salt marsh a mile north. The newly painted projects on the ridge, by contrast, didn't look like wastelands at all. But they were more broken, abandoned, and forgotten than the most decrepit building at the shipyard.

Someday, I thought, perhaps America would overcome its toxic racial past. Someday Martin Luther King Jr.'s words would come true, and people of all colors would sit down together at the table of brotherhood. Then those projects would just be well-kept buildings. But until then, they will be whited sepulchers, reminders of a shame that cannot be painted over and will not go away.

CHAPTER 19

THE BRIDGE

The Golden Gate Bridge

There are many Golden Gate Bridges. There is the industrial cathedral of orange steel that soars overhead at Fort Point, all latticework and flying arches and filigree. There is the vast Aeolian harp that appears from the Marin Headlands, whose Pythagorean strings seem to be playing the city behind them into existence. (This is only partly a metaphor: The great engineer who designed the bridge was a classicist who read the Greeks in the original.) There is the mysterious bridge one can see from Nob Hill on a gloomy evening, the south tower appearing at once tiny and vast as it rises out of the silver sea. There is the bridge as it appears from the top of Larsen Peak, marking the hidden strait like the world's biggest golf flag.

And those are just external views. There are also internal ones. For like all great human creations, the Golden Gate Bridge reflects and distills and deepens whatever one brings to it.

When I was writing this book, I stayed for a few weeks in the Berkeley Hills. In the mornings and late afternoons I would walk up to the Rose

Garden and look across the bay at San Francisco, perched on its narrow peninsula. It was often wreathed in fog while Berkeley basked in sunshine. On some afternoons when the fog was in, the bridge, directly opposite my perch, was completely invisible. Other days just the tip of one of its towers, 191 feet higher than the tip of the Washington Monument, pierced the fog.

At the time I was immersed in researching California Indians. They were not particularly drawn to San Francisco. Many more native people lived in the East Bay, with its better weather and abundant trees and mud flats, than on the narrow sliver of land across the water.

That knowledge, and the fact that I was observing the city from the outside, caused a Copernican shift in my sense of San Francisco. For the first time, I saw San Francisco as an undesirable outlier. It was an exposed spit of land—too far west, cut off, peripheral, a windy, gray, isolated peninsula across six and a half miles of water. Take away its two bridges, and it was virtually an island. And the mighty Golden Gate strait, a mile wide, haunted by towering fogs and scoured by one of the most powerful tidal movements on earth, was the most daunting barrier of all.

More than any other object, manmade or natural, the Golden Gate Bridge defines San Francisco's place in the world. But it does so in a para-doxical way. On the one hand, it is a supreme demonstration of man's abil-ity to tame nature. Old paintings and photographs taken of the Golden Gate before the bridge was built show a narrow gap in the coastal moun-tains, a void to which the eye and the imagination were inexorably drawn. The great structure filled that void, replacing a natural absence with a manmade presence. The Golden Gate Bridge represents the triumph of man over his environment. It was built during the Depression, yet more than any other modern American structure, it embodies the Renaissance optimism expressed by Hamlet: "What a piece of work is a man! How noble in reason! How infinite in faculty!" Hamlet's description of the sky, "this majestical roof fretted with golden fire," could be a description of the bridge itself.

As a feat of engineering, the Golden Gate Bridge ranks with any struc-ture ever built. The greatest challenge was the south tower, which had to be sunk in the open ocean, 1,125 feet offshore, through some of the most powerful currents on the planet.

But the bridge also draws attention to the very forces that it overcomes.

In crossing that turbulent strait, it highlights it. Every time one looks up from a thousand places in San Francisco and sees its mighty orange towers, or its magnificent profile, or the enormous shadow "H" it casts on the Marin hills, one is reminded that the city abruptly ends at an inexplicable gap in the coastal mountains, through which icy ocean waters rush twice a day. Every time one crosses it and looks down, one has a sense of the awe-inspiring power of that ocean, a power so vast that even the omnipotent bridge pales by comparison. And every time one looks back from the bridge at the white city, rising delicately from the sea on its narrow peninsula, one realizes just how fragile it is.

So the bridge returns San Francisco to the comforting, pre-Copernican center of the universe. But it also reveals just how close to the edge it is.

The bridge's history, too, reflects this charged encounter between nature and man. It was built to open Marin and Sonoma Counties to development, and to alleviate long lines at the ferries: The thousands of San Franciscans who had begun going on weekend excursions to Marin County frequently had to wait for up to three hours to put their cars on the Sausalito ferries. But the Sierra Club opposed the bridge because it feared it would desecrate its site. The original design submitted by Joseph Strauss, the engineer who was the project's Napoleonic driving force, was for a clunky monstrosity—opponents called it "an upside-down rat trap"—that would indeed have profaned the strait that in 1846 the self-aggrandizing explorer John C. Fremont christened Chrysopylae, or Golden Gate, after the Golden Horn of ancient Constantinople. (Fremont's desire to place San Francisco in the august lineage of the capital of the Byzantine Empire was more powerful than his sense of geography: The Golden Horn bears only a slight resemblance to the Golden Gate.) Fortunately, an engineer named Charles Alton Ellis took over. Strauss fired Ellis before the bridge was finished and did his best to make sure that Ellis received no credit. But the bridge designed by the unassuming engineer from Maine—who was finally given major credit for designing the bridge in 2007—is one of the most beautiful structures ever built by man.

Like the greatest creative works, the bridge blends nature and artifice exquisitely. No work by Robert Smithson or Andy Goldsworthy or Christo illuminates its site more profoundly. Like a Janus face, it faces in toward man and out toward the world. As Kevin Starr writes in *Golden Gate: The*

Life and Times of America's Greatest Bridge, "Although the result of engineering and art, the Golden Gate Bridge seems to be a natural, even an inevitable, entity as well, like the final movement of Beethoven's Ninth . . . The Bridge is a triumphant structure, a testimony to the creativity of mankind. At the same time, it also asserts the limits and brevity of human achievement in a cosmos that is as endless and ancient as time itself."

Seen in this light, the Golden Gate Bridge is the perfect metaphor for the city to which it provides such a sublime entrance. For San Francisco, too, is a bridge between mankind and the natural world. It, too, is suspended above an elemental power that could destroy it in an instant. And it, too, is a beautiful pennant flaunted exultantly in the face of that power.

As the symbolic western door of America, the Golden Gate Bridge inevitably summons comparisons to its East Coast counterpart, the Statue of Liberty. For countless immigrants, the first sight of the Statue of Liberty was something they never forgot. Standing as it does on the opposite end of the continent, and built after the great early-20th-century wave of immigration into the United States, the Golden Gate Bridge is not, like the Statue of Liberty, the symbolic gateway to the country. But it, too, has inspired overpowering emotions among those sighting it for the first time. Harold Gilliam memorably described standing at Fort Point one afternoon as a troop ship approached the bridge after the end of the Korean War: "The vessel was half a mile away, but the moment it passed under the bridge we were startled to hear a shout that rose from hundreds of throats and echoed across the water from the cliffs beyond. This was the place and the symbol every man aboard had been dreaming of during the months and years of exile, and it resulted in a spontaneous upwelling of sentiment and sound—a soldiers' chorus of total exuberance."

To cross the sea safely and return home is inscribed in our DNA. It is the theme of the epic that stands at the beginning of our civilization—the story of another old soldier who returned across the sea, after great trials, safely to his home. That was in another time. But we still read Homer's ancient tale, and will continue to read it as long as words exist, because in his perseverance, his will to survive, and above all his restless intelligence, Odysseus is the most profoundly *human* character ever created. He is the archetype of our species. He appears to have been created by someone standing miraculously outside the human race.

Odysseus was not a god. He was a mortal. But using only his wits, that cunning man tricked the Sirens, outwitted Polyphemus, survived the Clashing Rocks, strung the unstringable bow.

And—if we believe that some spark of the essentially human is passed on from generation to generation—built the unbuildable bridge.

There are very few words worthy of the 746-foot towers of the Golden Gate Bridge. Or of the brains and muscle and courage and skill that were required to build it. But the words spoken 2,000 years ago by a blind poet are.

"Tell me, Muse, of that man of many ways . . ."

CHAPTER 20

CALIFORNIO DREAMING

Former Point Rincon, near First and Harrison Streets

In 1836, the Richardsons got their first neighbor. Some savvy Yanks had realized there was good money to be made acting as resident agents for the hide and tallow trade. Jacob Leese, a trader from Ohio who was partners with two other pioneering businessmen, Nathan Spear and William Hinckley, built a two-story wooden house and store just to the south of the Richardsons' tent. It was the first building in Yerba Buena. To celebrate, Leese threw the first of what was to become an annual Fourth of July party. It was a legendary bash, talked about for years.

Leese invited everyone who was anyone: the American and British residents, the officers of the Presidio, the people from the mission, and the foreign officers of ships in harbor. Hinckley provided a six-piece orchestra, supplemented by two six-pound cannons borrowed from the Presidio.

It was San Francisco's first party, and Leese set the bar high. The American flag was raised for the first time, next to the Mexican flag, to great applause. When the sun was at its height, the ships fired a salute, to the cheers of the crowd. That evening, Leese held a grand banquet, followed by music and dancing that lasted until dawn the next day. After a short sleep, everyone headed to the village's favorite excursion site, Point Rincon. On the high ground that formed the southern end of the cove, near present-day First and Harrison Streets, the guests feasted, caroused, and enjoyed the beautiful view of the bay all day, returning to Leese's house in the evening to resume dancing. The party continued until the morning of July 6, when, according to William Heath Davis, "the ladies became so exhausted that the festivities ceased."

Leese had adopted one of the Californios' favorite pastimes, the *merienda*, or picnic. Tales of the period are full of mouth-watering descriptions of grand excursions in which dozens of revelers, accompanied by wagons groaning with sides of beef, roast turkeys and chickens, beans, tamales, fruit, *dulces*, wine, and brandy, would head off to a bucolic site at the edge of a lake or a glade. There the partiers would gorge on *carne asada* (meat broiled on a spit), race horses, play guitars, and sing all day.

Such grand fiestas were among the crowning glories of the California pastoral. That brief era lives in the state's mythology as a carefree, gracious time when generous-hearted, open-handed Spanish ranchers practiced the art of dolce far niente. As Nellie Van de Grift Sanchez puts it in the final words of her 1929 book *Spanish Arcadia*, "these wanderers from old Castile [sought] to make of this world a paradise, singing and dancing their happy lives away on the edge of the Peaceful Sea!"

Some of the myth is true. It really was a carefree, gracious time, and the Californios really were as happy and generous as any people who ever walked the face of the earth. Morever, during the few decades of the California pastoral, a peculiar combination of historical circumstances led many Anglo-Saxons and Hispanics to marry, creating a mixed-race society almost unheard of throughout American history. But beneath the surface of the Spanish arcadia were some all-too-human realities.

The Californios may have been the most loveable nouveau riche in history, but they were still nouveau riche, and their open-handed, generous-to-a-fault, profligate lifestyle was driven by status anxiety. As Douglas Monroy points out in his superb study, *Thrown Among Strangers: The Making of*

Mexican Culture in Frontier California, the rancheros "were of dubious lineage with regard to status, and to acquire social standing befitting their landed domains became their primary ambition." Part of their anxiety concerned their ethnicity. For the Spanish arcadia was not Spanish at all: Much as the dons liked to pose as "wanderers from old Castile," they were really mestizos from Mexico, who embraced their new identity as Californios primarily to distinguish themselves from the more recent immigrants from Mexico (many of them foundlings or convicts), whom they reviled as "cholos." And their willingness to marry their daughters to Yankee and British traders had at least some of its roots in the same anxiety. Monroy writes, "The arriviste gente de razón naturally gravitated toward respectable Anglos to counter the threat that the Mexican immigrants, whose numbers they correctly perceived as growing, posed to their shallowly rooted status and culture." The rancheros, to put it in urban slang, were "fronting."

But the fact that the rancheros suffered from status anxiety is far less troubling than the fact that the grand lifestyle that confirmed their status was built on the backs of Indians. Monroy argues that the Californio culture was, in the feudal sense, seigneurial. The lords of the manor were the patriarchs of a few dozen large extended mestizo families, the lucky beneficiaries of the land grants. In the middle, the "poor whites" were the lower-class Mexicans who worked for them. And at the bottom, the Indians, who did almost all the work, were the serfs.

As it had since Columbus set foot on Hispaniola, access to free or virtually free Indian labor made the rancheros' easy lifestyle possible. Almost to a person, contemporary observers commented on how little work the Californio men (the women were a different story) did. Juan Bandini, himself about to become a ranchero, commented, "Riding on horseback and lounging lazily is the gamut of their days, and the women bear all the responsibility of the house." Richard Henry Dana called the Californios' aversion to work "the California fever."

The trademark of the Californio lifestyle was unparalleled hospitality. Every traveler commented on it. José del Carmen Lugo accurately said, "The traveler could go from one end of California to the other without it costing him anything in money, excepting gifts he might wish to make to the Indian servants at the missions or on the ranchos." The head of the Hudson Bay Company, George Simpson, wrote, "They literally vie with each other in devoting their time, their homes and their means to the entertainment of a stranger." Mariano Vallejo noted that a hungry traveler could slaughter any cow belonging to anyone, so long as he left the hide where the owner could find it.

The Californios' approach to life, characterized by love of pleasure, an aversion to conflict, and a live-and-let-live attitude, was about to be destroyed by hard-charging Yankees. But many of the Americans who had lived among the Californios recognized that there was something rare and delightful about the way they lived, and bitterly regretted its loss. "The native Californians were about the happiest and most contented people I ever saw, as also were the foreigners who settled among them and intermarried them, adopted their habits and customs, and became, as it were, a part of themselves." So wrote William Heath Davis as an old man in 1889.

Davis knew the Californios intimately: Like Richardson and Leese, he married an *hija del país*. The wholesale sexual mingling between Californios and foreigners in the San Francisco area, as throughout Mexican California, is one of the most extraordinary anomalies in American history. No less than 15 percent of the marriages in California during the Mexican period were intercultural. Almost all the prominent traders in Yerba Buena married Californio women.

It would be unwise to exaggerate the degree of racial enlightenment possessed by either side. Foreign women almost never married Californio men, reflecting a gender taboo that was still in force more than 100 years later, when my Anglo mother scandalized her mother by marrying my Japanese American father in 1950, just two years after California became the first state to strike down a miscegenation law in the landmark *Perez* v. *Sharp* case. (My parents were unusual. Most members of my cohort—third-generation mixed-race Japanese Americans—have a white father, often a G.I., and a Japanese mother.) And as we have seen, the Californios tended to identify themselves as pure-blooded Spanish, a claim the foreigners were happy to take at face value: Marrying a "Castilian" was more acceptable than marrying a mixed-race Mexican.

But if marriages between Californios and Yankees were to a greater or lesser degree transactional, self-interested, and class-bound, they still resulted in a genuine intercultural mingling. And it went both ways: the foreigners embraced the Californio culture as much as the Spanish-speakers embraced the Anglo one. Edward Cleveland Kemble, who edited Yerba Buena's first newspaper, the *California Star*, called his town a "half-breed babe—[a] half Mexican and half 'foreign' prodigy." With the exception of Louisiana—and that was a slave state—no other place in the country except California could have been described as a "half-breed babe." (The first non-Indian child born in San Francisco, the daughter of Jacob Leese and wife Maria Vallejo—Mariano Vallejo's sister—was mixed-race.)

Not surprisingly, the Californios had complex, deeply ambivalent attitudes toward both the United States and Mexico. Leonard Pitt, in his classic 1966 study *The Decline of the Californios*, notes that "a vague and contradictory patriotism" led the Californians to stand by the mother country during war with America, and argues that "Californians remained, in their heart of hearts, Mexicans." On the other hand, many Californios saw Mexico not as their mother country but as a "stepmother," as Governor Alvarado, a proud *hijo del país*, put it. Some—Mariano Vallejo was the most prominent—admired the vigor, efficiency, and enlightened ideas of America and hoped it would conquer California. Others, perhaps the majority, wanted some kind of independence under Britain or France, but came to realize that was unrealistic. Most came to recognize that, sooner or later, America was going to swallow them up.

Starting in 1841, the year that the Bartleson-Bidwell party became the first wagon train to cross the Sierra, that future began to loom larger. A different, coarser breed of Americans—mountain men, trappers, overland emigrants—began to appear in the little cove. These Yankees had no interest in the Californios, their customs, or their society. They had come as outsiders and they intended to stay outsiders. Many held virulently anti-Mexican feelings, which became common after the Texas revolt of 1836. (The word "greaser" was originally used to refer to lower-class Californios who carried greasy bags of tallow on their backs to the Boston ships; later, Americans began using it as a derogatory term for all Californios.) They were trouble, and both the Mexican authorities and Californios knew it.

But the trouble came later. Until 1846, when the American flag was raised over Portsmouth Square not to kick off a party but to end a war, Yerba Buena was a place apart, a lost corner in the world where a band of eccentrics, color-line crossers and self-made men, and one remarkable woman, built a ramshackle utopia.

CHAPTER 21

THE
PUERTOZUELA

Pacific Avenue and Jones Street

From my office on the western slope of Telegraph Hill, I can see the saddle, the low point where Nob and Russian Hills meet. It's a thousand yards away, marked by a fortuitously lurid crimson apartment building on Pacific Avenue just below Jones Street. I have lived near that pass through the hills for more than a quarter of a century. The very first day I met my wife's two-year-old son, I pushed him up Pacific in a stroller. I've sweated up that damn hill on my bike thousands of times. An Asian man who lives in a little bungalow set back from the street sits on the sidewalk in his wheelchair on sunny days, smoking a cigarette. He always says, "You're halfway there!" as I pedal past him.

One of the benefits of riding a bike in San Francisco is that you end up following in the footsteps of everyone who has ever lived here, from the Yelamu to the Spanish to the Mexicans to the 49ers to the Beats. Your leg muscles are an infallible guide to the past. People have been avoiding the hills since time began.

Every low point in San Francisco's terrain collects history the way a fence in the desert collects tumbleweeds, and the saddle at Pacific and Jones has probably collected the most of all. According to Zoeth Eldredge, a leading historian of early San Francisco, the Spanish called it the *puerto suelo*, or "low pass"—*puertozuela* for short. The Yelamu must have traveled it. When Anza took his cryptic first tour of the eastern hills, he probably spurred his charger through the *puertozuela*. San Francisco's first street, a muddy path, angled up toward the pass. William Richardson rode over it on his way to the Presidio. Anyone on the northern side of the cove who wanted to get to the other side of Nob or Russian Hills would have taken it. The crowds that came to see San Francisco's first legal hanging in 1852, somewhere around Vallejo and Leavenworth, would have walked up it.

For decades, a little grocery called the New Russian Hill Market has stood on the *puertozuela*, on the northeast corner of Pacific and Jones. When I first moved onto Jackson Street in 1984, and for years thereafter, it was run by three elderly Italian brothers, one of whom lived in the apartment above it. The store must have been there, essentially unchanged, since the 1930s or 1940s. The place was like something out of Dickens's *Old Curiosity Shop*. It was absolutely crammed with odds and ends of homey merchandise— great bunches of dried red peppers tied with string hanging above the counter, salamis and cheeses randomly piled up, bottles of wine lurking in recesses where they had been gathering dust for decades, yellowing posters for Sam Spade whiskeys like Four Roses and Kessler ("Smooth as Silk") pinned up on the ceiling. The store was so old it had no refrigeration: The brothers kept their produce, milk, and perishable goods in ancient built-in wooden icebox units with heavy metal handles on their doors. Even though we knew they were Italians—from Liguria, I think, like many San Francisco Italians—my cousin and I called the old geezers "the Russians," after the sign on the store. After a while, we actually started to think of them as Russians.

One day, we found one of the Russians, a skinny guy with a thin mustache and a nervous face, crying. We asked him what had happened. He told us his brother—was his name Sal?—who had fat, spatulate fingers and always wore a wide tie that only went down his shirt about six inches, had passed away. "We worked together 12 hours a day. Hell, I spent more time with him than I did with my wife!" the old man told us, shaking his head as he rang up a loaf of bread. The oldest of the brothers (or maybe he was a cousin)—a smiling 90-year-old fellow who stood in the corner all day and spoke almost no English—died soon after, slipping gently down to the floor at a dance at the Italian-American Athletic Club in North Beach. "That's the way to go," said the skinny brother. "Talking to the girls with a glass of red wine in his hand." A year or two later he sold the business to a Palestinian family, who took out the ancient iceboxes and put in modern refrigerators. In a world-class example of poor marketing, they briefly taped a postcard of a keffiyeh-wearing youth throwing a rock next to the cash register.

For years, a large painting of the corner of Pacific and Jones hung somewhere in the San Francisco Center, the weathered "New Russian Hill Market" sign prominently visible. It was an odd painting because, aside from the *puertozuela*, which less than a dozen people have ever heard of, there is nothing particularly noteworthy about this intersection. It looks down on the Bay Bridge and Chinatown, but so does every other street on top of Nob Hill—and they're all a lot prettier than gray, utilitarian Pacific. Maybe someone realized that, because I couldn't find the painting when I went looking for it the other day. As for the latest version of the New Russian Hill Market, it went out of business a few months ago and was boarded up, but has now reopened. The *puertozuela* is still there, sparing San Franciscans' legs and lungs as it has for 5,000 years.

CHAPTER 22

THE LOTUS-EATERS

Former strawberry fields near Fort Miley, south of Lands End

When Jack Kerouac barreled into San Francisco after his 110-mile-an-hour cross-country trip in Neal Cassady's flame-throwing Hudson, he exulted, "Everybody in Frisco blew. It was the end of the continent; they didn't give a damn." Kerouac was talking about San Francisco in 1949, but he could have been talking about Yerba Buena in 1846.

In an attempt to explain the less-than-upright nature of Yerba Buena's citizens, historian Hubert Howe Bancroft wrote, "The presidio maintained the dignity of government and war, and the mission the dignity of religion, so that for the traffickers at the cove little dignity remained or was required." Leaving aside Bancroft's peculiar notion that there was only a limited quantum of dignity available in San Francisco, not to mention the fact that neither the mission nor the presidio had possessed any dignity for decades, Bancroft's assessment of Yerba Buena's population was right on the money.

One of Yerba Buena's leading don't-give-a-damners was a handsome young Brit named Bob Ridley. William Heath Davis describes him as a "regular English cockney . . . singular and comical, and . . . considered the funny man of the town . . . He imagined he was a ladies' man, and at times stirred up a little excitement among the feminines. He was a great teller of extravagant stories—a regular Munchausen—and withal was considered the life and the fun of the place."

In addition to these sterling qualities, Ridley was also an outrageous lush. He pops up here and there in the annals of Yerba Buena like an exuberant, slightly tarnished penny. One spring morning between 7 and 8 A.M., Davis—who was known as "Kanaka" Davis because his grandmother was native Hawaiian—was walking down one of Yerba Buena's dirt paths (it did not yet have streets) when he ran into Ridley. Ridley asked him, "How many London Docks [a grog made with rum and red wine] do you think I have taken before breakfast?" "About a dozen," Davis answered, "your usual allowance." "I can discount that," retorted Ripley. "I have taken 23!"

Excessive consumption of spirits appears to have been a virtual requirement for residency by the cove. In 1838 Nathan Spear, a future leading citizen who was reputed to be "fond of a glass of wine," placed an old 12-by-18-foot ship's house dismantled from the bark *Kent* on the beach on the northwest corner of Clay and Montgomery Streets, naming it "Kent Hall." This whimsical structure was the first building on the San Francisco waterfront. After Spear moved out of Kent Hall, the poop cabin became famous for housing the liquor case of Captain Grimes, a former privateer and businessman who stayed at Kent Hall when in town. His liquor case was filled with choice bottles, but he kept it locked, and in a kind of alcoholic version of *The Arabian Nights*, he would open it only if he deemed his company sufficiently entertaining. As a result, his thirsty friends were constantly telling him tall tales, hoping he would unlock the magic case. A worldly and well-read man, Grimes would disparage most of these yarns, but eventually would be taken in by some egregiously ridiculous tale. At that point the old sea dog would produce the key, open the case, and begin pouring the good stuff, to the great joy of all present.

Kent Hall was soon joined by some ramshackle grog shops, which catered to the runaway sailors who had begun to drift into Yerba Buena. A group of these tars were observed hanging around waterfront bars as early as 1840, beginning a tradition that would make the words "San Francisco waterfront" synonymous with "Sodom and Gomorrah."

But there was at least one resident in Yerba Buena who was not permanently pickled: an indomitable woman named Juana Briones. Briones is the most fascinating, and cryptic, character in Yerba Buena's early years. Her ancestors came up with Anza and Portola. Born in 1802 at the Villa Branciforte, an ill-fated Spanish rest home for soldiers in Santa Cruz, in 1812 she moved to the Presidio, next to El Polin Spring. The waters of the spring were believed to confer fertility, and they seem to have worked with her: by 1833 she and her husband, a soldier named Apolinario Miranda, had seven children. They moved to another house 1,000 yards east, just outside the Presidio wall: her ghostly presence lives on in the rectangular notch, now occupied by six houses, that dents the Lyon Street wall marking the Presidio's borders. At some point Briones set up a second home two miles to the east in Yerba Buena, building an adobe farmhouse near the present corner of Filbert and Powell, a few steps west of Washington Square. In those days, the water came up to Francisco Street, just four blocks away—hence the term "North Beach." A map drawn by Leese describes that waterfront as "La Playa de Juana Briones."

No one knows when Briones moved to North Beach—and thereby hangs a tale. According to her biographer, Jeanne McDonnell, it is possible that Briones moved to North Beach as early as 1826. If that is true, then she, and not Richardson, deserves the title "Founder of San Francisco." But in any case, she deserves an honored place in the city's history as the first—or second, if we count the widow Arballo, who skewered the pompous Font—in a long line of feisty women.

Briones's husband Apolinario was drunk and abusive, and somewhere along the line she left him. It was not easy for an illiterate woman to make her own way in the patriarchal world of 19th-century California, but Briones proved to be courageous and resourceful. She opened a dairy farm, pasturing her cows near the northeast corner of present-day Washington Square, and began selling milk to the crews of ships. William Thomes, who met her, wrote, "If the men had had some of the energy of that buxom, dark-faced lady, California would have been a prosperous state, even before it was annexed to this country, and we would have had to fight harder than we did to get possession." She helped runaways. She took the remarkable step of formally adopting an Indian girl, evidence of her egalitarian spirit. She was also a *curandero* or healer, using herbs and other medicines to heal the sick. Finally, she proved to be a first-rate businesswoman: she maintained title to her land and in 1844 bought a large cattle ranch in the Santa Clara valley (the seller was an Indian, which was highly unusual). The rammed-earth adobe she built there stood until 2011, when its owners prevailed after a long legal struggle and demolished it. A section of the wall was saved: Preservationists hope someday to move it to San Francisco and make it the centerpiece of a historical display about Briones.

Juana Briones died in 1889 at the age of 87, having lived under three flags and seen the village she helped found become a city of 300,000 people, eighth-largest in the United States. Of her, a historian wrote, "No other Spanish or Mexican woman [in 19th-century California] reached her position and maintained it through life."

Briones lived on the outskirts of town. The village's living room was the Plaza, a dirt square with bars on three of its four corners. (Until fairly recently, Geary and Leavenworth could beat that: The thirsty intersection had bars on all four corners.) There was a cheap *pulpería* or tavern, a joint called El Dorado run by a Dane, and the center of village life, a billiard parlor and bar on the southwest corner of Clay and Kearny, whose proprietor was a former Swiss sea captain named Jean-Jacques Vioget.

Like most of the human driftwood that collected on the cove, the popular Vioget could do a little of everything. In addition to being a mariner, he was an artist, a fine violinist, and a surveyor. This latter skill led Alcalde de Haro to choose him to make the first official survey of the village in 1839. Clanking through the sandy wastes on horseback with 100-vara-length chains, Vioget and a helper marked out the hamlet's 10 or so houses, along with about 40 lots and seven streets that did not yet exist. The map was conveniently stored behind Vioget's bar. When anyone wanted to purchase a lot, they had to ask Bob Ridley, who was working as Vioget's bartender, to pull it out. The map soon became so dirty and torn that it was almost unreadable. Ridley didn't last much longer; he died of alcoholism at the age of 32 out in the sticks at Mission Dolores, where he was running a ramshackle bar he whimsically called the Mansion House.

Running a bar that doubled as a recorder's office was presumably good for Vioget's business, but no saloon catering to a population of less than 100 people was ever going to be exactly raking in the doubloons (which were still in use in California). When Thomes visited Vioget's bar, he found the American proprietor "looking as though it would not take much to get him to commit suicide, as the Mexicans did not play billiards, and there was no vessel in port, except the *Admittance*." The bartender asked Thomes and his companions if they had enough money to buy a glass of *aguardiente*. When they told him they had money but "were not drinking much that morning," the man groaned, "Just my blanked luck," went into the saloon, and fell asleep.

Along with his other accomplishments, Vioget was a prodigious trencherman. One day, a Russian by the name of Hoeffener, a regular at Vioget's saloon who lived in the mostly Hispanic enclave at Mission Dolores and was teaching music to General Vallejo's daughters, challenged Vioget to an eating contest. Since no one suspected that Hoeffener was also a bottomless pit, Vioget agreed. A day was set and the merchants of the town invited. The chef was another beloved town character, known as Old Jack Fuller, a British cook and butcher who had, of course, married a Californio girl and was known—attentive readers will notice a subtle yet unmistakable pattern beginning to emerge—to "drink and tell tall tales."

The first course was plate after plate of pancakes. At the end of the round, Hoeffener was a plate ahead. Then came beefsteaks, also rapidly consumed. There followed several plates of *guisado* (a delicious Spanish meat stew), and many plates of *carne asada*. A large course of Spanish-style beans appeared, followed by tamales, of which each man ate at least a dozen. An immense pudding and several types of pies were then consumed, followed by black coffee. Vioget gave up during the pie course; Hoeffener, still eating, was declared the winner. The two men then got up and moved around, smoked, drank a little wine, and played billiards, apparently unaffected by the massive quantities of food they had just consumed.

Besides engaging in eating contests, trying to cajole old sea captains into opening their liquor cabinets, and consuming 23 drinks before 8 A.M., the good citizens of Yerba Buena had important business to transact—primarily figuring out ways to avoid paying duties on imported goods. Bribery, and the slothlike deportment of the local authorities, rendered this task manageable.

And so life went on in this "little corner of the world in which we were shut up," as one Yerba Buena resident called it, the same characters bumping into each other and rolling randomly away, like brightly colored balls on an old pool table. Here are a few of those balls:

Daniel Sill, the town blacksmith, an old mountain man from Kentucky who had crossed the continent and climbed the Sierra in 1830–31 and loved to go hunting on the flatlands between Rincon Hill and Mission Creek . . .

Francisco Cáceres, a former sergeant of dragoons who lived with his family in an adobe at the corner of Grant and Pacific, near the town's first brewery . . .

William M. Smith, a Georgian who had been a circus rider in Mexico and had hitched a shipboard ride to San Francisco in San Blas. Known as "Jim Crow" Smith because of his ability to imitate Southern blacks, he was a crack shot and a dangerous man when drunk . . .

A man named Finch, who owned a saloon on the northwest corner of Kearny and Washington and who, being illiterate, kept track of his customers by drawing symbols of them in his account books . . .

William Leidesdorff, an enterprising sea captain of mixed race (his father was Danish and his mother a mulatto from the Virgin Islands) who became the U.S. vice-consul to Mexico. He and his common-law Russian-Alaskan wife entertained at their cottage near the waterline, whose beautiful flower garden, tended by a Scottish gardener, was the pride of the village . . .

William Rae, the agent for the Hudson's Bay Company, a high-strung, hard-drinking Brit who boasted that the United States would never get its hands on California. He later shot himself, either because he had backed the wrong horse in one of Alta California's perennial political feuds or because he had been caught having an affair . . .

A "half-breed Indian and his wife" who lived at Broadway and Kearny . . .

John Evans, an oddly named Italian boatman who lived at Dupont (now Grant) and Clay . . .

John Tinker, a cheerful English castaway and grog-shop owner who always claimed that he was "growing younger every day," until one morning he was found dead in his shop . . .

With the exception of the blackberries that ripen in August and are scattered in odd places across the city, there are few wild berries to be found in San Francisco. But vast fields of wild strawberries used to cover the dunes near Lands End, and one of the favorite pastimes of the inhabitants of Yerba Buena and surrounding areas was to make excursions out to the ocean to pick them. People would come from as far as Santa Clara and Sonoma. It was a tradition that went back to the early days of the Spaniards, who had been told about the fields by the Yelamu.

In the spring of 1844, almost the entire village of Yerba Buena, 80 or 90 people, went on a weeklong strawberry picking excursion to the dunes near Lands End.

Across the country in Baltimore, the Democratic convention was beginning. The burning issue facing the party, and the country, was whether to annex Texas, which had declared itself a republic in 1836. Mexico had never recognized Texas's independence, and had warned the United States that annexation would mean war. The leading Democratic candidate, former president Martin Van Buren, opposed annexation, as did Whig candidate Henry Clay. Abolitionists warned that annexing Texas would create a "Slave Power." But theirs was a losing position. Fired with expansionist zeal, most Americans wanted the Stars and Stripes to wave not just over Texas but also over the vast, almost unknown Mexican territory called California.

The Democrats saw which way the wind was blowing. They rejected Van Buren and nominated an unknown pro-annexationist, James K. Polk, who defeated Clay and became president in 1845. Polk was determined to extend America's writ to the end of the continent. A phrase coined by a newspaperman, "Manifest Destiny," swept America, giving a quasi-divine imprimatur to the lust for territory. Some Democrats argued that the United States should annex all of Mexico.

Their most vociferous opponent was John C. Calhoun, a senator from South Carolina who, ironically, argued against the plan on racial grounds. Calhoun said, "We have never dreamt of incorporating into our Union any but the Caucasian race—the free white race. To incorporate Mexico, would be the very first instance of the kind, of incorporating an Indian race; for more than half of the Mexicans are Indians, and the other is composed chiefly of mixed tribes. I protest against such a union as that! Ours, sir, is the Government of a white race."

Before the excursion broke up, Don Francisco gave a grand *merienda*, to which he invited all the people who were camping in the area. He provided several bullocks and calves, which were roasted on spits over charcoal. Over Guerrero's cheerful protests, the prosperous Anglo merchants Davis, Rae, and Spear insisted on providing the wine. Several hundred men, women and children feasted on *carne asada* and wild strawberries.

As the sun set over the Pacific, songs in English and Spanish and laughter without language rose up from the camp at the end of the continent, the sound drifting over the strawberry fields in the purple twilight like a wandering soap bubble, until it vanished forever.

CHAPTER 23

THE LAST ROLL

The Cable Car Barn and Powerhouse,
Mason and Washington Streets

San Francisco has its rituals. When the Giants win, Tony Bennett's "I Left My Heart in San Francisco" wafts down over the ballpark. Every holiday season, the trees in Nob Hill's Huntington Park are lit up while members of the San Francisco Girls Chorus sing Christmas carols. Chinese New Year brings not just the big parade but nerve-shattering explosions at unexpected times all over town. And, of course, Halloween leads to a mass public display of behavior so outré it would have made Caligula blush.

But the deepest San Francisco ritual takes place late every night on a shabby street corner in the heart of the city.

The Cable Car Barn and Powerhouse is a big brick building, built in 1907 on the site of the wonderfully named Ferries and Cliff House Railway, whose barn was destroyed in the 1906 fire. The cable cars that used to run out to the Cliff House and all over town are long gone, but three gloriously outmoded lines remain, and the barn is their home. The building houses the guts of the system: the huge winding wheels that pull the inch-thick, wire-wrapped cables under the streets and the 510-horsepower motors that drive the wheels. It's also the place where the cars are stored and repaired. With its enormous squat brick chimney, the barn is a Victorian anachronism, like a kid's idea of a 19th-century factory.

The barn stands on one of those unfathomable corners where different urban realities dissolve into an ambiguous haze. The two-block stretch of Mason between Washington and Pacific is a twilight zone. As recently as a few years ago, much of it was positively decrepit, a decaying precinct of Chinatown. There used to be a huge fortune cookie factory on the corner of Jackson. The street has come up a little, with an architect's office and one or two buildings with new security systems, but it's still an odd mixed bag. John Street, half a block north, is lined with tenements. Across the street from the barn, on Washington, a sparkling new Chinese Recreation Center has replaced the old Chinese Playground, whose old green wooden sign always struck me as the acme of ethnic political incorrectness. (The "Japanese Playground"? The "Jewish Playground"?) Walk uphill on Mason, and it gets rich fast. Two steep blocks above, clearly visible on the summit of Nob Hill, looms the castlelike Brocklebank, the patrician apartment building where Madeleine lived in *Vertigo*.

Jackson is similarly elusive. Some barely respectable apartments rub shoulders with one or two swanky newcomers, million-dollar homes never before built this close to Chinatown. Once you get into Chinatown proper, all pretense at respectability disappears.

History is soaked into the ground here. During the city's wild youth, there was a brief attempt to make this area, which was called Spring Valley because water bubbled out of the earth at Washington and Powell, a fashionable neighborhood. But it was too close to the prostitutes who cruised down Stockton and Grant and the whorehouses and gambling hells on Pacific. One block away, at Pacific and Mason, stood the porch-encircled house of a crusading editor who bore the odd name James King of William. One night in 1856, as King began to walk the six blocks home from his Montgomery Street office, he was shot and mortally wounded by a corrupt supervisor named James Casey. The murder precipitated the formation of the Second Committee of Vigilance, the largest vigilante movement in American history.

The contested geography of this neighborhood played a crucial role in that still-controversial episode. King was a hyperbolic moralist whose shrill editorials, shrewd marketing, and use of sensationalism paved the way for the yellow journalism of the late 19th century, which reached its acme in William Randolph Hearst's *San Francisco Examiner*, the paper where I cut my journalistic teeth. (As a result of this, any errors or libels in this book are not my responsibility, but James King's.) King's crusade against gamblers and prostitutes earned him the undying loyalty of one powerful constituency: wives.

This is where Nob Hill's geography comes in. As historian Roger Lotchin notes in his superb *San Francisco 1846–1856: From Hamlet to City*, by 1856, middle-class San Franciscans had moved west, living on Nob and Russian Hills while working downtown. But in the area between, on Dupont and Stockton—today's Chinatown—large numbers of prostitutes still openly plied their trade. Because San Francisco was still very much a walking city, a "trip to the dentist, the doctor, the milliner, the husband's office, and sometimes even the church kept the situation explosive by renewing the contact between housewives and harlots," Lotchin says. A woman furiously spat, "Is it not wonderful that young men should spend their evenings, like dogs, smelling out all these vile excrescences, peering through the cracks and crevices of doors, windows and blinds in our crowded thoroughfares, in the full face of ladies and gentlemen going and returning from church?"

Racially, too, this area has long been a no-man's-land. Until the 1950s, the Chinese were not allowed to buy or rent west of Chinatown's unofficial border at Powell. When the restrictive covenants were removed, Chinese began buying properties on Nob Hill, eventually acquiring most of its lower slopes. Ironically, the whites who formerly kept the Chinese in a ghetto have now begun descending into that ghetto and buying out the Chinese.

So this is a deep San Francisco corner. And its dinginess makes it all the deeper. It is the perfect setting for a small urban coda.

The whole thing takes less than a minute. A little before half past one in the morning, the cable cars go home for the night. The last car runs up

Jackson, past the barn's car entrance. The gripman, weary after a shift working one of the most demanding jobs in the city, brings his car to a stop opposite dingy Auburn Alley. The conductor gets off and walks over to a railroad switch next to the tracks. If there are any autos behind the car, the gripman motions them to stay back. Then the conductor pulls the switch, the gripman releases the brake, and with a final clatter the old wooden car, free of the cable, rolls on gravity back into the barn.

A few minutes later, the sound of the whirring rope abruptly ceases, a sudden loud silence that informs anyone stumbling home that it is 1:30 A.M. And the city has called it a night.

CHAPTER 24

THE FARCE

Fort Point, previously the Castillo de San Joaquin

n the small hours of July 1, 1846, Captain John C. Fremont, his scout Kit Carson, and a few men commandeered a longboat at Sausalito, rowed across the Golden Gate, and climbed up to the ancient, abandoned Castillo de San Joaquin. By the dawn's early light they spiked 10 rusty bronze cannons, including three ancient pieces cast in 1623, 1628, and 1693, which were lying in the dirt, completely useless. The longboat's owner would later submit an exorbitant bill to the U.S. government for his services, which was rejected out of hand.

This heroic feat of arms was San Francisco's contribution to one of the most disgraceful episodes in California history: the Bear Flag Revolt.

Fremont was leading a company of army topographers on a mission of scientific exploration. He was also carrying secret instructions, now lost, regarding America's imminent acquisition of California. His orders were almost certainly to avoid conflict. But Fremont had a fatal Byronic streak, and it led him to encourage a pointless and unprovoked revolt.

The mountain men and adventurers who had begun trickling into the West had no connection to the Californios. They had long resented Mexican rule, and Fremont's saber-rattling presence gave them a green light. After the grandiloquent captain—whose presence had already aroused Mexican suspicions—ratcheted up tensions by rashly raising the American flag on a mountain near Monterey, a group of settlers seized 200 horses belonging to General Castro, the Mexican commander. Alarmed, Castro began to raise troops. On June 14 a group of 33 settlers, some of them extremely rough customers, stormed into the tiny hamlet of Sonoma and knocked on the door of Don Mariano Vallejo—the town's leading citizen, a staunch liberal, and, ironically, the most outspoken Californio advocate of an American takeover of California.

When Vallejo opened the door, the mountain men somewhat incoherently informed him that he was a prisoner of war. The courtly Vallejo brought out several bottles of his excellent *aguardiente*, which his captors avidly consumed. Fueled by brandy, they wrote out a document announcing the birth of what they styled the California Republic. One member of the party, William Todd (the nephew of Mrs. Abraham Lincoln), made a crude flag depicting a bear standing on its hind legs. Vallejo and several others, including Yerba Buena's second inhabitant, Jacob Leese, were marched away to jail at Sutter's Fort in present-day Sacramento.

The whole episode was a ridiculous farce. What the august founders of the California Republic did not know was that the United States was already at war with Mexico, and had been since May. American naval forces commanded by Commodore John Sloat captured Monterey on July 7. When the American flag was raised over Sonoma and Yerba Buena on July 9, the California Republic, such as it was—it was never recognized by any entity and passed no laws—came to an end. Its brief and inglorious life is nonetheless immortalized on the California flag, which features the grizzly bear and the words "California Republic."

Most of the American citizens of Yerba Buena, which in 1846 had a total population of about 200, favored an American takeover of California. John Henry Brown, who ran the old adobe City Hotel on the southeast corner of the Plaza, claimed that most of them also supported the Bear Flag Revolt. But several Yerba Buenans, including our thirsty old friend Bob Ridley, opposed the American conquest. When General Castro called upon all Mexican citizens to meet him in Santa Clara, Ridley and leading merchant William Hinckley heeded the call. Ridley was ordered to return to Yerba Buena and stop all boats from landing there. He had been home for only two days when two Bear Flag militiamen arrested him at gunpoint in the billiard room, told him they would kill him if he moved, and packed him off to jail, thoughtfully allowing him to take two bottles of liquor with him. This was the only time guns were drawn in Yerba Buena during the Mexican-American War.

On July 9, the U.S. sloop-of-war *Portsmouth* anchored off Yerba Buena cove and sent two dozen marines and carbineers ashore to take formal possession of the town. A sailor named Joseph T. Downey, writing under the name of Filings, captured the event in all its awful majesty. Disembarking at Clark's Point, the troops marched down Montgomery Street to the Plaza, accompanied by a single fife and drum. After a motley crew of 30 to 40 inhabitants were enticed to the Plaza by "threats, promises and entreaties," the American flag was raised above the old adobe Mexican customs house. After the cheers and the brays of jackasses had subsided, all present "unanimously voted to go where liquor could be had, and drink a health and long life to that flag. The Indians consequently rushed frantically to one pulperee, Captain Leidesdorff and the aristocracy to Bob Ridley's bar-room, and the second class and the Dutch to Tinker's [John Finch's bar]." Soon a cacophony of drunken "vivas" and "hip hip hoorahs" and "Got verdams" echoed from the four corners of the Plaza. At sundown, the authorities informed the revelers that the town was under martial law and that they had to return home. "But few, however were able to do so, and the greater part of them either slept in Tinker's alley or on the grass in the Plaza, and only woke with the morning's first beams, to wonder what was the cause of yesterday's spree."

In the months after the flag was raised, fears that the Mexicans would launch a surprise attack and retake Yerba Buena led to one of the most hilarious incidents in the city's history. The commander of the troops from the *Portsmouth*, one Captain Watson, came ashore late every night to stand watch. Watson tended to get thirsty during the night, so he always had hotelkeeper Brown fill his flask with whiskey before he started his watch. Brown was usually in bed by then, however, so Watson had come up with a cunning plan to alert him. He would rap on Brown's window twice and say "The Spaniards are in the brush," whereupon Brown would fill Watson's flask and he would go happily off to stand guard. One night, however, Brown drank more than usual and slept through Watson's raps. The displeased Watson, who had been imbibing even more freely than Brown, fired one of his pistols and shouted at the top of his lungs, "THE SPANIARDS ARE IN THE BRUSH!" Hearing the shot and the cry of alarm, the troops at the barracks in the customs house on the Plaza beat the long roll and rushed out to defend themselves. Thinking the Spanish really were in the brush, they opened fire, but succeeded only in hitting some scrub oaks that were waving in the wind. The next day Watson warned Brown that if he ever breathed a word of what had happened, he would be a dead man.

For Yerba Buena, the war was low comedy. But its ludicrous elements cannot disguise the fact that the conquest of California, like the entire Mexican-American War, was a case of naked expansionism. The U.S. government offered some flimsy justifications, but they were fig leaves. A young officer named Ulysses S. Grant, who gained his first combat experience in the war, later wrote, "To this day [I] regard the war . . . as one of the most unjust ever waged by a stronger against a weaker nation."

And for one of the village's leading citizens, the war was not a comedy at all. During the short-lived hostilities, Fremont imprisoned three of the sons of an old Californio man named José Berreyessa in Sonoma. The worried Berreyessa, accompanied by his cousins, two 19-year-old twins, went to see how his sons were doing. As they stepped off a boat in the North Bay, they were accosted by three of Fremont's men, including the famous frontiersman Kit Carson. When Carson asked Fremont what he should do with them, Fremont reportedly replied, "I have got no room for prisoners." Kit Carson and the other Americans shot the three unarmed men.

In *California: A Study of American Character*, published in 1886 and still one of the finest books ever written about California, the philosopher Josiah Royce bitterly attacked Fremont's conduct during the Bear Flag Revolt. Royce noted that the American consul in Monterey, Thomas O. Larkin, was secretly working to acquire California peacefully and that Fremont's loose-cannon adventuring undermined his efforts. Royce was outraged that Fremont had squandered an opportunity to deal justly and fairly with the Californios. Instead, the Grass Valley native wrote, Fremont "brought war into a peaceful Department; his operations began an estrangement, insured a memory of blood-shed, excited a furious bitterness of feeling between the two peoples that were henceforth to dwell in California."

Royce overstated the effect of the Bear Flag Revolt on the relations between the Californios and the Yankees who were about to flood in. Regardless of Fremont's actions, America was going to swallow California. But that knowledge would have been no consolation to Don Francisco.

De Haro was the first alcalde of Yerba Buena. He was the man who commissioned Jean Vioget to survey the village and one of the leading citizens in the town's early history. One of the most dramatic streets in San Francisco, rocketing down from the summit of Potrero Hill toward downtown, is named after him. His great gray tombstone adorns the north side of the Mission Dolores graveyard.

The 19-year-old twins who were killed in cold blood by men under the command of John C. Fremont—who also has a San Francisco street named after him—were de Haro's sons. For the rest of his life, the old man never got over their murder.

CHAPTER 25

A STREETCAR TO SUBDUCTION

The rope swing halfway up Billy Goat Hill,
near 30th and Castro Streets

I first stumbled upon Billy Goat Hill sometime in the 1980s. It was a steep, grassy, undeveloped hillside, located on a spur of Diamond Heights where it descends into upper Noe Valley. Two tall eucalyptus trees stood on a little saddle halfway up the slope. With its winding dirt trails, golden grasses, and random rocky outcroppings, it reminded me of the Berkeley Hills where I grew up, except that it was in the middle of a big city. I wandered around it for 20 minutes, then left. It was just one of those unassuming miracles that pop up in San Francisco, another breach in the urban wall. There are lots of them. I didn't go back to Billy Goat Hill for more than 20 years.

This spring, thanks to a man named Clyde Wahrhaftig, I finally made it back there. I'm glad that Wahrhaftig will always be associated in my mind with Billy Goat Hill. For both the man and the place represent everything that is best about San Francisco.

When I started poking around under this city's hood, one of the first things I wanted to learn about was its geology. San Francisco has some of the most extraordinary terrain of any city in the world, and after 40 years of wandering across it, I was curious about what I was walking on. I was really driven by the same impulse that leads people to look at the night sky: I wanted to blow my mind. The ground we stand on was formed by forces as inconceivably vast as those that created the stars twinkling in the sky. If you think of it that way, geology is just stargazing while looking *down*.

The circuitous path that led me back to Billy Goat Hill started when I was browsing the San Francisco Public Library's catalog. I came upon a book titled *A Streetcar to Subduction, and Other Plate Tectonic Trips by Public Transport in San Francisco.* The title enchanted me. It perfectly captured the juxtaposition of artifice and nature, the quotidian and the inconceivably vast, that epitomizes San Francisco. It made me want to climb aboard the J Church streetcar, ask for a transfer, and ride it to the center of the earth.

Which is pretty much what Clyde Wahrhaftig—the author of the book—did.

A Streetcar to Subduction has become an underground classic (no pun intended) and is hard to find, so I checked it out of the library. The photo on the back of the magazine-size book showed a lean-faced, white-bearded, white-haired man with keen, twinkling eyes looking out at the camera, his hand on a rocky outcropping. The accompanying biographical note said that Clyde Wahrhaftig was a geologist for the U.S. Geological Service and a professor of geology at U.C. Berkeley. He did field research in Alaska for almost 30 years. A committed environmentalist, he was the first chairman of the Geological Society of America's committee on the environment and public policy and served on the California State Board of Forestry.

Wahrhaftig was obviously a maverick. In his waggish note, he wrote that early in his career he "realized the advantages to health, safety and sanity in not knowing how to drive, and managed to get around on foot and public transportation, or by sponging on my friends." He was also a bit risqué. Telling readers how to get to Corona Heights, he wrote, "You are now in the heart of San Francisco's gay community. Don't get subduced." This type of witticism is not typical of geologists.

I already liked this guy. But I didn't yet know his whole story.

In *A Streetcar to Subduction*, Wahrhaftig takes the reader on a guided tour, via public transportation and foot, to seven geological sites in San Francisco and the Bay Area. Trip 1 is to Billy Goat Hill, via the J Church. Wahrhaftig chose Billy Goat Hill to open his book because the three most important types of rock found in San Francisco are exposed there, "in a deceptively simple and orderly relationship."

Simple and orderly—that had my English-major, 560-on-the-math-SAT name written all over it. I decided to take Wahrhaftig's magical mystery tour.

One spring morning after dropping my daughter off at school, I headed over Twin Peaks and through Diamond Heights. I parked halfway down insanely steep 29th Street, about 100 feet below the 679-foot elevation of Gold Mine Hill. It was a warm, hazy May morning, and the foliage was as bright and electric as the Riviera—wild blue pride of Madera rising up like psychedelic spears, waving poppies, profuse mustard, and screaming orange hibiscus. An intricate network of hills and ridges rose up ahead of me, to the right, behind—every direction except east. It felt like the topography of this area was the most convoluted in the entire city. It was simultaneously open and exposed, with long vistas to the north and east, and closed, tucked away, as comfortably dug-in as a hobbit's hollow. Later, when I looked up at Billy Goat Hill from the bottom of the valley on Church Street, I realized the landscape wasn't really that intricate. If I were in the Sierra, I wouldn't give it a second thought. It was just a spur of a hill. It was the grid, the famous San Francisco grid that imposes straight streets on uneven and precipitous ground, that made the terrain feel crazy.

I wandered through the streets for a while, then walked up 30th Street to the foot of Billy Goat Hill. I walked up a dirt trail to the flat spot by the eucalyptus trees, next to a rope swing, and looked back at the city. My jaw dropped. This might be the most beautifully framed view of downtown, from the most sublime viewing platform, in all of San Francisco. The sharp downhill slope of the hill, its irregular face, and its golden-grassed wildness set off the distant vista like a gem. Downtown, four miles away, looked like the Bottle City of Kandor—a discrete, sci-fi-like mass. The Bay Bridge aimed almost straight at me. Behind everything towered the lofty East Bay hills.

I looked around at the three-and-a-half-acre piece of hillside that offered this stupendous panorama. It was glorious and wild and free. It was surrounded by a charming, elegant, shaggy neighborhood. It was three blocks down to civilization. And no one knew about it.

Billy Goat Hill was once part of the vast open countryside that was Diamond Heights. For years it adjoined a quarry run by the notorious Gray brothers, George and Harry, who flagrantly defied city hall and their neighbors by continuing to set off illegal explosions at their two quarries, some of which hurled houses off Telegraph Hill and showered boulders upon schoolchildren. The Grays also had a habit of not paying their employees, which led to George's untimely demise in 1914, when a disgruntled worker shot and killed him right near where I now was standing.

A longtime resident named Buck Tergis explained how the hill got its name and how it was saved from possible development. "In the 1930s, my grandmother, Esther Benezra, who lived on Beacon Street, began grazing goats on the hill," Tergis told me. "That's why they call it Billy Goat Hill. There were horses and corrals around here. My mother, Sara Tergis, used to walk her dog on the hill. She and another woman named Sandy, who had a fox that she walked there, led the fight to keep the hill from being developed." Sara Tergis, the fox lady, and other neighbors—including Clyde Wahrhaftig, who wrote a paper about the hill's geological significance—succeeded in having Billy Goat Hill designated as a protected open space, under a proposition that funded the city's acquisition of such spaces. The city bought the land for $129,600 in 1977. In 1997, the hill was made part of the Recreation and Park Department's Natural Areas Program, which is also responsible for Glen Canyon and 29 other sites.

That was the new history. But I wanted the old. It was time to climb into Wahrhaftig's Wayback Machine. I opened *A Streetcar to Subduction*. The three kinds of rock in Billy Goat Hill, Wahrhaftig wrote, are pillow basalt, radiolarian chert, and graywacke. The oldest, pillow basalt, was found along 30th Street at the bottom of the hill. An outcropping of radiolarian chert stuck out near the two eucalyptus trees. And at the top of the hill, near Beacon Street, was exposed graywacke.

I walked down to check out what I thought were the basalt rocks, but they didn't look like pillows to me, and I wasn't sure if I had the right rocks. I found the chert, but I wasn't sure about the graywacke, either. I needed help.

To get it, I called a woman named Doris Sloan, author of *Geology of the*

San Francisco Bay Region, a book so clearly written even I could follow it. I asked her if she would spend a day showing me some of her favorite geological sites in San Francisco. She graciously agreed. When I mentioned Billy Goat Hill, and said I had gone there after reading *A Streetcar to Subduction*, she said that she had been Wahrhaftig's student. "He was an amazing man. He's the reason I became a geologist," she said. Did she want to go to Billy Goat Hill? "Clyde lived near there," she said. "But I've never been there." We decided to put it on our list of places to visit.

I picked Sloan up at the Glen Park BART station. At 82, she was as sharp and vigorous as a woman half her age, and her passion for the natural world in general, and geology in particular, was undiminished by a bad knee. We started out in Glen Canyon, then drove through Diamond Heights to Billy Goat Hill.

As we drove, Sloan told me something about the three kinds of rocks we were going to look at. Pillow basalt, radiolarian chert, and graywacke are the holy trinity of San Francisco rocks, the big three in the world-famous geological formation found in and around San Francisco known as the Franciscan Complex. Geologists came from all over the world to look at the Franciscan Complex rocks, Sloan said. Each of these rocks was formed by a different type of tectonic activity, in a different location. Wahrhaftig had explained this too, but it hadn't come alive for me. Sloan was a born teacher, and I began haltingly to understand. As she spoke, I realized that the way these rocks were created, and came to be here, is a more psychedelic tale than the most feverish acid trip in the addled annals of San Francisco.

We walked down 30th Street. Sloan quickly found the pillow basalt. This rock was formed by lava that erupted from the ocean floor 100 to 200 million years ago. It's called pillow basalt because the lava formed into pillowlike shapes when it cooled in the ocean water. It had the longest journey to get here—from the center of the Pacific Ocean, thousands of miles away. It rafted in on a now-subducted tectonic plate called the Farallones Plate—the same way the Farallon Islands, the world's most patient hitchhikers, came up from Southern California.

We walked through European grasses and mustard and wild radish, up the dirt path to the shelf by the eucalyptus trees, and found the chert outcropping. This was the next oldest rock, the one that was deposited on top of the basalt.

Radiolarian chert, Sloan explained, is made of the skeletons of one-celled animals called radiolaria. These tiny animals died and drifted slowly down through the ocean in what Rachel Carson memorably called "the long snowfall," finally landing on top of the basalt. For tens of millions of years, the silica skeletons of the radiolarians piled up. Pressure formed them into rock. The oceanic plate carried the basalt and chert to the east, where their fateful meeting with the westward-moving North American Plate took place 145 million years ago.

The subduction of the Farallones Plate under the continental plate was not a wham-bam-thank-you-ma'am affair. It lasted a Tantric 100 million years. During this time, a trench formed at the edge of the subduction zone. This trench played a key role in the creation of the rock we were about to look at.

We walked up the trail toward Beacon Street at the top of Billy Goat Hill. Near the top we found an outcropping of the last rock on Wahrhaftig's tour, graywacke. This rock is found all over San Francisco, particularly in its northeastern hills—Nob, Russian, and Telegraph. The dirt in my backyard probably contains pulverized graywacke. Graywacke is made up of sediments that eroded off the North American Plate and were carried into the aforementioned trench by massive underwater landslides called "turbidity flows." When the tectonic plates collided, these rocks were either carried down with the heavy Pacific Plate into the hot mantle where they metamorphosed, or they were scraped off onto the North American Plate.

Since much of that rock was 200 million years old, did that mean we were looking at an ancient landscape?

"No," Sloan said. "That's one of the hardest concepts to get across. The rock is old, but the landscape is very young. In geology, you have to have these two completely different time scales in your head at the same time. The underlying rock is old, but it has been through inconceivable changes over time, and the most recent changes, the ones that made the terrain appear the way it is today, are very recent—only a few million years old."

San Francisco is composed of three Franciscan Complex terranes. A terrane is a packet of rocks formed by the same processes during subduction. These terranes run diagonally and in parallel from the southeast to the northwest, like diagonal stripes on a flag. The northeasternmost terrane, which was the first one scraped off onto the continent, is called the Alcatraz

Terrane. Dominated by graywacke, it runs from South of Market to the Marina Green and includes Telegraph, Nob, and Russian Hills. The second packet, the Marin Headlands Terrane, runs from Visitacion Valley to Lands End and includes the great central hills—Twin Peaks, Mount Davidson, Diamond Heights, and Mount Sutro. Its primary rock is radiolarian chert. The third one is the San Bruno Mountain Terrane, which runs from San Bruno Mountain to Lands End and is made up of graywacke and shale.

In between these three terranes are two so-called mélange zones, mostly low-lying areas where rock that was crushed and mixed up during subduction (such rock is known as mélange) was eroded away by streams. The first, the Fort Point–Hunters Point mélange, is a narrow ribbon that runs between the Alcatraz Terrane and the Marin Headlands Terrane. It includes several large, hard blocks that were resistant to erosion: Hunters Point, Potrero Hill, Mint Hill, and Fort Point. The primary rock found here in this zone is California's state rock, serpentine, a metamorphic rock (as the name suggests, metamorphic rocks are transformed by great heat or pressure, usually far below the earth's crust). The second mélange zone, the City College mélange, runs from City College to Lands End and includes basalt, serpentine, and graywacke.

This might all seem as dry as, well, dust. But it ties the entire city together—and in a unique way. There is something strange and delightful about the fact that these diagonal zones, tangible evidence of the titanic forces that assembled San Francisco, join together completely disparate parts of the city. Someone living in the projects at Hunters Point shares the same terrane with the richest plutocrat in his Presidio Heights mansion. The wretched motels near the gaunt Cow Palace sit on the same kind of rock as the stunning sea cliffs at Lands End. The diagonal terranes are San Francisco's original Rainbow Flag.

"I'm delighted to have finally seen this place!" Sloan exclaimed as we looked out over the city. It had rained the night before, and in the clean air the view was as clearly etched as a Canaletto. "Clyde lived right over there on Valley Street, but we never came over here."

We descended three blocks to Church Street and civilization. Over sandwiches, Sloan told me how Wahrhaftig was responsible for her becoming a geologist—and his own extraordinary life odyssey.

"In 1970, at age 40, while I was working as a lobbyist for the Quakers in

San Francisco, I took a weeklong U.C. Extension geology course in the Sierra's Emigrant Wilderness," Sloan said. "I took the class because I wanted to see more of the sky than I could in my basement office. Clyde was teaching it. He was a great environmentalist, and he had decided to teach the class because he wanted the feds to protect a six-mile stretch of road leading into the wilderness. He figured he'd get a dozen people to write letters."

Sloan loved the week in the mountains so much she took the class again the next year. She discovered that she had a gift for explaining things and became Wahrhaftig's de facto assistant. By the end of the class, she had decided she wanted to study geology at Berkeley—at a time when there were no women geologists at the school.

Like most of his peers, Wahrhaftig was opposed to women geologists. "He'd say, 'I want to be able to pee where I want and say what I want,'" Sloan said. "This was the typical attitude of geologists at that time. The field was all male and very macho." But after Sloan told him she only wanted to get a master's degree so she could work in the public information office in the Ferry Building, he wrote Sloan a letter of recommendation and she got in. Although Wahrhaftig's sexual orientation was pretty obvious to Sloan, the chair of the department called her in and asked her, "Doris, are you really interested in geology, or are you interested in Clyde?" He simply couldn't imagine that Wahrhaftig was gay.

A critical part of a geologist's training, a rite of passage akin to a doctor's residency, was and is the "summer field class," an often arduous session during which the future scientists learn how to map, collect data, interpret geological structures—the nitty-gritty of the profession. "We went to the White Mountains. We had to hike down to Deep Springs every day and map it and then hike out. It was 100 degrees," Sloan said. "There were 22 guys and six women, four of us from Berkeley. All six of us women were incredibly feisty. One, Gail Mahood, later became a dean at Stanford.

"All summer we women worked incredibly hard and never complained. The women, some of whom were older, handled it much better than the men, who reverted to teenage behavior, whining and complaining. The tradition was that the two best students were offered a job at the USGS [the U.S. Geological Survey office in Menlo Park]. Well, the person who did the best mapping was a 35-year-old woman with a 9-year-old son. The person who did the best verbal description was me.

"It was an absolute milestone for Clyde. It opened his eyes. It was years before he came out, but he came back from that trip, and he started a program at the USGS to encourage and recruit women and minority geologists. Until then, he was all in favor of keeping the field exclusively male. It was the first such program at the USGS."

Sloan had never intended to make geology her career. But encouraged by Wahrhaftig, she went on to get her Ph.D. and get a job at Berkeley. "I've had an absolutely fabulous 20 years of teaching. An absolutely lovely time," she said. "And Clyde was completely responsible."

Sloan went on to talk about the final metamorphosis in Clyde Wahrhaftig's life. It was spurred by a terrible tragedy, one that devastated both the geology community and Stanford University. "The most important person in Clyde's life was a man named Allan Cox. They met in Alaska and Clyde convinced Allan to enter the field—Clyde was a few years older than Allan. They became lovers, and after that ended, they remained friends. Allan was a really brilliant, important geologist and a great teacher. But he had an eye for young boys, which Clyde never did. Clyde used to talk to him about it—this was long after they were lovers—and warn him that he would come to grief. I didn't know Allan that well myself; he was very aloof. But one day everyone was shocked and horrified to learn that Allan had died. He was mountain biking without a helmet and flew off the road and hit a redwood tree.

"It was a suicide. Allan had learned that the police were investigating a sexual relationship he had with a teenage boy, which allegedly began when the boy was 14 years old. Allan would have been disgraced, ruined. So he killed himself. The news was devastating for Clyde and for Allan's students. More than 1,000 people came to the memorial at Stanford Chapel."

Wahrhaftig was still in the closet. "Clyde was still a very private person," Sloan said. "Like many gay people of that day, he never really talked about his personal life." But two years after Cox's death, when the 70-year-old Wahrhaftig learned he was going to be given the Distinguished Career Award by the Geological Society of America, he decided to use the occasion to break through the last barrier. "I think it was a desire to make a difference," Sloan said. "To change the profession. And to reflect on what had happened to Allan."

In his speech, Wahrhaftig said, "Receiving this award for longevity has made me realize that my time to do good is running out. So I have decided to use the opportunity you have given me, by gracing my career with the adjective 'distinguished,' to do a little good with the accolade."

Wahrhaftig said that he had strived to nurture role models for black and Chicano geologists. Then he said, "I am now going to provide a role model for a minority that has been demanding a modicum of the civil rights the rest of the country possess—a minority that has managed to survive largely because it is invisible. It is a minority to which Allan Cox and I both belong. We are both homosexuals, and the force that caused us to do so much for each other, and because of each other, was homosexual love. The many of you who are familiar with the circumstances of Allan's suicide would have gathered from those circumstances and our close association that this was the case."

"I would not wish on anyone the life of repression, self-doubt, and dissimulation that Allan and I had to go through," Wahrhaftig went on. "No, the group whose attitudes I wish to affect are those of you who are not homosexual, but who may find yourself with students, subordinates, or colleagues who are. I ask you to recognize that homosexuals can make as much of a contribution to science and humanity as anyone else."

At the end of his speech, Wahrhaftig said that he hoped to encourage gay students who would like to be geoscientists but were afraid that being gay and being a geologist were incompatible. "I want my life, and Allan's and my relationship, to tell them that this is not so," he said. "If they are lucky, as we were, their love and their careers will sustain each other. And I hope that, by making this revelation here, I contribute in some small way to the creation of a society with a sufficiently intelligent, open, and compassionate attitude toward sexuality that suicides such as Allan Cox's will be a thing of the past."

Wahrhaftig's speech received a tremendous ovation.

Clyde Wahrhaftig was a Renaissance man. He was a first-rate pianist, a gifted artist, a lover of Proust and Bach, an activist, an environmentalist, and a great field geologist. He worked until the end of his life. Four years after he gave his speech, he died peacefully in his sleep in San Francisco.

There are exposed rocks all across San Francisco. Billy Goat Hill. Filbert and Kearny. Fort Mason. Jackson and Jones. McClaren Park. Tank Hill. Hudson and Mendell. Sacramento and Powell. Delta Street. O'Shaughnessy and Malta. Kite Hill. Armstrong and Ingalls. Fort Point. Shields and Head. Illinois Street. Corona Heights.

I will never know very much about those exposures. But they will never again be just rocks to me. They will be fragments of stars. And as I walk among them, I will think about the man who loved them, and who was made of similar stuff.

CHAPTER 26

THE DELIRIUM

The pedestrian bridge over Portsmouth Square,
southwest of Washington and Kearny Streets

No city in the world has ever come into existence the way San Francisco did. It was a creation ex nihilo, the urban equivalent of the big bang. During those years when the world rushed in and created an instant city, utter delirium prevailed. It almost seems preordained that San Francisco was to become the city of the Beats and the hippies, the counter-cultural capital of drug experimentation, for a radical alteration of consciousness was hard-wired into it from its beginning. The Sioux called gold "the yellow metal that drives white men crazy," and San Francisco during the Gold Rush years was, without doubt, one of the craziest cities in the history of the world. It was a wild Saturnalia, a carnival of self-invention, in which all the rules that governed self and society were suspended. As Kevin Starr put it, "for a few brief years, in far-off California, the bottom fell out of the 19th century." San Francisco was the center of that free fall. And no one who saw it could believe what they were seeing.

New York Tribune correspondent Bayard Taylor wrote, "Every new-comer to San Francisco is overtaken by a sense of complete bewilderment . . . One knows not whether he is awake or in some wonderful dream. Never have I had so much difficulty in establishing, satisfactorily to my own sense, the reality of what I saw and heard."

The three authors of *The Annals of San Francisco*, the 1855 tome that remains the best book about the Gold Rush city, were so overwhelmed when they tried to sum up their impressions of San Francisco in 1849 that they almost fell into stream of consciousness prose:

> And everybody made money, and was suddenly growing rich. The loud voices of the eager seller and as eager buyer—the laugh of reckless joy—the bold accents of successful speculation—the stir and hum of active hurried labor, as man and brute, horse and bullock, and their guides, struggled and managed through heaps of loose rubbish, over hills of sand, and among deceiving deep mud pools and swamps, filled the amazed newly arrived immigrant with an almost appalling sense of the exuberant life, energy and enterprise of the place. He breathed quick and faintly—his limbs grew weak as water—and his heart sunk within him as he thought of the dreadful conflict, when he approached and mingled among that confused and terrible business battle . . . The very thought of that wondrous time is an electric spark that fires into one great flame all our fancies, passions and experiences of the fall of the eventful year, 1849. The remembrance of those days comes across us like the delirium of fever.

Gold was discovered on January 24, 1848, on the American River near the town of Coloma in the central foothills of the Sierra Nevada. The discovery was hushed up, and the 800-odd citizens of San Francisco—which a year earlier, for commercial reasons, officially changed its appellation from Yerba Buena to the better-known name of the bay, mission, and presidio—did not get the news until March 15, when one of the town's two fledgling newspapers, the *Californian*, buried a small item about it, below a story about a private horse race. The other newspaper, the *California Star*, ran a similarly perfunctory item 10 days later. Such claims had proven to be false before, and the reports were greeted with skepticism. A letter in the

Californian opined, "I doubt, sir, if ever the sun shone upon such a farce as is now being enacted in California, though I fear it may prove a tragedy before the curtain drops." The barely 19-year-old editor of the *California Star*, Edward Kemble, visited Coloma to see for himself and pronounced the whole thing "a sham, as superb a take-in as ever was got up to guzzle the gullible."

But rumors kept trickling out about workers at Sutter's Fort paying for their purchases with gold, and they reached the ear of one of San Francisco's most prominent—and loudest—citizens, a shrewdly self-promoting businessman named Sam Brannan. Brannan was a Mormon who in July 1846 had arrived in Yerba Buena aboard the ship *Brooklyn* with 238 of his co-religionists, more than doubling the town's population. When they paid him in gold dust, he knew that the stories were true—and that he could make a killing.

When Brannan returned by steamboat to San Francisco on May 12, 1848, he pulled off one of the great publicity coups of all time. Holding aloft a quinine bottle full of gold dust in one hand and waving his hat in the other, Brannan marched down Montgomery Street at the water's edge and then up a block to Portsmouth Square, yelling at the top of his lungs, "Gold! Gold! Gold from the American River!"

What historian Richard Dillon called "the shout heard 'round the world" gave birth to the city of San Francisco, caused the largest mass migration in U.S. history, and changed our national character in ways historians are still arguing about. It was an earthquake too big to measure on any Richter scale.

The town emptied. Within three days, the male population of San Francisco went from 600 to 200. Everyone headed east across the bay, feverishly trying to get upriver to the gold fields. On May 29, the *Californian* ceased publication, its editor lamenting, "The whole country, from San Francisco to Los Angeles, and from the seashore to the base of Sierra Nevada, resounds with the sordid cry of gold! Gold!! GOLD!!! While the field is left unplanted, the house unbuilded, and everything neglected but the manufacturers of shovels and picks." The *California Star*'s Kemble gloated over the demise of his rival: "Gone to——. The *Californian* ceased issue with the annunciatory slip of Tuesday last. Verdict of inquest—fever." But the boy editor's last laugh was short-lived. On June 14, Kemble announced the demise of his own paper in one of the all-time great journalistic swan songs: "In fewer words than are usually employed in the announcement of similar events, we appear before the remnant of a reading community with the material or immaterial information that we have stopped the paper—that its publication ceased with the last regular issue. We have done. Let our word of parting be, *Hasta luego.*"

San Francisco was an empty shell. The city council no longer met, because its members had headed for the hills. Students in the school that had just opened joined them. Their teacher followed. Ships arrived in the bay, but their crews immediately deserted. Goods piled up on the wharves. Real estate values plummeted as owners sold out to raise money to go prospecting. By mid-July, according to one report, there were only seven able-bodied men in San Francisco.

Slowly but surely, the word spread. By June, gold seekers began arriving from Monterey and San Jose. Mexicans appeared in the fields by the summer. By autumn, most of the San Franciscans who had headed for the hills had returned, most of them either empty-handed or realizing that there was more gold to be made at home than in the diggings. But throngs of new Argonauts took their place: By October there were 8,000 men mining in the hills. By the end of 1848, the city's population had risen to 2,000. And after President Polk's December 1848 State of the Union Address, when he confirmed that vast quantities of gold had been discovered in California, the floodgates opened. It was, someone said, as though the continent had suddenly tilted and everyone had slid to the west.

They came from across the country and around the world, in that annus mirabilis of 1849. They were clergymen from New England and farmhands from Germany, frontiersmen from Missouri and peasants from China, clerks from New York City and students from Chile, black sailors from Boston whalers and fishermen from Hawaii. Some were wealthy and highly educated. Others were impoverished and illiterate. Pouring into California that year were 80,000 men, more than half of them in their 20s. What they all shared was a desire to strike it rich, and a willingness to throw over their old life to do it. All of them were about to embark on the greatest adventure of their lives. It was called "seeing the elephant." And San Francisco was the door through which they had to pass to see it.

It was a very strange door.

Just getting to San Francisco was an epic venture in itself. California was still a dangerous, little-known frontier: The first organized emigrant party, the Bartleson-Bidwell party, had crossed the Sierra just eight years earlier. There were only three ways to get to the West Coast. There was the sea route, starting in New York or Boston, rounding Cape Horn and beating up the coast of South America—an 18,000-mile trip that usually took five claustrophobic months. There was the sea-and-land route via Panama, which was much shorter but required a hellish trip through disease-ridden jungle. And there was the overland route, jumping off from Independence or St. Joseph, Missouri. This meant dealing with vast deserts, hostile Indians, and unknown mountains. (A few people, eager to avoid all these routes, paid a $50 deposit to fly on an "aerial locomotive"—the brainchild of the founder and first editor of *Scientific American*, no less—that would carry up to 100 passengers "pleasantly and safely" from New York to California in three days. Probably fortunately, what would have been the world's first dirigible was destroyed by a rowdy crowd.) Each of these routes had their advantages and disadvantages, but all were long, expensive, and arduous. Many 49ers died en route, their bodies tossed into the ocean or buried by the trail.

So when these thousands of young men first sailed through the magnificent entrance to the bay and set eyes on San Francisco, they never forgot it. And even had they not made a perilous journey halfway around the world, it was not a place anyone was likely to forget.

The first thing the 49ers saw when they sailed around Clark's Point at the base of Telegraph Hill was a forest of ships' masts. Hundreds of ships were crowded next to each other off the cove, forming "a perfect town upon the water." Most of these ships had been abandoned by their gold-crazed crews the instant they dropped anchor: Between 3,000 and 4,000 sailors had deserted by the end of 1849. One observer wrote that "these ships had a very old, ruinous, antiquated appearance, and at first sight, gave me an impression, that this new-born city had been inhabited for ages, and was now going to ruin."

These ships met varying fates. Some were reclaimed for their timber. (The beautiful yellow house at 825 Francisco Street, just east of the Norwegian Seamen's Church on one of the city's great blocks, was built out of wood salvaged from abandoned ships.) But most were simply left to rot, and their hulks were covered when the city expanded east into the cove. There are at least 47 ships buried beneath San Francisco's streets, ghostly reminders of the city's maritime beginnings.

Once ashore, the Argonauts found themselves in a place unlike any other on earth, a combination campground, casino, construction zone, battlefield, strip club, depot, garbage dump, stock exchange, and amusement park. The sheer spectacle was astonishing. Men in strange costumes speaking a babble of tongues hurried about everywhere, like ants in an anthill kicked by a giant boot. Most were heavily armed, having been warned (incorrectly, at least at first) that villains and desperados lurked on every corner. A doctor wrote, "Pistols were fired at rapid succession in every direction. Horses with their drunken riders were dashing through the town, the gay *serapa* and other gaudy trappings flying in the wind."

Thousands of tents were pitched anywhere and everywhere—on the flats, up the hills, on sand dunes. There were some wood-framed houses, and more were being built every day, but many structures were built out of any material that came to hand. A young German, Frederick Gerstacker, wrote, "Houses, if I may give them that name, were raised on the lightest possible frames, even basket-work, covered or stretched over with the lightest possible calico." At night, this vast, colorful "Canvas City" turned into a fairyland, as lanterns illuminated the tents from within and thousands of fires lit up the crescent-shaped cove and the surrounding hills.

San Francisco may have looked like a magic kingdom at night, but it was still the same barren, sandy, wind-swept place it was when William Richardson had erected his sail-shelter a few hundred yards above the beach 14 years earlier. One observer who climbed Nob Hill claimed he could not see a single tree as far as he could see. The westerly wind blew sand and dust into everything.

But far worse than the dust was the "mud plague" of 1849–50. The winter of 1849 may have been the wettest in the city's history, with as much as 50 inches of rain falling. There were no paved or planked streets and few sidewalks. Everything turned to mud up to four feet deep. William Smith Jewett, who was to become California's first resident professional artist, landed with a mining company—many 49ers traveled in organized companies, most of which dissolved soon after arrival—in December 1849. Carried by boat to the Broadway wharf, he and his companions beheld the lights of the city and started up Broadway, only to get so hopelessly stuck in the mud that they had to return to the ship to spend the night. One wag put up a sign saying "This street is impassable. Not even jackassable." Hauling goods was virtually impossible: An entire mule team, including the wagon, simply disappeared into the quicksand, never to be seen again.

The obvious solution was to plank the streets. But wood cost $400 to $500 per thousand feet and was all being used to build houses, so the instant city's inhabitants seized anything that came to hand. They tossed limbs of trees and brushwood into the muddiest places. When those were swallowed up, they threw in boxes, stoves, garbage, cases of tobacco, iron, sheet lead, salt beef, bags of rice and beans, even three barrels of revolvers. Montgomery Street merchants made stepping-stones out of boxes and barrels, forcing pedestrians to walk single file. Other paths were made out of empty bottles, which were so plentiful "a large city might have been built with them."

Weirdest of all, the ground of this strange town was covered with hundreds of *shirts*. "There were at that time, I really believe, not 10 square feet in the city, where a dirty, but in every other respect perfectly new shirt was not lying," Gerstacker observed. Laundry was so expensive—it cost $6 to $9 to wash a dozen shirts—that many 49ers simply threw their dirty shirts away and bought new ones. It was cheaper to send the laundry to Hawaii, or possibly even China, than to have it washed in San Francisco.

Laundry was not the only thing that was ruinously expensive in the city. Everything cost 10 to 20 times higher than elsewhere. When Bayard Taylor and a companion landed, they hired two Mexicans to carry their luggage several blocks, for which the porters charged $2 each—the equivalent of $50 each today. Taylor drily observed that this was "a sum so immense in comparison to the service rendered that there was no longer any doubt of our having actually landed in California." Lodging, for those lucky enough to find it, was astronomically expensive. Most 49ers stayed in squalid lodging houses, where as many as 80 men would huddle on the floor, with a few lucky ones occupying some filthy bunks. No mattresses or blankets were provided. Many men simply slept on the bare ground, or on crates.

Rents and real estate prices were exorbitant. A shack with a primitive fireplace rented for $800 a month, a store for $3,000. A building on Portsmouth Square that before the Gold Rush had rented for $10 to $20 a month now rented for $75,000 a year. A lot on Portsmouth Square that sold for $16.50 in 1847 sold for $6,000 in late-spring 1848. Before the end of the year, it sold for $45,000.

Food was also expensive: In the summer of 1849, a dozen eggs cost $12 and a loaf of bread worth 5 cents cost 50 cents. Most of the city's inhabitants were bachelors who were remarkably (but typically for their time) innocent of even the most rudimentary knowledge of cooking, cleaning, or anything domestic. As a result—and because few lodgings had cooking facilities—almost everyone ate in restaurants. (It is said that this is the origin of San Francisco's tradition as a great restaurant town.) There were culinary establishments for every taste and budget, from the high-end Delmonico's, where a meal could cost $10, to filthy dives where $1 would buy a meal of boiled beef, bread, and coffee. Many men ate standing up at street stands. Others frequented the "Celestial" (Chinese) restaurants that had already begun to open.

The prototypical Gold Rush restaurant was the "eating house," the culinary equivalent of the lodging houses. Dining in one of these joints was not for the faint of heart or slow of jaw. As a 49er described it, the ringing of various bells and gongs would set off a stampede of men toward two long rows of tables on which were placed "dishes of the most incongruous character . . . Boiled and roast meats, fresh and salt, potted meats, curries, stews, fish, rice, cheese, frijolis, and molasses, are served up on small dishes, and ranged indiscriminately on the table; there is a total absence of green vegetables." The men immediately began wolfing down whatever "fixing" was in front of them, ignoring requests to pass the dishes, and frequently using only a knife to "convey to the mouth both liquids and solids." In 10 minutes or less all the food was gone. The sated men picked their teeth with forks while waiters wiped off greasy spoons in preparation for the next seating.

The center of town was the old Plaza. Today Portsmouth Square, as it is now called, sits on the former boundary between the sterile Financial District and Chinatown, which is the opposite of sterile. That boundary no longer exists, because the square has become Chinatown's outdoor living room. On any given day, it is filled with hundreds of old Chinese, smoking cigarettes and animatedly kibitzing about mah-jongg games. It seems somehow fitting that the two elements that made up the Gold Rush, money and immigrants, still define the square.

There is really no place in San Francisco that conjures up the madness of the Gold Rush city, but the weird pedestrian overpass that spans Kearny Street and connects the square with the ugly Hilton Hotel at least is a good place to see where it all started. The bridge is a monstrosity and a profanation, but its strange location above the street jars one's customary perspective enough to allow the past to appear for a moment, like the Bay Bridge emerging from heavy fog.

Here is how the authors of the *Annals* describe the Plaza:

Take the plaza, on a fine day, for a picture of the people. All races were represented. There were hordes of long pig-tailed, blear-eyed, rank-smelling Chinese, with their yellow faces and blue garbs; single dandy black fellows, of nearly as bad an odor, who strutted as only the negro can strut, in holiday clothes and clean white shirt; a few diminutive fiery-eyed Malays, from the western archipelago, and some handsome Kanakas from the Sandwich Islands; jet-black, straight-featured Abyssinians; hideously tattooed New Zealanders; Feejee sailors and even the secluded Japanese, short, thick, clumsy, ever-bowing, jacketed fellows; the people of the many races of Hindoo land; Russians with furs and sables; a stray, turbaned, stately Turk or two, and occasionally a half-naked shivering Indian; multitudes of the Spanish race from every country of the Americas, partly pure, partly crossed with red blood,—Chileans, Peruvians and Mexicans, all with different shades of the same swarthy complexion . . . proud of their beards and moustaches, their grease, dirt and eternal gaudy serapes or darker cloaks; Spaniards from the mother country, more dignified, polite and pompous than even their old colonial brethren; "greasers," too, like them; great numbers of tall, goat-chinned, smooth-cheeked, oily-locked, lank-visaged, tobacco-chewing, large-limbed and featured, rough, care-worn, careless Americans from every State of the Union . . . bands of gay, easy-principled, philosophical Germans, Italians and Frenchmen of every cut and figure, their faces covered with hair, and with strange habiliments on their persons, and among whom might be particularly remarked numbers of thick-lipped, hook-nosed, ox-eyed, cunning, oily Jews.

This passage not only gives a sense of the dizzying variety of races, nationalities, and ethnic groups that filled the streets of San Francisco in

1849, it also reveals the unpleasant prejudices of its Anglo-Saxon authors—
who were, it should be noted, educated and upstanding citizens. Most of
their fellow Americans shared at least some of their benighted views, particularly toward "greasers"—an attitude that would make it easy for them
to justify stealing the land of the Californios whose former country they
had barged into.

This crazy cast—the Chilean Rosales described them as resembling a
throng of revelers "celebrating a vast and noisy masquerade ball"—rushed
about through the city's streets pursuing various activities, almost all of
them having to do with the making of money. Class distinctions meant
nothing. Bayard Taylor noted, "Lawyers, physicians and ex-professors dug
cellars, drove ox-teams, sawed wood, and carried luggage; while men who
had been Army privates, sailors, cooks, or day laborers were at the head of
profitable establishments and not infrequently assisted in some of the minor details of government." Another observer wrote, "A graduate of Yale
considers it no disgrace to sell peanuts on the Plaza."

But San Francisco's principal occupation, "the life and soul of the place,"
was gambling. The metastasizing city by the cove made Las Vegas look like
a convent. Its streets and alleys were packed with dozens if not hundreds of
shanties and tents used as gambling houses, most with saloons. Gambling
went on 24 hours a day, seven days a week. The El Dorado started out as
nothing but a 15-by-25 foot canvas tent, but its owners raked in so much
money that they quickly erected a building. Like the other top houses, it
boasted glittering chandeliers, live music, and beautiful women, whose
fleshy charms were amply displayed. On their walls hung what one discern-
ing viewer described as "French paintings of great merit, but of which female nudity alone forms the subject." (For decades, this leering artistic
tradition lived on in the 1930s-era bar called the Gold Dust Lounge on
Powell off Union Square. Sadly, despite a spirited defense by the bar's patrons and other connoisseurs of the city's rapidly vanishing stock of semi-
sleazy old joints, the Gold Dust was recently closed down—though it was
relocated to Fisherman's Wharf. The landlords' spokesman said, "Just because they claim that Janis Joplin once vomited there doesn't make it
historic"—a statement that, if true, would invalidate the entire premise of
this book.) The bright lights, strong drinks, erotic allure, and convivial
atmosphere of the gambling dens contrasted sharply with the miserable hov-

els where most 49ers lived. For the innocent young churchgoing Americans who had flooded into San Francisco, many of whom had never been away from home before, these "hells" were sinful, shocking—and irresistible.

Miners who had returned from the diggings were inexorably drawn into the gambling houses, where they frequently lost in a night what it had taken them months of backbreaking labor to gain. They joined fresh-faced boys of good families, and whores, and ruffians, and everybody in between. To escape San Francisco without at least taking a flyer in a gambling hell was to have missed an essential part of the elephant.

Gambling went hand in hand with another favorite San Francisco pastime, drinking. Undeterred by the fact that whiskey cost $30 a quart, the new San Franciscans imbibed the way they did most things: as if there was no tomorrow. In one of the wittier books about the Gold Rush, *Mountains and Molehills*, the English adventurer Frank Marryat wrote, with a noticeable lack of moral disapproval, "Drinking is carried on to an incredible extent here; not that there is much drunkenness, but a vast quantity of liquor is daily consumed. From the time the habitual drinker in San Francisco takes his morning gin-cocktail to stimulate an appetite for breakfast, he supplies himself throughout the day with an indefinite number of racy little spiritous compounds that have the effect of keeping him always more or less primed."

A city full of hot-blooded male adventurers in the flower of youth, far from the censorious eyes of authority figures, who had been supplying themselves throughout the day with an "indefinite number of racy little spiritous compounds"—surely one of the most mouth-watering descriptions of a taste ever penned—was a city sorely in need of women. But women of any kind, particularly "respectable" ones, were rare at first. In the first half of 1849, only 200 of the 10,000 immigrants who arrived in California were women. But the red-light districts of the world did their best to fill the need.

The first prostitutes to arrive in Gold Rush San Francisco, in 1848, were almost all from Mexico and Central and South America. They set up shop in a tent city on the southern slope of Telegraph Hill called Chiletown. Their American sisters began to arrive in numbers in the summer of 1849, when the first Cape Horn ships made harbor. Until then, there had been so few women in the city that a reported sighting of one would empty a saloon. Not surprisingly, they could make a staggering $200 a night. In *Mud, Blood, and Gold: San Francisco in 1849*, historian Rand Richards estimates that the total population of San Francisco at the end of 1849 was 20,000 to 25,000, of which only 1,100 to 1,200 were women—700 of them prostitutes. "Women were so scarce that men would take off their hats to the lewd women of the town," an observer wrote, although Spanish-speaking women were not afforded the same respect. ("The lewdness of fallen white women is shocking enough to witness, but it is far exceeded by the disgusting practices of these tawny visaged creatures" was a typical comment.)

This tolerant, even welcoming, attitude toward "the fair but frail," as prostitutes were euphemistically called, is displayed in an item that ran in May 1850 in the *Alta California*, the daily newspaper (California's first) that was born from the merger of the *California Star* and the *Californian*. Beneath arguably the best headline ever penned by a San Francisco editor, "Enlargement of Society," the story said, "We are pleased to notice by the arrival from sea Saturday, the appearance of some 50 or 60 of the fairer sex in full bloom." But only four months later the editors apparently decided that the enlargement of society had persisted for an unhealthily long time, for they dumped a bucket of rhetorical ice water over themselves and their readers. "We must confess our regret at the perfect freedom and unseemly manner in which the abandoned females . . . are permitted to display themselves in our public saloons and streets."

Prostitution helped inaugurate the proud San Francisco tradition of cosmopolitanism. By the end of 1852, it was said that there was not a single country in the world that was not represented in San Francisco by at least one prostitute—a fitting start for the city in which the United Nations charter was signed.

The few "honest women" in San Francisco were treated as virtual goddesses. Men would swarm around them, tip their hats to them, vie with one another to carry them in their arms above the mud. Any man rash enough to do anything indecent would have been instantly killed. One woman whose husband died got three marriage proposals in a week. Children were even rarer and more treasured. Grizzled miners would stop what they were doing, tears in their eyes, just to look at a child or tousle its hair. (One of

San Francisco's first literary stars, Bret Harte, wrote about such miners in his most famous story, "The Luck of Roaring Camp.")

For the vast majority of 49ers were not loners, nor—despite their temporary predilection for booze and gambling—hardened reprobates. They were ordinary young men. Some had fled stifling lives or trouble of one sort or another, but most just came to get rich, or at least to make more money than they could at home, and have an adventure while doing it. Very few of them planned to stay in California. They had left mothers and fathers, sons and daughters, brothers and sisters, friends and colleagues behind. They intended to return to them as soon as they had made their pile. And now that they found themselves at the other end of the continent, many of them were desperately lonely. Their poignant letters home are filled with worried questions about their loved ones, confessions of how homesick they are— and plaintive appeals to write.

Mail was the lifeline, the only connection the men in San Francisco had with the people they had left behind. As J. S. Holliday notes in his classic study *The World Rushed In: The California Gold Rush Experience*, the exchange of letters between them "began a dynamic process by which the entire nation was emotionally involved in the rush to California." In October 1849, the San Francisco post office was buried in 45,000 letters. In one month in the peak year of 1852, 45,000 letters came into San Francisco on ships and 40,000 went out. So desperate were San Franciscans for mail that they would stand in line all night at the post office when the Pacific Mail steamer was due.

It was inevitable that such a place would produce violently different reactions—sometimes in the same person. The 49er Isaac Baker wrote, "San Francisco. 'A beautiful country, romantic scenery, excellent harbor, a fine climate and plenty of game. This is the place for *me* in the winter season,' thinks I as I came on deck and looked around on the morning after we anchored. 'It's the most degraded, immoral, uncivilized and dirty place that can be imagined, and the sooner we are away from *here* the better for us,' were my thoughts five minutes after being landed on shore!"

Not a few visitors shared Baker's second opinion. In an almost absurdly bitter diatribe bearing the thumb-on-the-scales title *The Land of Gold: Reality vs. Fiction*, Hinton Rowan Helper wrote of California, "We know of no country in which there is so much corruption, villainy, outlawry, intemperance, licentiousness, and every variety of crime, folly and meanness. Words fail us to express the shameful depravity and unexampled turpitude of California society." His opinion of San Francisco was equally glowing: "Degradation, profligacy and vice confront us at every step . . . Nature wears a repulsive and haggard expression." With ponderous sarcasm, Helper concluded, "I may not be a competent judge, but this much I will say, that I have seen purer liquors, better segars, finer tobacco, truer guns and pistols, larger dirks and bowie knives, and prettier courtesans, here in San Francisco, than in any other place I have ever visited; and it is my unbiased opinion that California can and does furnish the best bad things that are attainable in America."

Little did the unhelpful Helper know that the lines he intended as a mortal insult to San Francisco would be so proudly embraced by its citizens that they would practically end up inscribed on City Hall.

CHAPTER 27

THE BALCONY

Larsen Peak, Golden Gate Heights, 14th and 15th Avenues

don't remember the first time I saw Larsen Peak. It was probably while driving down Lincoln Way with my dad when I was a kid. I vaguely remember thinking, "That's a weird hill." When I moved to San Francisco and began exploring the city, I noticed it again while wandering around in Golden Gate Park. It looked just as weird. But I never felt moved to go up there. It was a strange, steep peak rising up for no good reason out of the Sunset District, that vast flat stucco twilight zone that runs down to the end of the continent. Its rounded top had a Dr. Seuss–like clump of trees, and it was half covered with a bunch of ticky-tacky Daly City–style houses.

In those youthful days, I went for straight beauty. I had not yet learned to appreciate the charms of the banal. That led me to ignore not only Larsen Peak but also the entire western part of the city, with the exception of the beach and Golden Gate Park. It was only when I started doing the Knowledge that I began to truly explore the city's west side.

San Francisco is really two cities, East San Francisco and West San

Francisco. Its biggest hills—Mount Sutro, Twin Peaks, Mount Davidson, Diamond Heights—form the dividing line. The western part of the city is foggy, windy, mostly flat, and covered with acre after acre of modest middle-class houses. It belongs to the ocean. And it is an acquired taste.

If San Francisco were a beach town like Los Angeles or Honolulu—sun-stunned, hot, hedonistic, its beachfront architecture exuding a decaying Coney Island charm—its west side would be more immediately seductive. But San Francisco is not a beach town. Its west side is the coldest, foggiest, and windiest part of the city. Nor does the Sunset feel like a beach neighborhood. With the exception of a few zany, ramshackle houses on the Great Highway, its architecture is sober, solid, and uninspired. There are some art deco gems here and there, but mostly it's cookie-cutter stucco boxes. And a lot of it is just plain ugly. Nineteenth Avenue, the Sunset's main arterial, is as unlovely as they come.

And yet, the Sunset runs down to the Pacific. It is where America ends. You can see the ocean when you step out your door. The fog that sweeps over the avenues is wetter and closer to the source. The long, straight east-west streets aim at the horizon. The entire neighborhood is an infinity pool.

So it's a very odd place, the Sunset, simultaneously dumpy and glorious. I have come to appreciate that strange cocktail. And nowhere is it mixed more piquantly than in Golden Gate Heights, the anomalous little range of dune-covered hills that ends with Larsen Peak.

The four hills that make up Golden Gate Heights—Larsen Peak (officially known as Grandview Park), Rocky Outcrop, Golden Gate Heights Park, and Hawk Hill—offer superb views, but they are remarkable for another reason. They are the most dramatic remaining examples of the great sand drifts that once covered half of San Francisco. As such, they are a unique link with the city's pre-human terrain. To wander through the sand dunes that run down the western side of Golden Gate Heights Park is to walk across a tiny landscape that has remained largely unchanged for thousands of years.

The sand in those dunes originates in an unexpected place. Some of it comes from the sandstone cliffs at Fort Funston. But much of it comes from, of all places, the Sierra Nevada. During the last ice age, glaciers ground down granite rocks in the great range, and the resulting sediment was carried to the coast by the great rivers that were created when the ice melted.

Deposited offshore, the sand was eventually carried back onto the continental shelf. The prevailing winds blew untold volumes of it across San Francisco, creating the greatest dune system on the west coast and driving the 49ers mad. Considering that their lust for gold resulted in the devastation of California's rivers and foothills, which were torn apart by hydraulic mining, the Sierra sand that was blown in their face is a case of what goes around, comes around.

As it swept across San Francisco, the sand piled up when it hit obstacles. Golden Gate Heights, whose bedrock is made up of radiolarian chert, was such an obstacle. The thickest chert in San Francisco is located on the exposed crags that jut out off 14th Avenue, below a huge Spanish-castle-style house.

The vibe up here is completely odd. Five hundred steep feet below, the Sunset stretches off monotonously toward the majestic Pacific. Anonymous pastel houses look out at Point Reyes. A few yards farther south, at the corner of 12th Avenue and Quintara, the surreality reaches a Magritte-like pitch. A viciously beautiful outcropping of jagged chert stands on the corner, right next to some boxy 1950s houses that look too square for the Eisenhower administration. It's *Tyrannosaurus rex* meets *Leave It to Beaver*.

But climb the stairs to the 666-foot top of Larsen Peak—named after a kindly Dane who ran a dairy farm near here—and you can toss out your surreal cocktail, which is starting to get warm and flat, and pop the iced Dom Pérignon.

Golden Gate Heights is closer to the ocean than any other range of hills in town. It is the city's seafront balcony. And the view from Larsen Peak, intricate and vast, is one of the finest in San Francisco. To the north, the towers of the Golden Gate Bridge are almost directly lined up, with the complex mountains of northern Marin and Sonoma behind them. The towers of downtown gleam in the afternoon light. Across a disconcertingly deep gorge to the immediate east looms heavily wooded Mount Sutro, where Ishi, the last "wild" Indian in North America, roamed during his poignant final years. To the north is the great green rectangle of Golden Gate Park, running down to the sea in all its magnificent artificiality. Beyond the Presidio is the Golden Gate strait, hidden by a bump in the terrain, an invisible gorge. Past that are the imposing Marin Headlands and dreamlike Bolinas. To the south is Fort Funston, where the city peters out amid sandy cliffs. To the west stretches the flat Sunset—restored, from this height, to its native grandeur but marred by 19th Avenue and its gas stations. And at the end of the city, the sea.

The ugly 19th Avenue stretch of this magnificent view is worth pondering. For the vast majority of views in San Francisco are far more imperfect than this. They are marred by dreary neighborhoods, or ungainly buildings, or obstructions, or just by being aesthetically flawed. For every panoramic vista of the Golden Gate Bridge, there are a thousand truncated views of a tiny piece of it. For every Hokusai-like view of Mount Tamalpais, there are a hundred views of Mount San Bruno—a magnificent mountain, but one disfigured by radio antennas on its summit and tract houses running high up its flanks.

This imperfection is an essential part of San Francisco. It is its anti-postcard reality. And it holds a lesson.

In the 10 or so places I have lived in San Francisco, I have had all kinds of views, from the sublime to the uninspired. I am not going to say that I prefer the latter. But I have a place in my heart for all of them.

In February 1990, I was looking out the window of my room in San Francisco's Kaiser Hospital. The day before, I had had surgery for colon cancer. The oncologist had given me a 50-50 chance to live. Across the street was the stucco wall of a dreary little house, in front of which extended the almost-bare branch of a scraggly tree. It was the most beautiful view I have ever seen. It was a view of the world, which I loved and desperately wanted to stay in.

We all spend most of our lives looking at some version of that stucco wall and that scrawny tree. My brief moment of radiant contentment faded, and I do not pretend to possess any knowledge of how to make it stay. But if we are lucky, or wise, we learn to love that little view, the way a condemned prisoner loves the patch of sky he can see through the bars of his cell. All the views in San Francisco are beautiful.

CHAPTER 28

CITY LIMITS

The building formerly known as George's Log Cabin, 2629 Bayshore Boulevard, on the San Francisco–San Mateo county line

S an Francisco's extreme south is a lost world. Even when I was a taxi driver, I never really learned it. Most San Franciscans don't know it at all. It borders Daly City, whose greatest claim to fame is that Malvina Reynolds wrote "Little Boxes" about it, and a little strip of weird, steep-streeted, Christmas-cross bedecked Brisbane, whose once-beautiful lagoon was poisoned during the 30 years that San Francisco dumped its garbage into it. Nondescript, working-class, and devoid of tourist attractions, San Francisco's southern frontier is a ragged Cinderella scrubbing the pots of the glamorous Painted Lady neighborhoods of the north. In a sign of total cartographic contempt, one popular San Francisco street map simply omits the entire southern border and all the streets around it.

I've always been intrigued by borders. They endow their surroundings with a feeling of pointless specialness, a gratuitous drama. And the more banal and obscure they are, the more that feeling is heightened. Borders are like an anal manifestation of the Zen mind: Whatever they touch, no matter how insignificant, becomes important. Discovering a border in a place where the surroundings possess absolutely no charm, where the streets peter out meaninglessly, is like stumbling on a precious trinket dropped by an absentminded deity.

Doing the Knowledge for San Francisco obviously required me to know where it began and ended. So I set off to walk the entire six-mile-long line that separates San Francisco City and County from San Mateo County.

That ruler-straight line turned out to be oddly elusive.

One stormy day in late winter, I drove out to Fort Funston, the old army base on the coast whose enormous guns waited for an enemy fleet that never appeared. (I once saw a 1970s porno movie that utilized one of the deserted coastal batteries as a set—an admirably literal response to the 1960s admonition "Make love, not war.") Its crumbling cliffs are one of the last remnants of the vast sand dune system that once covered most of the city. I descended the sandy cliff below the hang-gliding platform and started walking south, looking for the border. I had a rough idea where it was from the city limits sign a few hundred yards east on Skyline Boulevard.

A heavy horizontal rain whipped into my face as I walked down the empty beach toward Mussel Rock, the sea stack where the San Andreas Fault, after running 600 miles through California from Mexico, heads out to sea before emerging in Bolinas, that wondrous old-hippie hideaway as sublimely cracked as the earth beneath it. The epicenter of the 1906 earthquake was about two miles offshore from Mussel Rock. I suddenly realized that, embarrassingly, I had never been this far south on Fort Funston Beach before—and it was one of the most spectacular places in San Francisco. Between the geological time bomb looming ominously offshore five miles away, the eroding yellow cliffs (which collapse from time to time during winter storms, sending houses crashing to the beach), the pounding surf, and the Wuthering Heights weather, it was a Götterdämmerung-like setting for the end of San Francisco, but there was no sign of the border. I climbed back up the cliffs looking for it, only to find the way blocked by the off-limits fairways of the patrician Olympic Club.

I went around to the eastern side of the golf club. Near the southern tip of Lake Merced, I found my first city limits sign. A few yards away from it,

I stumbled on what had to be the strangest historic site in San Francisco. At the end of a dead-end street used by pickup trucks serving a gated community I had never heard of, past a sad little picnic area and a nondescript gray house, stood a small ravine where, at dawn one day in 1859, David Terry, former chief justice of the California Supreme Court and an extremely hot-tempered and violent man, shot and mortally wounded U.S. Senator David Broderick in the last major duel fought in the United States. Two worn stone obelisks, terrifyingly close to each other, marked where the two men had stood. Ancient rage still hung over the place like mist.

I tried to walk east from the duel site but ran up against the fence of the mega-exclusive San Francisco Golf Club, another place I had never heard of. Why were all these lordly golf courses located on the city border, preventing honest citizens from going about their business? Consumed by such serflike thoughts, I went around it. The border reappeared in the Outer Mission, in a dreary neighborhood so confusingly hidden behind the twirled spaghetti strands of the 280 freeway, Alemany Boulevard, San Jose Avenue, and Mission Street that it might as well be behind a moat. (Which is probably why Patty Hearst took up residence there, a few hundred yards from the city limits at 625 Morse Street, when she was an SLA fugitive hiding from the police. They found her anyway.)

After a brief World-Historical Genius stretch at Goethe and Shakespeare Streets, the border crashed unceremoniously back down to earth at the County Line Cleaners. Its suicidal yellow waistcoat freshly scrubbed, it then intersected a long stretch of strange lunar-suburban streets descending from mighty Mount San Bruno. That big mountain, 1,314 feet high and four miles across, looms over and defines the entire southern part of San Francisco, but 95 percent of it is on the Daly City side of the line, and because they stood on rising ground on the lower part of the mountain, these streets didn't feel like they belonged to the big city at all.

After crossing gaunt Geneva Avenue near the vast Depression-era bread box called the Cow Palace, the border ran along the industrial edge of one of San Francisco's least-known neighborhoods, Visitacion Valley, once home to the terrifying Geneva Towers, two Eichler-built high-rises that became housing projects so nightmarish (think snipers and bodies being hurled from windows 20 stories up) that even the police were afraid to enter them. I found myself in a twilight zone of industrial buildings, ringed by ambiguous roads that petered out in the middle of nowhere. I walked around a vast See's Candy plant, only to find my way blocked by an inexplicable fence. On the old stagecoach and toll road, Bayshore Boulevard, the boundary was clearly marked, then disappeared among the weedy railroad tracks.

I crossed Bayshore and headed east into a weird oasis of small Spanish-style houses called, for reasons that are unclear, Little Hollywood. I had never been here either. This two-block-by-five-block neighborhood, squeezed between Highway 101 and Bayshore and in the lee of the least-climbed major hill in the city, 500-foot Bayview Heights, was so cryptic it made Visitacion Valley look like Times Square. Past three laughing Latino kids playing in front of their house and an old black man changing the oil in his truck, I came to a little hilly park on the neighborhood's edge. When I walked up to the top of the park and looked through the fence, I found myself staring with astonishment at a sculpture garden. Then I saw a flock of circling seagulls and heard the sound of bulldozers, and realized that the sculpture garden stood on land owned by the city dump. I'd been to the dump a dozen times and never known that this hidden neighborhood butted up against it.

I walked east down a forlorn street. It dead-ended at Highway 101, but there was an opening in the bushes and some sort of overgrown no-man's-land running along next to the freeway. I stepped over some old tires, pushed through the bushes, and bushwhacked through weeds and anise plants and a couple of gnarled trees. After about 30 yards, the no-man's-land petered out. Peering out from the bushes next to the guard rail, a few feet away from cars going 65 miles an hour, I saw the Brisbane city limits sign at the side of the freeway, 20 feet away.

This was the ultimate border hidey-hole. If it were Checkpoint Charlie, I would have had a chance to make a dash for West Berlin before the guards swung their machine guns around and opened fire.

That was the last city limits sign. I went through a tunnel that crossed under the freeway, which took me past some sterile modern high-rise apartments beneath Bayview Heights, and wandered along the edge of the bay near Candlestick Park. But that was it. The unmarked border vanished for good into the mucky bay somewhere south of an empty little beach.

I had come to the end, but there was one more border to explore. And this one turned out to be the strangest of all.

Leafing through an Arcadia book about Visitacion Valley, I found a photograph of an old log cabin, occupied by various nightclubs over the years, which sat directly on top of the San Francisco–San Mateo county line. According to the book's authors, the building's owners had painted a line down the middle of the floor, right over the county line.

To understand the purpose of this line, it's necessary to know a little about the peculiar history of San Mateo County. That county is now a staid and ultra-respectable place, dominated by wealthy peninsula communities like Burlingame, Hillsborough, and Atherton, but the matron used to be a trollop. Starting as early as 1856, gambling, dueling, prostitution, and drinking flourished in the northern end of the county, whose laws were much laxer than San Francisco's. Between 1890 and the early 1900s, an estimated 30 percent of San Mateo County's businesses were saloons. By 1900, the county also hosted boxing and dog racing, the latter disallowed in San Francisco. One now-defunct municipality located just west of the Cow Palace, Bayshore City, made its money entirely from dog racing; when the sport was outlawed in 1939, Bayshore City died. An ancient roadhouse just over the city line, the still-going 7 Mile House, was variously a stagecoach stop and a whorehouse, a speakeasy, a biker bar, and a mobbed-up gambling den that was busted twice by the FBI. During Prohibition, San Mateo County was a hotbed of bootlegging: Under cover of fog, shiploads of booze from Canada were dropped in coves off Half Moon Bay, picked up by obliging artichoke farmers, hauled on sleds to the road, and trucked into San Francisco. Female speakeasy owners known as "whisper sisters" poured drinks for police chiefs and mayors, who also enjoyed the company of the county's numerous women of easy virtue. Small wonder that throughout the 1930s and 1940s, San Mateo County rejoiced in the title "the Most Corrupt County in California."

San Franciscans in the first half of the 20th century, by some unhappy twist of fate forced to endure life in an uptight, Calvinist burg where the booze stopped flowing at 2 A.M., naturally saw San Mateo County as their southern playpen, a pre-Castro Cuba, a den of iniquity whose merry or paid-off officials turned a blind eye to the bacchanalian vices that should rightfully have belonged to the big city.

Hence the line painted on the floor of the old log cabin. At 2 A.M., all a customer had to do was step over that line, yell "O for a beaker full of the warm South," and he or she could keep partying all night long with impunity.

I had hit the jackpot. Not only had I located the border with exquisite precision, I had found the bar I had been looking for my entire life.

A little research revealed that the building that had once been the old log cabin was still standing and was now owned by the A. Silvestri Company. Silvestri is a well-known San Francisco family business that manufactures and sells garden statuary. In fact, one of their fountains—of Bacchus, by happy coincidence—stands in my backyard. Sandra Silvestri, who runs the business, agreed to show me the log cabin. So I drove down to the company's big Visitacion Valley showroom, located just on the San Francisco side of the border, across Bayshore from the log cabin.

Sandra Silvestri was giving directions in Spanish to three Mexican employees who were moving some pieces into the showroom. A successful middle-age businesswoman with a no-nonsense air warmed by Italian earthiness, she told me that the seeds of her family's business were planted in the early 20th century, when her great-grandfather Arcangelo and grandfather Adorno came to America from Bagni di Lucca, a region home to many of San Francisco's Italian immigrants. Experienced at working in plaster, the two men got jobs in 1916 creating the decorative molding for Bernard Maybeck's Palace of Fine Arts. They also started a workshop where they made little figurines of saints, which they peddled door-to-door, mostly to other Italian immigrants. When the Great Depression came, Arcangelo and Adorno returned to Italy, but they emigrated again to San Francisco in the 1950s, joined by Sandra's father, Alfeo, and other family members. "They started pouring concrete into molds, instead of plaster and alabaster, and making bigger objects like St. Francis statues and pagodas," Sandra said. "And they started selling wholesale to nurseries." The business took off in the 1970s. The company that started with poor immigrants peddling tiny statues door-to-door now grosses millions of dollars, has 50 to 70 employees, and is an anchor in a neglected part of the city. "When we walk into a community meeting, the police cheer," Sandra said.

She took me across the street to the log cabin, which her family purchased in the 1970s. "It had been abandoned for a few years and was filthy. The roof was caving in," she said as we waited for the light at Bayshore. The company used it as a showroom until 2001, when they bought the place across the street.

The cabin was a conventional frame structure, but the logs were real redwood. A San Francisco city limits sign stood right outside the door. "Look at this," Sandra said, pointing down. Embedded in the sidewalk was a round, cast-iron disk about eight inches across, which read "Survey monument SF-CAL," the words circled by eight stars. "It's an old marker for the city limits," she said. "One day someone stole it. And you know who it was? An old man with a cane! I had installed a video camera in front of the building for security, and on the film I saw him lean down and pick it up. He could hardly walk!" She laughed, then said, "I don't know if his conscience started bothering him, but a few months later it appeared again." Before it was returned, she had asked the city about replacing it. They said they didn't know anything about it or any marker like it. It is apparently the last one in existence.

Uneasily wondering if my San Francisco mania was pointing me toward the fate of that light-fingered old man, I followed Sandra into the building. We found ourselves standing in a cavernous, high-ceilinged room with a weird split-level roofline and big vertical support beams. To the left was a vast stone fireplace, at least 10 feet wide. Dozens of old fiberglass molds for statues and fountains rested on the floor. The oddest thing was that the entire interior was covered with shaggy redwood bark. It was like a Dean Martin–style cocktail lounge decorated by Daniel Boone. It was one of the stranger buildings I'd ever been in, and it kept getting stranger the farther we went into it.

"The stage area was straight ahead," she said. "The bar was to the right. It was a beautiful bar—60 feet long and made out of mahogany. We had to cut it up—there was nowhere for us to put it."

And the famous line on the floor? "That was right here," she said, pointing down. "It was painted yellow." The line ran from around the center of the front door back to the stage area. Since the bar ran parallel to the line, and was on the San Mateo side of the building, anyone standing at the bar did not have to move to keep legally drinking at closing time. I wondered whether the line was just a gimmick, or whether the police ever stormed in to arrest miscreants, only to run into an invisible wall that stopped them in their tracks like Marcel Marceau.

The place was enormous, 6,000 square feet, a warren of weird old rooms. In the attic, a 10-foot-long old grain-storage unit with pull-out bins sat along one wall. Pulling aside a shaggy piece of bark, Sandra said, "If you look through here, you can see where there are little windows looking down on the floor. They used to have gambling in here, and the owners could look down from above to make sure no one was cheating." She thought there had been a brothel here too.

In the 1930s the log cabin was called Sam's Lodge, Sandra said. In the 1950s it was known as George's Log Cabin. Later it became Roman's Cantina, the Polynesian Hideaway (where the owner's beautiful wife danced the hula and her kids performed the fire dance), and finally the Moonrose Forest.

The Moonrose Forest had its own peculiar story. When I had Googled "George's Log Cabin," I came upon a Web site called Rock Archaeology 101, which chronicles obscure rock venues of the 1960s and 1970s. According to the leading blogger on the site, someone named Corry, the notorious British band the Deviants—who were reportedly the first rock group to call themselves punks—played at the Moonrose Forest ("formerly George's Log Cabin") on November 14, 1969. Why, Corry wondered in his post, had this legendary group ended up in an unknown club at the edge of the city?

An old knotty pine bathroom still had the original graffiti on the walls. I looked for any sign of the infamous Deviants, their American career fizzling out in this obscure roadhouse on the edge of town. Or Dan Hicks, or Sly Stone, who, Sandra said, had played here once. But I couldn't find any. Someone had scrawled "Nita and Riley from Lodi, November 3, 1963"—19 days before America lost its president and its innocence. "Hootenanny forever 1959–1960." "The moon lasts 4-ever." And this sad little complaint, preserved in knotty pine: "Can't get a man without playing on his marriage problems."

We left the melancholy ghosts in that wood-paneled time capsule and walked back into the main room. It was invincibly cheerful, as if decades of good times had somehow collected in its shaggy bark.

Outside, standing on Bayshore, I took a last look at the building formerly known as George's Log Cabin, the Moonrose Forest, the Polynesian Hideaway, Roman's Cantina, Sam's Lodge. They were all gone now, and so were most of the numberless men and women who had once danced and laughed here, gone across a border no one can find. To the north, on the other side of McLaren Ridge, the big city hummed heedlessly along. To the south, across the city line, the sign of the ancient, formerly sinful 7 Mile House thumbed its nose at the commuters roaring past. And to the west, an invisible line ran through miles of uncelebrated streets, each of them hiding its own universe of stories, until it hit the distant sea, where it vanished for good.

CHAPTER 29

THE TORCH

The Palace Hotel, New Montgomery and Market Streets

Gold Rush San Francisco was no paradise. For many, it was a living hell, and the visitor to Portsmouth Square had only to stumble south through half a mile of sand dunes to find its ninth circle. The majority of 49ers camped out in a 1,000-tent city centered on where the present-day Palace Hotel stands at New Montgomery and Market Streets. The neighborhood was called Happy Valley, but for many of the men who lived there, that name must have felt like a cruel joke. Disease, widespread throughout the instant city, plagued Happy Valley. Poor sanitation and San Francisco's acute water shortage were to blame. Drinking polluted water from "hundreds of little seep-hole wells two and three feet deep," almost everyone who stayed there got dysentery. The disease, marked by bloody diarrhea and abdominal pain, is often fatal.

A 49er named John McCrackan described wandering through Happy Valley for hours, trying to find the tent of a man suffering from severe dysentery. Himself ill, McCrackan reported that "it [was] very unpleasant wading through" what he called a "perfect desert of sand." He finally found the sick man and had him taken to the hospital, but it was too late; the man died the next day. McCrackan wrote to his family, "It is dreadful to think of his coming out here to suffer so much, and to die at last."

Death was as present in San Francisco as in a medieval city. One observer related coming upon a well-dressed young man lying dead on the ground, apparently of exposure, on Washington Street.

The authors of the 1855 *Annals of San Francisco* saw the tragic side of the new city clearly. "San Francisco was like the scene of a great battle. There were victorious warriors braving and flaunting on all sides, while hope swelled the breast of every unwounded soldier. But, unheeded amid the crash and confusion of the strife, lay the wounded and dying, who had failed or been suddenly struck down in the melee."

There were a lot of wounded and dying. One physician estimated that one in five people died within six months of reaching San Francisco. Others went mad. Others returned home, disappointed and ashamed.

But people from around the world kept coming to the ragged, jagged, brawling city at the end of the continent. They were initially drawn by the dream of getting rich, but some of them found other rewards.

What San Francisco offered, for those first few strange years before it came back down to earth, was unprecedented freedom—from family, from work, from church, from one's own past. For most Americans, whose entire lives might be expected to play out literally within a few square miles and figuratively within an even smaller area, that freedom was a wind more exhilarating than an April breeze blowing in from Ocean Beach. Lawless, self-regulated, radically democratic, licentious, compassionate, lonely, and fearless, the city by the bay was a place apart.

Above all, San Francisco was *alive*. The painter John David Borthwick said of it, "People lived more there in a week than they would in a year in most other places."

Thoreau, the cold-blooded moralist of Walden Pond, balefully denounced the Gold Rush as a disgraceful race to get rich quick. He was partly right: It *was* a rush to get rich quick. But Thoreau missed something quick, alive, and unknowable in that wild stampede. Greed brought the 49ers to San Francisco. But something happened to many of them along the way.

At the end of *The Shirley Letters*, perhaps the finest literary document to come out of the gold rush, Louise Clappe wrote, "My heart is heavy at the thought of departing forever from this place. I like this wild and barbarous life; I leave it with regret . . . Here, at least, I have been contented."

Clappe was writing about a mining camp on the Feather River, but she could have been speaking for the thousands of others whose lives had been transformed by their time in San Francisco.

The Gold Rush shaped the 49ers' lives in too many ways to describe, but two in particular stand out. First, it blurred class distinctions. Bayard Taylor wrote, "A man who would consider his fellow beneath him on account of his appearance or occupation would have had some difficulty living peaceably in California." San Francisco's famous tolerance, its embrace of oddballs and outcasts of all stripes, its impatience with East Coast notions of propriety, can be traced back to the radical egalitarianism of its early days.

The second is harder to describe, but it has something to do with the euphoric self-transformation that Louise Clappe experienced. To an extent unique in American history, many of the participants in the Gold Rush were educated, thoughtful men who were aware of the historic nature of their odyssey even as it took place. And what some of them came to realize was that the quest that had taken them to the far West had been its own reward. In Buddhist terms, theirs was a mindful journey.

Whether by some nebulous chain of causality or mere serendipity, that peculiar combination of adventurousness, acquisitiveness, reflectiveness, and, above all, independence, has remained deeply inscribed in San Francisco's character. This has always been a city of thoughtful rogues, greedy do-gooders, irreverent theologians, socialist entrepreneurs, hedonistic environmentalists, sensitive newspapermen, philosophical rockers, and high-minded sensualists. And through the years, these mavericks have carried, like an unruly band of Olympic torchbearers, the rebellious, restless, life-affirming fire that was lit in 1849.

CHAPTER 30

THE PARK

Golden Gate Park

Parks are infallible signs of civilization, and Golden Gate Park is no exception. The great verdant rectangle that runs from the Haight to the sea came into existence because 20 years after its chaotic birth, San Francisco had finally outgrown its wild youth and was ready to settle down.

It was a tumultuous passage. In the years following the Gold Rush, San Francisco underwent a literal and figurative trial by fire. Between December 1849 and May 1851, it burned six times, the most destructive series of fires ever to befall an American city. At the same time, its citizens had to confront the dark side of the limitless freedom upon which their city was founded.

At the very beginning, the city's lawless, every-man-for-himself ethos was liberating. But Hobbes soon replaced Rousseau. In 1849 the "Sydney Ducks," a band of Australian ruffians, and the "Hounds," a gang of former Mexican War soldiers, began terrorizing the town, the latter specializing in "patriotic" assaults on Chileans. Other criminals ran amok, their misdeeds rarely punished. San Francisco's merchants and businessmen were willing to overlook corruption and rampant crime as long as their own tills kept jingling. But after a series of egregious crimes, they decided to take the law into their own hands, forming a first Vigilance Committee in 1851 and a second in 1856. The second, with 6,000 members, was the largest vigilante movement in American history. A genuinely revolutionary movement—its real aim was not so much to punish criminals as to destroy the corrupt political machine—it remains the most contested episode in the city's history.

While San Francisco battled for its soul, it kept relentlessly growing. In 1850, it had 35,000 people; in 1860, 56,800. By 1870, its population had swelled to 149,000, making it the 10th biggest city in the United States (New York, the largest, had 942,000). The city comprised only about nine square miles; few people lived west of Divisadero or south of 24th Street. San Francisco was not particularly densely populated—New York had five times more people per square mile—but its houses were built right next to one another, and it sorely lacked open spaces or parks. As early as 1855 the authors of the *Annals of San Francisco* had complained, "There seems to be no provision made by the projectors for a public park—the true 'lungs' of a large city . . . Not only is there no public park or garden, but there is not even a circus, oval, open terrace, broad avenue, or any ornamental line of street or building or verdant space of any kind." Portsmouth Square, Washington Square in North Beach, and Union Square to the west were the only open spaces in the city.

Nor was it a particularly attractive city. Two panoramas taken by Edward Muybridge in the early 1870s show a sprawling, dumpy town of boxy buildings and warehouses, with smoke rising up from factory chimneys. Museums, civic buildings, and monuments barely existed. San Francisco's lack of civilized amenities reflected its obsession with money, a fact observed by the underwhelmed British novelist Anthony Trollope: "I do not know that in all my travels I ever visited a city less interesting to the normal tourist, who, as a rule, does not care to investigate the ways of trade or to employ himself in ascertaining how the people around him earn their bread." (Trollope's complaint was echoed during the dot-com years, and is being heard again today, as the city fills up with high-paid techies. It would be a colossal irony if high-spirited, eccentric San Francisco ended up as a boring, money-obsessed burg.)

One might think that San Francisco's spectacular setting would have offered its residents some aesthetic solace. But its natural surroundings do not seem to have made a great impression on its inhabitants. There were several reasons for this. First, San Franciscans had less contact with those surroundings than they do now. There were well-known beauty spots, like the city's favorite promenade, Long Wharf. One of the city's many long piers—de facto streets, lined with saloons and auction houses and stores— Long Wharf extended 2,000 feet into the bay from the foot of Market Street. Climbing Telegraph Hill and visiting the Cliff House and the crumbling Mission Dolores, out in the country, were also popular pastimes. But these were Sunday excursions, not routines of daily life. Because the upper reaches of the hills were still inaccessible by road, and there were few tall buildings, views were harder to come by. Rhapsodies about the city's vistas are not common in the literature of the day.

Equally important, perhaps, was the city's roughness. The fact that the natural world was still incompletely tamed made it seem more threatening and alien than sublime. Moreover, the very idea of contemplating nature for pleasure and enlightenment, although promoted by visionaries like John Muir and embodied in the 1860s passion for the *pasear*, camping trips taken by middle-class families to the Coast Range or the Russian River, was still new. And it ran counter to the heedless, nature-ravaging, money-mad ethos that had built the city. The vast natural park that surrounds San Francisco, more beautiful than any man-made one, was not perceived as such.

Deprived of beauty, and having finally made up their minds to stay in the instant city they had created, San Franciscans were ready to put down roots—literally. They had sown their wild oats; now they wanted to plant trees. They began clamoring for a great city park.

They were part of a national movement. Before the 1830s, the idea of a city park scarcely existed in America. But as the country became increasingly urban, parks were seen as necessary—to ameliorate crime and other city-related pathologies, to reconnect with nature, and to establish a city's civilized bona fides. Like every other 19th-century American city, San Francisco had a number of so-called pleasure gardens, privately owned enterprises described by one historian as "a unique artifice—a blend of circus, museum, rural dale, and sometimes saloon." Russ's Gardens at Seventh and Harrison, the Willows at Valencia and 19th, and Woodward's Gardens at

14th and Mission (which featured a lake, a museum, a zoo, an aquarium, and a racetrack for Roman chariot races) were all popular, but they were insufficient for a city whose citizens had always been accustomed to living publicly. Moreover, the lofty self-image of the place that John C. Fremont had implicitly compared to Byzantium demanded a park that would rival Hyde Park or the Bois de Boulogne, not a glorified beer garden adorned with stuffed bears. In 1865, a petition given to the Board of Supervisors stated, "No city in the world needs . . . recreation grounds more than San Francisco."

The city turned to the master planner of urban parks, Frederick Law Olmstead, who in 1857 with Calvert Vaux had submitted the winning design for New York's great Central Park, still being finished in 1870. Olmstead looked at the endless sand dunes that made up the city west of Divisadero, known as the Outside Lands, and concluded that no park in San Francisco would "ever compare in the most distant degree with those of New York or London. There is not a full-grown tree of beautiful proportions near San Francisco." Olmstead instead proposed creating a "sea gate" on the site of today's Aquatic Park, a sunken parkway along Van Ness, and a park in Hayes Valley. But in 1870, San Francisco officials (led by a self-dealing politician who stood to make a pile by leveling the hills) decided to establish a park in the Outside Lands anyway, choosing a three-mile-by-half-mile rectangular area ending at Ocean Beach. At 1,017 acres, the park would be 20 percent larger than 843-acre Central Park.

The skepticism and derision that greeted this decision can only be understood when one realizes just how windswept and inhospitable the park site, and all of western San Francisco, was. Great sand dunes covered most of it. Roads were almost nonexistent. The incessant breeze blew sand so violently that it was difficult to get a horse to face west. And plants would not take. William Hammond Hall, the park's first engineer and superintendent, set about the Herculean task of domesticating this wild terrain.

The most critical problem facing Hall was how to hold the sand in place. A hardy plant with long roots was needed. From camping out in the dunes, Hall knew that the native lupine was a likely candidate. But when he planted soaked lupine seed, the sprouts were covered by the wind-blown sands before they could take hold.

An accident provided the solution. One day, a saddle horse's nosebag of soaked barley spilled onto the sand dunes. The horse refused to eat the sandy barley, so it was left on the dunes. When Hall returned to the spot a week later, he discovered that it was covered with barley sprouts. Hall mixed the barley and lupine seeds together and scattered them on the sand. It worked. The barley grew fast enough to protect the lupine. The sand that had been piling up for centuries had been conquered.

The rest was easy. Guided by Olmstead's vision of an urban green space that would feel as natural as possible, Hall and his legendary successor, the irascible, hard-drinking Scot John McClaren, created what Harold Gilliam called "the city's greatest work of art." San Franciscans fell in love with the vast emerald rectangle instantly—"The desert has been made to bloom as the rose," a newspaper exulted—and they have remained in love with it ever since.

In one crucial respect, Golden Gate Park is inferior to certain other great city parks. New York's Central Park, London's St. James's Park, and Paris's Luxembourg Gardens all offer a sublime contrast between city and nature. That contrast is an essential part of their magic. The fact that you can look up and see the Dakota Apartments filtered through the branches of elm trees deepens the drama of Central Park. You never entirely escape the city, and that urban presence illuminates the park like a poignant sunset. There is a human sadness, a romance, to Central Park that exists only in the old belle epoque eastern end of Golden Gate Park, around the Music Concourse and the Children's Playground. In the same way, the fact that the Luxembourg Gardens sit right in the middle of Balzac's "humming hive" and St. James's Park is next to Buckingham Palace makes them feel almost otherworldly. In these urban works of art, the frame is as important as the painting.

Golden Gate Park, on the other hand, has no frame. It gets no help from its surroundings. Situated in a low-rise residential district of undistinguished buildings far from the city's center, it lacks the dramatic sense of being an urban oasis.

But Golden Gate Park's weakness is also its strength. For it possesses a quality none of the above-mentioned parks do, one singularly appropriate to its city: It feels wild. It is shaggy and labyrinthine and confusing. There are places in it so hidden away and hard to find that few people have ever set foot in them. You can get lost in the place. After visiting it frequently for 30 years, I had barely scratched its surface. It wasn't until I began systematically exploring it that I really got to know it. And it took months.

The paradox of Golden Gate Park is that its wildness is almost completely man-made. (North Lake, part of the semi-natural Chain of Lakes and one of the most beautiful spots in the park, is an exception.) Every inch of the park had to be won, in a grinding battle that lasted years. The loss of San Francisco's great sand dunes, a natural marvel misguidedly seen as a barren desert, is tragic. But cities always violate nature. And what replaced those dunes is a second nature of singular grace. In a city whose very existence represents a complicated, sometimes failed, but ultimately triumphant negotiation between man and the world, Golden Gate Park is the crowning glory.

CHAPTER 31

HILL OF HATE

Pacific Union Club (the former Flood Mansion);
California between Mason and Cushman Streets

O n California Street, on the summit of Nob Hill next to Huntington Park, stands an imposing brownstone mansion that houses
the city's most exclusive private club, the Pacific Union. I've lived
in the neighborhood for almost 30 years, my kids grew up playing in Huntington Park, I've walked past that mansion hundreds of times, but I have
no idea what, if anything, goes on in there. I've never even seen anyone go
in or out besides tradesmen. Behind those thick stone walls, the club's aging all-male members may be partying as inanely as Bertie Wooster and his
fellow Drones, but it's impossible for a passing plebian to know. The brownstone's blank walls, curtained windows, and general aura of "tradesmen use
back door" are an invisible moat. The one time I dared to walk up the
club's stairs and peer in its portcullis-like entrance, I felt like Frodo trying
to sneak into Mordor.

Still, the unfortunately acronymed PU Club has an anachronistic charm.

Sitting on a bench in Huntington Park on a spring Sunday, with dogs and their owners milling around the splashing tortoise fountain, sunbathers lying on the lawn, and kids playing in the sandbox, the idea that just across Cushman Street retired captains of industry are drinking sherry and reading freshly ironed papers is reassuring in a retrograde sort of way, like stumbling upon a store that specializes in ascots.

But the bluebloods on Nob Hill did not always rest so easy in their club chairs. For years, the mansions on the summit inspired not bemused curiosity but venomous rage. Rabble-rousers in the depths pointed up at the hubristic towers that lined California Street and vowed to hang their inhabitants. On more than one occasion, angry mobs stormed the heights, like medieval armies besieging a lofty castle. Only one of those detested castles still stands: the brownstone on California Street. The great fire of '06 destroyed the others. It is a fossil, the only tangible evidence of a vanished archaeological strata of hatred.

The brownstone was built by silver. In 1859, vast deposits of silver-nitrate ore were discovered on the slope of barren Mount Davidson in Nevada Territory. The Comstock Lode, as it was called, turned out to be rich beyond belief. Over the next 20 years, the mines near Virginia City produced over $350 million ($6 billion today), the greatest mining bonanza in history.

Almost all that money flowed directly to San Francisco. San Francisco investors capitalized and controlled the Comstock mines and mills, and reaped staggering profits from the tons of silver ore miners dug out of the earth. By the mid-'60s, the city was experiencing its biggest building boom since the Gold Rush.

The bonanza fueled a delirious orgy of stock speculation. San Francisco had always been a gambler's town, but during silver's 15-year heyday, virtually the entire population succumbed to a gambling mania unlike any it had seen before or would ever see again. What made speculating in mining stocks so addictive was that their values fluctuated so wildly. A rumor that a new vein had been found could cause the value of a mine's stock to go up 10 times; it could plummet a week later. As a result, anyone could make a fortune literally overnight, and many did. The entire city buzzed with tales of chambermaids who bought the rooming houses they had worked in a few weeks earlier and of former ditchdiggers riding down newly fashionable

Kearny Street in opulent carriages. Between January and May 1872, the market value of the shares traded on the San Francisco exchange went from $17 million to $81 million.

But the market was rigged. A few powerful men—bankers, brokers, and owners—had inside information about what was happening in the mines, and they used it to manipulate the market. When the bubble burst in June 1872 and stocks crashed, losing $60 million in value in 10 days, thousands of small investors were bankrupted, but insiders made vast fortunes.

The game's fundamental corruption had been exposed, but so long as there were profits to be made, people ignored it. Another bonanza led to another frenzy of speculation. San Franciscans dreamed of a future of universal prosperity. But in 1875, the biggest crash of all wiped out the West Coast's leading bank, the Bank of California, and permanently burst the bubble. (After the bank failed, founder William Ralston mysteriously died while swimming off Aquatic Park.) By 1877, according to John Hittell's 1878 *History of San Francisco*, the two leading mines had lost $140 million in three years, or $1,000 for every white adult in the city.

A keen-eyed Scottish observer who had arrived in San Francisco in 1879 described this great transfer of wealth in starkly geographical terms. Robert Louis Stevenson wrote, "From Nob Hill, looking down upon the business wards of the city, we can decry a building with a little belfry, and that is the stock exchange, the heart of San Francisco; a great pump we might call it, continually pumping up the savings of the lower quarters into the pockets of the millionaires upon the hill." Treasure Island, indeed.

Four of those millionaires—John Mackay, James Fair, William O'Brien, and James Flood, the so-called Silver Kings—controlled the biggest Comstock mines. Of the four, Flood was the shrewdest. He was the ablest at manipulating the market. He became the most detested by a public that had once worshipped him. He was the man who built the brownstone mansion on California Street.

Like his fellow Silver Kings, Flood had risen from obscurity. Wisely deciding that the most bulletproof scheme in San Francisco was anything involving liquor, Flood and fellow Irishman William O'Brien opened a saloon, which they called the Auction Lunch. It quickly became popular, known for its excellent free lunch (for years, most saloons in San Francisco offered lavish free lunches) and first-rate drinks. O'Brien carved corned beef and ham in one corner, while the nattily dressed Flood presided over the bar.

Flood was shrewd and insatiably ambitious. He picked up bits of information from brokers who stopped in for a drink and began to cautiously play the market. Soon he become wealthy and decided to quit bartending and open a brokerage house around the corner. He and O'Brien met Fair and MacKay, formed a firm, and in 1872 bought some unproductive properties in the Comstock called the Consolidated Virginia Mine. Exploratory tunnels revealed the richest layers of silver ore ever discovered. In the blink of an eye, the four partners became unbelievably rich.

The former corned beef carver and the former cocktail mixer had completely different ways of spending their vast wealth. O'Brien, a modest man known as "the jolly millionaire," spent his days in the back room of McGovern's Saloon, playing a card game called pedro with old cronies from his first days in California. But Flood had more lavish tastes, and he wanted the public to notice them. He liked to drive through the city's streets in the finest carriages, their sides polished until they shone, with coachmen in plumcolored livery. In 1878 this Donald Trump precursor built a palace in Menlo Park called Linden Towers, a fantasia of white turrets and gables, topped with a 150-foot tower, that became known as "Flood's wedding cake."

Flood was richer than God, but like many of San Francisco's nouveau riche, he lacked social polish. As Hittell observed, "Nowhere else will such bad manners be found in families possessing so much wealth." The genteel residents of Menlo Park, predominantly conservative Southerners, called Linden Towers "the beautiful atrocity" and were filled with what one writer described as a "boundless lack of enthusiasm" for having a former bartender as their neighbor.

But Linden Towers was not enough for Flood. He needed to display his wealth and power in the ultimate setting, the place where every self-respecting plutocrat on the West Coast was building his showplace mansion: Nob Hill.

The summit of the 376-foot-high hill had only recently become *the* place to live in San Francisco. In the city's early years, the Clay Street Hill, or Fern Hill, as it was variously called, was barely populated. (The etymology of the name Nob Hill is disputed; it probably derives from "nabob," a wealthy person.) Dauntingly steep, especially on the southern and eastern sides that adjoined the growing city, and covered with sand dunes, it was an insurmountable barrier to the city's expansion. Horse-drawn buses and streetcars could not climb it, and its slopes were considered too sheer to build houses on. A local newspaper called it "a Sahara of desolation," a wind-swept expanse of sand and lupine, with a few live oaks tucked away here and there.

At some point during the early years, several large families erected a shantytown on the very summit of the hill, a ramshackle collection of huts cobbled together out of scrap material and surrounded by a barnyard through which cows, pigs, ducks, and chickens wandered. This strange Dogpatch looked down from its squalid heights to the bustling city below, like a fog-swept northern cousin of the dreamlike Technicolor Rio favela in Marcel Camus's *Black Orpheus*.

Nob Hill's Wuthering Slums period ended at 5 A.M. on August 1, 1873, when a 37-year-old British immigrant named Andrew Hallidie, looking down Clay Street from the summit on Jones, called "All aboard," released the grip, and started the world's first cable car rolling downhill into a thick mist. Three hundred and seven vertical and 2,800 horizontal feet later, the door to Nob Hill had been opened. That same year, rancher and thorough-bred breeder James Ben Ali Haggin built the first mansion on the hill, a sixty-one-room house at Taylor and Washington Streets.

Haggins's pile kicked off a mansion-building frenzy among San Francisco's newly, and obscenely, rich. Chief among these were a quartet of capitalists even wealthier than the Silver Kings, the so-called Big Four—Leland Stanford, Collis Huntington, Charles Crocker, and Mark Hopkins. Flush with the staggering profits they had made from their railroad monopoly, the Associates, as they were also known, vied with one another to build the most opulent palaces, which were lined up like enormous wooden peacocks on California Street. Stanford's 1876 mansion, where the Stanford Court Hotel now stands on California between Powell and Mason, was typical in its almost ludicrous excess: A reception room boasted an onyx table cut from a faulty pillar taken from St. Peter's in Rome, and its picture gallery featured artificial plants filled with mechanical birds that would burst into song at the touch of a button (whether their song kept a drowsy emperor awake is not recorded). Hopkins's 40-room mansion above it, where the Mark Hopkins Hotel now stands, was topped by so many towers, steeples, and gables that it looked like a caricature of a medieval castle.

Naturally, Flood had to keep up. In 1882 he bought a block on California Street and began building a 42-room mansion. Fittingly, the foundation of Flood's house was quarried by what in effect was slave labor. In a story on a visit made by various poobahs to Folsom Prison, the December 11, 1883, *Alta* blandly reported, "A large number of prisoners are now engaged in the quarries getting out massive blocks of granite for the foundation of the proposed residences of the bonanza millionaires on Nob Hill." Not even the pharaohs who built the pyramids had a better labor arrangement.

The construction and completion of the house was big news. San Franciscans oohed over its opulent interiors, but what really fascinated the town was the bronze fence that surrounded the mansion. The elaborately wrought fence cost $30,000 (at least a million dollars in today's money) and was looked after by an employee whose sole job was to polish it.

In those pre–high-rise days, the ostentatious palaces atop Nob Hill were visible all over town. Today there is only one place in San Francisco where a viewer can experience the same sensation: the northwest corner of Union Square, from where the massive Mark Hopkins Hotel seems to float like a castle in the air. To the workers toiling below, the mansions on the heights were infuriating, a constant, gloating reminder that their betters were literally lording it over them.

In 1886, the year Flood finished his mansion, the *Alta* (which had been acquired by his fellow Silver King James Fair) ran a piece headlined "A Socialistic Gathering. Citizens Urged to Raid the Mansions on Nob Hill." The piece opened: "Nearly 300 people assembled in the open space at the foot of Clay Street yesterday forenoon, to listen to the mouthings of several socialists and anarchists who were speaking from the elevation of a heap of garbage. The tenor of the language used by them soon became of the most rabid and incendiary character, and in the course of an hour or so the scoundrels were inciting their auditors to make a raid on Nob Hill. They were to pillage and destroy every residence in that locality and divide the plunder equally."

That raid never materialized. But by then, popular anger at the robber barons on the hill had been simmering for more than a decade.

The year 1877, the peak of the mansion-building craze on Nob Hill, witnessed the beginning of an unprecedented American political insurgency known as the Great Upheaval. Driven by a severe economic depression, the Great Upheaval started with a nationwide railroad strike, included the Haymarket Square bombing and the Pullman strikes, and took in the rise of numerous radical labor and farmers' political parties. In San Francisco, the Great Upheaval manifested itself in the rise of an extremely strange figure named Denis Kearney, and the political party he started, the Workingmen's Party of California.

Kearney and his followers subscribed to a kind of inverted Tea Party ideology: They were anti-capitalist demagogues who played the race card. They accused greedy businessmen of using cheap Chinese labor to replace white workers and break their nascent attempts to organize. The charge was not unfounded, and when added to the anti-Chinese attitudes already held by many whites, it led to a poisonous resentment that soon turned violent.

The Chinese, who had begun arriving in 1849, were initially accepted by San Franciscans. But whites began turning against them when railroad magnate Crocker began importing workers from Canton to blast his Central Pacific line through the Sierra Nevada, paying them far less than what he paid white workers. When the economy slumped after the Civil War, and the completion of the transcontinental railroad did not bring the expected boom to San Francisco, the slogan "The Chinese Must Go!" began to be heard. And when manufacturers began replacing white workers with Chinese and using Chinese workers to break strikes, resentment turned into hatred. In 1869, Chinese workers were used to break a strike by boot and shoe workers; four years later, at least half the boots and shoes manufactured in California were made by Chinese. Chinese also dominated garment manufacturing and cigar making. In 1873 the city had 115 cigar-making plants employing 3,480 workers, almost all Chinese.

Enraged by what they saw as an unholy alliance between capitalists and their Chinese "slaves," San Francisco's rapidly growing population of workers demanded a solution to the "Chinese evil." The political clout of the workers forced politicians to adopt anti-Chinese platforms, and both San Francisco and the state passed a series of Chinese exclusion acts. In 1875, San Francisco prohibited Chinese laundries from operating in non-fireproof buildings and imposed other restrictive laws. In 1876, state Democrats tried to bolster their reelection prospects by announcing a Senate committee to investigate the "Chinese issue"; the results were printed in pamphlets and distributed widely throughout the city. The committee's "findings" can be summed up by the testimony given by Judge David Louderback of the San Francisco Police Court: "I think they are a very immoral, mean, mendacious, dishonest, thieving people, as a general thing."

In 1877, the Comstock mines were in terminal decline, unemployment was soaring, and a major drought had caused the grain crop to fail. Large numbers of unemployed workers began gathering at a sandlot at McAllister and Market Street, listening to orators inveigh against the "coolies" and the crooked businessmen who employed them. On July 24, 1877, a speaker named James D'Arcy whipped the crowd into such a frenzy that it set off en masse to destroy Chinatown. The workers burned a laundry at the corner of Turk and Leavenworth to the ground, pulled Chinese prostitutes from their houses and raped them, and beat every Chinese man they found on the street. These were the worst riots San Francisco had ever seen.

The next day, 5,000 men gathered at Fifth and Mission. After more incendiary speeches, the mob headed into the streets, vandalizing six Chinese businesses and trying to burn the Mission Bay docks of the Pacific Mail Steamship Company, which transported Chinese to the West Coast. When firemen and police arrived, the rioters cut the fire hoses and climbed a bluff near First and Brannan to hurl rocks at their adversaries below. One hundred members of a just-formed citizen's militia called the Committee of Safety, led by an old vigilante chief named William Coleman, charged up the steep hillside, swinging pick handles. After a pitched battle in which a committee man was shot and mortally wounded, the "Pick Handle Brigade" finally drove the mob off.

Kearney had been a member of the Committee of Safety, but now he switched sides and began haranguing the crowds at the sandlots, denouncing the "moon-eyed lepers" and their businessmen masters, whom he called "miserable felonious bank-smashers." In October he formed the Workingmen's Party of California, whose platform poured contempt upon "thieves, peculators, land grabbers, bloated bondholders, railroad magnates, and shoddy aristocrats," and vowed "to vote the moon-eyed nuisance [Chinese] out of the country."

A weird amalgam of socialism and racism, the Workingmen's Party intrigued no less a figure than Karl Marx. In 1880 Marx wrote, "California is very important to me, because nowhere else has the upheaval most shamelessly caused by capitalist concentration taken place with such speed."

On the evening of October 29, Kearney led 3,000 followers up Nob Hill to Charles Crocker's mansion at California and Taylor. Crocker owned the entire block, with the exception of one lot owned by a German undertaker named Yung. When Yung refused to sell to Crocker, the magnate took revenge by erecting a 30-foot-high fence that surrounded Yung's cottage on three sides, almost completely blocking the sun. Kearney cited this "spite fence" as an example of the limitless arrogance of the corrupt rich. He warned that if Crocker did not tear down the fence, he and his followers would give Crocker "the worst beating with the sticks a man ever had." As his torch-carrying supporters roared in approval, Kearney shouted, "If I give an order to hang Crocker, it will be done . . . The dignity of labor must be maintained, even if we have to kill every wretch that opposes it!" The mob marched down California Street to Stanford's mansion, but its bark was worse than its bite, and it dispersed.

Kearney's moment in the sun was brief. His Workingmen's Party won more than a third of the seats at the California Constitutional Convention, but the party was wracked by internal dissension and failed to achieve anything. Legislation calling for an eight-hour workday was toothless, and various anti-Chinese campaigns in San Francisco were overturned by the courts. (At a national level, however, the anti-Chinese campaign succeeded, culminating in the draconian Chinese Exclusion Act of 1882, which essentially froze America's Chinese population until it was repealed in 1943.) By 1880, the party that had fascinated Karl Marx was defunct. In a fitting conclusion to his hollow, opportunistic career, Kearney himself returned to being a conservative businessman and pillar of the community.

The confused, contradictory, and volatile reactions the magnates on Nob Hill inspired among San Franciscans mirrored the nation's complex reaction to what Mark Twain and Charles Dudley dubbed the "Gilded Age." That money-mad era profoundly confused Americans because it revealed the contradictions in their most cherished beliefs. Just when Jacksonian democracy had established that every man was as good as a king, a new national elite, the plutocracy, emerged. Class, which had barely existed before, appeared at precisely the moment when anti-class ideology had triumphed. As the rich got richer and the poor got poorer, America was becoming a nation of city dwellers, leaving its old small-town and agrarian values and verities behind. Americans desperately strove to reconcile their Horatio Alger–like belief in individual effort and their Calvinist admiration for wealth as the external sign of inward rectitude with their increasing awareness that many of the men who got rich had done so by cheating. Small wonder that San Franciscans were uncertain what to make of the huge mansions on the hill.

Meanwhile, a breezy new perspective was being heard from. On August 18, 1877, the *Daily Union* gave prominent play to a "Letter from Kate Heath" about her visit to " 'Nob Hill' and its Railway." Writing in a witty, intimate style that feels strangely contemporary, Heath described riding in a cable car up to a Nob Hill mansion next to an elderly moneybags. "I was so near him I could have poked him in the ribs with my guilty forefinger, and he was gray and wrinkled, and when he breathed he wheezed; yes indeed, he actually wheezed, and when he stopped the car, he walked off goutily and gingerly, as though neither his lot in life nor his palace on the hill were worth bragging of, after all. Poor man! I've no doubt in the world he'd have liked my lungs, my sound feet, and my hair that I'd just freshly crimped over Hyperion curlers."

Heath's teasing compassion is a breath of fresh air after the lugubrious moralizing of so many of her male colleagues, whether they were Nob Hill haters or Nob Hill defenders.

But perhaps the last word on the mansions on the hill should go to a failed 49er, a good-natured, good-hearted man from Buckport, Maine, named Franklin Buck. Buck had tried everything—mining, running a store, speculating, selling lumber, raising hogs—and had never made any money. Now, in 1880, at age 55, he and his wife, Jennie, were ready to retire to the Napa Valley. But on the way, he returned to visit San Francisco, the city that had enthralled him when he sailed through the Golden Gate as a 24-year-old.

The Bucks wandered around town, amazed by the changes, taking in the sights and visiting old friends. "I still think it is the finest city to live in the U.S.," Franklin wrote in one of the last of the letters that he had been faithfully sending to his sister for almost 40 years. He marveled at the great wooden mansions of Stanford, Flood, Crocker, and the rest of the magnates.

"It was a kind of melancholy satisfaction for Jennie and me to stroll around and gaze upon these splendors and try and guess which house our twenty dollar pieces went into . . . for here is where it all gets to. These magnates own the mines, the state of Nevada and all the people in it."

Buck had spent the best years of his life searching for treasure, and never found it. Now, just when he was abandoning his dream, he realized that the riches that had eluded him had ended up in these vast palaces on California Street. But he was content. He had lived his life the way he wanted to. In his final letter to his sister, from Oakville, he wrote, "I have given up the idea of ever finding a rich mine or making a fortune in stocks. I have given it a fair trial and such things are not for me so I am setting out trees and fixing myself comfortably for life right here."

There are many ways to look at the Flood Mansion. It is the dream house of the luckiest bartender in history, symbol of an age of ruthless greed, target of a vengeful mob, survivor of a cataclysm. But I like to think of Franklin Buck approaching the big brownstone, looking at it for a moment with a rueful smile, and then walking away to plant his trees.

CHAPTER 32

HAPPY TRAILS

*Dirt trail between Clarendon and Belgrave Avenues,
a few feet west of Tank Hill*

One of the most marvelous things about San Francisco is its dirt trails. I'm not talking about trails in parks—every city has those. No, I mean trails in the city itself—dirt trails running right through the middle of swanky residential districts, and staid middle-class tracts, and run-down slums, and just about everywhere else. As far as I know, this makes San Francisco unique. In all my extensive wanderings through dozens of cities in the developed world, I have rarely come across a single dirt trail. In modern cities concrete covers everything, and what isn't covered is fenced off. But not in San Francisco. This city fought the earth, and the earth frequently won. As a result, there are whole stretches where between dirt trails, stairways, hillsides, natural areas, back lanes, and just plain unclassifiable open spaces, you can avoid setting foot on the asphalt grid at all. It is San Francisco's secret circulatory system, a network of divinely dusty capillaries.

Take, for example, the dirt trail half a block from my office on Telegraph Hill. Filbert Street, the steep street at the north end of my alley, Varennes, is filled night and day with tourists huffing and puffing and smiling their way up to Coit Tower. Very few of them notice a little metal gate through a fence on the hillside above the Garfield School. It bears two little hand-painted signs, one of which says "Please shut gate" and the other "Farewell." If you swing open that sweetly enigmatic gate, you find yourself on a dirt trail that heads north. It meanders along, past anise plants and random rocks, until it emerges onto Telegraph Hill Boulevard above the dead-end of Greenwich Street. I sometimes end up parking in front of the apartment building there, and that trail is the most direct route to my office. It feels like a divine cross between a mountain trail and the secret tunnel that leads to Toad's pantry in *The Wind in the Willows*.

Or take the nameless little trail that runs just west of Tank Hill, between Clarendon and Belgrave, two of the most beautiful and expensive streets in the city. Like most of the city's dirt trails, this one is the result of a patch of hillside simply falling between the cracks: The land is presumably owned by the city, but it's between two houses and it's too narrow to do anything with. But someone, a kid or a kid at heart, has made a trail there. It is covered with pine needles that have fallen from a big Monterey pine and it looks out at the Golden Gate Bridge. For 30 seconds, as you walk along it smelling that dusty pine needle smell, you are in the Sierra foothills.

Or the unmarked trail that runs west of Beacon Street at the top of Billy Goat Hill. I discovered it one afternoon when I saw a bobcat in the foliage next to a monstrous modern house at 275 Beacon. Following the bobcat, I walked up the hillside and found myself on a densely wooded trail that emerged at the Walter Haas Playground on Diamond Heights Boulevard. I had no idea I was going to come out there. The great thing about trails is that you don't know where they're going to end up.

Equally delightful are the city's unpaved streets and lanes. There are only a few of these left. Since Brewster Street in Bernal Heights has been paved over, Glen Park now holds the James Taylor title as Country Road Capital of San Francisco. Poppy Lane, off Sussex, wanders along for 400 or so blissful yards, probably the longest dirt road in town. But even more of a trapdoor into permanent summer vacation is nearby Ohlone Way. This path lives up to its evocative name, dreaming along in dusty splendor past anises and daturas and blackberries and morning glories and prickly pears.

Great cities invite you to love them in extreme close-up, to love every inch of them. And the more eccentric, convoluted, broken, and uneven they are, the more there is to love. The tenements on the Lower East Side in New York City, the decaying wooden houses above the waterfront in Istanbul, the fading rose-colored buildings in the magical little grid south of the Spanish Steps in Rome, the bombed-out villas near the Vucciria in Palermo—it is precisely the irregularity of these places that allows your heart to get a grip on them, like a climber finding a tiny hold that will not give way. Shimmering Venice has the most beautiful inches of any city in the world. San Francisco cannot compete, because it does not have streets made of water. But it has the next best thing: It has dirt trails. They make this city a place where mystery is measured in soft footsteps, and magic in clouds of dust.

CHAPTER 33

THE BALLOON

*Nameless lawn past the balustrade at the dead end of
Vallejo Street, east of Florence Street*

The most enchanting view of downtown San Francisco is found from a little-known place high on Russian Hill called Ina Donna Coolbrith Park. It is not so much a park as a winding paved path that meanders along the steep eastern face of the hill just off Taylor Street, making two loops before rejoining the Vallejo Steps. A few old green benches line one side of the cracked asphalt path. The hillside is luxuriant with towering Monterey pines and century plants, jade and potato, oleanders and manzanita shrubs and golden grasses.

This lane offers such an unexpectedly close-up view of the city that it almost feels illicit, as if you've stolen into a locked-off castle turret. The skyscrapers of downtown rise up less than a mile away, with the Transamerica Pyramid filtered through the branches of an enormous pine. The banners of Chinatown wave gaily in the foreground, against a background of old brick buildings. By day, Broadway is just a wide street; at night, illuminated by the gaudy signs of the last of the topless bars, it acquires a spurious neon romance. Beyond the city, three of the four towers of the magnificent suspension span of the Bay Bridge are visible, leading the eye to the bridge's mighty keystone pier, Moran's Island, the deepest bridge pier in the world, more massive than the Great Pyramid at Giza. The cable cars roll past a block below, on an amiably disheveled block of protean Mason Street that marks the border of the northern reach of Chinatown. To the left, Coit Tower soars like an Italianate exclamation mark.

Even today, when it is easily accessible, the top of Russian Hill feels like a place apart. But in the 19th century, when only a steep goat trail connected the heights with the town below, it felt like it was floating above the earth. So, at least, a writer named Emma Frances Dawson wrote in an 1896 short story titled "A Gracious Visitation": "I live in a region of remote sounds. On Russian Hill I look down as from a balloon; all there is of the stir of the city comes in distant bells and whistles, changing their sound, just as the scenery moves, according to the state of the atmosphere. The islands shift as if enchanted, now near and plain, then removed and dim."

If you cross Taylor and head uphill on the Vallejo Steps, you come to the summit of Russian Hill. Here, just east of an elegant stone balustrade, is the most delightful patch of grass in San Francisco. This little lawn with the stunning view has no name, but I think of it as Robin Hood Place, because it steals from the rich and gives to the poor. It stands on hallowed, and very expensive, San Francisco ground. Right next to it is one of San Francisco's great houses, architect Willis Polk's anti-Victorian shingled duplex at 1013–1019 Vallejo. Like a number of houses atop Russian Hill, this masterpiece escaped the 1906 fire. Polk also designed the balustrade, as well as the larger one at the Jones Street end, and four cottages on Russian Hill Place. A few steps away is little Florence Street, one of the most exquisite and exclusive lanes in the city. The two oldest shingle-style houses in the city, designed by an ethereal Swedenborgian minister named Joseph Worcester, stand at 1034 and 1036 Vallejo. Every square inch on the summit is soaked in history—and money. But that cheerful little lawn at the very top is a commons, open to all. I sometimes walk up there with a go-cup, the knowledge that I am a plebian trespasser making the cocktail taste even better.

Actually, some of the summit's denizens would have heartily approved of such bibulous trespassing. For they were trespassers themselves—bohemians and free spirits who for a brief time sent a zany jolt through San Francisco and the country with their lighthearted, invincibly youthful approach to life and art. Here on the summit of Russian Hill, at the end of the 19th century, a merry band of young writers and artists and architects came up with a little magazine called the *Lark*. The *Lark* was not profound, or even particularly original. But it was playful, witty, sophisticated, and self-mocking. And it did leave a legacy, albeit one written in invisible ink. It was fun.

Fittingly, the *Lark* came into existence because of a prank. A teetotaling dentist named Dr. Henry Cogswell had donated a number of fountains to the city, each of them featuring a life-size statue of Cogswell himself proferring a glass of refreshing, nonalcoholic water to the onlooker. One of the statues stood at Market and California, near the Ferry Building. This statue offended a 27-year-old man named Gelett Burgess, a Bostonian who was teaching topographical drawing at U.C. Berkeley. Burgess found it outrageous that visitors to San Francisco, of all the gin-joint-filled burgs in the world, should be confronted by a fatuous cast-iron sermon for abstemiousness the moment they set foot on the city's main street. So late one January night in 1894, Burgess, his friend Bruce Porter, and two other cronies, threw a rope around Dr. Cogswell's iron torso and dragged him off his pedestal.

Demonstrating an admirably lax attitude toward vandalism, the *Examiner* lauded the mystery miscreants, lambasting the statue as "an eyesore" that "dried up the artistic fountain of the soul." When Burgess, reveling in the praise, told friends what he had done, U.C. officials got word of his involvement and fired him. Cast out of bourgeois respectability, Burgess embraced a bohemian lifestyle. His first step was to leave his modern apartment at Green and Leavenworth and move to a dilapidated old house at 1031 Vallejo, on the summit of Russian Hill.

In the late 19th century, San Franciscans wanted modern houses, with indoor plumbing and electricity. New houses were popping up in Pacific Heights, the Western Addition, and the Mission District. The old houses on the summit of Russian Hill, even though they had panoramic views of the Golden Gate, downtown, and the bay, were not in high demand. According to an 1890 article in the *Chronicle*, Willis Polk discovered his future home when, wandering around at night "in quest of inspiration," he came upon a deserted old house with all of its windows broken and decided to move into it if he could. The story is probably apocryphal, but the summit was not exactly ritzy. A nearby site at about that time was occupied by a poor old Irish woman's shack and filled with trash through which goats roamed. Of his one-story-plus-an-attic house, one of 15 modest structures built in the 1860s on that stretch of Vallejo, Burgess wrote, there was "no queerer, quainter, crookeder a house, nor a house in worse array, of more tatterdemalion an aspect and cock-sided disrepute than the chunk of queer cottage at No. 1031 Vallejo Street."

Russian Hill had long been an artists' haunt. In the late 1860s, the poet Ina Coolbrith (after whom the park was named), Bret Harte, and Charles Warren Stoddard met frequently at Coolbrith's house on the hill, plotting out issues of a magazine called the *Overland Monthly*. The tradition was continued by a charismatic middle-age woman named Kate Atkinson, a fellow Unitarian with whom Burgess had become close. Atkinson hosted dinner parties at her house at 1032 Broadway (built in 1853, the house still stands), where the guests included Burgess, Willis Polk and his wife, artists and designers Bruce Porter, Florence Lundborg, and Porter Garnett, and printer Charles Murdock. Polk also hosted a group called the Roseleaves for select fellow members of the Bohemian Club, a writers' and artists' club. (It later underwent a hideous, Gregor Samsa–style metamorphosis into an exclusive retreat for the likes of Donald Rumsfeld.) During one of his brief stays in town, Robert Louis Stevenson, who was universally beloved by San Francisco's artistic community, attended a Roseleaf party. Burgess and Porter and their pals also gathered at a cabin in the redwoods they called Camp Ha-Ha. (In a pleasing continuity, the novelist Herb Gold, author of a book on bohemias, lives on the summit of Broadway, across from Atkinson's old house.)

Burgess and Porter—whom Burgess regarded as the true artistic genius and free spirit, and with whom he remained friends for more than 60 years—played the part of bohemians to the hilt. The diminutive Burgess, who was known as "the Walking Peanut," wore a knee-length cape with a huge lapel carnation, Oscar Wilde's trademark. The much taller Porter favored gloomy bohemian clothes. As they walked on the goat trail that ran down the steep Vallejo slope to the "Lower Town" (North Beach, Chinatown, and Kearny Street), they must have been a peculiar sight.

The duo closely followed the avant-garde tendencies of the day, in particular the aesthetic and decadent movements, with their art-for-art's-sake credo. They read the London magazine the *Yellow Book*, kept up with French post-impressionist painters, and were intrigued by Oscar Wilde and Aubrey Beardsley. Porter, who had visited the studio of Edward Burne-Jones, was a proponent of art nouveau. The two men were painfully aware that San Francisco was a provincial backwater, whose best writers and artists inevitably decamped for New York. (They would not be the last San Franciscans to grapple with this problem.) Possibly inspired by a Chicago magazine called the *Chap-Book*, they decided to launch their own. As Burgess later wrote, "we had been watching the literary movements of the time very narrowly, and the impulse to strike for California grew in us. There was a new note of personal expression then becoming dominant, but not in the *Revue Blanche*, not in the *Yellow Book* nor yet in the *Chicago Chap-Book* did we seem to hear the tune ring true. Yes, we must demolish Decadence and its 'precious' pretensions."

Thus was born the *Lark*. In place of pessimistic Decadence, Burgess and Porter extolled a Western optimism that drew its strength and inspiration from nature. Instead of preciousness, they celebrated nonsense and childish whimsy. Burgess's most famous poem appeared in the first issue:

I never saw a purple cow,
I never hope to see one;
But I can tell you anyhow,
I'd rather see than be one.

Rubbing shoulders with the nonsense were brief romances, parables, French-influenced poems, and little essays. They surrounded their text with remarkably creative graphics, including hand-drawn drop caps, unusual typefaces, startling borders, and weird creatures drawn by Burgess called "Goops." The bubbly nuttiness of the contents was evidenced by the back cover of issue no. 10: a spoof ad, with an illustration by Willis Polk, for a new book by Polk called *L'arkitecture Moderne*. "The edition will be limited to three copies, printed on palimpsest parchment, bound in half-chicken leather, crushed mouse-skin, or Irish bull," the copy solemnly intoned. This light-as-a-feather magazine cost five cents.

The public loved it. Reviewers felt that the *Lark* had somehow captured the spirit of the fin de siècle. The *New York Times* wrote, "It is a thin, small creature, but incredibly, even impossibly, 1895. And as for contents, it is all written by 'Les Jeunes,' those of California, forsooth, and delightfully young men they are." The *Boston Budget* agreed: "*The Lark* is a reaction against the decadent spirit. It is blithe, happy, full of the joy of life and the Greek within us. A herald of the dawn of a new century." There were dissenting voices—the *New York Tribune* called it "one more hysterical magazine . . . from the realm remote from the moorings of intelligence"—but they were decidedly in the minority.

The *Lark*'s biggest impact, not surprisingly, was on its hometown. San Francisco, which had seen a blossoming of talent in the 1850s and 1860s with Mark Twain, Bret Harte, Ina Coolbrith, Joaquin Miller, and others, had been in a literary doldrums for several decades. The *Lark* inspired a cultural revival. Les Jeunes, as the magazine's creators took to calling themselves after the *Times* review came out, blew fresh air through the town's Victorian sensibilities, just as they had toppled the self-satisfied statue on Market Street.

Les Jeunes' finest achievement, out-*Lark*ing the *Lark*, was a one-issue magazine called the *Petit Journal des Refusées*. Trapezoidal-shaped, filled with demented graphics based on old wallpaper designs, pursuing the conceit that every piece in it was rejected by made-up journals like the "Polynesian Monitor," its margins crawling with what Burgess called "Goops, square trees and cubical suns, striped elephants and plaid hippopotami, architectural monstrosities, falling tears, lighting flashes and deformities unmentionable," it was a miraculous little bit of anachronistic Far West Dada, a simultaneous precursor of *Zap Comix*, the *Onion*, the *Believer*, and *Mad Magazine*. Looking at its original pages, protected beneath plastic covers in the History Center of the San Francisco Public Library, it is hard to believe that something this crazy was published in 1896.

The *Lark*'s flight lasted just two years—which, considering its gossamer nature, was actually a solid run. By the end, the fizz had gone out of the bottle. "Our mood was too spontaneous, or rather too enthusiastic to last, for we had dwelt over-long with gayety; there was the world's sober work to do," Burgess recalled. "And, jealous of the *Lark*'s prestige, which had suffered from no carelessness in our devotion, after two years of the frolic, we brought the essay to a close before it could be said that the fire of our initial enthusiasm had grown cold."

Les Jeunes claimed to take their inspiration from the superb natural setting of San Francisco. Burgess wrote, "For here Nature came to our very doorsteps and bade us to be of good cheer. To our doorsteps . . . in a literal sense, for from my window on Russian Hill, I commanded a whole half circle of ocean, channel, harbor, islands and mountains, and saw the hills change from green to yellow, from yellow to red and from red to brown, as we swung past the vernal equinox. Who would not call such a terrible, awful, beautiful land his home, and, loving it with the passion of youth, endeavor to liberate it from the worship of dead gods and useless rituals!"

But neither Burgess nor any of his collaborators attempted to capture this "terrible, awful, beautiful" nature. The *Lark* features some poems and essays that gaily celebrate nature and living for the moment, but they lack depth and darkness. At their worst, they evince a pallid, oversophisticated, effete tone that recalls Watteau's paintings of shepherds. A deeper response to nature, a truly independent California literature, would have to wait for greater artists, like Robinson Jeffers and John Steinbeck.

Burgess was besotted by San Francisco's beauty, but he was unable to turn his personal immersion in that beauty into lasting art. This is a common-enough theme in San Francisco's history that it raises the perennial question: Is this city so beautiful that it turns its would-be artists into stupefied Lotus-Eaters? At least some of the time, the answer seems to be yes.

But one does Burgess and his friends an injustice by weighing them against heavyweights. They were not great artists, but they did not claim to be. They created a madcap, funny, smart, life-affirming little magazine, one that still breathes the spirit of youth and fun. And they knew enough to bring down the curtain before their act got old.

The true spirit of Les Jeunes, and the best qualities of Burgess the man, comes across in his little book *Bayside Bohemia*. Looking back on the long-gone days when he and Porter Garnett created the *Petit Journal des Refusées*, Burgess wrote, "I doubt if there is any place in the broad world, save San Francisco, where such insane, misspent endeavor could be possible; where two men, no longer in their first youth, would toil for a month to produce 16 pages of such fantastic rubbish as we perpetrated in my office on Sutter Street. But my blood had not yet begun to cool, nor has it yet, thank

God,—I would link arms with any other such madman as Porter Garnett, in any other such absurd enterprise, today, at the drop of a hat!"

Fun, like friendship, leaves no tangible traces. It rises into the air and vanishes like a balloon. But from that little lawn on the summit of Russian Hill, when the sun begins to set, you can still sometimes see that balloon floating out toward the ocean, in the shape of—what else?—a purple cow.

CHAPTER 34

THE FRONT DOOR

The Ferry Building

It is best seen at night. It is better still if a white shroud of fog—that ghostly mantilla that Dashiell Hammett called "thin, clammy and penetrant"—obscures the soulless towers behind it. But above all, it must be seen from the water. Only then do its ghosts rattle their anchor chains.

The Ferry Building has loomed up at the watery end of Market Street since Ulysses S. Grant was president. Its clock famously stopped at 5:16 A.M. on April 18, 1906. Modeled after the Giralda, Seville Cathedral's minaret turned bell tower, A. Page Brown's long, elegant gray pile still functions as a ferry terminal, and as the home of a popular (and extremely expensive) farmers' market. There was universal rejoicing when the wretched Embarcadero Freeway was torn down after the 1989 earthquake, bringing one of San Francisco's most beloved landmarks back into view. But what was revealed is an enormous tombstone for a city that no longer exists.

Actually, the Ferry Building commemorates not one but two vanished cities: the workingman's city and the city of the bay. Those lost cities were not identical, but they overlapped, and they died at about the same time. Soon after the bay ceased to be San Francisco's heart and soul and became just a pretty backdrop, the laborers and truckers and merchant sailors and all the other working Joes who used to own this town began to vanish from the city's streets. There is poetic justice in the fact that the vast, unknowable bay evokes an equally vast, unknowable city—and country, for that matter—that no longer exists.

Until 1936, when the Bay Bridge opened, San Francisco could be reached only by water or from the peninsula. The overwhelming majority of people came across the bay by ferry. Which meant that the Ferry Building was the city's front door.

In 1913, 60,000 commuters crossed the bay by water twice each workday. They walked off the boat and up the Y-shaped gangways into the Ferry Building, strolled across its marble mosaic floors, and exited through its massive arches onto the Ferry Plaza. What greeted them was controlled chaos—and a city planner's dream. Streetcars, horses, cable cars, railroads—there was more transportation running around than in a Richard Scarry book. The streetcars, timed to arrive at the Ferry Plaza when the boats came in, hauled most of the passengers, but the cable cars were workhorses too. They clanked all over town, along the flats and up the hills, rattling along at a civilized six miles an hour, the pace of a slow runner. On the water, 23 ferryboats plied the turbid bay waters from 5:30 A.M. to 11:35 P.M. Fast Key System boats carried passengers to Berkeley and Oakland in 18 minutes, where they were met by electric trains. It was so efficient that San Franciscans routinely commuted to U.C. Berkeley. On weekends, 30,000 people rode the ferries on cheap pleasure outings. The "Moonlight Excursion to Mt. Tamalpais—Up on the Crookedest Railroad in the World" cost $1—10 cents more for a round trip to Sausalito and $1.50 for dinner at the Tavern at the Top.

The heart of the waterfront was East Street, now the Embarcadero. The scene there in 1913 is captured in a wonderful panoramic photograph included in Nancy Olmsted's *The Ferry Building: Witness to a Century of Change*. With its shabby stores and bars and earnest billboards, the picture is a relic of a handmade San Francisco, a pre-corporate San Francisco, a San

Francisco still hospitable to people walking the street with very little money in their pockets. Olmsted gives a lovingly detailed description of it:

At 16 East Street between Mission and Market, Yosemite beer is advertised in stained art glass at five cents a glass. The owner is confident that beer won't cost more in his lifetime. San Francisco's waterfront is a workingman's hangout; he can choose between "Can't Bust 'Em" or "Boss of the Road" overalls. He can put away a dozen oysters on the half-shell at Herman Dree's Sidewalk Oyster Bar at 2 East Street, and wash them down with Jackson or Albany (brewed locally) or imported Bohemian Lager. He might drop into the Ensign Saloon (front door on Market, backdoor getaway on East Street) . . . It's "Big Doin's at Calistoga on July 4th!" Coca-Cola is recommended for "relieving fatigue." Los Angeles is $12 away—round-trip on scenic Southern Pacific; and a hotel room costs as little as 15 cents for a chicken-wire separated stall at the Cosmopolitan.

East Street belonged to the men who went down to the sea in ships. A 91-year-old sea captain named Fred Klebingat, who first sailed into San Francisco in 1909, stood with Olmsted in front of the Ferry Building in 1980, looked at the old photograph, and recalled the old days on what was called, fittingly, the City Front. "If you walked into the Ensign Saloon and called 'Captain,'" half the men in the place would look up," Klebingat said. As a broke young sailor, he relied on one of San Francisco's great saloon traditions, the free lunch. "If it wasn't for the free lunch, I don't think we would have survived. There was Feige Hansen in the middle of the block between Mission and Market, known as the 'Hash House.' It served 'cannibal sandwiches' as free lunch. There were slices of pumpernickel with raw hamburger and a slice of onion on top. Of course, first you had to buy a couple of steams for five cents." Klebingat recalled talking with a couple of broke pals: "'How much you got?' 'I got a nickel.' 'I got a dime. That's 15 cents. Enough for three of us—let's go to Sanguinetti's for lunch.' Sanguinetti's would serve you a scoop of steam beer, some spaghetti and Italian bread, and all the fish you could eat for a nickel. Now his place is called Fisherman's Wharf."

Traffic at the Ferry Building, whose first incarnation opened in 1875, increased every year between 1888 and 1933. In 1930, the year that saw the greatest volume of ferry traffic on the bay, 43 boats carried 47 million passengers and more than 6 million vehicles over a dozen routes. Fifty to 60 thousand people crossed the bay between San Francisco and Alameda County every day. At the evening rush hour, the Ferry Plaza was black with people rushing to catch the 5:15 ferries home. This superbly efficient and organized mass transit system handled more people than any transportation hub in the world except London's Charing Cross Station.

The piers north and south of the Ferry Building were the city's muscular heart. The waterfront bustled. In 1933, the nadir of the Depression, 7,000 ships pulled in and out of the port's 82 docks. In a fascinating book titled *San Francisco in the 1930s: The WPA Guide to the City by the Bay*, an anonymous author evokes its atmosphere:

> The smells of copra, of oakum, raw sugar, roasting coffee and rotting piles, and mud and salt water creep up the darkened streets . . . Even before the eight o'clock wail of the Ferry Building siren, the Embarcadero comes violently to life. From side streets great trucks roll through the yawning doors of the piers. The longshoremen, clustered in groups before the pier gates, swarm up ladders and across gangplanks. The jitneys, small tractor-like conveyances, trailing long lines of flat trucks, wind in and out of traffic; the comical lumber carriers, like monsters with lumber strapped to their undersides, rattle along the street. Careening taxis, rumbling underslung vans and drays, and scurrying pedestrians suddenly transform the water front into a traffic-thronged artery.

It was the workingman's heart of what was still, at least in demographic terms, a workingman's town. Of the city's 600,000 residents (400,000 of them male), 150,000 were blue-collar males and 150,000 white-collar workers. Even during the Depression, those down on their luck could still get by in San Francisco.

But if workers made up the bulk of the city's population, they did not call the shots. Led by a shipping magnate appropriately named Robert Dollar, employers had crushed attempts by the riggers and stevedores to form a union. Throughout the 1920s, big business interests successfully imposed their so-called American Plan—empty patriotism, then as now, being employed to disguise naked greed—which mandated open shops and gave employers control of the crucial hiring halls used to assign daily work on the waterfront. Longshoremen were forced to go through a humiliating and corrupt process called the "shape-up," in which they were forced to mill around a bribe-taking "straw boss" who decided who would work that day.

By 1934, the longshoremen, led by a terse, lean Australian named Harry Bridges, had successfully unionized. In May, 35,000 West Coast waterfront workers went on strike, demanding a coast-wide contract, higher wages, shorter hours, and an end to the shape-up. Negotiations brought the two sides fairly close, but an ideological chasm and mutual mistrust prevented a settlement. Tensions mounted and violence flared as employers and police tried to forcibly open the port. On July 5, 1934, the waterfront exploded. Hundreds of police and thousands of strikers clashed at the foot of Rincon Hill. Near Steuart and Mission Streets, a policeman fired into a crowd with a shotgun. Three men fell—one dead, one dying, one seriously wounded. Seventy-five others were shot, clubbed, or hit by tear gas canisters. It would forever be known as "Bloody Thursday."

In the arbitration agreement that followed Bloody Thursday, almost all of the longshoremen's demands were met. It was one of the great triumphs for organized labor in U.S. history.

But the 1934 waterfront strike proved to be the high-water mark not just for San Francisco's organized labor movement but also for its traditional workforce. Vast changes—in industry, in technology, in society, and on the world stage—were afoot that would utterly transform the city.

The ferries were the first to go. The bridges and the automobile doomed them. By 1939 the number of annual passengers on Southern Pacific ferries had dropped to about 10 million, compared with more than 22 million in 1920. Also in 1939, the worst streetcar jam in the city's history clogged downtown streets, while the Ferry Plaza stood empty. In 1941, the mighty side-wheeler *Eureka*, now one of the floating museums on the Hyde Street Pier, made its last trip to Sausalito. By 1950, there were only four ferry routes and 13 boats. In 1958, the last ferryboat sailed. Ferry service would not be resumed until 1964, and then it was only a shadow of what it once was.

Herb Caen, keeper of so many of the city's sacred fires, recognized what had been lost: "A bridge is only a bridge, a highway in the sky. Ferryboats were close to the foaming heart of the matter—something to love."

Like a heartbroken old spouse, the port began its final decline. Trucks were replacing trains as freight carriers, but they were hard to maneuver on San Francisco's cramped docks, and hard to drive through its increasingly congested streets. Fewer and fewer ships used the port.

The coup de grâce was announced in 1958, the same year the last ferry ran. That was when the first containerized freighter sailed through the Golden Gate. Container shipping requires space and facilities, and San Francisco could not compete with Oakland. Just 24 years after Bloody Thursday, one of the world's great working ports was nearing the end.

And behind the City Front, the brawny man's-man city that had existed since the Gold Rush was dying too. Heavy industry was leaving San Francisco. Factory workers were being replaced by secretaries and clerks. Skyscrapers for the new financial district were replacing docks and cranes. The great postindustrial transformation that was to change all American society had begun in San Francisco. Over the next two decades, it would result in a completely different city.

Women, pouring into the workforce after World War II, played a far bigger role. The middle class grew enormously, driving the new consumer culture but also making it possible for transgressive bohemian movements like the Beats and the hippies to spring up. And in San Francisco, the members of that ascendant middle class were far from the petit bourgeois Babbits imagined by doctrinaire leftists. Urbanist, worker-identified, and cosmopolitan, they were much more liberal than their counterparts in, say, Los Angeles.

So it is appropriate that it was three middle- and upper-class Bay Area women who helped launch the crusade that would save the bay. Ironically, they did so at precisely the same time that it ceased to define the city's identity.

Familiarity, even love, does not necessarily mean knowledge—let alone wisdom. And during the century that San Franciscans engaged most intimately with the bay, they neither knew it nor had the wisdom to realize that they were destroying it.

From the human point of view, San Francisco Bay is the world's greatest natural harbor. From nature's point of view, it is a unique estuary, a meeting of freshwater and saltwater unlike any other. Forty-two miles long, an average of 11 miles wide, and 460 miles square, the bay is fed by 85 watersheds that drain 40 percent of California's land. The movement of water through the estuary is so complex that scientists are still studying it. Around it are 46 cities, 7 million people, six ports, and 135 parks, refuges, and preserves. It hosts 120 species of fish, 1,000 to 3,000 sea lions, 600 harbor seals, and 500 pairs of great blue herons. Every August, 700,000 waterbirds arrive. In late April, as many as 500,000 migrating western sandpipers may be on the bayshore in a single day. Above all, it is an environment in constant flux: In 1997, torrential rains changed the salt composition of the bay from 79 percent to 22 percent. In short, it is a natural miracle.

From 1848 until around 1961, none of that meant anything to the human beings who lived in increasingly large numbers on the bay. People viewed the great estuary as an infinitely renewable or indestructible resource—if they even thought about it at all. Factories poured toxic substances into the bay. Butchers, farmers, and manufacturers all used it and the streams leading to it as a dump. As Ariel Rubissow Okamoto and Kathleen M. Wong note in *Natural History of San Francisco Bay*, before 1970 "raw sewage traveled directly from toilets into the bay via more than 80 points of discharge." The bay stank. It was too dangerous to swim in. And it was being relentlessly filled up. In Gold Rush times, the bay is estimated to have had 787 square miles of open water. By 1960, that had shriveled to 548. Even more devastating was the mania to "reclaim" swamps and wetlands. By 1950, only 50,000 acres of tidal marsh remained, a quarter of the original area.

No one cared, because no one even had access to the bay. Incredibly, only four miles of its entire 276-mile circumference below the delta were open to the public.

In 1961, a planner named Mel Scott—remember that name—made a survey of the bay for a conference cosponsored by U.C. Berkeley Extension and a citizen's group called Citizens for Regional Recreation and Parks. Led by a handful of planners and activists, including Scott, Jack Kent, and Dorothy Erskine, the group argued that regional planning was necessary to protect the Bay Area's natural resources. As he did his research, Scott realized that most of the tidelands around the bay were privately owned, and extensive plans were under way to fill in vast stretches of the bay and its wetlands.

Around this time, Sylvia McLaughlin, a U.C. Berkeley regent and the wife of a mining magnate, began noticing that the bay was shrinking. She was accustomed to looking out the window of her Berkeley Hills house to admire the view. Now the water was disappearing. "We could all see it being filled in," she told Okamoto and Wong. "Then I saw the headlines in the *Daily Gazette*, how the city was going to double its size in the name of 'progress.' And every time I went downtown, I'd see these huge trucks rumbling down to the bay, filled with dirt and refuse from university building projects."

McLaughlin shared her concerns with two friends, Kay Kerr, the wife of U.C. president Clark Kerr, and Esther Gulick, who was married to a professor. To their horror, the three women realized that the city of Berkeley was planning to fill in 2,000 acres of the bay—with zero community input. They invited the leaders of 13 environmental organizations to meet in Gulick's living room. Scott, Kent, and Erskine were present as well. "Kay gave a pitch about the bay being filled in and they all agreed something must be done, but said they were too busy saving birds and redwoods and wilderness," McLaughlin recalled. "So they all wished us luck and filed out the door, and we sat down and started our own organization, Save the Bay."

Using mailing lists from the Sierra Club and other groups, the three women sent out hundreds of letters, calling attention to the destruction of the bay and asking for a $1 contribution to join their group. The response was overwhelming. An avalanche of $1 contributions poured in. They got extensive media coverage. Powerful politicians came on board. In 1965, the McAteer-Petris Act created the San Francisco Bay Conservation and Development Commission (BCDC) to safeguard the bay. It was the first coastal zone management agency in the world. Today nothing goes into the bay without BCDC signing off on it. And you can swim in the water.

Three women with no experience in politics or activism had led the successful fight to save San Francisco Bay—and helped create the American environmental movement. In *The Country in the City*, Richard Walker says, "Nothing was more essential to the Bay Area's green culture. It all goes through Save the Bay."

So if the Ferry Building is a tombstone, it is also a beacon. The bay is no longer San Francisco's front door. And the army of men who worked on the wharves and the ships is gone. But thanks to a different army, the great estuary has been preserved for future generations. If Eagle, who in Ohlone mythology helped create the world, were to fly over the Ferry Building, he would tip his wings.

CHAPTER 35

A TALE OF TWO EARTHQUAKES

274 Shipley Street, between Fifth and Sixth Streets

We are drawn to disasters. Apocalyptic events have a weird erotic pull: At this very moment, Godzilla is destroying Tokyo again on some cable channel. But they are inaccessible. They're too frightening, too alien, too vast. The great earthquake and fire that destroyed San Francisco in 1906 is no exception. We can list the buildings that were destroyed and the number of people that were killed, but the experience itself is impossible to imagine. Unless you were there. I wasn't there in 1906. But I was there in 1989. It wasn't as big of a disaster, but it was big enough. And it's the one I know.

What follows is a tale of two earthquakes, placed side by side, like tectonic plates.

At 5:12 A.M. on April 18, 1906, about six miles below the ocean floor just north and west of Mussel Rock, Daly City, the rocks along the eastern edge of the Pacific Plate, the largest tectonic plate on earth, suddenly broke free from the rocks on the western edge of the North American Plate and lurched violently forward. Enormous shock waves raced toward San Francisco at 7,000 miles an hour, furrowing the earth like a plow. Four seconds later they arrived.

A policeman named Jesse B. Cook was on duty at Washington and Davis, near the old produce market. He heard "a deep and terrible rumbling." As he looked up Washington Street toward Nob Hill, he saw the street rising up and down like an undulating snake and coming at him. "It was if the waves of the ocean were coming toward me, and billowing as they came," he said.

A man named Clarence Judson, who lived at the then Siberia of what is now 47th Avenue near Judah Street, was preparing to take his daily early-morning dip in the Pacific. As he waded in up to his armpits, an unusually large breaker almost knocked him off his feet. The undertow began to carry him out. "Instantly there came such a shock," Judson recalled. "I was thrown to my knees. I got up and was down again. I was dazed and stunned, and being tossed about by the breakers, my ears full of salt water and about a gallon in my stomach. I was thrown down three times, and only by desperate fighting did I get out at all. It was a close call."

Judson ran around looking for his clothes. "I thought of lightning, as the beach was full of phosphorus," he said. "Every step I took left a brilliant, incandescent streak." When the quake hit, Judson was probably the closest person in San Francisco to the San Andreas Fault.

Reporter James Hopper of the *Call* was awakened in his room at the Neptune Hotel on Post near Mason. "Right away it was incredible—the violence of the quake. It started with a directness, a savage determination that left no doubt of its purpose," Hopper wrote. "It pounced on the earth as some sidereal bulldog, with a rattle of hungry eagerness. The earth was a rat, shaken in the grinding teeth, shaken, shaken, shaken, with periods of slight weariness followed by new bursts of vicious rage."

The sound of the tortured earth was dreadful. One musician said it sounded "like a thousand violins playing off key."

Tuesday, October 17, 1989, 5:04 P.M. *I am holding a cold beer and standing in the back room of my apartment on Jackson Street, getting ready to watch the Giants*

play the A's in the World Series. A jolt hits the room. What? Oh—big one. Stop.
Coming south to north. Keeps on rolling. Sharp rises. Definitely big.

I'm a Bay Area native. I've been through a few earthquakes. But every time one
hits, I wonder exactly what I should be doing and know I'm not doing it. Sometimes
it vaguely occurs to me that there's nothing I really could do anyway. But I've never
grasped this in any part of my life, and earthquakes are no exception. They come in
fast and low, under the radar of consciousness, and unsettle things in your mind that
you didn't even know were in there.

The shocks last for more than 5 seconds, maybe closer to 10. I look up and see the
jerry-rigged bookcase over my computer begin to swing out of the wall and come for-
ward. Five shelves and about 300 books. Are they going to? No?—they slowly rock
forward and then crash heavily, landing on the desk and the floor. A heavy volume
slides across the rug and ends up touching my toe. Okay, I'm okay.

Wait, the TV is out. Is it unplugged? Did the building blow a fuse? I stumble
around indecisively for a few minutes.

Reporter Fred J. Hewitt was near San Francisco City Hall when the quake struck. "I was thrown . . . on my back and the pavement pulsated like a living thing. Around me the huge buildings, looming up more terrible because of the queer dance they were performing, wobbled and veered." In the Mission District, Officer Henry N. Powell wrote, "Valencia Street not only began to dance and rear and roll in waves like a rough sea in a squall; but it sank in places and then vomited up its car tracks."

The Valencia Hotel at 18th Street and Valencia, an intersection that is now hipster central, was built on the old Laguna de los Dolores. It "telescoped down on itself like a concertina" in a few seconds. Forty people were killed immediately, and more drowned in the subterranean waters of Mission Creek—an ironic fate, considering the city was about to burn down because there was no water. The four elements seemed to be vying with each other to see which could kill the most people on this intersection: Those who survived the earthquake and the waters of the creek were burned to death the next day. A total of more than 100 people died in the Valencia Hotel, the highest recorded number to die in any one building in the city.

San Francisco fire chief Dennis Sullivan was in bed on the third floor of the Chemical Company No. 3 firehouse at 410 Bush at Kearny, just opposite Claude Lane. When the quake hit, he struggled to his feet and rushed into the next room, where his wife, Maggie, was sleeping. A cloud of dust prevented him from seeing that there was a gaping hole in the floor, created when the cupola of the California Hotel next door had fallen 60 feet and sliced through the firehouse. Maggie, tucked in bed, fell three stories to the basement and lay still swaddled in her sheets, miraculously unhurt.

Chief Sullivan was not so fortunate. He landed on the floor of the basement next to a boiler, the impact fracturing his skull, breaking his ribs, and puncturing his lungs. But his most serious injuries were caused by a jet of boiling steam from the broken boiler. Rescuers pulled their severely burned chief out and rushed him to the hospital, but he died four days later. Sullivan was the one man who possessed the knowledge, experience, and leadership abilities that might have saved the city from the fire about to consume it. A plaque on a firehouse at Bush and Mason honors his memory.

5:25 P.M. *I get on my mountain bike and zoom north down Jones, turn right on Pacific. It's a hot day. The Bay Bridge is there as always. I don't bother to look at it. I careen down Mason, then Vallejo. I ask a cop at the Central Station when we're going to get power back. He says he doesn't know. It's citywide.*

North Beach. I turn left onto Stockton, and as I go past two stalled buses and shoot across Columbus, the absolute and glorious improbability of it all hits me, the city stunned into a new life, during the World Series yet, and I break into a loud and exuberant laugh. I want to shout out "The damndest fine ruins!" And I don't even know there are any ruins.

I swoop around a pedestrian. This quake is nothing, just a nudge in the ribs from the earth, a good joke from its igneous guts. I turn into that crazy six-way intersection and pull up in front of Gino and Carlo's.

William James, author of *The Varieties of Religious Experience* and one of the fathers of pragmatism, was asleep in a house in Palo Alto, where he was living for a year while teaching at Stanford. When the quake hit, all the chimneys in the house collapsed and bricks crashed into the living room. James ran into his wife's bedroom, saying, "This is an earthquake. Are you frightened? I am not, and I am not nauseated either." What James's wife thought of her husband's response is not recorded.

Later James wrote of the experience: "In my case, sensation and emotion were so strong that little thought, and no reflection or volition, were possible in the short time consumed by the phenomenon. The emotion consisted wholly of glee and admiration: glee at the vividness with which such an abstract idea or verbal term as 'earthquake' could put on when translated into sensible reality and verified concretely; and admiration at the way in which the frail little wooden house could hold itself together in spite of such a shaking. I felt no trace whatsoever of fear; it was pure delight and welcome."

5:25 P.M., Gino and Carlo's, Green and Stockton. *The TV is dark. A bunch of people are leaning over the bar, listening to a radio. I hear something indistinguishable about a "Cypher-structure" collapsing. This cryptic "Cypher-structure" or "Cypress-structure" phrase, with no explanation, is repeated a number of times. A hysterical reporter comes on the air; he's almost incoherent. "They're not gonna play," says a dyspeptic-looking middle-age man at the bar. A Financial District–type woman next to me is pretty shaky, pounding them down. The bartender suddenly announces it's free drinks for everyone. "Thanks for staying!" As I drink a straight shot of Jack Daniel's, I hear reports that people are dead on the freeway. There are helicopters flying around. It's all very garbled. Somebody says there's a fire in the Marina.*

"The vibrations ceased and I began to dress," James Hopper wrote. "Then I noted the long silence. Throughout the long quaking, in this great house full of people I had heard not a cry, not a sound, not a sob, not a whisper. And now, when the roar of crumbling buildings was over and only a brick was falling here and there like the trickle of a spent rain, this silence continued, and it was an awful thing. But now in the alley some one began to groan. It was a woman's groan, soft and low."

Hopper's eyewitness feature on the quake and fire was the finest piece of writing to emerge from the disaster. (The world-famous Jack London, who was enticed to write a 2,400-word essay himself when *Collier's* magazine offered him the unheard-of figure of $500, admitted that Hopper had outdone him.)

Hopper made his way down Post toward Union Square. "In the morning's garish light I saw many men and women with gray faces, but none spoke. All of them, they had a singular hurt expression, not one of physical pain, but rather one of injured sensibilities, as if some trusted friend, say, had wronged them, or as if some one had said something rude to them."

Jack London noticed the same silent restraint. "As remarkable as it may seem, Wednesday night, when the whole city crashed and roared into ruin, was a quiet night. There were no crowds. There was no shouting and yelling. There was no hysteria, no disorder. I passed Wednesday night in the path of the advancing flames, and in all those terrible hours, I saw not one woman who wept, not one man who was excited, not one person who was in the slightest degree panic-stricken . . . Never in San Francisco's history were her people so kind and courteous as on this night of terror."

Examiner reporter Hewitt must have been in a less stoic part of town. "Each and every person I saw was temporarily insane," he wrote. "Laughing idiots commented on the fun they were having. Terror marked their faces, and yet their voices indicated a certain enjoyment that maniacs have when they kill and gloat over their prey . . . All humanity within eyesight was suffering from palsy."

6:05 P.M., Columbus and Green. *Looking west behind Russian Hill, I see a huge hanging pall of orange and black. I jump back on the bike. I'm going to check out that fire. Big smoke—this is kind of serious. I head out Columbus, over Bay. Bay is pretty clogged. I squeeze past the cars and turn right on Fillmore.*

6:15 P.M. *I see it. It's the first evidence, the first of a long accumulation of events and visions that gradually dig a dark tunnel under the exaltation of being alive and at large. It's at the corner of Cervantes and Fillmore. A big three-story apartment house, one I've gone by a thousand times on the way to Marin or the Marina, has completely buckled. The building has been brought to its knees. It leans over at a demented angle. The first story was squished, crazed, splintered; in parts it's only two feet high. It doesn't seem possible that anyone could have survived in there. It doesn't seem possible that I'm seeing this.*

(I later found out that a three-and-one-half-month-old infant and two adults, a 40-year-old woman and a man, died in there. That was one hour earlier.)

The police turn me back after Fillmore. I circle around Chestnut, come in at

Pierce. I keep riding. The flames are getting closer, casting dancing patterns on the pavement.

A policeman named Harry Walsh, standing on Mission Street, looked east toward the docks to see dozens of frenzied long-horned cattle stampeding toward him. Some Mexican vaqueros had been driving a herd of cattle from the wharves to the stockyards in the southern part of town; when the earthquake hit, they ran off, leaving the panic-stricken animals to fend for themselves. As the maddened cattle ran along the sidewalk between Fremont and First, a warehouse collapsed, killing most of them. Walsh shot the wounded cattle to put them out of their misery, but realized he had only six bullets left and more longhorns were rushing toward him. He asked a man named John Moller, who owned a saloon on the street, for ammunition.

"There was no time to think. Two of the steers were charging right at us while I was asking him to help, and he started to run for his saloon. I had to be quick about my part of the job because, with only a revolver as a weapon, I had to wait until the animal was quite close before I dared fire. Otherwise I would not have killed or even stopped him. As I shot down one of them I saw the other charging after John Moller, who was then at the door of his saloon and apparently quite safe. But as I was looking at him and the steer, Moller turned, and seemed to become paralyzed with fear. He held out both hands as if beseeching the beast to go back. But it charged on and ripped him before I could get near enough to fire." Moller was fatally gored.

6:25 P.M., Beach and Divisadero. *The stench of gas is heavy; a lot of mains have ruptured. It's a four-story apartment building that's lighting up the sky. I'm across the street and the heat is so intense I'm sweating. Eighty or 90 firefighters are there. It's a five-alarm fire. (Each alarm brings one truck and three engines.) Big yellow five-inch hoses, 1,000 feet long, are running down the street. They vanish around the corner, where they connect up to a fireboat pumping water out of the bay. Later a fire marshal praised that fireboat, which had been in mothballs. "She saved the Marina," he said.*

As the west wall falls in with a crash, I think, There's nothing anthropomorphic about nature. It fucks you, or it doesn't fuck you. And you don't get to say anything about it. The world is not made to man's specifications. In the next few days the whole city dimly realizes this, feels the weird backwash of this meaningless force, and everybody is uneasy for a long time.

I ride off. Darkness is falling. A block away from the fire, at Scott, a house has collapsed forward, leaning off-line seven or eight feet. My God, there's damage everywhere here. People are still streaming on foot or on bike toward the flames, but now the cops are starting to turn them away. A crowd is gathered at a roadblock. A Latino man of 40 or so is shouting at a cop. "You have to let me go in there! My family is in there! Before I do something crazy!" He's on the edge of hysteria.

An old woman, standing in front of a house with severe cracks in it, says something angrily to her daughter in Italian. Her daughter shakes her head and says back with exasperation, "No, Mom, you can't light candles!"

On the way back home, for the first time I realize what it's like to be in a big city without lights. A motor scooter almost runs me down. Intersections are unknown pools. Approaching headlights are completely blinding. I wish I had lights. I'm riding on faith.

The neighborhood now called South of Market used to be called South of the Slot (after the "slot" of the Market Street cable car). It was the poor side of the tracks. In 1900, the population density there was second only to that of Chinatown, making it one of the most crowded neighborhoods in the United States. Thousands of poor, transient, immigrant, and working-class San Franciscans were packed into the wood-framed hotels and apartments that lined streets like Sixth, Howard, Folsom, and Harrison and alleys like Shipley, Clara, Natoma, and Tehama. Most of this area was built on what used to be a tidal marsh surrounding Mission Bay, part of the vast stretches of San Francisco that had been reclaimed from Mission Bay, Mission Creek, and the swamps, marshes, streams, and pastures that used to surround them. This "made land" was known to be unstable as soon as it was created.

A striking thing about the 1906 disaster is the way that death and destruction stalked the city's vanished waters. Like an unforgiving palimpsest, horror traced the places that had once been beautiful. It's as if nature had taken revenge on the city for having profaned her.

Sixth Street is now one of the last remaining vestiges of San Francisco's old Skid Row, filled with crazy people, parolees, street hustlers, and assorted lost souls. In 1906 Sixth Street was less Bosch-like but still pretty rough around the edges. Four cheap boardinghouses lined it between Howard and Natoma. They stood on what had once been a marshy pond known as Pioche's Lake. The five-story, 300-room Brunswick House stood on the corner of Sixth and Howard. Lined up next to it, going north toward Natoma Street, were three other large boardinghouses: the Ohio, the Lormor, and the Nevada. More than 1,000 people were living in these buildings, and most of them were asleep at 5:12 A.M.

The shock waves, coming from the west, hit South of Market like an enormous sledgehammer, literally shoving the land up against Rincon Hill to the east. As the earth jerked violently to the east, the watery soil under the cheap structures liquefied. Their foundations sank unevenly into watery sludge, the intolerable pressure cracking joists and vertical beams.

The Nevada House was the first to go. It began tilting crazily to the south, then completely collapsed onto the Lormor. The Lormor in turn fell over against the Ohio, and all three buildings collapsed like dominos against the Brunswick, which fell over on Howard Street like a drunk.

Two doctors were staying nearby and arrived at the Brunswick House within minutes. "There was a terrible, low, heart-rending cry of utter resignation" from the people trapped in the building, one of the doctors reported. Many of the people on the top floors managed to crawl out. But hundreds in the floors below were either crushed to death or trapped beneath tons of beams and plaster. Those who survived cried for help. Rescuers began frantically digging at the rubble. But they did not have much time. For almost as soon as the Brunswick House fell, it started to burn.

8 P.M., Jackson and Hyde. *As I pass a little candlelit bistro, a voice yells out my name. Wonderful coincidence in the hot darkness: It's my cousin Jonathan, who's sitting and having a beer. I use the phone of his friend to call my parents. Everybody's fine, including my sister, who lives in Santa Cruz, and my brother, who owns a home right next to the Cypress Structure. I have finally figured out what that means—a section of the freeway.*

10:45 P.M. *Jon and I jump on our bikes. No lights, hardly any cars. There's a very strange but familiar quality about this night. Heading down the eastern edge of Nob*

Hill, we both realize what it is: We feel like we're in the High Sierra. The warm smell of burned wood, the darkness, the stars. The buildings loom up like mountains. You can imagine these hills without buildings. The city has temporarily returned to the land.

11 P.M., Rincon Hill. *We race past the big 76 clock at the Harrison Street entrance to the Bay Bridge. Up the ramp, onto the bridge. "This is the only time in our lives we'll ever get to do this!" my cousin shouts at me. I see flashing lights coming onto the bridge from the west. The monstrous gray structure is abandoned. We lose our nerve and go back after a few hundred yards.*

11:30 P.M., Sixth near Bluxome and Townsend. *Harsh moonlight yellows the police barricade that cordons off this little street, which runs parallel to the freeway. I know Bluxome well. It's a few hundred yards from the Yellow Cab lot where I worked for years. A building partially collapsed here, raining tons of brick and metal onto cars below. Five people died, including a man decapitated in his car. You can see the devastated roof to the east of the alley.*

The hulks of two flattened, chewed-up, burned-out cars sit in the middle of the street, well beyond the building that collapsed. We ask a cop how they got out there. He says they pulled them out there to try to recover the bodies.

It's a horrible sight. These lives were ended by bricks or fire for no reason. At least it must have been fast.

This is feeling more and more insane. It's hot, we're riding around on flimsy silent vehicles through an empty, dark city under a lurid moon, and in a few utterly unconnected places there are these sudden endings. It's completely random, like the V-1 bombs that fell on London during World War II.

The 1906 earthquake ravaged San Francisco, but it was the fire—or rather the 52 separate major fires that were caused by the quake—that destroyed it. Whether or not the city could have been saved is a question still debated today. San Francisco's firemen had been the pride of the city since the Gold Rush days, and the fire department one of the finest in the world. But the fire department was betrayed by the negligence of the city fathers and let down by two crucial decisions by unprepared leaders.

Fire chief Sullivan had pleaded with city officials for years to modernize San Francisco's water system and stockpile dynamite that could be used to create firebreaks. But the corrupt and incompetent administration of puppet mayor Eugene Schmitz, political boss Abe Ruef, and the Board of Supervisors—a bunch of paid-off hacks who were so greedy that they would, in Ruef's immortal phrase, "eat the paint off a house" (Ruef would have eaten the primer)—refused to allocate the money for the necessary improvements. Then, when the quake hit, most of the water mains broke, leaving the firefighters with empty hoses to fight the largest urban conflagration in American history. The tragic death of Fire Chief Sullivan left the department leaderless in its hour of need. Finally, Mayor Schmitz and General Frederick Funston made two fateful decisions. First, Funston called in the U.S. Army and Schmitz ordered troops to shoot looters on sight. Second, the authorities decided their only recourse was to try to stop the fire by making widespread use of explosives—even though they lacked dynamite and had no experience in using the weak explosives they did have. The two decisions were understandable, but together they probably doomed the city.

Former fireman and firefighting expert Dennis Smith argues in *San Francisco Is Burning: The Untold Story of the 1906 Earthquake and Fire* that the presence of often undisciplined and trigger-happy troops, combined with Schmitz's draconian shoot-to-kill order, prevented San Franciscans from fighting the fire themselves—which they could have successfully done. (The old Mint at Fifth and Market, for example, was saved by its workers.) Again and again, residents or neighbors were needlessly driven from their houses or offices by zealous troops and police, and the buildings they had been defending were left to burn or blown up. San Francisco archivist Gladys Hansen estimates that 500 people, many of them innocent, were shot by soldiers—one-sixth the total number of casualties. Another historian of the earthquake and fire, Philip Fradkin, agrees with Smith and Hansen that Schmitz's looting order was disastrous. He also concurs that the incompetent use of explosives created more fires than it stopped—including the fire that consumed Chinatown and the one that destroyed Russian Hill and North Beach.

Different decisions might, perhaps, have saved much of San Francisco. But nothing could have saved the hundreds of people trapped in the wreckage of the buildings near Sixth and Howard.

In the moments after the quake hit, a third-floor lodger in the Nevada House named William Stehr tried to decide whether to jump out the window to the roof of the Lormor House next door. As he thought it over, the Lormor House suddenly collapsed with a tremendous roar. Then he heard the Brunswick House collapse. He reached for the door and tried to open it. At that moment, Stehr said, "I felt the floor tilting and sinking under me, and I knew the house was going down like the others. So I hung on instinctively to the door handle while the whole floor dropped. As it sank, I felt three distinct bumps as the lower floor collapsed in turn under the weight of the roof and top story. With each bump came a frightful crash and cracking of timbers and glass and the cries of other people in the house who were being destroyed. The cries of the people who were being killed, especially the women, were dreadful to hear."

Stehr was knocked unconscious but managed to drag himself out of the wreckage when he came to. He could hear the horrible screams of people as the fire caught them, then an equally horrible silence. Rescuers hacked frantically at the rubble with axes, trying to free a little girl. As the flames became intolerably hot, other men held a wet blanket between them and the fire. They pulled the little girl to safety just as the flames raced over the spot.

Most of those trapped were not as fortunate. Another man who managed to escape one of the collapsed boardinghouses said he overheard a conversation between two people trapped in the rubble. One person said, "I'm not hurt, but there's a beam across my back and I can't get out from under it." The other replied, "I'm caught too, it's my wrist. Don't worry, they'll get us out." They did not know that flames were already beginning to eat at the timbers that trapped them. Minutes later, they were burned alive.

A few blocks away, near Mission and Third, another man was trapped under tons of rubble, with only his head protruding. Flames from a fire that had started in a Chinese laundry two blocks away on Howard Street were rapidly approaching. "Don't leave me here to die like this," the man begged again and again. A large middle-age man stepped forward, leaned over, and spoke quietly to the trapped man for a minute, his hand holding the back of his head. Then he stood up, drew a revolver, took aim, and killed the man with a single shot to the head.

More people died near Sixth and Howard than anywhere else in the city. The total number of fatalities will never be known, but it was probably at least 300, and possibly 500 or more. For decades, the official death count for the entire disaster stood at only about 450 people. This low figure served the needs of city officials and businessmen, who as soon as the flames were out began trying to convince the world that all was well, San Francisco was open for business, and there was nothing to fear. It was not until 1980, when Gladys Hansen began trying to compile a complete list of all those killed in the earthquake and fire, that the absurdly low death total was revised up 3,000—and that historians began to grasp how dreadful the carnage was South of the Slot.

Midnight, Folsom and Sixth Streets. *Sixth has been hit hard. It's buckled up in the middle, sloping away on each side. There's heavy damage around here. We swing down Shipley Street, a bizarre little South of Market alley whose buildings offer the most dramatic remaining evidence of the 1906 catastrophe. Shipley subsided by as much as five feet after the quake, taking the buildings on the street down with it. When the streets were raised, many of the buildings ended up half-buried. Some of them also lean noticeably to one side or the other, or backward. They're still inhabited. They seem to have made it through this one okay.*

Wednesday, October 18, 12:30 A.M. *We hear the sound of sea lions barking as we come over Leavenworth on Nob Hill. We light candles and fall asleep.*

While the South of Market fires raged out of control, a slower-moving blaze had started in the wholesale district, near Clay and Davis, and begun methodically moving to the west. Firemen hoped to hold the line at Sansome Street, but soon had to fall back, fighting block to block. Meanwhile, a catastrophe had erupted behind them. At 9 A.M. that morning, an unknown resident of a house at Gough and Hayes kindled a fire in his or her kitchen stove, not knowing that the flue had been damaged. Sparks ignited the wall. Because all the firemen were fighting other blazes, the fire quickly spread to the west, south, and east. The "Ham and Eggs" fire, as it was called, would eventually burn a larger area than any other fire.

11:30 A.M. *Hot again. Steamy. Impossible to get a paper. I walk 15 blocks—Polk, Van Ness, California, Broadway. A pile of bricks has fallen off a roof and smashed the back window of a car on Clay. Finally I give up and listen to the radio.*

It's useless to work. I get on my bike and ride out with a friend to the beach and the park. In Golden Gate Park a bizarre holiday atmosphere prevails. At 25th

Avenue big piles of masonry litter the street. Many buildings are damaged. It's amazing that more people who had been walking on the streets weren't killed.

Baker Beach is crowded. Naked bodies. Apocalyptic tales and sentimental anecdotes fill the airwaves. I feel like I should be more disturbed. All the national media say I should be. Pious pronouncements are everywhere. A pathetic moralizer in the sports department at the New York Times *says they should call off the Series. I am, however, unhappy to discover I have only $9.25 in the bank.*

Along the waterfront and in the old Barbary Coast, U.S. Navy Lieutenant Frederick Freeman led his men in an all-out fight to save the city's streets and its vital wharves, hauling heavy hoses over the hills, blasting sea water pumped out of the bay, rushing to every hot spot without orders or authority, taking it on himself to try to save what he could. Working for three days with almost no sleep, Freeman was everywhere, his trademark cry—"Okay, men, let's sock it to 'em!"—inspiring those he commanded to find strength when strength was gone. As Smith movingly recounts in his book, Freeman never received official credit for his actions during the fire. Later this decent man's life took a terrible downward spiral: Suffering from depression and with a drinking problem, he was abruptly cashiered from the Navy after a ship under his command was torpedoed. He was denied medical help and a pension and died of cancer, a sad and forgotten man. But in San Francisco's most desperate hour, he was its greatest hero.

8 P.M., Jackson and Jones. *The entrance to my apartment building is terrifyingly dark. I'd been so hedonistic at the beach I'd forgotten to buy candles. This is like a play emergency. I roast a chicken with garlic and lemon and cook couscous. My beer is miraculously cold. What a quake. Send money.*

11 P.M. *Stir-crazy. I ride through silent North Beach; it's still blacked out. A few people are drinking in Gypsy's. I head out the Embarcadero, using the headlights of passing cars to see if the road is safe. I circle the base of Telegraph Hill, pass Pier 39, and go through Aquatic Park and out to the end of Municipal Pier. The foreground is black, but downtown—including the Transamerica Pyramid, which sits in the exact center of a gentle bowl—glitters. It looks like a great ship just coming over the horizon.*

Midnight. *I head down Divisadero near Hayes. The whole north side of town is dark and dead. I want some warm place with lights and human beings. Two ragged kids in black leather are going into the Kennel Club. It seems too young and vicious in there. I head over to Haight, a bit warily. A friend lives on Baker and Fulton; she said that when one of her neighbors went out to the car to listen to the radio, a guy appeared, stuck a gun in his face, and said, "Give me the car, motherfucker."*

I go into Nickie's BBQ. It's packed. Great calypso music is throbbing. I don't feel like dancing. Being in here is like watching your last candle going out in a cave. The darkness is pressing in from the outside.

By Thursday, San Franciscans had begun to realize that the entire city might burn. Tens of thousands of people flooded into parks, squares, any open spaces where they would be safe from the flames.

As most of the city fled, one sound was heard everywhere, a monotonous noise so omnipresent it almost drove some people mad: the scraping sound of trunks being dragged along the ground.

Firemen made a desperate stand on Powell Street, hoping that Union Square would provide a firebreak. But they had to give up when the flames jumped the street and ignited the roof of a building on Bush Street. Nob Hill was now doomed. Within hours, the ornate mansions that had once thumbed their noses at the city below burned to the ground. The last chance to stop the fire would be Van Ness, two blocks away.

More photographs were taken of the San Francisco disaster than any event in history to that time. The most famous photographer in San Francisco was Arnold Genthe, a poet with a camera whose photographs of old Chinatown are as eloquent as Eugène Atget's photographs of fin de siècle Paris. Genthe's studio and apartment was on 790 Sutter Street, and all his small cameras were damaged by falling plaster. So he walked down to a camera shop on Montgomery and asked the owner if he could borrow a camera. "Take anything you want. This place is going to burn up anyway," the owner told him. Genthe took a 3A Kodak, stuffed his pockets with film, and wandered through town taking photographs. At some point he stopped on Sacramento Street just east of Taylor, near the summit of Nob Hill, and shot a picture looking downhill at the flames consuming downtown.

The resulting photo was voted one of the 10 best news photographs of all time. What makes it so striking is the strange contrast between the inconceivable destruction—the vast billowing clouds of smoke that cover downtown, the apartment building whose front wall has fallen off, the heaps of rubble in the street—and the group of people sitting casually on chairs in the foreground, looking for all the world like they are watching a movie of a disaster instead of the thing itself.

Friday, October 20, 11 A.M. *The weather has changed: It's gusty, moist. Rain is coming. I bike to the top of the steepest street in town, Filbert at Hyde. I ask an old man there if he suffered any damage. Not a thing, he replies, except a big brass amphora that went spinning around. Two minutes later, at the bottom of the hill across Gough, I see houses severely damaged on Francisco Street.*

11:10 A.M., Marina Middle School. *This is a disaster-relief point. The schoolyard is a hive, with long lines of mostly patient, almost all well-to-do Marina residents. (Joe DiMaggio stood in line here, I later learned.) City officials are sitting at little school desks. It's bureaucratic chaos. "Three days!" shouts out a man. "You haven't cleared me to go in, and my house isn't even damaged!" Inside the school, dozens of clean-cut young people are volunteering for the Red Cross. I talk to an old, laughing man leaning on a handcart. "I lost my wife!" he says. "I hope I don't find her!" He's going to get some things out of his sister-in-law's house in the cordoned-off area.*

Inscribed on the walls of the school are a number of immortal names—Pericles, Michelangelo, Shakespeare, Aristotle, and Archimedes. It was Archimedes who said, "Give me a lever and a place to stand, and I will move the earth."

As firemen began blowing up the buildings on Van Ness, the fires to the southwest raged out of control. The Ham and Eggs fire had joined the South of Market fires and raced deep into the Mission, killing the people trapped in the Valencia Hotel who had not already been crushed or drowned. The flames consumed almost everything between South Van Ness (then called Howard) and Dolores as far south as 20th Street, and were threatening to climb over the hill and burn the entire district.

Then, miraculously, a hydrant at 20th and Church, at the panoramic top of Dolores Park, was found to be working.

A small group of exhausted firemen began pulling their heavy engine up Dolores Street. Yelling like soldiers charging into battle, 300 refugees who were camped in the park ran to join them. Inch by inch, blocking the wheels after each pull, the crowd and the firemen dragged the engine up to the hydrant. It took more than an hour. When the firemen connected their hose to the Greenberg hydrant and a great jet of water shot out, the crowd cheered again. Finally armed, the firemen dragged the hose down the hill to the flames on Guerrero and Lexington and faced down the raging inferno along 20th Street. Three thousand San Franciscans joined them. Shoulder to shoulder, San Francisco's finest—firemen, policemen, and citizens—battled the flames. It took seven brutal hours, but they held the line. The fire would not cross 20th Street.

The so-called golden hydrant is still there. It is painted gold every April 18.

11:30 A.M., Pierce and Chestnut. *The cops won't let me in, but I luckily run into a friend who lives there. In one collapsed building you can look right through a smashed wall at a big white chair and an ottoman facing a TV. The sight is somehow obscene.*

People are packing their belongings. Ahead of us, two old women walk with dignity in their best clothes. The older one, who is at least 80, is carrying a tightly furled umbrella.

We go into my friend's trashed apartment. "Let's drink everything," she says. We sit there and toss down the last of her cognac, then take care of her Bushmills miniature, then her E&J brandy, then her rum.

Saturday, October 21. *I hear they pulled someone alive from the Cypress Structure.*

The fire that burned Nob Hill roared to the west, but a mighty stand along the Van Ness corridor stopped it. That should have been the end. But in a bitter final twist, just when the fire had been contained, the unnecessary demolition of a building filled with inflammable chemicals at Vallejo and Van Ness started a new blaze. This fire, blown by westerly winds, climbed Russian Hill—where a few houses on the summit were saved by determined owners and neighbors—and burned North Beach to the ground. Only a few houses atop Telegraph Hill, soaked with wine, survived. In a life-and-death evacuation on the northern waterfront, as many as 30,000 refugees were saved from the advancing flames by a motley flotilla of boats, including junks, lanteen-rigged Ligurian fishing boats, tugs, pleasure craft, naval ships, and anything else that would float. It was San Francisco's Dunkirk.

Then it was all over, and there was nothing for San Franciscans to do except look around at what someone called "the damndest fine ruins" and start rebuilding.

The 1906 earthquake and fire was the greatest disaster ever to befall an American city. The Galveston hurricane of 1900, which is estimated to have killed at least 6,000 people, is its only possible rival, but Galveston's population was 37,000; San Francisco's was 400,000. Outside of war, the blaze that destroyed the heart of San Francisco was the largest metropolitan fire in history. During the four days that the inferno lasted, more than 3,000 people were killed, 28,188 buildings were burned, 522 blocks leveled, and 200,000 people were left homeless. San Francisco's entire downtown (except for one small area), its three most historic neighborhoods (Nob, Russian, and Telegraph Hills, except for a few blocks on the summits of the latter two), the Civic Center, much of Hayes Valley, a big swath of the Mission, and the entire South of Market area down to Townsend Street—all were utterly destroyed. The 4.7-square-mile, 3,000-acre burned area was six times larger than that consumed by the Great Fire of London in 1666, and twice as large as that lost in the Chicago fire of 1871. Its perimeter was 9.3 miles long. If you lay a map of the burned area over a map of Manhattan, it would run from Houston Street all the way to 65th Street and cover at least half of the east-west area between them.

The ruins looked like the bombed-out wastelands of Dresden, Tokyo, or Hamburg in World War II. It was the closest thing to an urban apocalypse this country has ever seen.

Midnight, October 19, Clay and Jones. *The end of another day spent chasing the quake, across a once-familiar place that has become big and unknown. I look down the steep hill into Chinatown. The bridge is stretched across the darkness. The lights on its suspension cables abruptly end at the point where it has collapsed.*

Thousands of buildings rest on the unquiet earth. The lights in downtown have come back on, but Nob Hill is cloaked in a strange intimate darkness. For a moment it is absolutely still.

Atop that silent hill, it seems fitting that the titanic forces that created this frag-ile sand castle at the edge of the sea should be the same ones that destroyed it once before, and have just tried to destroy it again. We are drawn to this place because of its beauty. But that beauty is the tip of a deadly iceberg. At the beginning of the Duino Elegies, *Rilke wrote, "For beauty's nothing but the beginning of terror, which we are still just able to endure." The line could be posted on top of every hill in town.*

San Francisco offers a rare gift: a chance to live face-to-face with the inhuman universe. That gift comes at a price. But it is one that those of us who live here are willing to pay. To dance on the brink of the world . . .

I push off into the night. The hill takes me, the wind whistles past. As I fly down, I want to say some words in homage to my city. And to the earth—restless, carrying its weight of unknowable power—that lies beneath it.

CHAPTER 36

CITY BEAUTIFUL

Grant Avenue and Post Street

C*hristmas shopping.* That's the first and only thought that came into my mind when I walked down to Grant and Post a few days ago. For years, I stood here at retail shopping ground zero, another consumer in the madding crowd. Fancy stores, money changing hands, full shopping bags, "Angels We Have Heard on High" wafting from somewhere, well-dressed people walking fast, foggy afternoons in late December. I don't have any associations with this corner beyond those. But I do have an impression. Every time I've been on this corner, I've always had a subliminal feeling of urban elegance. I never knew why I had that feeling. Now I do. And that knowledge has permanently altered the way I see not just this intersection but San Francisco's entire downtown.

Downtowns are usually invisible. You're too busy shopping, running errands, trying to get to the bus, or just lost in your own thoughts to notice the buildings you're scurrying past. There are exceptions, like Manhattan's Fifth

Avenue, whose mind-blowing verticality makes it impossible, at least for a visitor, to ignore. But most people never look up.

It isn't just distractions that make San Francisco's downtown—by which I mean the retail shopping area around Union Square—easy to miss. Downtown suffers for the sins of the Financial District and lower Market Street, which were blighted by the mindless construction of soulless high-rise buildings that started in the late 1950s and peaked in the late 1970s. This "Manhattanization" transformed San Francisco's low skyline, which had allowed the myriad gentle curves and dramatic slopes of its hills to be seen, into one indistinguishable from Houston's. For a mess of pottage, they killed something unique. The Union Square area was not invaded by these over-grown Legos, but urban ecology is delicate, and the towering mediocrities to the east and south of downtown cast a long shadow, literal and figurative.

Very few people who walk down Grant Avenue realize that they are walking down a street that a leading California architectural journal once called the greatest architectural street in the world. That claim is exaggerated, but it's not completely baseless. Once I started paying attention, I realized that this street and those around it are indeed distinguished, a harmonious ensemble of elegant buildings. That harmony was responsible for my subliminal impression of elegance.

Urban architecture turns out to be the last cheap thrill. All you need is a little curiosity, and a few books, and you get a free lifetime pass to an entirely new city.

There is nothing spectacular about most of the buildings around here. In fact, only architectural historians even recognize them as possessing an identifiable style. Mention San Francisco architecture, and most people simply think of wooden Victorian houses with ornate facades and bay windows. But downtown San Francisco is a treasure—a largely intact time capsule from the greatest era of city building in American history, the early 20th century.

San Francisco's downtown is so cohesive because it was built at basically the same time. Almost the entire downtown came into existence between 1906 and 1931, with the majority of it going up between 1906 and 1912. Paradoxically, what was responsible for this development was the greatest calamity ever to befall an American city, the earthquake and fire of 1906. It is almost axiomatic that the Great Quake destroyed a beautiful, romantic city and gave birth to an inferior modern one. But as architectural historian Michael Corbett argues in his fascinating 1979 book *Splendid Survivors: San Francisco's Downtown Architectural Heritage* (which meticulously ranks every architecturally significant building in downtown San Francisco as part of a campaign to halt Manhattanization), the disaster could be seen as a "fortunate catastrophe." By sweeping away a cluttered and ungainly Victorian downtown, the fire literally cleared the ground for a human-scaled new district whose dignified buildings possess a rare unity of design.

The architects who rebuilt San Francisco were inspired not just by a design aesthetic but also by an entire vision of what a city could be. The City Beautiful movement made its triumphal debut at the 1893 World's Columbian Exposition in Chicago. Architect Daniel Burnham and a distinguished team designed an entire city-within-a-city for the fair, whose chest-beating rationale was to celebrate the 400th anniversary of Columbus's "discovery" of America. Burnham's White City, as it was called with unintentional irony, was a monument to grand, rational planning, featuring wide, symmetrical boulevards and imposing white Beaux-Arts buildings of uniform cornice height. The Beaux-Arts style took its name from the École des Beaux-Arts in Paris, which many of America's (and San Francisco's) leading architects attended. Inspired by the buildings of imperial Rome, the Italian Renaissance, and the French and Italian baroque, Beaux-Arts architecture aspired to capture the classical virtues of order and harmony in a grand but flexible style.

The City Beautiful movement, as reflected in Burnham's White City and its Beaux-Arts buildings, had an enormous impact on American city planning and architecture. Spurred by the increasing squalor and poverty of America's inner cities depicted in works like Jacob Riis's *How the Other Half Lives* (1889), City Beautiful proponents embraced reformist goals, some of which now appear laughable. They believed a city rebuilt according to their plans would not only achieve the obvious good of removing slums and tenements, it would also inspire and uplift the urban poor with its vision of a shared civic life.

The City Beautiful movement was a creature of its time—idealistic, in hindsight naïve in its belief in the ameliorative power of beauty, but well-meaning. And its effects on American cities, from Detroit to Washington to Chicago to San Francisco, were overwhelmingly positive.

At the turn of the century, many prominent San Franciscans were profoundly dissatisfied with their city. Allan Pollock, manager of the St. Francis Hotel, warned his fellow citizens that upstart Los Angeles was making itself more enticing to visitors than San Francisco, which had "little really attractive" to offer tourists or residents. Pollock was particularly harsh on his city's architecture, denouncing its wooden buildings as "hideous in design and flimsy in finish—architectural shams of lumber and paint." At Pollock's urging, a group of notables formed the Association for the Improvement and Adornment of San Francisco, electing former mayor James Phelan president. Phelan was equally concerned about the city's future. He said it was time for San Francisco to become "a great and wonderful city, or wander aimlessly to an uncertain end."

Phelan was so impressed with Burnham's White City that he invited the architect and planner to draw up a plan to remake the entire city. Burnham accepted and arrived in San Francisco in fall 1904. His custom, when working on city plans, was to find a high point from which to look down upon his urban canvas, and he asked Phelan to provide him with a house on 910-foot-high Twin Peaks, whose view of downtown is jaw-dropping. Phelan agreed, and Burnham's former student, Willis Polk, built Burnham a cabin on a spur of the hill in Diamond Heights.

Burnham famously said, "Make no little plans. They have no magic to stir men's blood and probably themselves will not be realized." He was true to his word. His plan called for the entire city to be remade to look, as one architect commented, "like Paris, with hills." At the heart of his vision was a series of Parisian *rond-points* (roundabouts) and open spaces, with wide radial and diagonal streets cutting through the 19th-century grid. A Roman-inspired civic center at Van Ness and Market would form the city's center, from which would radiate nine wide boulevards. Following Burnham's precept that every citizen should be within walking distance of a park, the area around Lake Merced, in the southwestern corner of the city, would be transformed into a vast public green space, even bigger than Golden Gate Park. The Panhandle would be extended all the way to the civic center. The streets on Nob and Russian Hills would be taken off the grid and rebuilt to follow the circular contours of the hills. Telegraph Hill was to be crowned with a templelike structure, with Italianate villas ringing its base. As for Twin Peaks, it would be crowned with a majestic "Athenaeum" consisting of "courts, terraces and colonnaded shelters," the latter "arranged after the manner of the great Poecile of the Villa Hadrian." In the center of the Athenaeum, "the moral and geographical center of the city" overlooking the Pacific, would stand a "colossal figure symbolical of San Francisco."

Some of Burnham's ideas, like Baron Haussmann's for Paris, were too grandiose for their site. His Greco-Roman plan for Telegraph Hill, as former San Francisco city planning director James McCarthy noted in his introduction to the facsimile reprint of the 1906 plan, would have destroyed "the tight little medieval Italian hill town that we cherish today." Others might not have translated well to the automobile age: His grand boulevards might have turned into ugly ring roads. And Burnham—who was later criticized by Louis Sullivan and Frank Lloyd Wright for excessive fealty to classicism—ignored the city's rich architectural history, evinced in the shingled redwood cabin Polk built for him, as well as its Victorian and Spanish colonial heritage.

But many of Burnham's ideas were decades ahead of their time. For example, he proposed combining small backyards in residential areas to form a chain of parks, 25 years before such a plan was implemented in Sunnyside Gardens in Queens. His proposal for one-way streets was also prescient—and not adopted in San Francisco until 1942. His still more visionary call for the city's downtown to be closed to traffic has yet to be adopted.

In September 1905, Burnham presented his vision to an enthusiastic audience at the St. Francis Hotel on Union Square. Burnham's plan wowed the city, and the Board of Supervisors commissioned a fancy $3,000 book illustrating the plan. Copies of it were sitting in City Hall on April 18, 1906, when the San Andreas Fault slipped and buried them, along with much of San Francisco.

At first, it appeared that the catastrophe was a divine intervention on Burnham's behalf. The sudden disappearance of the old city made his Olympian plan seem feasible. But resistance from business interests, a political scandal, the opposition of the *San Francisco Chronicle*, and the need to rebuild immediately doomed Burnham's dream. The only major part of his plan that was largely realized was the Civic Center, a spacious group of elegant Beaux-Arts buildings that is widely considered America's finest ensemble of public buildings outside Washington, D.C.

But the ideals of the City Beautiful movement and the Beaux-Arts style did not die with Burnham's plan. They shaped and guided the architects who rebuilt downtown. Those architects embraced the École's classical aesthetic, but they were equally concerned with making buildings that worked—ones with good light, adequate retail space, and so on. Design extravagances were always subordinated to functional considerations, which is why few of the downtown buildings possess the majesty of the Civic Center. Yet they are quietly creative in their design and in their details, and built to last.

The happy results of this dignified, modest aesthetic are still apparent on Grant Avenue, where many leading retail stores previously located a block east on Kearny Street moved after the fire. Take the Shreve Building and the Head Building, at Grant and Post. The two tallest buildings on the street, both built by William Curlett, they face each other on opposite sides of Post. The Shreve Building was built in 1905 and rebuilt after the fire, the Head Building in 1909. Both are fine three-part vertical blocks with unobtrusive Renaissance/baroque ornamentation. The Shreve is clad in luxurious Colusa sandstone, the Head in the terra-cotta favored in downtown buildings after the great fire, in which stone facings performed poorly. But what makes these buildings noteworthy is the way they function in tandem. Exactly the same height, they simultaneously form an imposing gate to Union Square, the city's urban heart one block west, and denote the heart of the shopping district on Grant, in a perfect location halfway between Market Street and the Chinatown Gate.

A similar matched set of buildings anchors Grant's beginning at Market Street. On the west side of Grant stands the Security Pacific National Bank, built in 1910 by Bliss and Faville. A variant of a classical temple, it is based on a design that is extremely hard to screw up, the Roman Pantheon. Facing it on the east side of Grant is the Wells Fargo Bank, also built in 1910, by Clinton Day (who built one of San Francisco's most beloved buildings, the City of Paris—torn down in 1980 and replaced by an inappropriate Philip Johnson pile). Also a modified Roman temple design, its elegant curved front on Market Street demonstrates the eclectic flexibility of the Beaux-Arts style. Across O'Farrell Street from both banks is another first-rate 1910 building, the Phelan, built by Curlett. Like most of the post-fire buildings in downtown, the flatiron Phelan has a "commercial" lower section used for window displays and an "architectural" upper section—an intelligent way of reconciling the needs of Mammon and beauty. This trio of buildings lends gravitas to an important Market Street gore.

Most of the post-fire buildings in the area are relatively conservative, but a few are daring. Close to the Chinatown Gate, the Pacific Telephone and Telegraph Building (Coxhead and Coxhead, 1908) tweaks the classical idiom with enlarged details, distorted elements and peculiar finesses, like the weird and wonderful entrance arch. Across Grant from the Shreve Building is the richly detailed 1908 Hastings Building by Meyer and O'Brien, whose sculptured female heads looking down from the top story lend it a piquant baroque air.

There are dozens more fine buildings like these, on Grant, Post, Sutter, and adjoining streets. Few of them are masterpieces like Willis Polk's stunning glass-curtained 1918 Hallidie Building or Albert Pissis's 1892 Hibernia Bank Building, which now languishes on the blighted first block of Jones Street near a methadone clinic, but was regarded by Pissis's contemporaries as the finest building in the city. In a way, though, that's precisely the point. They are proof that professionalism, when it is guided by a superior design aesthetic and informed by a shared urban vision, can produce beautiful buildings whose sum is more than their individual parts.

So the next time I'm Christmas shopping at Grant and Post, with the carols drifting down above the hurrying crowds, I will look for something besides the window displays. I will look for a past world that still lives, in buildings embodying a civic vision that has not lost its power to inspire. Quietly but eloquently, those buildings proclaim their message of harmony, restraint, and grace. Angels we have heard on high, indeed.

CHAPTER 37

TRYING TO FIND CHINATOWN

Tien Hou Temple, 125 Waverly Place

My earliest memory of San Francisco is of a visit to Chinatown with my parents at night. A phantasmagorical kaleidoscope of glittering lights, exotic buildings with winged roofs, hordes of mysterious people packing the narrow streets—I felt like I had been transported to a parallel universe where a perpetual night was perpetually illuminated.

Childhood visions don't die; they become ghosts. And somewhere that dream Chinatown still haunts me, a platonic original that seems more real than the actual one. For me, everything that is unknown and alluring and intricate and deep and wondrous about cities, especially cities at night, goes back to that flickering neon memory.

It was, of course, all an illusion. As I grew up, I realized that the otherworldly Chinatown of my memory was a parlor trick, conjured up with strings of 100-watt bulbs. Concealed beneath Chinatown's romantic veneer was a very unromantic slum, where thousands of impoverished people were squeezed into decaying tenements. By day, the City of Magical Night looked pretty dreadful.

But that judgment, too, turned out to be an illusion. In fact, it was a bigger illusion than my childish belief in a fairy-tale Chinatown. For the paradoxical truth is that Chinatown's fake surfaces are authentic in their own strange way. And still more paradoxically, those glittering facades can even be seen as appropriate symbols of a neighborhood whose inhabitants have transcended the constraints of poverty. It may not be in the way that I imagined, but Chinatown is indeed a magical place.

The Chinese who began arriving in 1848 were drawn to San Francisco for the same reason all the other 49ers were: the desire to get rich. Also like most other 49ers, they did not intend to stay.

The first Chinese immigrants, relatively few in number, were welcomed. In 1850, Mayor John W. Geary invited the "China boys," as they were called, to march in the funeral procession for President Zachary Taylor. In a ceremony in Portsmouth Square, a justice said, "You stand among us in all respects as equals." The governor urged that they be given land grants, and naturalization was offered.

The China boys sent a warm response to the mayor. But they did not want to become U.S. citizens, even though doing so meant they would not have to pay the tax imposed on foreign miners. They had no interest in becoming Americans. They were, in sociological parlance, "sojourners": They were just passing through.

There were a number of reasons why the Chinese did not regard the United States as their home. As Erica Y. Z. Pan points out in *The Impact of the 1906 Earthquake on San Francisco's Chinatown*, the Chinese government opposed emigration: To live abroad for a long time or to become a citizen of another country was treasonous, and families of émigrés could be executed. The émigrés had left their families behind because they planned to return. Of equal importance, there was an enormous cultural rift between the Chinese and the Americans—one created by both parties. As Pan writes, "They had come to make money, not to obtain citizenship. Their homes would always be in China where their ancestors had lived. It was their belief that once a Chinese acquired citizenship in the U.S., he became a lost son to China. More important was the conviction that China was a more civilized country than the United States. There was no incentive to acquaint themselves with a 'barbarian' culture or language."

American racism and hostility exacerbated Chinese separatism. In the gold mines and in San Francisco, where the Chinese had begun to settle around Portsmouth Square after one of the disastrous fires destroyed the area, the Yankees made it clear that the only use they had for the Chinese was as cheap labor. And soon, they rejected even that.

The initial trickle of Chinese immigrants, almost all of them Cantonese from the Pearl River Delta in Guangdong Province, soon became a flood. By 1853, 4,000 had arrived and Chinatown, centered on Sacramento and Dupont (Grant), was considered a separate district. The Chinese took the jobs white men would not take, like doing laundry, and would work for much lower wages. By the late 1860s, Chinatown was a large retail, service, and entertainment district that contained almost two-thirds of the Chinese in San Francisco.

Anti-Chinese sentiment exploded in the dark decade of the 1870s. Attacks on Chinese miners and the completion of the transcontinental railroad led thousands of unemployed Chinese to return to San Francisco, where they encountered angry whites who had been thrown out of work by the depression of 1873. By this time, the Chinese dominated the shoe-making and sewing industries and had gained a virtual monopoly on clothing manufacturing and cigar making. (In the 1870s, the first union labels in the United States appeared on cigar boxes to distinguish cigars made by the Cigar Makers' Union from those made by Chinese.) The Chinese became scapegoats, their worst tormentors the Irish working class. Attacks upon Chinese, especially those outside Chinatown, forced those who had moved into other neighborhoods back inside. For a Chinese to venture west of the quarter's unofficial western border on Powell Street was to risk being set upon by hoodlums (the word, of uncertain etymology, originated in San Francisco).

White San Franciscans feared that the Chinese were taking over the city. In 1869 Dr. Li Po Tai began buying real estate, the first Chinese to do so. False rumors soon spread that the Chinese owned one-tenth of the city. In 1878 the *Sunday Chronicle* reported that the "Mongolian Octopus . . . has fastened its tentacles from Sacramento to Jackson on Dupont." The alarmed legislature passed a law in 1878 forbidding aliens debarred from citizenship to acquire title to real estate. As a result, at the time of the 1906 earthquake and fire, only 39 owners of property in Chinatown were Chinese. The majority of landlords were absentee white owners who charged their tenants double the normal rent.

For the overwhelmingly male population packed into the 12 blocks of Chinatown (for a long time almost all the women were prostitutes who had been shipped to America against their will), the neighborhood provided a refuge, an island of China in an alien land. It was, in effect, a ghetto—but it was a ghetto created by both external racism and internal inclination. As Pan notes, "It was a blessing for most Chinese who could not read English to have a corner of their own that resembled their hometown. Nevertheless, the congregation of this alien body was also their curse, for the place was too different from the rest of the city. It was an un-Americanized colony with its own colors, which seemed to stand in open mockery of the melting pot. Small wonder that many white San Franciscans resented its presence." Comments like "We hate the Negro because they are citizens. We hate the yellow dogs because they will not be" were widespread in the 19th century.

But as the Chinese put down roots in San Francisco, their attitudes toward America began to change. Increasingly, they began to feel that this country where they had spent so much of their lives was their home. Assimilation was spurred by Christian missions, and by the fact that many Chinese worked as domestic servants for white San Franciscans, who came to value and respect them. The desire to avoid persecution may also have played a role. Many Chinese were now willing to be naturalized.

Anti-Chinese violence reached its peak with the sandlot-orator-instigated riots of 1877, when more than 500 men stormed Chinatown from two directions and were beaten back by two phalanxes of police, one on Pine and one on Broadway. Five years later the notorious Chinese Exclusion Act was passed, which essentially froze Chinese immigration for decades.

If the Chinese were viewed with suspicion and contempt, Chinatown was seen as a menace to health and morality—"the shame of the city." It was dirty, overcrowded, and filled with brothels, opium dens, and gambling parlors. White San Franciscans did nothing to ameliorate these conditions, but they nonetheless cited them as a reason to tear down Chinatown or to move it as far away as possible.

The movement to get rid of Chinatown began as soon as there was a Chinatown. In 1882, a city supervisor proposed that the Chinese be moved to government reservations or else be "separated under police guard in a tent city near the city cemetery." Another group proposed to send all the Chinese back to China in a flotilla of ships. The nadir of these efforts took place in 1890, when the city suddenly declared Chinatown a hazard to public health and ordered its residents to move to a special site far away from the city, on pain of arrest. Federal courts, which consistently struck down San Francisco's attempts to force the Chinese out of town, declared the ordinance unconstitutional.

Not surprisingly, the very vices that so outraged white San Francisco proved irresistible to tourists. The more journalists, politicians, and moralists wrote outraged screeds about the district's brothels, opium dens, white slavery, (nonexistent) underground tunnels, gambling cellars, and hatchet men, the more tourists flocked into Chinatown, panting to see the unspeakable depravity for themselves.

Then came the 1906 fire. As they surveyed the smoking rubble of what had once been Chinatown (which was immediately looted by soldiers and citizens), the city fathers thought they had a golden opportunity to get rid of the despised quarter once and for all. "San Francisco may be freed from the standing menace of Chinatown," wrote the *Merchants' Association Review*. The *Oakland Monthly* editorialized, "Fire has reclaimed to civilization and cleanliness the Chinese ghetto, and no Chinatown will be permitted in the borders of the city." The Chinese were segregated and so poorly treated in San Francisco's refugee camps that President Roosevelt, facing diplomatic fallout, chided the city for its shoddy treatment of them.

Anti-Chinese sentiment made strange bedfellows. Mayor Eugene Schmitz and his crony, political boss Abe Ruef, were the archenemies of former mayor and City Beautiful proponent James Phelan, but they all agreed that the Chinese had to go. (Phelan's anti-Chinese and anti-Japanese bigotry is an ugly blot on his otherwise stellar civic record.)

Even before the quake, industrialist John Partridge had proposed building an "Oriental City" to replace Chinatown at San Francisco's longtime dumping ground, Hunters Point. Now Schmitz, Ruef, and Phelan came up with the same idea. The city convened a Subcommittee for the Permanent

Relocation of Chinatown, headed by Ruef, with Phelan a member. But when Ruef and Phelan tried to push through the relocation to the slaughterhouse district, they ran into immediate resistance.

Chinatown notables, who hitherto had prudently avoided any direct confrontation with the white establishment, initially remained silent. But empowered by an awareness of legal rights and political and economic power they had not previously known they possessed, they stood up for themselves for the first time. At a meeting on May 10, they said Hunters Point was too far away and they wanted to rebuild in the place they had always lived. Knowing that officials feared the loss of the revenue they generated, they warned the subcommittee that if they were not allowed to return to Chinatown, they would permanently move to Oakland, where most of them had ended up after leaving the refugee camps.

The all-powerful Six Companies, familial (surname-based) and district-based fraternal associations that essentially ran Chinatown, forgot their past quarreling and worked together to ensure the neighborhood's return. They realized that anti-Chinese attitudes would actually work in their favor: If they rebuilt Chinatown quickly, whites would not live there and "that way Chinatown would be easier to hold," as a Chinese newspaper pointed out. Their second trump card was white greed. Chinese merchants quickly began signing long leases at high rents from the white landlords who owned most of Chinatown.

In the face of unified and unwavering Chinese resistance, the San Francisco establishment admitted defeat. In June, after 25 committee meetings, Ruef asked for his committee to be dismissed. Phelan admitted that "legally the city had no right to prevent the Chinatown property owners to rebuild upon their own premises."

Reconstruction in Chinatown began almost immediately. By June 10, 12 businesses had opened in temporary structures. It took only two years to rebuild the entire quarter, a year ahead of the rest of the city.

The Chinatown that arose from the ashes of the old was greatly improved. Streets were widened, alleys were terminated or run through, and new buildings were fireproof, sanitary, and well ventilated. But the most striking change was to its appearance.

The original Chinatown consisted of drab Western-style buildings. They were later painted in bright colors with a few added Oriental motifs, but otherwise they were conventional. The post-quake Chinatown, by contrast, reveled in its exoticism, flaunted its otherness. And to achieve the desired look, its white architects, working with Chinese merchants, invented a "Chinese" vernacular that had never existed.

Knowing that their community had almost been erased, the Chinese aimed to placate the city by replacing the bad old Chinatown with a new, cleaned-up "Oriental City." More important, they, along with all the other stakeholders in Chinatown, realized that making Chinatown look more "Chinese" would attract tourists. As models, they had three recent proposals: the self-contained Chinese city proposed for Hunters Point, a planned Chinatown in San Mateo that was to consist of imitation Chinese houses, and a Japanese plan to buy up property in South Park, where a number of Japanese were already living, and create a Japanese colony called "the Young Tokio." None of these came to fruition, but they helped inspire the design for the new Chinatown.

As architect and historian Philip P. Choy notes in *The Architecture of San Francisco Chinatown*, the white architects searching for a "Sino-architectural vernacular" knew only about "pagodas and temples with turned-up eaves and massive curved roofs, forms and expressions that were already centuries old." And they had to create this "Chinese" look using Western construction techniques. The buildings they created used forms that in Chinese architecture are structural elements, like pagodas and complex roof supports, in a purely decorative way. They turned iron fire escapes into pseudo-balconies decorated with Chinese motifs like the "Double Happiness" character, and employed neoclassical design elements like loggias, corbels, coffer soffits, and dentils to simulate Chinese architecture. It was, in effect, a Potemkin Village.

Waverly Place is ground zero for this early-20th-century ethnic-themed Disneyland. One of the oldest streets in the city—formerly known as Pike Street, it was home to a brothel run by the notorious Belle Cora as well as her famous Chinese counterpart, Ah Toy—Waverly on its west side features an unbroken line of "Oriental" buildings that creates a magical effect. As Choy notes, "the illusion created is a masterful design solution, unique and indigenous, for it is neither East nor West. Rather, it is decidedly San Francisco."

Deception is an odd quality to be the foundation of a legendary neighborhood. Deception for the purposes of attracting tourists and placating a hostile white establishment seems even more dubious. And so Chinatown poses a semiotic riddle, one that goes all the way down to its essence. Standing on Waverly and looking up at the Tien Hou Temple and the buildings that adjoin it, should one see them as "authentic" or not? Is Chinatown a fake?

On one level, it obviously is. Chinatown's buildings are obviously not "authentic," if by that we mean organically connected to indigenous Chinese architecture. But they are authentic in a deeper sense.

Partly this is simply because they are old. Even the cheesiest and most artificial historical object becomes authentic once it gets old enough. But it goes beyond that. For the new Chinatown was authentic the moment it was created. It was never really Disneyland—or if it was Disneyland, Disneyland was reality. Chinatown was an organic expression of the desires of its inhabitants, an accurate reflection of a subculture at a given moment in historical time. The Chinese were a mercantile people, and the tourist-friendly fairyland they created reflected that. In a deeper sense, it reflected their in-between status as foreigners who were turning into Americans. Chinatown's appearance captures one critical moment in the long process by which an immigrant group, once outsiders and subjected to bigotry, intolerance, and violence, becomes a part of America. Paradoxically, the buildings created to fetishize Chinese-ness can be seen as the concrete embodiment of the melting pot.

As Pan argues, the 1906 catastrophe helped catalyze the integration of the Chinese into San Francisco in a number of ways. First, it began to change the attitudes of white San Franciscans. San Franciscans had always prided themselves on their tolerance and cosmopolitanism, and when President Roosevelt chided them for their mistreatment of the Chinese in the refugee camps, they were ashamed. The courage of the Chinese who helped clear the streets of rubble, and the loyalty of the Chinese domestics who risked their lives to save their families' children, impressed white San Franciscans. After the new Chinatown was built, a magazine apologized for past sins: "We have unwittingly perhaps held up to the public gaze for too long the more sensational phases of Chinese life. We have concentrated our vision over much on the differences between their lives and ours . . . and thus the racial gulf that separates the yellow and white peoples of the earth becomes increasingly widened instead of being bridged."

But the cataclysm also changed the attitudes of the Chinese. For the first time, they had spoken up on their own behalf. They had skin in the American game. And in the aftermath of the disaster that destroyed their neighborhood, they acknowledged their own share of responsibility for its problems.

After 1906, Chinese community leaders set out to clean up Chinatown's vices. They cracked down on idol worshipping, white slavery, the opium dens, and the gambling parlors. True, the anti-vice campaign was mostly driven by self-interest, just as the creation of an "Oriental City" was. But profound changes nonetheless followed both developments. Marketing is all-American, and the act of marketing their Chinese-ness to Americans made the Chinese more American. They became more deeply integrated into society, more open to Western ideas. Some began to cut their queues. As Pan sums it up, "They were moving toward the mainstream of American culture, even as they held on to their old Chinatown home."

But even if Chinatown's architecture is authentic in some sense, it also feels disturbingly like a false front, lipstick on a pig. Those never-neverland buildings may have been conjured up by the Chinese themselves, but their exotic facades conceal grinding poverty. Within Chinatown's 16-block area are packed 18,000 to 20,000 people, making it the second most densely populated part of the United States, after New York City's Chinatown. And these impoverished people are jammed into crumbling, century-old SROs with communal bathrooms and kitchens, or equally decrepit apartments.

I have been inside those tenements. My wife and I once went on a house-buying tour of one. It was a ramshackle, rotting building on Himmelmann Place, off Pacific above inner Chinatown, that had been divided into about 10 apartments, each one a small room crammed with people. Some of the tiny spaces were divided by sheets. In one room, a child of about 12 was doing his homework sitting on a top bunk bed, his head bent because the ceiling was so low.

This is how most of the people in Chinatown live. It's a slum with Orientalist architecture. It is a living museum, and the main attraction for the tourists who gawk through it is its "exotic" impoverished inhabitants. It's hard not to think that a visit to Chinatown is just a genteel form of slumming.

But there are slums and then there are slums. For cultural reasons, the Chinese have been able to rise above poverty and overcrowding. Chinatown has virtually no crime, and most of its inhabitants either choose to live there or put up with living there as part of a cost-benefit calculation. The head of that kid on the bunk bed was touching the ceiling, but he was doing his homework. Once you dig deeper into Chinatown, you realize that it serves a vital function for its inhabitants. And, most critically, there is no way to fundamentally alter it without destroying it.

Cindy Wu is the community planning manager for the Chinatown Community Development Center, a nonprofit agency whose mission for 35 years has been to improve the lives of Chinatown's residents. The CCDC has acquired and rehabbed 2,300 units of affordable housing in Chinatown and runs a variety of social services programs for its residents. "The main group of people living in Chinatown are seniors aging in place," Wu said. "There's a disproportionate number of them, more than anywhere else in the city. They live in SROs—40 percent of the housing in Chinatown is SROs. It's suitable for these seniors. It suits their lifestyle. It gives them independence. They can walk to the store, see their friends." Families living in SROs, most of them low-income immigrants for whom Chinatown is their first stop, and single working people make up the rest of the population.

The critical question facing Chinatown, Wu said, is what to do about its housing. "It's aging housing stock, most built after the quake. It's in poor condition, but it's affordable. The issue we face is how to upgrade this housing stock, make it seismically safe and healthy, while also maintaining affordability."

The key players in this process are the owners of the buildings. And this is where it gets interesting. Wu said that most of the landlords are the family associations, the surname-based fraternal groups with ancient roots in Chinese culture, that have dominated Chinatown for most of its history. The rentals work by word of mouth, and tenants who share the surname have an advantage in getting in, Wu said. "These are the people we work with," she said of the landlords. "But it's not easy, because they're like trusts. There isn't one person you're dealing with, and each family association has its own structures and politics. Also, according to what we hear, they've owned these buildings outright for a long time. So they don't need to make mortgage payments. They're all different—some are more proactive about maintaining their buildings, others are not."

The CCDC does drop-in counseling for tenants and receives complaints about substandard housing or illegal practices like denial of kitchen access. But Wu said the CCDC worked proactively with the family associations and the city building inspectors to improve the buildings: "We don't just call the inspectors. We don't want to lose the unit." What this means is that except in the case of egregious violations—and many of those no doubt exist as well—the CCDC and the city allow the status quo to prevail. At best, their efforts are a case of two steps forward, one step back.

I learned for myself that the city has no intention of cracking down on Chinatown. Soon after I became an involuntary slumlord, I called the city building department, fearing that I might be legally liable for housing so many people in a single building. The inspector I talked to laughed. "Maximum occupancy laws? I've never heard of them being enforced in San Francisco," he said. Left unsaid was the obvious fact that if the city enforced its codes strictly, it would have to close down Chinatown.

And if Chinatown went away, so would its residents. Wu said the average SRO rents for about $500 a month, although new rentals are going for $600 or $700 and some are as high as $1,000. In a building being demolished to make way for the new Central Subway, Wu said, some tenants were paying in the $200s—this in a city where mediocre one-bedroom apartments can rent for $3,000.

These rock-bottom rents make it impossible to fundamentally alter Chinatown. It isn't feasible to add much housing stock in such a tiny, crowded area, nor does the city or anyone else have the limitless funds that would be needed to buy up the tenements, remodel them, and return their tenants to them at the same rents. (It should be noted that many of the Chinese landlords do not seem to be driven by greed—or if they are, they're penny wise and pound foolish. They'd make much more money getting rid of their impoverished tenants, gutting the buildings, and selling them or renting them at market rates. Wu said that so far, with the exception of one building on Washington Street, that has not happened.)

The conundrum facing the CCDC, the city, and all the stakeholders in Chinatown is that the status quo—maintaining a crowded slum in the heart of the city—is unpalatable, yet the alternative would be much worse.

What keeps Chinatown alive, Wu said, is immigration. "And immigration isn't ending. We still get new immigrants coming to Chinatown. I don't want to sound too sappy, but they're beginning their American dream. They come to Chinatown, then after a few years they move to the Excelsior or Visitacion Valley. Chinatown helps them get started. With all the social services here, it gives them the tools. There's no crime, and the small businesses are doing fine. I don't mean to be nostalgic about Chinatown, and I wasn't here in the old days, but it serves a very important purpose."

In any case, the only alternative would be to reenact the city's most disastrous planning decision: the razing of the "blighted" Western Addition in the name of "urban renewal." "I've heard calls for high-rise buildings to be built in Chinatown that would create a more mixed income range," Wu said. "But anytime you do demolition and relocation, you lose lots of people. Fifty to 60 percent tenant retention is considered a success, and that's unacceptable. The cost of new construction in the city is such that if you build a two-bedroom condo, it costs $500,000. If you put those condos in, you're going to displace a lot of people. That kind of displacement is what we're trying to prevent. Demolish and rebuild doesn't work. So we are left with rehabbing the existing buildings."

The bottom line is that for all of its problems, Chinatown is still one of the most dynamic neighborhoods in the United States.

"My family came over from mainland China in the early 1980s," Sarah He told me. He is the operations director for the Chinese Progressive Association, another Chinatown nonprofit whose mission is to improve living conditions and develop local leadership from the ground up. "I was nine when we came. We lived on the edge of Chinatown in a studio on Bush, right near the Chinatown Gate. My mom was a seamstress, and my dad worked in a Chinese barbecue shop. There were four of us in 400 square feet, including the kitchen and bathroom. After five years we moved to the Excelsior District. My uncle had a house there.

"I had major culture shock in the Excelsior. All of a sudden I had a backyard to play in, but no stores and no tourists. It was a long way to Chinatown, but we made our way back every weekend—we figured out the buses. My parents went back for the food and the sense of community. It was like they were coming home. My mom was still working in Chinatown, but my dad was starting to drive and get work around San Francisco.

"My parents still live in the Excelsior. They saved up enough money to buy a house 10 years ago at Cambridge and Silver, near McClaren Park. They shop on San Bruno Street. There's a Chinese community there that's getting more vibrant. I now live in Daly City. But I feel a strong connection to my old neighborhood."

There are tens of thousands of stories like Sarah He's in Chinatown, and across San Francisco and the Bay Area.

So it all came full circle. That intoxicating vision of Chinatown I had as a child, that dream landscape lit by lanterns, turned out to be real in a deeper sense than I could have imagined. The city, whose primary revenue stream is tourism, did not have to feel guilty about wanting to preserve Chinatown. Yes, Chinatown has serious problems that need to be addressed. Yes, it is a ghetto. But it is a ghetto that works. For once, what's good for the Chamber of Commerce also turns out to be good for the poorest San Franciscans.

Chinatown is a living demonstration that crowded and squalid conditions cannot defeat determined and hardworking people. In that sense, its 16 blocks contain nothing less than the entire American immigrant experience, played out anew with each generation. That experience has not been easy. Like many other immigrants, more than most, the Chinese have faced racism and prejudice. But, also like other immigrants, they have overcome them to make a better life for their children. By night, the streets of Chinatown are magical; by day, they are crowded and dirty. But to walk them, by day or by night, is to walk the history of America.

CHAPTER 38

DESERTED CITIES OF THE HEART

The Great Highway and Balboa, former site of
Playland at the Beach, and many other locations

Like all cities, San Francisco is constantly changing. Some of those changes have been salutary—the creation of a magnificent park at Crissy Field, the destruction of the Embarcadero Freeway, the installation of public street seating—but many more have been dreadful. What follows is an unsweet list of 16 things that have disappeared forever from San Francisco, leaving it a much lamer place than it was before.

The list does not include anything I did not experience myself, so the truly monumental, Les Halles–like losses will not be found here. Like the great ferry fleet, or the 1853 Montgomery Block, or the Belt Line Railway at the base of Telegraph Hill, or the sprawling old Produce Market that used to stand where the sterile Golden Gateway Apartments now are. Those icons are not on the list, but the ones included are heartbreaking in their own right. If a common theme connects them—besides the preponderance of bars—it is that they all date to a time when the city was cheap and unpretentious and amiably vulgar and infinitely more eccentric. Read 'em and weep.

1) *Playland at the Beach.* The old amusement park at the Great Highway and Balboa was the city's last low-I.Q., high-kicks, comic book link with a sleazy, fun-loving America, the low-democratic country of dames and John Dos Passos sailors and crazy-eyed carnies that spilled gloriously all over the place before liability lawsuits and sanitized corporations vacuumed it up.

2) *Portofino Caffe and Frank's Extra Bar.* There are still Italians in North Beach, but these two moribund and lovely little places harkened back to the golden days of Joltin' Joe. The fact that no one was ever in them made them even more shrinelike.

3) *Minnie's Can-Do Club.* This was the last jazz and R&B club on Fillmore, a solitary hip outpost at uptown Pine Street after redevelopment had gutted the street that once jumped all the way down to Hank's 500 Club. To be in that mixed-race crowd in 1974, with Dave Alexander pounding the 88s and Minnie working the bar, was very heaven.

4) *U.S. Restaurant.* A venerable North Beach joint with brisk middle-age Italian waitresses in starched blue uniforms, it was the last restaurant in San Francisco to unapologetically serve completely unambitious food.

5) *Musée Méchanique.* This wonderful little collection of antiquated moving toys lost its nostalgic mojo when it left the Cliff House for Fisherman's Wharf. At least the sublime and demonic Camera Obscura is still out there.

6) *Hamm's Brewery sign.* A huge beer mug that filled and overflowed at 16th and Bryant, it was the zenith of neon advertising's Godlike period and served the essential function of making San Francisco mysterious from the freeway.

7) *Monkey Island at the zoo.* Unsanitary, decrepit, and weird, this moated jumble of enormous concrete blocks was an irresistible spider monkey favela that must have inspired thousands of future zoologists.

8) *Surf Theatre.* It ran every film in the Janus Film Festival. It was a block from the beach, and its perch at the end of the N line and the continent somehow seeped into the atmosphere. Maybe it's just because that was where I saw *Jules and Jim* and *Black Orpheus* and *Red Desert* for the first time, but no subsequent cinematic experience has ever come close to the ones I had in that little stucco building on Irving and 47th Avenue.

9) *Sam Wo.* The most recent addition to the list (it closed in 2012), this absurdly narrow, filthy Chinatown noodle house was presided over by Edsel Ford Fong, the rudest waiter in the world. (See no. 11). If an eatery's greatness is measured by the number of drunken 2 A.M. meals consumed in it, Sam Wo was the greatest restaurant in history.

10) *Fun Terminal.* The sordid downtown counterpart of Playland, this low-class arcade stood opposite the (also departed) Transbay Terminal. Haunted by sad *Last Exit to Brooklyn* hustlers and lost souls. Inspired the title of the seminal Mutants album.

11) *Persian Aub Zam Zam Room.* Actually this little WWII-era bar on Haight is still there, but it isn't the same without its weird owner/bartender Bruno, who with silken malevolence would summarily kick out patrons who did not order a martini or otherwise behave in accordance with his impossible-to-divine requirements. There is a special restaurant and bar on the 10th level of hell reserved for Edsel Ford Fong and Bruno, where they will never be served.

12) *Keystone Korner.* Bill Evans, Grant Green, Rahsaan Roland Kirk, Bobby Hutcherson, Herbie Hancock, Charlie Haden—all the greats played there. Those of us who hung out there didn't know that, after 1983, there would never be another New York–class jazz club in town.

13) *Vacant lot at the end of Reed and Priest Streets.* On the very summit of Nob Hill, accessible by two wondrous little dead-end streets, stood a patch of unclaimed dirt covered with foxtails. The ultra-swanky Montaire destroyed this miraculous hidey-hole.

14) *VFW bar at the Beach Chalet.* Bikers, nomads, and assorted losers drinking long-necked Buds underneath the glorious Lucien Labaudt murals while the ocean crashed across the highway.

15) *Gjoa.* The great Norwegian explorer Roald Amundsen's ship *Gjoa*, the first ship to sail through the Northwest Passage, stood at the Great Highway until 1972. The beautiful sloop, facing the Pacific, was the final triumphant link with the centuries-long search for the Strait of Anian that led to the discovery of California.

16) *Danny's Dynasty and the Rickshaw.* Two bars that faced each other across Ross Alley in Chinatown. The alley is so narrow that if you were thrown out of one, you would literally land inside the other, saving cab fare if not face.

CHAPTER 39

PORT OF EMBARKATION

Fort Mason, former San Francisco Port of Embarkation

Y ou could put a plaque to memorialize World War II on hundreds of places in San Francisco, because the war touched everyone and everything. You could put one on the old Bethlehem Steel shipyard at 20th and Illinois Streets, where six days after Pearl Harbor the workers came up with the slogan "Keep 'em sliding!"—after the Army's "Keep 'em flying!" You could put one on the sidewalk on Fillmore Street, where hopeful merchants had erected metal arches after the 1906 quake, when the street briefly became the city's main drag. Those merchants had sacrificed the proud arches to one of the scrap-metal drives that kept the tanks rolling off assembly lines. You could put a plaque on Saints Peter and Paul Church in North Beach, which lost many of its parishioners in the first months of the war when hundreds of Italian American men enlisted. You could put one on the Chinese Playground, which volunteered the services of

Chinese kids who were master kite builders when the military needed model airplanes for training.

But one place stands out above them all: Fort Mason, formerly known as the San Francisco Port of Embarkation. For it was from its piers that 1,647,174 troops shipped west—two-thirds of all the troops sent to the Pacific theater. For many thousands, who would not survive the island hells of Tarawa and Kwajalein and Iwo Jima, it was the last piece of American soil that they would ever touch.

The war changed San Francisco externally. It became an instant citadel, the "American Singapore." A submarine net stretched under the Golden Gate Bridge. Catalina Flying Boats roared over the bridge, searching for Japanese submarines. Massive gun emplacements and machine gun nests ringed the bay. These defenses protected a vast network of military bases, shipyards, factories, and munition plants that stretched across the entire Bay Area. The huge Naval Shipyard at Hunters Point, the four Kaiser Shipyards in Richmond, and others worked around the clock. During the war, the Kaiser Shipyards built more than 747 ships, many of them the indispensable workhorse Liberty ships, a record never matched by any shipyard before or since. One Liberty ship was built in less than five days. By 1943, the Bay Area had become the largest shipbuilding center in the world.

Before the United States entered the war, in a radio broadcast urging America to provide support to Great Britain during the dark year when it stood alone, President Roosevelt had called the United States "the great arsenal of democracy." That arsenal was to play a decisive role in the ultimate Allied victory. And San Francisco was a vital part of it.

The city was packed as never before or since, not just with military personnel but also with tens of thousands of migrant civilians—blacks from Texas and Arkansas and poor whites from Dust Bowl states who had streamed into California, lured by shipyard jobs. (The "Okies" were subjected to almost as much discrimination as the blacks.) A staggering 94,000 people migrated to San Francisco between 1940 and 1943, most in less than one year. Despite frenzied government housing construction at Hunters Point and elsewhere, there was not nearly enough housing for all these newcomers. Workers packed into tiny rooms, vacant lots, gymnasiums, spare rooms. Servicemen slept in movie theaters. Families doubled up. Some workers slept in the same bed in shifts.

But the war also changed the city in invisible ways, reaching into its citizens' hearts and souls. San Franciscans had always been highly individualistic, but the common goal of winning the war united them. One of the most remarkable manifestations of this unity was the explosion of wartime neighborhood block clubs. These neighborhood groups, often led by women, took charge of organizing civil defense, first aid, food supplies, firefighting, and other emergency needs. In *The Bad City in the Good War: San Francisco, Los Angeles, Oakland, and San Diego*, Roger Lotchin argues that "it is very likely that [the clubs] contributed further to making San Francisco the collection of neighborhoods it was already famous for being."

But if the war created a sense of shared experience, a feeling of being a part of something larger than oneself, it also heightened a deeply subjective sense of strangeness, newness, unpredictability. Almost 200 years after Anza had chosen the site for the presidio, San Francisco had finally become a true frontier garrison city. As a result, life there during the war was a whirlwind—exhilarating and sometimes terrifying.

San Franciscans learned the realities of war firsthand on Christmas Day 1941, when hundreds of wounded soldiers, orphaned children, and other survivors of Pearl Harbor, along with the remains of those killed, arrived on a convoy of ships. No official announcement was made, but the city saw the convoy of camouflaged ships moving through the Golden Gate. Thousands of anxious people, not sure if their loved ones were on the ships, drove down to the waterfront, only to be turned away by armed sentries. A fleet of ambulances and taxis drove the wounded—far more of them than had been reported in the newspapers—to hospitals as an emergency call went out for nurses to report to Eddy and Octavia. Hundreds of female volunteers greeted the refugees and soldiers, dispensing hot coffee and cigarettes and making sure every child got a toy. The *Chronicle* ran a photo of a sad, confused-looking little girl clutching a teddy bear. There was no way to conceal the trucks that drove away with the black coffins. It was not a Christmas any San Franciscan who was there would ever forget.

Death was a constant presence. Fear of a Japanese attack was real: Japanese submarines sunk freighters off the coast and shelled an oil refinery in Santa Barbara. Blackouts were frequent. As the war went on, it hit closer and closer to home. Everyone had a relative or a friend in the service, and everyone knew what it meant when the dread Western Union man knocked on the door. Gold stars denoting mothers who had lost sons were displayed on windows all over town.

In 1943, the city turned out to honor the survivors of the cruiser U.S.S. *San Francisco*, which had engaged in a heroic point-blank shootout with Japanese warships in the naval battle of Guadalcanal. Its commander, San Francisco–born Rear Admiral Daniel J. Callahan, and 77 men were killed in what was perhaps the last ship-to-ship engagement in military history. The battered cruiser had staggered into Mare Island Navy Yard for repairs, and the 100 surviving members of her crew were sent ashore. Some were in bathrobes, carrying canes and crutches. As the sailors, sitting silently and ill at ease and looking straight ahead, were driven in jeeps down Market Street, 100,000 San Franciscans, standing three deep on the sidewalks and leaning out of office windows, roared and applauded and whistled. Today the twisted, shell-torn bridge of the ship stands at Point Lobos, in the most spectacular place in the city, facing the great circle route from San Francisco to Guadalcanal.

Omnipresent death mingled with ceaseless change. People—workers, family members, friends, lovers—were here one day and gone the next. Uncertainty gripped everything. Thousands of lonely young men were always in town, celebrating their last nights before going off to war. Carpe diem was the city's motto. Bars and clubs were packed. Authorities winked at prostitution, although many of the soldiers were small-town innocents who were just looking for a nice girl to talk to. Love, deep respect, and dread made a cocktail of unbearable poignancy. An electric charge filled the city, a sense that life mattered, that it was for keeps.

In *I Know Why the Caged Bird Sings*, Maya Angelou, an immigrant from Alabama who had only recently moved to San Francisco, captured this feeling eloquently: "The air of collective displacement, the impermanence of life in wartime and the gauche personalities of the more recent arrivals tended to dissipate my own sense of not belonging. In San Francisco, for the first time, I perceived myself as part of something. Not that I identified with the newcomers, nor with the rare Black descendants of native San Franciscans, nor with the whites or even the Asians, but rather with the times and the city . . . To me, a thirteen-year-old Black girl, stalled by the South and Southern Black life style, the city was a state of beauty and a state of freedom."

John dos Passos, who had described the raw feeling of Market Street in his great *U.S.A.* trilogy, wrote an evocative essay about the city's atmosphere for *Harper's* magazine in March 1944. He went up to the top of Coit Tower in a rainstorm, where for a moment he saw, through the shifting mist, a long line of gray freighters at anchor. "Two young men in khaki are standing beside me, squinting to see through the rain-spattered glass. 'Boy, it won't be long now,' says one. 'You mean before we are stuck down in the hold of one of those things.' 'You said it.'" They notice he is listening and shut up. The city was filled with young men like those.

San Francisco served two crucial functions during the war. It was a vital part of the great arsenal of democracy, and it was a great liberty town. As the last stop, San Francisco got to play her favorite role, the whore with a heart of gold. And for once, she could play it completely straight. She *was* a whore with a heart of gold, offering the solace of her beauty, her nightclubs, her booze, her tattoos, and her beautiful girls—and they were all beautiful—to a bunch of scared 19-year-old kids who were about to enter hell.

The war changed the city in a million ways, some good, some bad, some too ambiguous or huge to sum up even now. But if you were to ask any San Franciscan who was there, they would tell you that what the war did to them was not important. What was important was what they did for the war. And when it was over, they could say, as Albert Camus said of his fellow Parisians on the August night their city was liberated, "We did what was necessary."

CHAPTER 40

THE END
OF THE ROAD

1546 Grant Avenue, formerly the Place

O n January 14, 1949, a former Columbia University halfback named Jack Kerouac, his pal Neal Cassady, Cassady's first wife, LuAnne Henderson, and a man named Al Hinkle piled into Cassady's 1949 Hudson and barreled out of New York City, heading for San Francisco. Hinkle is unknown to history and is only mentioned here because on the trip east with Neal to meet Kerouac, in an apropos curtain-raiser to what would become the most mythic American road chronicle since Huck Finn headed down the Mississippi with Jim, he had left his newlywed wife stranded in Arizona.

The 26-year-old Kerouac had just finished his first novel, titled *The Town and the City*. But Scribner's and Little Brown had both rejected the 1,183-page manuscript. Angry and depressed, Kerouac wrote a despairing letter to his equally unknown and equally ambitious friend, a brooding, sexually frustrated, intellectual poet named Allen Ginsberg: "I am lost. The only thing to do is to give up—I am giving up."

But Kerouac was revived by Cassady. The young Dionysus from Denver—athlete, sex junkie, car thief, motormouth, semi-sociopath, and wannabe writer—sent Kerouac passionate letters proclaiming they were "blood brothers." Inspired, Kerouac started a new book, which he described as "an American-scene picaresque . . . dealing simply with hitch-hiking and the sorrows, hardships, adventures, sweats and labours of that." The book would be called *On the Road*.

When they arrived in San Francisco, Cassady yelled, "No more land! We can't go any further 'cause there ain't no more land!" Then he abruptly dropped Kerouac and LuAnn at the corner of O'Farrell and Grant and went to rejoin his second wife, Caroline. "You see what a bastard he is?" Lu-Ann said to Kerouac as they stood penniless on the corner. "Dean will leave you out in the cold any time it's in his interest."

It was not an auspicious visit. "I stayed in San Francisco a week and had the beatest time of my life," Kerouac wrote. He and LuAnne walked all over town, looking for food money. They were so broke they hit up some drunken seamen in a Mission Street flophouse, who offered them whiskey. But Kerouac, and Allen Ginsberg, would return to the place Kerouac called "the fabulous white city of San Francisco on her eleven mystic hills."

That the Beats would come to San Francisco seems preordained. They were city poets par excellence: Their dark romantic vision needed mysterious streets and evil towers. (Film noir, which came into existence at the same time as the Beats, manifests the same love-hate relationship with the city.) Kerouac loved San Francisco, calling it "really the most excited city in America." His descriptions of it have an intensity born of the fact that in those days before air travel, getting there still felt like an epic feat. "Whoo, Frisco nights, the end of the continent and the end of doubt, all dull doubt and tomfoolery, goodbye," Kerouac rhapsodized. And it was in San Francisco that Kerouac and Ginsberg launched the pedal-to-the-metal literary movement that would inspire youth across the country, outrage the Man, and give a name to a generation: the Beats.

One San Francisco neighborhood is indelibly associated with the Beats: North Beach. The connection makes sense. North Beach had been edgy since the Gold Rush days of the Sydney Ducks, the Hounds, Chiletown, and the Barbary Coast. The holy trinity of cheap sex, sketchy bars, and low rents have always attracted writers and artists, and North Beach and environs, in particular its southern edge, became San Francisco's artistic quarter. The tradition kicked off with the Montgomery Block: Built in 1853, it hosted various impecunious artists' colonies until the 1940s. Its most famous turn-of-the-century watering hole was Coppa's, whose walls were covered with a demented collection of murals, mostly by Porter Garnett, depicting various lascivious, off-the-wall, and generally crazed artists and writers. The Black Cat Café, which opened in the 1930s, was another bohemian haunt (and later a gay bar of historic import) just up the street on Montgomery. The nearby Iron Pot was a favorite of artists, including Hassel Smith, Sam Francis, Jean Varda, and Benjamin Bufano.

From the 1930s on, the neighborhood's politics also played a role in attracting writers and artists. As the poet and City Lights founder Lawrence Ferlinghetti recalled, many of North Beach's Italian American residents were anti-Mussolini leftists. They were part of San Francisco's strong left-wing, pro-labor, pacifist, and anarchist tradition, one exemplified by the city's leading literary figure, Kenneth Rexroth. It was nurturing soil for the rebellious Beats.

And finally, there was simple geography. North Beach is to San Francisco as the Campo de Fiori is to Rome: a sacred space. There is a reason that Juana Briones, the city's mother, ran her dairy ranch on what is now Washington Square. Protected by Nob and Russian Hills on the west and Telegraph Hill on the east, with Columbus, the hinge of an ancient geological syncline, running diagonally between them, North Beach is San Francisco's lyrical heart, its oldest and most beloved quarter.

Beat ground zero was upper Grant Avenue. The three blocks between Vallejo and Filbert were lined with weird and wonderful watering holes: the Place, the Co-Existence Bagel Shop, the Coffee Gallery, Caffe Trieste. The hepcats also frequented City Lights and Henri Lenoir's bar Vesuvio on Columbus. (Bill Morgan's *The Beat Generation in San Francisco: A Literary Tour* provides an exhaustive list of the sites.) But the event that launched the movement, triggered the San Francisco Renaissance, and made Allen Ginsberg the most famous poet in America took place not in North Beach but in the Marina, on a street now filled not with angelheaded hipsters but with upscale pickup bars.

Ginsberg ended up in San Francisco after Carolyn Cassady caught him having sex with Neal at their San Jose home and threw him out. In the city, Ginsberg made what turned out to be his last attempt to live a "normal" life: He cut his beard and hair, put on a suit, got a job as a market researcher (!), and moved into an apartment at 755 Pine on lower Nob Hill with a pretty ex-roadhouse singer and her son. But when Ginsberg confessed that he and Cassady had been lovers, the singer moved out. Although Ginsberg soon met his longtime partner, Peter Orlovsky, he had hit rock bottom. At 29, he described his life as a "monstrous nightmare." He had been unable to write since coming to San Francisco and was considering applying to graduate school.

But in August, Ginsberg sat down at a typewriter—which he never worked on—and started to improvise in the spontaneous style Kerouac had taught him, using long lines inspired by both his poetic mentor William Carlos Williams and by jazz saxophone solos. "I saw the best minds of my generation destroyed by madness, starving mystical naked . . ." Ginsberg was off like a ski jumper, a lifetime of rage and yearning like a great wind at his back. But as Steven Watson notes in his superb history of the Beats, *The Birth of the Beat Generation: Visionaries, Rebels, and Hipsters, 1944–1960*, the crucial creative moment came when Ginsberg typed the line "who let themselves be fucked in the ass by saintly motorcyclists, and screamed with joy / who blew and were blown by those human seraphim, the sailors, caresses of Atlantic and Caribbean love." Watson writes, "At this point mentally declaring the poem unpublishable, Ginsberg felt free to 'write for my own soul's ear and a few other golden ears.'" By the end of the day he had written seven pages.

San Francisco makes one appearance in Ginsberg's poem, and it's a doozy. A few days after he started his long poem, wandering through downtown San Francisco stoned on peyote, Ginsberg stared up at the Sir Francis Drake Hotel. Its upper stories, crowned with the star above the Starlight Room, suddenly appeared to him to be a robotic death's head, glowing red—the fearful embodiment of soulless capitalism. The clanging of the Powell Street cable car sounded like the word "Moloch," the ancient god to whom the Ammonites offered child sacrifices. Ginsberg sat down in a cafeteria off Union Square and began writing. His nightmare vision became the "Moloch" section of the poem he called "Howl." Modern American poetry, not to mention drinking at the Starlight Room, has never been the same since.

Two months later, Ginsberg mailed out 100 mimeographed cards that read: "Six poets at the Six Gallery. Kenneth Rexroth, M.C. Remarkable collection of angels all gathered at once in the same spot. Wine, music, dancing girls, free satori. Small collection for wine and postcards. Charming event."

The Six Gallery was a cooperative art gallery in a former auto repair shop at Fillmore and Greenwich. (It subsequently became a rug store where, sick transit, I once bought a kilim.) On October 7, 1955, Ginsberg, Ferlinghetti, and Peter Orlovsky drove to the gallery in Ferlinghetti's battered Austin. A large crowd had gathered, among them Jack Kerouac, who was too shy to read himself but collected money and returned with gallon jugs of cheap red, which he handed to the audience. Rexroth, the poets' father figure, introduced the readers: Ginsberg, Philip Lamantia, Michael McClure, Philip Whalen, and Gary Snyder.

Ginsberg came to the lectern about 11 P.M. He started out slowly, but as he got deeper into the poem, he began to sway rhythmically, waving his arms, intoning the long lines like a cantor. When he finished reading 12 minutes later, he recalled without false modesty, he dissolved in "tears which restored to American poetry the prophetic consciousness it had lost since the conclusion of Hart Crane's *The Bridge*." Rexroth was also in tears. The audience was ecstatic, stunned, overwhelmed. Lamantia said the atmosphere was "like bringing two ends of an electric wire together."

Afterward the dazed and euphoric poets went to Sam Wo in Chinatown and then six blocks north on Grant to the Place. They all knew something big had just happened. That night, Ferlinghetti sent Ginsberg a telegram that consciously echoed one of the famous salutations in American literature, Emerson's message to Walt Whitman after reading *Leaves of Grass*. "I greet you at the beginning of a great career," Ferlinghetti wrote. "When do I get the manuscript?"

Ferlinghetti published *Howl and Other Poems* the next year. When the San Francisco police arrested Ferlinghetti and bookstore manager Shigeyoshi Murao on obscenity charges, the ensuing trial and publicity made Ginsberg and his poem world-famous. In 1957, *On the Road* was published to a rave review in the *New York Times*. In 1959, the last and strangest of the three seminal Beat works, William S. Burroughs's *Naked Lunch*, was published abroad by Olympia Press; its American edition appeared in 1962.

By then, the Beat moment had passed. The wild success of *On the Road* created a media feeding frenzy, the first of its kind. Watson describes the Beats as "American literature's first rock stars," and the comparison is apt. In the first example of commodified dissent, the media both reported on and created the Beat Generation. The popular TV show *The Many Loves of Dobie Gillis* featured a goateed, bongo-playing Beat character named Maynard G. Krebs. Tour buses drove down upper Grant, filled with spectators looking for "beatniks"—the witty phrase coined by Herb Caen just after Sputnik launched. Vesuvio featured a sardonic sign, now on display at the Oakland Museum, that said "This is the only authentic bohemian atmosphere this side of Daly City." The "angry young men" and their "real gone chicks" were explored in a million pop-sociology pieces. In a precursor of Beatlemania, women went crazy over the handsome Kerouac, babbling on the phone to his unfortunate girlfriend, "You're young. I'm 29, and I've got to fuck him now!"

But Kerouac's overwrought fans, male and female, were lusting over a figment of their imaginations. They mistook him for his wild hero Dean Moriarty (Neal Cassady), but he was nothing like Cassady. Kerouac was a shy, religious, sexually insecure, politically conservative man, who was also an alcoholic. He was unequipped to handle the notoriety. To celebrate his success, he went on a five-week drunken spree in New York, but the availability of "girls girls girls" did nothing to soothe his uneasy spirit. Eventually he moved back in with his mother, where his already virulent bigotry—he was racist and anti-Semitic—worsened. When he died at age 47, he was drinking a quart of Scotch a day. He was never able to regain the innocence, the vulnerability, the sense of reaching for something that could never quite be grasped, that made *On the Road* a sad and brilliant flare in the American night.

The glory and the curse of the Beats was that they insisted on an art of utter spontaneity, of unmediated expression, of naked self-expression—an art as raw and dangerous as life itself. At their best, the Beats were able to touch primal wellsprings. But their insistence on collapsing the distinction between art and life held two opposite dangers. On the one hand, it threatened to tip them into madness, drugs, or death. And on the other, it could lead to formal sloppiness. Intensity of living does not always translate into artistic achievement.

In this sense, San Francisco was the perfect city for the Beats. For more than any other American city, San Francisco represents the apotheosis of unmediated experience. Its beauty can overwhelm the artistic response to it. Artists here are always at risk of merely gesturing at the self-sufficient world—a good move for a Zen master, not so good for an artist. Whether San Francisco itself can be held responsible for the Beats' artistic shortcomings is dubious, but variations on this critique run throughout the city's history, and when there's this much smoke, artistic fires must have gone out somewhere. San Francisco's tendency toward navel-gazing provincialism, itself largely the result of the city's stupefying beauty, did not help. As Kevin Starr notes in explaining why Frank Norris, one of the city's greatest writers, did his best work in the East, "San Francisco's isolation might give rise to a splendid originality, but it could also lead to narcissism and a self-justifying tolerance for the third-rate." Kerouac himself said he thought that "California is white like washlines and emptyheaded."

The Beats flamed out fast, but their free-spirited rebellion still inspires. It does so because one day the young Allen Ginsberg sat down at his typewriter and dared to tell his truth, because Jack Kerouac was able to transform a road trip into an odyssey that would fill a generation with excitement and hope. The Beat meteor shot through long ago, but late at night in North Beach you can sometimes still see its traces, like the taillights of a big car hurtling west.

CHAPTER 41

THE HAUNTED HOUSE

1712 Fillmore Street

A geologist would call the block of Fillmore Street between Post and Sutter a "triple junction." It's one of those three-way collisions where a swanky part of town crashes into a seedy one, while a completely different quarter sideswipes both of them. In 1974, my cousin Jonathan and I were house-sitting four blocks away, at Pine and Buchanan, in a majestic, decaying Victorian with a big psychedelic mandala painted in an alcove.

We didn't know it at the time, but our building was a weird precursor to the Summer of Love. In 1965, that stretch of Pine Street had been a pre-Haight hippie scene, with half a dozen houses filled with longhairs and dealers. The downstairs unit had been home to the legendary hippie newspaper the *Oracle*. Across the street, at 2111 Pine, a rooming house once stood; some of the itinerant musicians there played in a vanished after-hours jazz club three blocks away called Bop City. The rooming house was managed by a guy named Bill Ham, who invented psychedelic light shows.

Our block was mostly black and pretty run-down. We used to walk down to Kim's Market at Pine and Fillmore (now a Kiehl's, which sells $50 bottles of shampoo) to buy our daily $2 ration of sausages, carrots, and potatoes. If you turned right on Fillmore, in a block you would come to California Street, the city's great north-south dividing line. California was and is the unofficial border of Pacific Heights, the swankiest neighborhood in town. Turn left and you would quickly end up in the unswankiest neighborhood in town.

Past Kim's Market, as you walked toward Bush, the block was a grab bag, with a venerable Japanese restaurant rubbing shoulders with a jumping jazz and R&B joint called Minnie's Can-Do Club. In the block after Bush, things started to become disheveled, a no-man's-land traversed by Japanese, blacks, and a few confused tourists looking for Japantown. Once you crossed the ugly, multi-lane Geary Expressway, you were in the heart of black San Francisco.

Some years after I moved out of the neighborhood, I happened to find myself on Fillmore between Post and Sutter. I remember being subliminally aware that there was something odd about the east side of the street. Its feng shui was wrong. In particular, there was something weird about a row of five stately Victorians. But I couldn't put my finger on it.

It took me a few decades, but I finally learned why that block felt off. Those five Victorians were not built there. They were saved from the wrecking ball, raised up from their original sites, and plunked down on Fillmore. The block felt weird because the setbacks were too deep.

It is appropriate that this line of Victorians stands out. For one of its buildings has a history so rich and strange that an entire book could be written about it. The house at 1712 Fillmore is San Francisco's version of Joyce's 7 Eccles Street. It is a universe on a 27 1/2-by-93-foot lot.

In or around 1895, a three-story Victorian, built in the exuberant Queen Anne style that was the last hurrah of Victorian architectural excess, was erected at 1690 Post Street, just east of Buchanan, in the Western Addition. The name Western Addition is a link with the Gold Rush days, when the city did not even include all of Nob Hill. In 1851, San Francisco's western limit was Larkin Street, a few yards west of my house on Jackson. A year later, the booming city extended its boundary 13 blocks west to Divisadero.

The area north of Market Street between Larkin and Divisadero became known as the "Western Addition." Despite the fact that the "addition" is now 160 years old, the name has stuck. A more suitable name, considering the way the city has treated the neighborhood and its residents, might be the "Western Subtraction."

The Western Addition was a solidly middle-class and upper-middle-class neighborhood. Streetcar lines carried its merchants and professionals to their offices in downtown San Francisco. By 1900 its residents were mostly native born, three-quarters of them to immigrant parents from countries like Germany, Austria, Ireland, and France. A significant number of them were Jews, mostly from Germany, attracted by San Francisco's lack of overt anti-Semitism and business opportunities. By the 1870s, Jews made up 7 to 8 percent of the city's population, the highest percentage in any city west of New York.

The first of the neighborhood's three great transformations was a result of the 1906 fire. Displaced working-class people from the burned-out downtown and South of Market areas poured in. The stately single-family Victorians were divided into rooms and flats. The neighborhood became more densely populated, poorer, and much more ethnically diverse. Large numbers of working-class Filipinos, Mexican Americans, and Jews moved in. So did the two ethnic groups whose fates would become entwined in the neighborhood, and in that wooden building on Post Street: African Americans and Japanese.

Blacks began arriving in San Francisco before the Gold Rush, but never in great numbers until World War II. As Albert Broussard notes in *Black San Francisco: The Struggle for Racial Equality in the West, 1900–1954*, the lack of factory jobs and the distance from the South discouraged black immigration, but so did the "politely racist" attitudes held by many white San Franciscans. The early city had no racial covenants for blacks and no ghettos, but it was only the fact that there were so few blacks that created the illusion of unusual tolerance: The white citizens of San Francisco shared many of the racial prejudices of their fellow white Americans. After 1906, increasing numbers of blacks moved into the Western Addition. By 1930, almost half of all the 5,000 blacks in the city lived in the neighborhood.

So did most of the Japanese. The first Japanese immigrants arrived in San Francisco in 1869, establishing the first and oldest Japantown in the United States. (One of the most influential early immigrants, a devout Christian and future newspaper editor named Kyutaro Abiko, established an agricultural colony of fellow Japanese in Livingston in the Central Valley, soon followed by a colony in Cortez, near Turlock. My Japanese grandparents emigrated to the Cortez colony in the early 1920s; my Nisei father was born in nearby Turlock in 1925.)

The first Japanese in San Francisco lived in South Park and on Dupont (Grant) in Chinatown. Like many other ethnic groups, they moved to the Western Addition after 1906. The willingness of the neighborhood's landlords, many of them Jewish, to rent to Japanese did not sit well with many whites: In 1907, the *Chronicle* ran a scare piece about the Japanese "invasion" of the Western Addition titled "A Greater San Francisco or a Lesser Nagasaki—Which?"

The Western Addition was one of the most diverse neighborhoods in the country; writer Jerry Flamm calls it San Francisco's "Little United Nations." The Japanese population was a mixture of older, first-generation (Issei) immigrants, most of whom were not U.S. citizens, and their second-generation (Nisei) children, almost all of whom were citizens. For convenience, I will refer to them all as Japanese Americans.

At some point after the quake, the majestic Queen Anne Victorian at 1690 Post Street was divided into apartments. Sometime before 1920, the Nippon Drug Company opened on its ground floor. In 1930 the co-owner of Nippon Drugs was a man named J. Hatsuto Yamada, who lived eight blocks away at Bush and Divisadero.

By 1940, more than 5,000 Japanese Americans were living in Japantown. There were more than 200 Japanese-owned businesses. Some owned property; the exact percentage is unclear. Many worked as domestic servants, the famous "Japanese houseboys."

Japantown on the eve of the war was a bustling enclave. It had 40 churches, 17 schools and kindergartens, a department store, and dozens of small businesses. Culturally, it was a scramble: There were four traditional baths but also American-style diners serving hot dogs, ham and egg sandwiches—and fried noodles.

Then came Pearl Harbor. After word got out, hostile whites drove through the neighborhood, staring creepily at its inhabitants. The authorities immediately began arresting "suspicious" Japanese. An incident reported in the December 9 *Call-Bulletin* reveals the round-up-the-usual-suspects nature of this early venture into Homeland Security. Under the headline "Enemy

Aliens Arrested Here," the paper gravely reported that three Japanese men had been arrested on suspicion of taking a photo of an army transport, "although no camera was found."

"No camera was found" could have been the motto for the entire hysterical, fear-and-race-driven episode that followed. Californians in general and San Franciscans in particular had long viewed the Japanese as even worse—more ambitious, more evil, more underhanded—than the despised Chinese. Journalist and historian Carey McWilliams described the hostility as the "California-Japanese War." In 1900 the San Francisco journal *Organized Labor* opined, "Chinatown with its reeking filth and dirt, its gambling dens and obscene slave pens, its coolie labor and bloodthirsty tongs, is a menace to the community; but the snivelling Japanese, who swarms along the streets and cringingly offers his paltry services for a suit of clothes and a front seat in our public schools, is a far greater danger to the laboring portion of society than all the opium-soaked pigtails who have ever blotted the fair name of this beautiful city."

In February 1942, President Roosevelt signed Executive Order 9066, expelling "all persons of Japanese ancestry, including aliens and non-aliens," from West Coast military zones. Every Japanese person in San Francisco was ordered to register and report at various sites for processing. Stripped of their belongings except for what they could carry, they mustered at 2020 Van Ness and then were sent to "assembly centers," mainly the Tanforan Racetrack in San Bruno. Most of San Francisco's Japanese residents, including Nippon Drugs co-owner Hatsuto Yamada, were sent to the Topaz internment camp in Utah, one of 10 hastily built "relocation" camps scattered across the barren stretches of the country. (My father and his family, from the Central Valley, were mustered at the Merced Fairgrounds, where my dad had once shown his 4-H Club chickens, and imprisoned at desolate Camp Amache, official name Granada, in Colorado.) By April, Japantown was empty.

Sometimes the silences left by cataclysmic events are the loudest reminders. While researching the city directories, I compared the 1942 listings (compiled before the internment order) from "Yamada" to "Yamazaki" with the 1943 listings. In 1942 there are 32 listings—Yamada, Yamagata, Yamaguchi, Yamamoto, Yamasake, Yamazaki. In 1943, there are none. The names, and the people, are simply gone.

The forced removal and imprisonment of 110,000 people, most of them

American citizens, for no reason other than their race, was one of the great injustices in U.S. history. But the sudden departure of 5,000 Japanese from the Western Addition proved a boon to another victimized group of Americans: blacks.

As we have seen, World War II was responsible for the great influx of blacks into San Francisco. Before the war, the city had fewer than 5,000 black residents. By the end of the war, 32,000 blacks, drawn by good-paying shipyard jobs and the opportunity to get out of Texas or Louisiana, were living in the city.

The jobs were there, but there was literally nowhere for the newcomers to live. Some found housing in the apartments that were quickly constructed in Hunters Point, but thousands more units were needed. San Francisco was not an egregiously bigoted city, but many white landlords refused to rent to blacks, and overtly racist actions were not unheard of.

In this charged situation, the empty apartment buildings and houses in Japantown were a godsend. Because the neighborhood was already racially mixed, its landlords were happy to rent to blacks. Between 1940 and 1950, the black population of the Western Addition went from 2,144 to 14,888. Citywide, the demographic change was even more startling: San Francisco went from having 4,846 black residents in 1940 to 43,502 in 1950.

In one of the stranger urban transformations in American history, the area around Post and Buchanan went from being a Japanese neighborhood to a black one virtually overnight. Maya Angelou, who as a 13-year-old had moved into a building near that very corner, wrote: "The Yamamoto Sea Food Market quietly became Sammy's Shoe Shine Parlor and Smoke Shop. Yashigira's Hardware metamorphosed into La Salon de Beauté owned by Miss Clorinda Jackson. The Japanese shops which sold products to Nisei customers were taken over by enterprising Negro businessmen, and in less than a year became permanent homes away from home for the newly arrived Southern blacks. Where the aromas of tempura, raw fish and *cha* had dominated, the aroma of chitlings, greens and ham hocks now prevailed."

The old neighborhood was gone, and overnight its new inhabitants made it their own. And the neighborhood they created, before the city destroyed it, was one of the most jumping places on the planet. It was called the Fillmore, a.k.a. the Harlem of the West. Or just the 'Mo.

Within months, the Fillmore was exploding with life—and its crown jewel was its jazz clubs. By a coincidence as exuberant as an Art Blakey snare drum roll, the Fillmore's incarnation as a black neighborhood at the beginning of World War II exactly coincided with one of America's great artistic achievements, a rival to abstract expressionism: the birth of modern jazz, in its first incarnation—bebop.

The virtuoso improvisational style created by Bird and Diz and Monk and Max Roach and Bud Powell ushered in a new age of intense, deeply personal, and harmonically advanced music. It took serious chops to play bop. To use a phrase coined by Mark Schorer, the great English professor across the bay at U.C. Berkeley, it was "technique as discovery." And what they discovered, during a thousand jam sessions, was an American soundtrack of genius and joy.

For more than 15 years, the Fillmore was the hottest jazz, blues, and R&B scene outside New York. Everybody in the 'hood and plenty from outside dressed to the nines and hit the streets to drink, party, and listen. The mile-long stretch of Fillmore and its side streets was packed with more than 2 dozen clubs. All the greats came: Charlie Parker, John Coltrane, Miles Davis, Dizzy Gillespie, Billie Holiday, and Dexter Gordon, to name just a few. Even Art Tatum, a.k.a. God, played the 'Mo.

In 1949, the old Victorian at 1690 Post underwent its strangest transformation yet. Shuttered-up Nippon Drugs reopened as Vout City, a club run by a jazz guitarist, pianist, composer, and singer named Slim Gaillard. Gaillard was a weird and wonderful character, a musical cousin of Lord Buckley. In addition to speaking eight languages, Gaillard made up his own, which he called Vout—hence the name of his club. Jack Kerouac immortalized Gaillard in *On the Road*. He describes going to see him at "a little Frisco nightclub" where "great eager crowds of young semi-intellectuals sat at his feet and listened to him on the guitar, piano and bongo drums . . . He does and says anything that comes into his head."

Shockingly, Gaillard turned out to be a terrible businessman, and Vout City quickly folded. The building's owner, Charles Sullivan, had to find a new tenant. Sullivan approached John "Jimbo" Edwards, one of the first black car salesmen in San Francisco, who decided to open a café called Jimbo's Waffle Shop in the former Vout space. When local musicians discovered it had an unused back room, they started using it for after-hours jam sessions. Jimbo changed its name to Bop City, word got around, and soon every jazz musician who came to San Francisco started heading there.

The cover photograph of a book about the 'Mo's glory days, *Harlem of the West: The Fillmore Jazz Era*, by Elizabeth Pepin and Lewis Watts, captures an indelible moment. A heartbreakingly young, innocent-looking tenor player stands on the stage. He and fellow tenor man John Handy and trumpeter Frank Fischer are listening to altoist Pony Poindexter soloing. The young man is leaning slightly forward, his eyes half shut, a slight smile on his face. He is listening so intently, so gently, that his whole body seems to be a receptacle for sound. The young man is John Coltrane.

Bop City carried the torch for 15 glorious years. But by the early '60s, musical tastes had changed. Jazz was not as popular with either whites or blacks. The club featured more R&B. In 1965, owner Charles Sullivan closed it down.

Sullivan was a remarkable man. He was born in Monroe County, Alabama, to an illiterate mother. He ran away from his adoptive father at age 13 and made his way to San Francisco. When the war broke out, he was the only qualified black machinist in California. He tried to get a job at the shipyards, but the union refused to hire blacks. Sullivan got 50 white machinists to testify on his behalf, but it took the personal intervention of President Roosevelt to get the union to hire him. During the war years he began opening bars and liquor stores in the Bay Area, including a liquor store just down the street from Bop City at 1623 Post. It was the first liquor store in San Francisco to make free deliveries. Branching into entertainment, he became the leading black music promoter on the West Coast.

The same year that Bop City closed, Sullivan played a key role in the birth of the music that would permanently relegate jazz to the high-art, low-audience niche. Sullivan loaned his dance license for the Fillmore Auditorium to a young promoter named Bill Graham. The Airplane, the Dead, Big Brother, Zappa, and other rock bands played there in 1966 and 1967, kicking off a musical revolution as profound as the one that created jazz.

Sullivan himself met an unhappy fate. In August 1966 he was found dead near Fifth and Bluxome Streets, shot in the heart. The case was never solved.

The ghosts of Vout City and Bop City haunt San Francisco, evoking a fabled time and neighborhood that will never return. But those legendary clubs were themselves haunted by a ghost—the ghost of Nippon Drugs, the business that had occupied the building for decades.

When Hatsuto Yamada returned to San Francisco from Topaz, he opened a new drugstore two blocks away at 1698 Sutter. The 1945–46 city directory shows that "Jas. H. Yamada" gave up his old residence on Divisadero and moved to 1950 Bush, between Laguna and Buchanan. Whether he owned the old building and sold it before being shipped off to the camp, or rented it, is not clear. But he never returned to 1690 Post.

Yamada renamed his new store Jim's Drug Company, after the "James" that he apparently began calling himself after the war. One wonders what "Jim" thought as he walked past his old store, now bearing the ironically similar name "Jimbo's."

After the war, some of the internees returned to Japantown, but many did not. As Reid Yoshio Yokoyama notes in one of the few studies of Japanese resettlement in San Francisco, many evacuees, believing ethnic enclaves exacerbated racism, thought it would be better to disperse. The major Japanese American organization, the Japanese American Citizens League, took the same position. JACL president Saburo Kido, who visited Japantown in late 1944, wrote that returning Japanese Americans would face four problems: housing, jobs, hostility from labor unions, and relations with blacks. Kido warned, "Since [blacks] occupy the former Japanese residential district, they will resent being displaced by returning evacuees."

A confidential government report echoed Kido's fears, predicting that "the release of Japanese from War Relocation Authority Camps will be the cause of friction and racial clashes when the Japanese arrive back in California."

Despite such concerns, about half the former residents of Japantown returned. They found that housing was indeed a major problem. Those who had been renters found that their apartments were occupied by others. Property owners, who may have constituted as much as half of the returnees, fared better, but not always. There were 13 occasions on which their property was seized by the government. At first many stayed in hostels or slept on cots. But gradually the Japanese Americans found places to live.

Work was also hard to find. Anti-Japanese sentiment continued to run deep for years after the war. (In 1949, the famous Japanese Tea Garden in Golden Gate Park was still being referred to as the "Oriental Tea Garden." The Hagiwara family, who had lovingly tended it for three generations, was not allowed to return to it; not until 1958 did ownership of the garden return to the Japanese community.) Many businesses would not hire Japanese: Some owners said their veteran workers would kill any "Japs" who were hired.

In late August 1945, more than 60 members of the AFL Machinists Union threatened to strike after they learned that a 37-year-old Nisei named Takeo Miyama had been placed as a mechanic with the Municipal Railway. Mayor Roger Lapham and State Senator Jack Shelley tried to convince the workers not to strike, but they refused to back down. Miyama was going to withdraw, but after a three-hour meeting with JACL and War Relocation Authority officials, he decided he would go to work, saying that he "would be betraying other Nisei and other minority groups if he abandoned his fight for a job." Miyama showed up for work at the barn the next morning, and the machinists put down their tools.

Facing 60 angry men, 2 men rose to defend Miyama. Both of them were bus drivers and part of a different AFL union. The first driver was a black man named Robert Gray. As the *Pacific Citizen* reported, Gray said, "When Negro bus drivers went to work for Muni there was some fuss at first, but soon everybody got used to it. If you boys let this man go to work, you'll find it'll be the same way." The second driver was an American Indian named James Burns, who said, "Do you want the sort of thing here that goes on in the old South?" But the machinists refused to yield, saying that because Miyama had not fought in the war, they would not work with him.

At this moment the chief radio technician at the barn, Harold Stone, spoke up. Just five months earlier, Stone had been awarded a Silver Star for bravery when his carrier, the U.S.S. *Franklin*, was devastated by Japanese dive-bombers on March 19 and 807 men were killed—the most casualties on any American warship during the war except the *Arizona*, sunk at Pearl Harbor. Stone said, "I didn't go out to fight in the Pacific so people with differently colored skin would be discriminated against when I got home." The war hero's speech made the difference. By a better than 2-to-1 margin, the machinists voted to stay on the job.

By 1946, 2,500 Japanese Americans had resettled in Japantown, about half of its original population. Within two years, the population was back to its old size. But most of these were newcomers. San Francisco State University professor Ben Kobashigawa found that only one-third of the 1,952 Japanese surnames listed in the directory were prewar names. By 1949 a lively but smaller Japantown was centered at Post and Buchanan, with 150 instead of 400 businesses.

It is difficult to get a clear picture of the relationship between blacks and Japanese-Americans after the war. Research is scanty, and neither group is interested in reopening any old wounds that may still exist. After her family moved to Japantown, the young Maya Angelou was struck by the fact that the Japanese seemed to have vanished into thin air, leaving not even a memory. "No member of my family and none of the family friends ever mentioned the absent Japanese," she wrote. "It was as if they had never owned or lived in the houses we inhabited." Keenly aware of the irony of one victimized people taking the place of another, Angelou wrote, "A person unaware of all the factors that make up oppression might have expected sympathy or even support from the Negro newcomers for the dislodged Japanese." Blacks did not feel such sympathy, Angelou believed, for all-too-human reasons: They were doing well, and because the Japanese weren't whites, they didn't have to fear or even consider them.

Some blacks shared the negative views of the Japanese held by most of society. The NAACP took only a tepid stand against internment. But many blacks had a more favorable view. A reporter for the *Afro-American* newspaper, Vincent Tubbs, went to San Francisco during the evacuation. During the course of his stay, Tubbs's attitude became more sympathetic to Japanese Americans, and he noted that the black community's attitude had also changed. Tubbs came to understand that, like blacks, the Japanese Americans had been victimized solely because of their race. He said that many blacks referred to Japanese Americans as their "good friends."

As for the returning Japanese Americans, they mostly wanted to avoid conflict and resume their lives. Some Issei, and to a lesser degree some Nisei, may have held racist attitudes, but if so, they did not express them. More likely the returnees were simply wary of their new neighbors. In *Making Home from War: Stories of Japanese American Exile and Resettlement*, one aged Nisei, who was sent with his family to live in Hunters Point, describes running away in fear as a child when he saw a large black man on the street, and offers a poignant apology for something that had clearly troubled him his entire life.

"In general, I would say the relations between the blacks and the Japanese were friendly, not chummy," 86-year-old Yokio Takakuwa, whose family returned to their home in Japantown after being interned, told me. "We tolerated each other and were decent to each other. There wasn't that much contact." Certainly the predicted clashes did not take place. When a black group, the Carver Club, put forward "Should the Japanese be returned to the West Coast?" as a debate topic, no one was willing to argue the negative side. There were numerous documented acts of black kindness toward the Japanese Americans: A black landlord saved Honnami Taieido's stock during Taieido's internment, allowing him to reopen his art goods store. The first cleric to welcome the returnees was a black minister, who invited them to join his church in San Francisco. In Oakland, black neighbors were among the first to welcome back a returning dentist and his wife. A number of black families took Japanese Americans into their homes.

During the 1950s and early 1960s, San Francisco's Little United Nations experienced a renaissance. Japantown, or Nihonmachi, was now a thriving Japanese American neighborhood adjoining a thriving black neighborhood. The two worlds collided at Post and Buchanan: Jimbo's Bop City was right next to one of the oldest Japanese businesses in the city, Uoki Sakai's fish market.

Judy Hamaguchi was a Nisei girl who grew up in a subdivided Victorian flat on Post Street, right next to Bop City. Despite the crowded conditions, she described Nihonmachi as a "great neighborhood for a child to grow up." Hamaguchi said that Jimbo Edwards would sometimes help her and her toddler brother cross the street to the Miyako restaurant, where her mother was a waitress.

The Western Addition was far from perfect. It had crime and drugs and high unemployment, and a lot of its buildings were decrepit and overcrowded. But for all of its faults, it was a living neighborhood—until the city decided to fix it.

The destruction of the Western Addition was the result of a perfect storm of good intentions, unconscious racism, naïveté, greed, and technocratic optimism. It was San Francisco's cardinal sin, and the city is still living with its legacy.

Most accounts of the Western Addition debacle emphasize the high-level planning decisions made after the war. But the die was cast during the war. The residents of Japantown had not even been shipped off to Tanforan when city officials began worrying about what to do with their run-down neighborhood. An April 16, 1942, *Chronicle* editorial headlined "Quick Action on Rehab of Jap Houses" read, "Departure of the Japanese from San Francisco presents an opportunity that will not come again to lift the face of a dreary section of the city—and at the same time creates a danger of the kind we are so prone to neglect until now. A blight now, the 20 blocks of 'Little Tokio' will become an outright slum if left alone. What to do? There's the rub." The paper acknowledged the city had only limited options, since the soon-to-be-imprisoned Japanese owned as much as 60 percent of Japantown.

There matters stood for a year. Then the flood of black shipyard workers into Japantown caught the attention of the authorities. In June 1943 the extreme overcrowding of the neighborhood led a city commission to investigate conditions. Its findings were alarming. In its story about the dire situation there, the *Chronicle* interviewed Robert Flippen, the respected black director of the just-built Westside Courts project, at Bush and Baker. Due to racist policies, they were the only wartime housing projects in San Francisco open to blacks. Flippen told the *Chronicle*, "I know of one place where 15 people live in one room—cook, eat and sleep there. They have no toilet facilities. For that purpose, they go to a filling station or out into the street. These 15 are 4 families. They sleep in shifts . . . They are willing to live in anything and a certain kind of landlord knows it."

The *Chronicle* reported, "All participating in the effort to find a solution emphasized that it is not a racial problem, but a social and health hazard that would be the same if the district were overcrowded with whites."

Japantown was indeed severely overcrowded, and city officials appear to have believed they were simply taking urgent action to clean up a health menace. But there was cultural and racial topspin. The fact that the "slum area" had been first a Japanese and then a black neighborhood clearly led officials to view Japantown as a kind of urban cancer that needed to be cut out. It was only the war that prevented the city from wielding its scalpel. And when the war ended, the scalpel came out.

In fact, the war whetted America's appetite for wielding the scalpel. It is no coincidence that "urban renewal" became a national policy after the war. If America could defeat the Nazis and the Japanese, why couldn't it solve inner-city blight by simply destroying the inner cities and building new ones? There may be an unconscious connection between the "strategic bombing" that left Berlin a heap of rubble and the urban renewal that eviscerated America's inner cities.

The federal government played a critical role in the nationwide campaign to remake inner cities. The 1949 Housing Act allocated $1.5 billion for urban renewal, defined as redevelopment of "blighted areas." The federal government would pay two-thirds of the costs of "renewing" such areas.

In 1947, the city hired the respected planner Mel Scott, a former journalist, to look into redeveloping the Western Addition. Located near downtown and with a politically weak population, it was a prime location for pro-growth forces.

Scott's role in what was to come was heartbreaking. He clearly meant well. He was not a racist. In his 1959 *The San Francisco Bay Area: A Metropolis in Perspective*, he defended the black residents who flooded into the Western Addition during the war, saying that "most of them were products of a social system that resolutely kept them 'in their place.'" He was one of America's first anti-sprawl and open-space advocates. And as we have seen, his 1961 survey triggered the movement to save the bay, a fact that qualifies him as one of the city's heroes. But Scott's report on the Western Addition was a product of the ignorance and hubris that marked urban planning at that time, and it sent the city down a terribly wrong path.

His official 74-page report asserted that rehabilitation would not work: "Nothing short of a clean sweep and a new start can make of the district a genuinely good place to love." A shorter version of the report, titled "New City: San Francisco Redeveloped," featured an illustration of a white couple standing on the balcony of a high-rise, looking out over the city. The text was hopeful modernist Muzak: "It is a green city. Broad lawns, trees, ample flowers form a setting for your 10-story apartment house. You look down on tree-lined walks and attractive spots for relaxation." The next page featured a ludicrously propagandistic double-page photo-collage depicting the blighted old neighborhood, "with its death-trap intersections" and "alleys in which juvenile gangs plotted mischief that sometimes ended in murder." Decaying Victorians, a wrecked car, a junk-filled yard, an overflowing trash can with a liquor bottle crudely drawn atop it, and a building with cartoon-like flames painted on it form the background against which two vaguely Filipino-looking urchins look out in mute appeal, next to a young white delinquent covering his face. With his striped double-breasted coat, jeans and pre-Elvis pompadour, he looks like he stepped out of the pages of Graham Greene's *Brighton Rock*.

Tactfully, no ominous black hoodlums are pictured in the report—in fact, no black people are depicted at all. But the city had no plan to include minorities in the "new city of space and living green." Noting that few of the "colored and foreign-born families" could afford to live in the new neighborhood, Scott asked the city to ensure they would be adequately housed in "future projects." The key word, and the one that revealed the limits of 1947 liberalism, was "future."

James Baldwin famously said, "Urban renewal is Negro removal." In his study of the Western Addition debacle, Jordan Klein correctly argues that it is too simplistic to reduce the entire complex movement to that motive. But as he also correctly notes, "in the Western Addition . . . urban renewal was 'Negro Removal' *by design*."

On June 3, 1948, despite resistance from black and Japanese American residents, the Board of Supervisors declared the Western Addition a blighted area and designated it for redevelopment. The San Francisco Redevelopment Agency was duly created in 1948, but for 10 years it did almost nothing. Then, in 1959, Justin Herman took charge. He was the man who was most responsible for urban renewal—and, ultimately, Negro removal—in San Francisco.

Herman was a dynamic, politically connected leader who made things happen. The city acquired the properties in the area by eminent domain and began bulldozing them. In 1960, Geary Boulevard was demolished and work began on the enormous Geary Expressway.

This third great transformation of the Western Addition turned out to be the most catastrophic of all of them. Redevelopment was supposed to be a win-win-win: Corporations and real estate interests would grow, the city would increase its tax base and clean up blighted areas, and the neighborhood's residents would be compensated for their losses and relocated in better housing. If the third part did not happen, the whole endeavor would be a failure. As Herman himself wrote, "Without adequate housing for the poor, critics will rightly condemn urban renewal as a land-grab for the rich and a heartless push-out for the poor and nonwhites."

Herman's words turned out to be prophetic. There was no adequate housing for the poor, because the planning for it was fatally flawed from the beginning. Klein lists the five critical mistakes. First, the destruction of housing units was not phased: Thousands of units were demolished, and new housing not built for years. As a result, by the time housing was available, the community had scattered. Second, the redevelopment plans relied on invalid, overly optimistic predictions of turnover and vacancy. Third, the income of the displaced people was overstated. Fourth, the planning ignored segregation and racial covenants. Fifth, it relied on SROs as replacement housing, but no one wanted to live in SROs.

Facing the destruction of their community, the residents of the Western Addition organized. In 1967 a coalition of progressive ministers and community leaders, including black leaders like Hannibal Williams and Japanese American ones like Yori Wada, formed the Western Addition Community Organization (WACO) to try to save their neighborhood. They picketed the SFRA, organized, and blocked bulldozers. WACO won some legal battles, managed to delay redevelopment, and got additional housing built, but it was too late. The battle was lost.

By the time the bulldozers fell silent, 883 businesses had been closed, 20,000 to 30,000 residents displaced, and 2,500 Victorian houses demolished. Most of the displaced people left the neighborhood for good.

The old, racially mixed neighborhood around Japantown was trashed. The Geary Expressway, designed in part to carry commuters to department stores on Masonic that no longer exist, was not only an ugly gash, it became a Berlin Wall separating blacks and Japanese Americans. The corporate Japan Center gutted Japantown. With the exception of old people, few Japanese Americans live in Japantown today.

What happened to Fillmore Street was worse. The heart and soul of black San Francisco was torn out. The loss only exacerbated a crisis fueled by unemployment. The demise of the shipyards and the disappearance of construction jobs forced blacks to look for work in service and tourism, where all too often they faced discrimination. "It's the same old loaded dice for a Negro in San Francisco," said a Fillmore resident. "They just sugar 'em up a little." As for the big housing projects built in the 1960s, they proved to be far more efficient petri dishes for growing crime and social pathologies than the crumbling old Victorians they replaced.

Minnie's Can-Do Club, the last of the great Fillmore clubs, died in 1974. Much of the Fillmore stood empty until the 1980s. Only one of the original businesses on Fillmore remains: the New Chicago Barber Shop at O'Farrell. Its proprietor, Reggie Pettus, coined the phrase "Fillmo' no' mo'."

The phrase could apply both to a neighborhood and a community. There are fewer and fewer blacks in San Francisco. Late one summer night in 2011 I walked the entire length of Fillmore, from Geary to Haight. I saw only one black person.

Trying to make amends for the past, in 1995 the city created the Historic Fillmore Jazz Preservation District in the heart of the old Fillmore. In a well-meaning attempt to revitalize the area, the city poured $15 million into loans to launch four jazz-themed restaurants and clubs, including a swanky San Francisco branch of the great Oakland jazz club Yoshi's. But it hasn't worked. All four businesses have had to repeatedly go back to the city for more money. They're too expensive for the black residents of the area and not enough nonresidents are coming in. The peculiar, sterile vibe of this stretch of Fillmore, with its high-rises and empty public spaces, doesn't help. But the real reason the "jazz district" is a failure is simple: Jazz isn't popular. Yoshi's was losing so much money it had to start booking non-jazz acts. The whole enterprise reeks of artificiality and museum culture and guilt.

As the Victorians crashed to the ground across the Western Addition, architectural preservationists and historians began cataloging them. A number of the most significant buildings were saved, but most were destroyed.

In the late 1970s, the Queen Anne Victorian at 1690 Post was slated to be razed as part of the Japantown renovation. But in another attempt at rectification, the Redevelopment Agency decided to make it part of a city-subsidized retail development called Victorian Village. Along with five other buildings, it was moved two blocks, to where it now stands, at 1712 Fillmore.

There can be no happy ending to the tragedy of the Western Addition, but there has been one for the haunted house. The building that once housed Nippon Drugs and Jimbo's Bop City is now home to Marcus Books, the oldest African American bookstore in the United States. I walked in there one fall day. The proprietor, Karen Johnson, was sitting behind the counter. She was a distinguished-looking black woman with a short gray Afro and the sardonic, dry wit of a book person. I asked her about the building's history and what she knew about Bop City. "My parents started the store in the 1960s," she told me in a soft voice that was at once steely and wry. "Dr. Julian and Raye Richardson. [Raye Richardson was the head of the Black

Studies Department at S.F. State.] It was one block up from here on Fill-more. My dad was a friend of Jimbo's. He used to go hear music there."

We talked briefly about the redevelopment fiasco. Johnson's contempt was glacial. "The store was in various locations during redevelopment," she said. "It was at Fillmore and Turk. Then we moved to Leavenworth and Golden Gate. There was a community groundswell to bring our store back to the neighborhood. Our family bought this building after it was moved. It had stood empty for seven years. They butchered it when they moved it. They messed up the plumbing, stole all the Victorian details, the fireplaces. We've been here since 1981. We're the only black business that returned to the Fillmore."

I asked Johnson where the famous back room that hosted the after-hours club was. She walked around to a table of books that stood in the center of the long, narrow room. "All of this was the back room," she said. "The restaurant in front was an add-on." She picked up a copy of *Harlem of the West*, the book with the amazing photograph of John Coltrane on the cover. "This picture was taken right here," she said. "Isn't that the coolest thing ever?" We stood there for a moment, seeing the ghosts.

I said goodbye to Johnson and walked out onto the street. It was still a scattershot scene. A Burger King and a senior housing place stood across the road. A handsome Indian restaurant was catty-corner from a Goodwill store.

I turned and looked back at the old purple building. It had been through most of San Francisco's history: The lighthearted 1890s. The great earth-quake and fire. The Little United Nations days when kids of all colors went to the same schools and lived on the same street. The decades when it was the Nippon Drugstore, run by a well-dressed man named Hatsuto—later James—Yamada. The Vout City interlude-orooni. The 15 years when it was Jimbo's Bop City, a legendary jazz club run by a black man who used to walk a little Japanese American girl across the street to find her mother. The years when everything around it was torn down. The day it was jacked up and moved. The years it stood empty. And the 32 years it has been a book-store, owned by a family who remember what needs to be remembered.

I walked over to Geary. People hurried down the sidewalk. The traffic roared underneath. Like a great river, the city flowed indifferently on.

CHAPTER 42

IF YOU WERE A BIRD

Lily Pond, 200 yards west of Hippie Hill, Golden Gate Park

I n 1965 San Francisco was rolling comfortably along on post-Eisenhower cruise control, a prosperous, increasingly corporate city busy tearing down its poor neighborhoods and historic buildings and throwing up high-rises and freeways. For all its vaunted bohemianism, its power structure was deeply conservative. Tough, working-class Irish Americans had dominated San Francisco politics since the city's birth, and an Irish Catholic old boys' network ran the city—Mayor Jack Shelley, Police Chief Tom Cahill, and Judge Raymond O'Connor of Juvenile Court, with Archbishop Joseph Mc-Gucken wielding spiritual and temporal power offstage. The old Beat haunt, North Beach, had been taken over by topless clubs. In Berkeley, the free speech movement had galvanized students the year before, but there was no evidence that anything weird was brewing.

Yet in 1965, a strange delirium began to grow in San Francisco. You couldn't call it a movement. You couldn't really call it anything. What name could you give to a way of life held together only by LSD and rock music? But whatever it was, it got stronger and stronger. And by the summer of 1967, it had become so powerful that 75,000 young people from around the world flooded into the Haight-Ashbury. They called it the Summer of Love, and it remains one of the most enigmatic episodes in American history.

I just missed getting both extremely loaded barrels of it. I was only 14 in 1967, a few years too young to experience that summer's once-only craziness. (When it comes to recollections of the Summer of Love, don't trust anybody under 63.) But the hippie era was not confined to a three-month or even a three-year period. It was a cultural H-bomb whose metaphysical radiation spread far and wide, and its half-life has still not expired. Growing up in Berkeley, I was close enough to ground zero to be dazzled, discomfited, and derailed. I lived out my own version of the sixties. It was not particularly noteworthy—hair down to my ass, wonderful and scary acid trips, black velvet coats, adolescent dreams of total Rimbaudian freedom, dropping out of Yale, going to work at a shipyard, reading Nietzsche, working dead-end jobs, returning to U.C. Berkeley after another acid trip—and I bring it up only because it demonstrates that everyone who was touched by the sixties lived it out in a unique way. Infinite permutations and variations and different spiritualities and politics and types of humanity were all subsumed under the rubric of "hippie." The received image of a woo-wooing, it's-all-so-cosmic hippie is about as insightful as the "LSD Story" episode on *Dragnet*.

The hippies did not appear out of a void. They were creatures of a disturbed leisure society. Beneath its prosperity, America was haunted by dark realities: the assassination of JFK, the escalating Vietnam War and the draft, the eclipse of the civil rights movement, and the rise of black militancy. The fissures in American society that had been covered up by the great resolve-driven unity of World War II were widening and could no longer be ignored. As Charles Perry notes in his insightful *The Haight-Ashbury: A History*, in dealing with this situation, the original hippie community drew on the bohemian ethos of self-discovery and self-assertion, as most recently enunciated by the Beats. But the hippies differed from the Beats in important ways. The Beats tended to see themselves as victims, they identified with blacks, and their writings had a nihilistic tone. The hippies didn't see themselves as victims, identified not primarily with blacks but with American Indians, and rejected nihilism. In short, they were less alienated from society than the Beats were, and for that very reason more independent (but also more naïve). With their raging against the cold war and the Man and normative sexuality, the Beats were trapped in the Hegelian dialectic of the master and the slave. The hippies simply walked out of jail.

Like all revolutions, the hippie one was ignited by specific local actors and events, from the benefit for the San Francisco Mime Troupe thrown by a young ex-businessman named Bill Graham, to the canine-loving Pine Street communards who opened a concert hall called the Family Dog, to the advent of the "heavy hippies" known as the Diggers, who provided free food, sarcasm, and gravitas to the carnival. The trail is too convoluted to retrace here, but one aspect of it is too weird and wonderful to pass up. If something as shapeless and free-form as the hippie phenomenon can be said to have a beginning, it came when the self-invented San Francisco band the Charlatans went to play at the self-invented bar the Red Dog in Virginia City, Nevada.

This gig united the ethos of the Old West and the nascent hippie one in a weird and wonderful way. When the town sheriff went to the club's opening night, he politely asked one of the club's owners, a peyote-eating wild man named Don Works, if he could check his revolver at the door. Works took the sheriff's gun, expertly twirled the chambers, fired two shots into the floor, and handed it back, saying, "Works fine, sheriff." The ghost of Mark Twain, who worked in Virginia City as a reporter before his ill-fated stint as a scoop-grubbing "lokulitems" in San Francisco, would have cracked up.

The dances rocked on, the bands got better, the acid kept coming, and the word got out. By summer 1967, tens of thousands of young people from across the country and around the world were making their way to the Haight-Ashbury.

City hall was none too thrilled about the invasion. As David Talbot recounts in *Season of the Witch*, the authorities refused to help deal with the urgent health crisis that erupted, leaving David Smith, founder of the Haight-Ashbury Free Clinic, to fight his noble battle single-handedly. But other key players in the city reached deeper into San Francisco's wild and roistering past and welcomed the hippies. *Chronicle* editor Scott Newhall had no personal affinity for the hippies—he was a jazz and martini guy—but he made sure his paper defended them. Herb Caen showed up on New Year's Eve at the Fillmore to welcome in 1967 by dancing to Jefferson Airplane. The *Chronicle*'s tolerant tone played a crucial role in shaping the Bay Area's attitudes toward the hippies.

In the end, the hippie explosion was really about three things—grass, rock, and acid—and what they did to people's minds. That's why you can't really write a history about it. It's like writing the history of a moving, infinitely fractured dream. As a piece in issue no. 9 of the hippie newspaper the *Oracle* put it, the Haight was "an abstract vortex for an indefinable pilgrimage."

Or, rather, for tens of thousands of indefinable pilgrimages—hundreds of thousands, if you count all the people around the country who didn't physically make it to the Haight but traveled there nonetheless. Leonard Cohen once said, "The revolution has to take place in every room," and the secret history of the hippie era is found in documents like the following letter sent to the *Oracle* by a young woman from New York:

Dear *Oracle* People,

This is a plea for help.

I am being held prisoner. I am the prison that holds me captive and I can't seem to escape myself.

Up until a few months ago when I took my first trip, I thought there was no reason to be alive and was about to settle on merely existing . . . trying to get by the next fifty years or so that way. But I saw that there is more.

But New York City is an awful place. The Lower East Side cannot be believed as to what it does to human dignity and freedom. It seems everyone is looking West and all anyone talks about here is when they are leaving for the Coast.

I am afraid. What if it isn't as it seems . . . as acid has shown me life ought to be. I've heard so much . . . read so much. Your paper is beautiful, beautiful, beautiful. But because I'm not just stifled by the environment but by myself . . . it is a very hard thing to summon the courage to act and come there. Like anyone, I've been stepped on a lot and have reacted by learning the futility of my words and rarely find the courage to do more than smile at a friendly face . . .

If someone has read this far—please, please could someone, would someone take the time to write me and tell me the right things so I won't be afraid to come to San Francisco. Please . . . something concrete—a name, an address— something to come to. I need direction and I think maybe I could give a lot if someone would help me . . . or even better, need my help. Thank you.

Love,

V.M.

NYC

The entire history of the era we call the sixties, everything good, bad, and indifferent about it is contained in that one heartbreaking line: "What if it isn't as it seems . . . as acid has shown me life ought to be." There is, of course, no answer to that question. But what remains inspiring about the hippies, for all their foolishness and narcissism, is that they tried to find out the answer. They pursued intense experiences for their own sake. As much as Cabrillo and Portola, they were explorers, but the terra incognita they ventured into was inside them.

Forests have been sacrificed by people pondering the legacy of the sixties. There is a sense in which the question is irrelevant. What is the legacy of an epiphany? The societal impact of a vision? When a reporter at the Human Be-In, the gathering at the Golden Gate Park Polo Field, which as much as any event was the climax of the era, asked Allen Ginsberg if it would last, he replied, "How do *I* know if it will last? And if it doesn't turn out, who cares?" There was no odometer for those inner voyages, no gold medal awarded after a wrestling match between an angel and the spirit of gravity. But there is a human legacy: All those people who listened to the music, sought the light, took the acid, or smoked the grass opened the doors of perception in their own way, and emerged when it was all over to carry on their lives, to find new ways to make connections with the ineffable, or just to live as deeply and richly and decently as they could. The true motto for the sixties was Nietzsche's aphorism "Not the intensity but the duration of high feelings makes high men."

Not everyone was able to walk down from the magic mountain and keep going. Some people burned out; others became California cartoons, simultaneously blissed-out and prone to inane conspiracy theories. But many did, and America is better off because of them. The spirit of the sixties, which is really just another way of saying the free spirit, lives on in the enriched lives of a million normal people.

And it lives on in the music that drove the sixties. It would almost have been an ex post facto repudiation of the whole crazy episode if its soundtrack had been all Paul Revere and the Raiders and the Strawberry Alarm Clock. But it wasn't. A masterpiece like Jefferson Airplane's *After Bathing at Baxter's*, still as avant-garde as it was the day it was released (Bill Graham hated it, saying, "There's nothing on it you can hum"), captures the creativity, the daring, the brains, the sheer vitality that pulsed through San Francisco during that once-in-a-lifetime explosion.

You could choose a hundred sites in the Haight to epitomize the hippie era. But unlike the Beats, whose rebellious noir spirit comes to life in darkened streets, the site cannot be urban. The corner of Haight and Ashbury does not evoke the spirit of the sixties any more now than it did when busloads of gawkers drove past it with Richard Brautigan holding up a mirror to the windows. The hippie era needs open skies.

So it's better to wander into Golden Gate Park. First to the Children's Playground, in honor of the essentially childlike, innocent nature of the whole crusade. Then across the big meadow to Hippie Hill, where the unruly tribes once gathered. And then over the road to the Lily Pond (formerly known, in an apropos coincidence, as Hobo Lake), one of the most magical places in the park, whose giant tree ferns and ancient chert folds give it the look of a dinosaur-haunted grotto in the Jurassic era. Who knows how many hallucinated pterodactyls rose into the air here in those bygone days?

And from there, anywhere. As the Airplane sang in "The Ballad of You and Me and Pooneil":

If you were a bird and you lived very high
You'd lean on the wind when the breeze came by
You'd say to the wind as it took you away
That's where I wanted to go today . . .

CHAPTER 43

THE GREATEST
of THESE

18th and Castro Streets

There are many heroes in the history of San Francisco. There is Father José María Fernández, the city's first whistle-blower, who lost his position and his mental health standing up for the Indians in his charge. There is U.S. Navy Lieutenant Frederick Freeman, shouting "Sock it to 'em!" as he fought the inferno on the wharves. There is Donaldina Cameron, who dedicated her life to saving Chinese girls from sexual slavery. There are the three Muni employees, black and Native American and white, who stood up for a Japanese American man who wanted to work. There are the three faculty wives who led the fight to save the bay. There is David Smith of the Haight-Ashbury Free Clinic, who stepped forward when the Summer of Love threatened to turn into the Summer of Death. There are the neighborhood groups that organized to stop the freeways, and the preservation groups that stopped the wanton destruction of the city's architectural heritage, and the citizens' groups that fought the razing of the Western Addition.

But of all the heroes in the city's history, the ones who most truly epitomized the spirit of the gentle saint for whom the city was named were San Francisco's gays and lesbians during the AIDS crisis. Confronted with an unprecedented and unthinkable horror, San Francisco's gay community transformed itself into a gigantic family—comforting the sick, burying the dead, fighting for justice, and demanding that society live up to the ethical tenets without which no civilization is worthy of the name. It was an epic of compassion, commitment, and love that went largely unseen, but can stand shoulder to shoulder with any heroic feat performed in any war.

To anyone who had a front-row seat for the erotic bacchanalia that was the Castro in the late 1970s and early 1980s, the idea that any kind of heroism would come out of it, other than the ability to have sex with eight men in one night, would have seemed about as likely as Mother Theresa becoming a pole dancer. As a taxi driver, I had that seat. For years, several nights a week, I got to observe the Castro in its full glory. And it was a sexual madhouse that would have led Tiberius to sell his Capri villa and buy a one-way galley ticket to San Francisco.

Before we revisit that epic debauch, however, we need to briefly trace the history of gays in San Francisco. Despite the city's loose reputation, open homosexuality scarcely existed before the 1930s. Cross-dressing "queens" promenaded down Market Street, and there was some action in the Tenderloin and in the old Embarcadero YMCA, but the city's gay population was small and secretive. That began to change during World War II, when servicemen, straight and gay, flooded into town and bars like Mona's, Finocchio's, and the Black Cat Café began catering to a bohemian crowd that included gays and lesbians.

The Black Cat was one of the most intriguing bars in America. The onetime haunt of John Steinbeck and William Saroyan, it began to attract increasing numbers of homosexuals in the 1940s, who happily mingled with Beat poets and longshoremen. The bar became a center of the so-called homophile movement, a groundbreaking advocacy movement that included the Mattachine Foundation and the Daughters of Bilitis. The Black Cat's most famous performer was José Sarria, an amazingly ahead-of-his-time figure famous for performing Bizet's *Carmen* in drag on the city streets, where he would merrily dodge the vice cops. Sarria urged the bar's patrons to be open about their sexuality and at closing time would lead them in a rousing version of "God Save Us Nelly Queens," set to the music of "God Save the Queen."

The unamused authorities, determined to stamp out "sexual deviancy," or at least force it deep underground, harassed the Black Cat mercilessly, finally forcing it out of business in 1963. In 1961, police raided the Tay-Bush Inn (located, unsurprisingly, at the corner of Taylor and Bush) and arrested more than 100 homosexuals, the largest such raid in the city's history.

But the forces of sexual repression were barking up the wrong city. The publicity created by the homophile movement began to draw national attention to the gay scene in San Francisco. The crucial event, oddly, was a two-part *Life* magazine series in June 1964 about homosexuality in the United States. The article's claim that homosexuals preferred California because of its "easy hospitality" (an unexpected legacy of the Californios) became a self-fulfilling prophecy. A character in Jack Fritscher's 1990 "memoir-novel" *Some Dance to Remember* says, "An engraved invitation to every faggot in America wouldn't have caused more of a sensation."

Gays and lesbians began moving to San Francisco. An ill-advised 1965 police raid on a homophile gathering at California Hall on Polk, which infuriated the numerous straight attendees, proved a watershed in police relations with the city's homosexuals. No longer would the city's police have carte blanche to harass gays and lesbians. (The Reichstag-like California Hall seems to attract police idiocy: In 1984 cops got in trouble for handcuffing a gay cadet to a chair onstage, where a hooker gave him a blow job.)

The floodgates opened. Between 1969 and 1978, close to 30,000 gay men moved to San Francisco, along with thousands of lesbians. By the mid-'70s, gay men had claimed four distinct neighborhoods: Polk Street, the Tenderloin, South of Market, and Castro Street. As Josh Sides notes in *Erotic City: Sexual Revolutions and the Making of Modern San Francisco*, "At no time in the history of the world had as many openly gay men claimed as much urban terrain as they did in San Francisco during the 1960s and 1970s."

When I moved to town in 1971, there was more gay action on Polk than on Castro. But that soon changed. The Twin Peaks bar at Market and Castro opened in 1972; it was one of the first gay bars in the country to have picture windows, a development fraught with symbolism. And once a critical mass was reached, the party was on.

For 10 years or so, starting around 1973, the Castro District was the world's biggest sexual candy store. They were giving it away all night, every night. Driving down Castro Street you almost had to put your windshield wipers on, there was so much testosterone being sprayed around. Guys were grinding pelvises on every corner. There were more hard-ons than in a pool full of ninth-grade boys being taught how to swim by Brigitte Bardot. It was so out of control that as a straight man, I had to make up a thought experiment to understand it: Imagine if you and several thousand other young, good-looking, horny straight men were plunked down in a vast pickup bar filled with every conceivable variety of attractive women, all of whom—here is where the thought experiment requires considerable willing suspension of disbelief—wanted to have sex with you, not after four dates, or two months, or some unspecified period of time that they could use to ascertain that you were not a bozo, but *immediately*. Tonight. In 10 minutes. Change the women to men, and that was the Castro. The whole scene can be pretty much summed up by the immortal Flight of the Conchords song "Too Many Dicks (On the Dance Floor)." Except that there weren't too many. There were enough for everyone.

As a taxi driver, I got hit on a lot in the 2 A.M. desperation. I confess I trimmed my sails into the prevailing sexual winds a few times. One time a gay man on the corner of Fillmore and California was trying to flag a cab. I pulled up at the same moment another cab did. The fare looked at both of us, wavering. To my eternal shame, I batted my eyes at the guy. Saying coquettishly, "Oh, I'm in a *Yellow* mood today," he chose me. I felt like a low-down lying ho', but I took his $5 anyway.

It was all good clean dirty fun, and it seemed like it would go on forever. But a dreadful visitor had slipped into the party, like the costumed figure of Death slinking through Rio's Carnaval in *Black Orpheus*. Its presence was announced on December 10, 1981, when the gay newspaper the *San Francisco Sentinel* ran a story by a registered nurse named Bobbi Campbell. The piece opened, "I'm Bobbi Campbell and I have 'gay cancer.' "

That September, Campbell had noticed he had some purple spots on his feet. He went to the doctor, who diagnosed Campbell as having an extremely rare disease called Kaposi's sarcoma. Normally KS, as it came to be called, was found among elderly Jewish or Italian men, but for some reason, a lot of gay men were getting it. Campbell courageously decided he wanted to be the "KS Poster Boy," alerting gays to the dangers of this mysterious new disease. A few weeks later, he convinced the Star Pharmacy, on the corner of 18th and Castro, to put up photos of the purple blotches that had begun to cover his body.

Anyone who has ever been diagnosed with a potentially fatal disease can remember exactly where they were and what they were doing when they got the news. One's life divides into Before Diagnosis and After Diagnosis. Campbell's poster had that effect on a young graduate student in creative writing named Ed Wolf. In David Weissman's deeply moving 2011 documentary *We Were Here*, Wolf recalls the night he saw the poster.

I'll never forget it. There was a great double feature at the Castro, *Casablanca* on the big screen. I ran down to the Star Pharmacy because we were going to smoke some dope and I didn't have any papers, and on the window there were these little Polaroid photos that this young man had taken of himself. The first one was of him opening his mouth, and inside there were these little purple splotches. And big purple splotches on his chest. There was a handwritten note that said something like, "Watch out, guys. There's something out there." Oh my God, it made this huge impact on me. Then I got stoned and watched the movie, but the whole movie I was just thinking about that. I went to see the movies with this friend of mine named Michael. And he had woken up recently with this splotch in his eye. He kept going, "What is this? What is this?" He had been going to the eye doctor. It turned out to be KS in his eye. So it was right there in the movie line with us. Like it was already there.

"It" was not only there; it was already widespread. HIV probably arrived in San Francisco in 1976. By 1979, 10 percent of the city's gay men were probably infected. By June 1981, about 20 percent were infected. If there were 1,000 gay men in the Castro Theatre that night, 200 were probably infected—and more than half of them would die.

The posting of Bobbi Campbell's photos was like the tolling of a dark bell. And what made it more terrible was that it tolled not just for individuals but also for an entire community. As more and more gay men came down with dreadful, little-known diseases like *Pneumocystis carinii* pneumonia, and as more and more of them began to die, every gay man in San Francisco realized that he, too, could die. By 1997, 15,548 San Franciscans had died in the epidemic—more than all the Californians who were killed, wounded, captured, and missing in World War II. It was one of the most horrific ordeals ever visited upon any community of people in the world.

But even as the disease relentlessly spread, the party in the Castro raged on, like the Masque of the Red Death in Poe's nightmarish story. Cognitive dissonance prevailed: Men standing in line at the vast Club Baths at Eighth and Howard jokingly called the address "AIDS and Howard" but went in anyway. After a media scare in the summer of 1982, the attendance at the bathhouses, the primary vectors of infection, went up. Public health officials who suggested that the bathhouses be closed down were denounced as moralistic homophobes. In 1983, when AIDS activist and Democratic political aide Bill Kraus called upon gay men to change their lifestyle by giving up the bathhouses, writing, "We gay men can transform this epidemic into our finest hour," he was called a "sexual Nazi" and a self-hating gay.

This reaction was tragically misguided, but it was at least partly understandable. As Randy Shilts argues in his groundbreaking book *And the Band Played On*, the gay community reacted to the epidemic with the classic five stages of grief: denial, anger, bargaining, depression, and acceptance. In 1983, it was still in the anger stage.

Straight San Francisco was still slower to spring into action. In a move that summed up prevailing attitudes, Mayor Dianne Feinstein in December 1982 reluctantly vetoed a domestic partners bill that would have given gay couples the same rights as married ones. Feinstein was the most progressive Democrat in the country on gay issues, and San Francisco the most enlightened city. But as Shilts points out, "For all the acceptance gays had gained, homosexuality was still not accepted as equal in the city they called Mecca. A prevailing morality that viewed homosexuals as promiscuous hedonists incapable of deep, sustaining relationships ensured that it would be impossible for homosexuals to legitimize whatever relationships they could forge." Even the liberals who supported gay rights tended to stereotype gays as free spirits and free agents who eschewed family and other commitments. Gays were seen as a lot of things, but caregivers were not one of them.

But from the earliest days of the epidemic, some San Franciscans had rolled up their sleeves and gone to work. One of the places where they worked was Ward 5B at San Francisco General Hospital, the nation's first AIDS unit. Almost all the patients at 5B were dying. And everyone who worked on the ward, in those early days when AIDS was as frightening as Ebola, was a volunteer.

One of those volunteers was Ed Wolf. In *We Were Here*, he recalled how he responded to an appeal from an organization called the Shanti Project, asking people to be buddies with people who had AIDS. The sensitive, serious Wolf had not been a successful cruiser in the gay bar scene, but when he met the man he was assigned to befriend, he said he realized that "my way of being with gay men was perfect." He took the Shanti training and began working at 5B. There he made a discovery that touched him profoundly. "This is where I started to encounter lesbians coming to work on the AIDS unit with all these gay men who were dying," Wolf said. "It was so moving because certainly gay men were not making a whole lot of room for lesbians, let's put it that way. So I got this sense of this group of people who were really caring for these men who were dying." From cleaning bedpans to donating blood to the most crucial task of all, simply providing loving support to frightened young men who were about to die, San Francisco's lesbians were in the front ranks of the fight from the beginning.

They were joined by other San Franciscans, straight and gay. The city was still reeling from the 1978 assassinations of Mayor George Moscone and Supervisor Harvey Milk and the appalling massacre at Jonestown, but its citizens rose to the occasion. Like Eileen Glutzer, a young woman who had come to the Haight-Ashbury in the hippie era, stayed in the city, and become a registered nurse. Glutzer volunteered to work on 5B. As she told Weissman, "I remember my mom saying, 'Why do you have to do this?' Because I've already put my mom through a lot of stuff. And I remember saying to my mom, 'Mom, I didn't choose it. It chose me.' Because you're there. And this terrible thing is happening, and you're a nurse, and you can help. And sometimes that's just helping somebody die. But you know, I couldn't turn my back to it."

Or a retired grandmother named Ruth Brinker. When Brinker realized that many people with AIDS were suffering from malnutrition, she started a meal service called Project Open Hand. The charity that started with meal deliveries to seven people grew to serve more than 1,000 meals a day.

But the foot soldiers in the great war were gay men. Death is a touchstone: It strips people down to their essential nature. And the AIDS epidemic revealed a strength, a compassion, and a grit in San Francisco's gay community that had been obscured by the wild partying. In a deeper sense, the crisis *created* the gay community. Organizations sprang up everywhere, dedicated to everything from providing housing to lobbying for more funding to medical care to psychological support to pet care. These community efforts, combined with the city's increasingly muscular response, became known as the "San Francisco model." To this day, it remains the international standard for fighting AIDS.

But the deepest, darkest battles took place inside gay men's hearts and minds. By a dreadful irony, a culture devoted to youth and physical beauty was ravaged by a disease that destroyed both. The hideous visibility of AIDS made an already terrifying disease still more terrifying. When I was diagnosed with colorectal cancer at age 39, I used to dread having to go to the hospital and mingle with other cancer patients: I once saw a middle-age man who was obviously dying, and the sight was too frightening. But there was no hiding AIDS. The first time I saw a man with full-blown AIDS on Market Street, I thought he was 80 years old. It wasn't until I got closer that I realized he was probably only 30. There were so many emaciated men in the Castro that it looked like Auschwitz. Those suffering from KS were covered with purple blotches and spots. Infected gay men in San Francisco saw men who were worse off than they were every day. Those who were not infected had to confront the gaunt faces and ravaged bodies that could soon be theirs—and until the first viable AIDS test was introduced in 1985, they had no way of knowing if they carried the virus. This meant almost every gay man in San Francisco was living under a sword of Damocles, knowing that the next time he looked in the mirror he might discover that he had contracted a disease that would not only probably kill him, but would also disfigure him and possibly blind him and destroy his brain.

The Castro was ravaged by something that felt like more than a disease. It felt like a medieval Triumph of Death—and whited sepulchres like Jerry Falwell were quick to assert that the plague was "God's judgment." And it was not just right-wing bigots who failed the simple test of human empathy. Some parents of dying AIDS patients did as well.

Standard hospital protocol gave biological families the right to decide who saw patients in the critical care unit. On Ward 5B, one mother refused to allow her dying son's longtime lover to remain in the room. "I'm his mother and I don't want any faggots in this room," she said. "And I don't want any of those nurses who are faggots. They did this to him." The young man began to cry but was unable to speak because he was on a ventilator. He died a few days later and never saw his partner again. As a result of this episode, AIDS nursing coordinator Cliff Morrison instituted a new policy. Henceforth, the patients on 5B would decide who could visit them.

So San Francisco's gay men became each other's family. They took care of each other and laughed with each other and held each other's hands when they were scared and, when the time came, buried them. To me, the most overpowering image in *We Were Here* is a still photograph of a heartbreakingly young man with KS. His sweet face is covered with purple spots. He is smiling radiantly at the camera. Next to him are two other men, equally young, and on their faces are the same radiant smiles. It is a San Francisco Pietá.

In *Plays Well with Others*, his novel about being a young gay artist in AIDS-ravaged 1980s New York, Allan Gurganus says, "Maybe more important than any single work of art we had yet made—we'd founded this ragged-ass impromptu village. Insane, fleeing towns of ten thousand in order to found another just two hundred strong. But its unity would lead us, goad us, bully us—toward our greatest masterpiece—the nursing, cheering, burying of our own." Gurganus's words are just as true of the gays of San Francisco. As Bill Kraus, who did not survive the epidemic, said, it was their finest hour.

Today Castro Street has bounced back. It may not be the nonstop party that it once was, but it's full of life. Walking down it, it's hard to imagine the plague years, and it's almost too painful to try. All those young men died and they will never come back. But something besides death came out of those terrible years. It is not something that is easy to put into words. But St. Francis of Assisi, who gave away all that he had when he saw a poor man in need, would have recognized it, and bowed his head.

CHAPTER 44

ROTA FORTUNAE

South Park

The first time I saw South Park it was 1972 and I had recently moved to San Francisco after leaving my shipyard job in Newport News. My father was one of the inventors of biofeedback, and when I came back to the Bay Area, he got me a job running a sleep experiment paid for by the company that invented the waterbed. The company was hoping to be able to run ads saying "Scientific research proves you sleep better on a waterbed." Every night for a month or so, I hooked up electrodes to the heads of subjects and monitored their sleep cycles, which I recorded on an EEG machine. It was a peculiar experience, trying to stay awake all night in a little office next to the Chinatown Gate on Bush and watching the automatic pens on the machine make cryptic spiky patterns on the unfurling paper as the subjects' brain waves jumped and twitched. Unhappily for the waterbed company, the results proved inconclusive. But I was getting paid, and the job left my days free to wander around San Francisco.

One afternoon I took a long walk south of Market Street. I walked for hours. I went down the old Skid Row on Third Street, past a dingy hofbrau and bar called Breen's, which had a faded sign that read "Sliced before your eyes since 1925." Bums slumped in doorways. I walked down Folsom. I had no idea where I was. It was all gray and industrial. I walked and walked. Cities were new to me, and it was all fascinating. Late in the afternoon, going up Second Street, I saw what looked like a little park. I headed toward it.

I found myself in a peculiar little oval. It looked like a Dickensian mews that had seen better days. There were a few decaying Victorian houses on it, next to some run-down buildings that looked like auto parts stores or the like. The center of the oval was a decrepit patch of grass, covered with litter and dog shit, ringed by a few sad benches. A bum stumbled across the grass holding a pint bottle. At the far end of the oval, five or six old black men were standing around a rusty trash can in which a fire was burning. Acrid black smoke blurred the weary late afternoon sky. I walked reverently by the men. I felt like I had stumbled on a dark and holy and weirdly ancient urban secret, one that I had been looking for without knowing it. I never forgot that moment.

Flash forward 28 years to 1999. San Francisco is a dot-com madhouse and its lunatic heart is South Park. The desolate oval where those old bums once warmed themselves at garbage-can fires is filled with young hipsters in neo-Beat haircuts and $300 shoes, all holding on for dear life to a rocket heading for the money stratosphere at the speed of stupidity. Every 10th person sitting with a laptop at Caffe Centro is a multimillionaire. Most of them are under 40. A lot of them are under 30. They are working for start-ups that have big plans to sell pet food online. The VC boys are throwing $10 million at anything with a ".com" at the end. On Jones Street atop Nob Hill, where it's impossible to park, people are simply leaving their Mercedes and BMWs on the sidewalks at night, writing off the $200 ticket. It's a money orgy.

I'm in the middle of the pile. Four years earlier, I had left my union job at the *San Francisco Examiner* to help launch an online magazine called Salon.com. Salon had started out as eight people sharing a floor with an architect's office on Main Street. Most of us were former *Examiner* staffers who were lured away by Salon founder David Talbot. Only later did Talbot inform us that he had started the whole thing with only a $75,000 investment. We had no idea what we were doing. We started out publishing biweekly and put original artwork on every story. In 1999, we're a daily, the Internet has driven the financial world insane, and Salon has just gone public. The stock is trading at $10 a share. I have 85,000 stock options. I am 46 years old and am rapturous at the idea that I and a few other ink-stained wretches will be the first journalists in the history of the world to get rich. On the back of an envelope I scrawl the names of the cars I want to buy. A Jaguar, a Morgan . . . Will that leave enough for the country house?

Flash forward 13 years to 2012. South Park is quiet. There are no more bums and garbage-can fires, but the hipsters who used to sit on the grass like a flock of rich pigeons are gone. After the dot-com bubble burst in 2000, the city emptied out like a bawdy house full of politicians during a raid. So did my bank account. Thinking it would go up—ah, the eternal recurrence of tulipmania!—I never sold my Salon stock. It became worthless, and because I had compounded my idiocy by exercising my options, I had to pay $110,000 in taxes on money I never made. Salon stumbled along, breaking stories and carrying on the San Francisco tradition of maverick journalism—and losing lots of money. It turned out that there was no business model for a general-interest online publication with a large paid staff. Eventually I, along with a lot of other people, was laid off.

I take some solace in the fact that the whole bizarre dot-com episode was in the finest San Francisco tradition. The city was discovered as the result of a series of comedic errors, settled by drunks and runaways and mavericks, and exploded into urban existence as a result of a mass outburst of greed unparalleled in history. A few got rich, but most did not. For some 49ers, the gold rush was a disaster. But for most, it was a great adventure, one they would not have missed for anything. At the beginning of his ur-Gonzo masterpiece *Roughing It*, the former miner and San Francisco newspaperman Mark Twain dedicated his book to his friend Calvin H. Higbie, "in memory of the curious time when we two were millionaires for ten days." Twain knew that after you've seen the elephant and are left with only a big pile of shit, all you can do is laugh.

So yes, it would have been nice to have gotten rich. But I got to work for almost 15 years at a magazine where we published what we wanted and had no bosses except ourselves. That was worth more than a pile of stock options. So at least I tell myself.

It's fitting that South Park was the center of the dot-com boom and bust, for South Park is San Francisco's ultimate boom and bust neighborhood. In 1854, an Englishman named George Gordon laid out 17 elegant brick houses on an oval surrounded by Second, Third, Bryant, and Brannan Streets. The reason Gordon chose this site is found in the 1856 *San Francisco Directory*, which describes it as "the only level spot of equal area, free from sand, within the city limits." The floral park inside the oval was surrounded by a wrought-iron fence to which only residents had the key, a patrician setup still irritatingly observed in Gramercy Park in New York City. South Park became the city's first fashionable neighborhood, home to Senator William Gwin (who built the city's first ballroom) and other Southern aristocrats, who threw grand dress balls, musicales, theatricals, and less formal gatherings called "kettledrums." But South Park's *Gone with the Wind* period did not last long. In 1869, a road was cut through the hill at Second Street, ruining the character of the neighborhood. Soon the social elite had moved to Nob Hill, which had been made accessible in 1873 when the cable cars began running.

South Park never recovered its cachet. It was home to the city's first Japantown, then was swallowed up by the vast working-class area known as South of the Slot. Today South Park has benefited from the gentrification at Mission Bay and AT&T Park, but it has not regained its dot-com glory. It remains an ex-patrician remnant.

I don't find myself in South Park that often. But whenever I do, I feel like I'm looking at a stage set of my own life. It's one of those odd places in the city whose history mirrors my own. It's been up and it's been down, and then it's been up again and down again. It's hosted Scarlett O'Hara barbecues and hobo-jungle campfires. It's seen dot-com moguls and dot-com bankrupts. And it's still there, waiting to turn again, a Great Wheel of Fortune flattened into an oval off Second Street.

CHAPTER 45

THE SAND CASTLE

Aquatic Park

Of all the places in San Francisco, Aquatic Park is the one I've had the most fun in. The little stretch of sandy beach at the foot of Polk Street enchanted me from the first time I saw it 40 years ago. And since then, it has remained an old friend, like Rat and Mole's river in *The Wind in the Willows*—a companion whose conversation never palls, whose countenance never darkens, whose spirit remains forever carefree.

A big part of the beach's charm is its tiny size. Only 400 yards long, it's protected by the gently curving Municipal Pier on one end, and by the old wooden buildings that house the venerable Dolphin and South End Rowing Clubs on the other. Its toylike quality is heightened by the enormous ship model in reinforced concrete that faces it. Architects Mooser and Mooser's spectacular 1939 streamline moderne building, now the Maritime Museum, looks like a beached 1930s ocean liner, complete with portholes, deck rails, and funnels: You expect P. G. Wodehouse and Cole Porter to appear on the top deck in white flannels, martinis in hand. It was built as an "ultra-modern" public bathhouse, and the *WPA Guide* to San Francisco made the showers sound like they were designed by Jor-el of the planet Krypton: "Each person returning from the water passes through a photo-electrically operated chlorinated shower and foot bath on his way to the dressing rooms and fresh-water showers. He dries himself in currents of warm air and re-trieves his street clothes from metal containers that will be sterilized with live steam before they are reissued." (In later years, some of the clothes stashed there needed all the sterilizing steam they could get: Until it was lamentably closed in 1990, the bathhouse was the only free indoor public shower in San Francisco, and attracted its share of homeless people.)

Best of all, this postage-stamp beach is shoehorned into the heart of the waterfront, at the foot of swanky Russian Hill. Van Ness Avenue, the city's main north-south artery, dead-ends at one end of it. Hyde, the fabled ski ramp conjured up by Tony Bennett when he sings "where little cable cars climb halfway to the stars," ends at the other. The city's other beaches are destinations. But you stumble upon Aquatic Park on a stroll down Colum-bus Avenue. It is the ultimate urban amenity: a beach in the middle of town. It's like the ersatz "beaches" they create every summer along the Seine in Paris, except it's real.

Actually, whether Aquatic Park is real or fake is an unanswerable ques-tion. It's a real beach: You can wade into the bay here and swim until you drown, as banker William Ralston did in 1875 when his financial empire collapsed. But it is also artificial—although the "artifice" simply restored the shoreline to something closer to its original state. In keeping with the city's founding mania for paving over any and all bodies of water it could, the original cove at Aquatic Park, known as Black Point Cove, was filled in with debris from Chinatown after the 1906 quake. When the park was cre-ated in the 1930s, workmen clearing the cove found jewelry, watches, pieces of jade, and foreign coins. The beach was created by using tons of sand from the excavations for the underground garage at Union Square. So Aquatic Park is not only a blend of nature and artifice, it is a literal cross-section of the city.

It is also a testament to the New Deal. During the Depression, the proj-ect stalled because the city ran out of money. WPA workers—laborers, engineers, artists—stepped in and finished the job. Like another one of San Francisco's artistic gems, the superb murals at Coit Tower, Aquatic Park is a testament to enlightened government action. It is fitting that this quasi-socialist cove graces the northern waterfront of the most liberal city in America, a gratifyingly permanent stick in the eye of Fox News.

Finally, Aquatic Park is a link, through the Dolphin and South End Clubs, with San Francisco's lost world of joyous athleticism and benign machismo. Even before the Dolphin Club was founded in 1877, small swim houses dotted the cove. Carleton Watkins's 1867 photograph of four naked boys in the water captures the innocent spirit of a time when the whole city would turn out to watch a race between rival rowing clubs and when "international tug of war" was all the rage.

Aquatic Park is the private beach for every San Franciscan who lives downtown. It's mine too. I can bike there from my house in five minutes. Coming down Polk Street on a sunny day, the frozen ship with its flying pennants, the enigmatic sea behind it, always reminds me of a de Chirico painting, with the mystery but without the melancholy. It is the one place in my world that is reserved only for fun.

So many of the best times of my life have been spent on that little beach that the place and my memories of it have become inseparable, like a perfect Bill Evans chord in which the melodic and the dissonant notes merge. Celebrating Zachary's pirate-themed birthday with my family. Playing our diving-into-the-water-for-a-football game with Jonathan. Marking each one of Celeste's summer vacations—there will not be many more—with a father-daughter swim. Riding my bike along the old Belt Line tracks. Listening to the monotonous *congeros*. Wandering out to the end of the collapsing old pier and looking back at the white city. Buying a Hamm's from the grumpy old man with bad teeth who ran the long-gone hot dog stand and always opened the beer from the bottom, for reasons that were never explained. Lying in the hot sand. Sitting on the old cracked creosote-smelling boards next to the Dolphin Club, and marveling at how little is required for happiness.

CHAPTER 46

TAKING IT
TO THE
STREETS

Sacramento and Leidesdorff Streets

The city that existed when I moved here in 1971 is long gone. Many of San Francisco's working-class people have left, or moved into outlying neighborhoods like the Excelsior, the Outer Mission, or the Bayview. Its black community has been decimated. And the middle class has been battered by a combination of poor public schools, high rents, and stratospheric home prices. Ironically, the people who are most protected are the very poor, who have powerful allies defending them. As historian and open-space activist Greg Gaar told me, "San Francisco is starting to be like Paris before the revolution—only the very rich and the very poor live here."

San Francisco's inexorable move toward becoming a rich man's city began in the mid-1970s, when real estate values exploded. At least four separate tidal waves of money followed, each tsunami washing away a few more cops, teachers, artists, and plumbers. In the late 1970s and 1980s, there was an influx of young financial-industry types, who clustered in the Marina, tied sweaters around their necks, and drove Porsches. In the late 1990s, the dot-com-ers blasted inanely through, spending half of their companies' available capital on Super Bowl ads and dropping thousand-buck tips on strippers. In the first decade of the new millennium, there were the investment bankers, stockbrokers, hedge fund managers, and mortgage brokers who made a killing on the housing bubble. And today, there are the second-wave techies, who are flooding in at a rate that exceeds even that of the dot-com era. San Francisco draws more venture capital money than any other American city. A staggering 1,700 tech firms are now based here, employing a total of 44,000 workers—many of them highly paid enough to afford $3,000-a-month one-bedroom apartments or down payments on modest houses that cost $800,000.

The ramifications of this latest invasion are most obvious in the Mission and South of Market neighborhoods, favored techie turf where real estate prices have gone through the roof. But the whole city has become so expensive that people making an ordinary salary cannot move here. San Francisco is on the verge of becoming a gated community.

For close to 40 years, San Franciscans have been asking the same questions, and today they're more urgent than ever. Can the city survive all this money? Will ordinary people be able to live here? Will the city still nurture artists and mavericks and dissenters? Will it still be San Francisco?

I don't have the answers any more than anyone else does. It may be that money will finally flatten the city out, homogenize it, kill its spirit, run down its freak flag once and for all. But the city has experienced booms before and survived. And its history suggests that it would be unwise to predict anything—good, bad, or indifferent—about its future.

The most pressing issue is the increasingly exorbitant cost of housing. But even this will not completely change the nature of the city. San Francisco is becoming a city divided between those who are grandfathered in and those who are rich enough to buy their way in. Those who get shafted are the young and middle-class people who want to move here. This is deplorable, and the lack of churn and fresh blood is inevitably going to lead to cultural stagnation. Oakland, Brooklyn West, where many young artists and creative people have moved to escape San Francisco rents, is coming on fast: Its First Fridays, dazzlingly multiracial street parties, are hipper than anything happening across the bay, or probably in the country. But again, San Francisco has been expensive, albeit not quite so expensive, for decades, and the city has muddled through, still just as left-wing, if not as eccentric, as ever. The de facto urban socialism known as rent control keeps enough oddballs and nonplutocrats here to keep San Francisco from becoming Monaco. It's a Rube Goldberg–like solution, it's unfair and inequitable, but it sort of works.

San Francisco is the "limousine liberal" of cities. It's too bad it's not still the *deux chevaux* liberal of cities, but at least it's still liberal.

Still, anyone who isn't concerned about San Francisco's future is not paying attention. Some unique combination of class and politics and ethnicity and geography and history and a dozen other ingredients have gone into making it the place that it is. Some of those ingredients have changed, and some of them don't exist anymore. It's worth fighting to save what can be saved, to ensure that this city remains ornery and compassionate and out of step with the American mainstream. But nostalgia—which San Franciscans are prone to indulge in far too much—is a fool's game. And it is ultimately antithetical to the city's spirit. Born in a frenzy, destroyed in a catastrophe, the destination of renegades and dreamers, San Francisco has constantly reinvented herself. There are many prayers that one could say for her as she approaches the 250th anniversary of her founding, but the one that matters most is that she stay forever young.

On the dismal, rainy morning of January 20, 2012, I found out that she still was.

The Occupy San Francisco movement started in the fall of 2011. Inspired by Occupy Wall Street's protest in New York's Zuccotti Park, protesters set up a few dozen tents in Justin Herman Plaza, across from the Ferry Building. (If those protesters had known who the plaza was named after, they might have moved.) Like the other Occupy protests in cities across the country, the San Francisco movement was an outburst of pent-up popular anger in the wake of the great financial crisis of 2008. The protesters were outraged that predatory, unregulated financial institutions were bailed out, while average Americans lost their life savings or got kicked out of their houses. At a deeper level, the Occupy movement was driven by a sense that the fundamental American social contract—the promise that if you work hard and play by the rules, you will do all right—had broken down. The movement's slogan, "We are the 99 percent," resonated with millions of people fed up with the enormous gulf between the richest Americans and the rest of the country, and by a political and economic system that increasingly seemed to be bought and paid for by the 1 percent.

The protesters who came out to Justin Herman Plaza at the beginning were a mixture of recent college graduates, veteran lefties, homeless people, young anarchists, people down on their luck, and a few employed people. They were a motley crew, but they stayed around. The movement was essentially theatrical, but in a media age, theater is a legitimate political tool, and Occupy offered a counter-narrative to the Tea Party. The more aggressive stance on income inequality President Obama took in 2012 was made possible in part by the political cover the movement gave him.

So, Occupy San Francisco made its mark. But winter came, the authorities kicked it out of its encampment, and people drifted away. Then, on January 20, organizers were ready to launch Occupy Act II. They had called for a day of protests in San Francisco's Financial District.

At 6:20 A.M. that day, I rode my bike through the rain to the 52-story Bank of America building. The schedule on the Occupy Web site said there was supposed to be a 6 A.M. squid fry in front of Goldman Sachs—the squid theme derived from *Rolling Stone* writer Matt Taibbi's description of Goldman Sachs as a "great vampire squid wrapped around the face of humanity." But when I arrived, there were only four protesters there. One of them, wearing a bedraggled squid costume, was a 69-year-old retired psychology professor named Eleanor Levine. I asked Levine what brought her out at six in the morning.

"I'm out here to bring attention to the irresponsible financial practices of Goldman Sachs," Levine said. "I also want to bring attention to the concept of corporate personhood [which was behind the Supreme Court ruling in *Citizens United*]. Corporations are not people. This company played a role in bringing not just the country but the world to financial ruin. People have to face up to what Goldman Sachs has done. Their CEO made $28 million." Asked if the dreadful weather had prevented more people from joining the protest, she said calmly, "Yes, the rain put a damper on the turnout, but more will come." Her pink tentacles waving, she walked cheerfully off.

I approached a mustachioed man in a yellow poncho inscribed with the words "Money 4 Housing and Education, not 4 Banks and Corporations." Alex Carlson, 34, was a San Francisco paramedic who said the biggest reason he came out was to protest America's lack of educational opportunities. "I couldn't get into school just to get an EMI license. I had to beg a teacher to let me into his class. Nursing was my real goal, but there's no money for nursing schools. It's crazy because there's a nursing shortage and there's going to be a crisis of care when the baby boomers die off."

Carlson said he had come out at the crack of dawn in the rain because he felt he had to. "Like everyone else, I'm just trying to carve out a little life for myself, but my knife is getting shorter and shorter," he said. "I'm not a crazy activist person. I have a wife and a young son. Camping out isn't an option for me. But I was able to come out today, so I did. And I'm proud."

I walked down a block to a building housing Wells Fargo, where people protesting the bank's role in the national foreclosure crisis had chained themselves in front of the entrances on all four sides. A crowd was gathered on Leidesdorff Street, where the great self-taught 19th-century radical Henry George, whose passionate insistence that land was the rightful possession of all citizens inspired George Bernard Shaw, once lived. In an entranceway, about eight people were squeezed in, their arms inside big yellow PVC pipes that were connected together. A policeman came up and politely informed them that they were creating a public health risk and would be arrested if they didn't leave. Dozens of police waited on the corner.

A fresh-faced young woman with glasses was sitting among the crowd in the entrance, with a sign that said "Give us our homes back." I asked her why she was there. "My parents had their home in Southern California foreclosed," she said. She said her name was Sarah Lombardo and she was 28 years old. "They couldn't make their payments because of medical costs. My mom had breast cancer, and my dad had a stroke. They were told to leave in two weeks, and our house was auctioned off. Now they're living in an apartment, but their credit was destroyed, so they had to pay three times the normal deposit."

Lombardo said her mom was a purchasing agent, and her dad was a factory worker. "I'm the first one in my family to go to college." She said she came to the protest because she wanted "to put a face to the statistics." It was a face that looked like it belonged to the girl next door, or to your daughter.

She said that now that she had finished college, it made it possible for her to be arrested. "It's for a good cause."

I asked her if she had ever been arrested before. "No." Was she afraid? "No, I'm not scared."

Later, behind a cordon of police, I watched as protesters on the north side of the building were arrested, frisked, and loaded into a police van. I rode off on my bike to cover some more actions. When I came back, Lombardo and the rest of the group of people in the doorway had been arrested.

I walked up Sacramento. A few blocks down the street once stood Fort Gunnybags, the headquarters of the Second Vigilance Committee, whose members, inspired by a Roman ideal of civic duty, formed themselves into a citizen's army that ousted their corrupt government.

Back up at 555 California, beyond the big turd-in-a-plaza artwork jokingly called the "Banker's Heart," I came upon an older man in a suit, carrying a sign that said "Give Us Our City Back." I was intrigued: He was definitely not the usual Occupy protester. But when I asked him who he was, he turned out to be even more unusual than I could have expected. He was Warren Langley, the 69-year-old former head of the Pacific Stock Exchange.

What brought a man with his background out to protest?

"I was in the industry. I worked for an option trading firm that was sold to Goldman Sachs. So I played the game on the other side. But I have two grandkids and two daughters, and I became increasingly concerned that their future wouldn't offer them the same opportunities that I had as a young man. The income inequities in our society are a huge problem."

Langley said he first heard about the Occupy movement from his pal Ben Cohen, of Ben and Jerry's ice cream. "He was scooping ice cream for them in New York. And he told me, 'These are the real deal.' So one day I was eating lunch at the Ferry Building, and I walked across the street to the camp and started talking to these young people. And they were the real deal. They're folks who lost their jobs, or are just out of school and can't get a job. I could bring my credibility to the movement, so I decided to get involved."

Across the city that day, hundreds of protesters snarled traffic, got arrested, held sidewalk teach-ins, and generally served notice that they were mad as hell and weren't going to take it anymore. It was Occupy's last major street action, although hundreds of activists came out on September 17, 2012 to celebrate the movement's one-year anniversary. Since then, the movement has become more focused, taking aim at specific issues like home foreclosures, health care, and education. Spin-off groups like Occupy Bernal Heights and Occupy SF Housing have held marches and succeeded in saving a number of homes from foreclosure.

No one knows what the future will hold for the Occupy movement, or for progressive politics in America in general, any more than anyone can predict what will happen to San Francisco in the decades ahead. But on that miserable January day, Eleanor Levine and Sarah Lombardo and Alex Carlson and Warren Langley and the hundreds of other people who came out in the rain served notice that the dissenting city, the visionary city, the compassionate city, the city of the vigilantes and Henry George, of the antiwar fight and the green movement and the gay rights struggle, was still around.

CHAPTER 47

GENIUS LOCI

The lawn at the base of Coit Tower, Telegraph Hill

Telegraph Hill is quintessential San Francisco. If you compressed the entire city between two tectonic plates, it is the diamond that would emerge. All the beauty and mystery and romance of this white seaport at the end of the American trail are found here, reduced to their purest form. Telegraph Hill is the city's genius loci.

At a modest 284 feet, Telegraph Hill doesn't even break into the list of the 30 highest hills in town. But what makes it the San Francisco hill par excellence—old-timers simply call it "the Hill"—is its location. In a city of unexpected hills, Telegraph is the most unexpected of all. The historic, storied part of the city is its northeast corner, and Telegraph Hill is squeezed into the northeasternmost part of that corner. Its sheer eastern side rises gratuitously up a few steps away from the bay, as improbably as a sperm whale breaching in a swimming pool. On the vast canvas that is San Francisco, Telegraph Hill is the section drawn by a child, an impossibly steep isosceles triangle with a toy-castle tower atop it, right below a smiling wild-haired sun.

The same sublimely playful quality hovers over the dense, loving way the hill's terrain has been worked on. Its slopes, some of which are more like cliffs, are covered with a network of old wooden steps and blind alleys and dead-end streets more intricate than any in town. The Filbert Steps and Greenwich Street Stairs are the most celebrated, but at every turn you find yourself in some cul-de-sac, or facing an unexpected precipice, or stumbling upon a tiny park, or at the corner of two streets so steep you feel like you're on a Dr. Seuss set.

Take the intersection of Filbert and Kearny, just below the steps that go up to Coit Tower. It is one of the city's holy corners. The long view down the steps to the bottom of the hill at Filbert and Grant (memorialized with a plaque as "Poet's Corner") is suffused with as much history and melancholy as the Montmartre alleys down which the little boy runs in *The Red Balloon*, that unforgettable homage to Paris and childhood and magic. Look left down ridiculously steep and narrow Kearny, and the skyscrapers of downtown mark the cove where Esteban Richardson watched quarreling bears, wolves, and coyotes. Yet this place of magnificently condensed urbanism also faces the majestically inhuman Marin Headlands across the windblown Golden Gate. It is the classic San Francisco encounter between civilization and nature, the known and the unknown, the near and the infinitely far. And the vista is exquisitely harmonized by the facing slope of Russian Hill, which forms the far side of a U-shaped valley whose center is marked by the glorious spires of Saints Peter and Paul Church.

Like a billiard ball dropping into the corner pocket, history has always sought out Telegraph Hill. In *A Child's Christmas in Wales*, Dylan Thomas immortalized the village of his childhood as the "sea-town corner," and the lovely phrase fits Telegraph Hill perfectly. During the city's wild beginnings, when its connection to the outside world was by ship, the Hill's corner location, overlooking both the Golden Gate and the heart of the city, made it indispensable. In 1850 a semaphore, called the Marine Telegraph, was placed on the hill's summit to inform the city when ships came through the Golden Gate—hence the name Telegraph Hill. The various positions of the semaphore's arms denoted different types of vessels and were widely known by San Franciscans—a fact that resulted in one of the best one-liners ever delivered in the city. During a Gold Rush–era performance of a play called *The Hunchback*, an actor entered with outstretched arms, loudly declaiming, "What does this mean, my lord?" Before the other actor could respond, some wag in the audience shouted out, "Side-wheel steamer!," bringing down the house.

As the corner hill, overlooking both Yerba Buena cove and the bay, the Hill witnessed all the decisive events in the city's early years. It was on Loma Alta, as the Spanish called it, that the indomitable Juana Briones gathered the herb that gave the cove its name. When the Hounds ran riot in 1849, they charged up Telegraph Hill on horseback, firing at the fleeing Chileans. When the vigilantes aimed their cannon at the jail on Broadway and demanded the jailer hand over Casey and Cora, solemn crowds watched from the slopes above. Telegraph Hill has loomed over all the fabled maritime events in the city's history—the entrance of the U.S.S. *Portsmouth* at the end of the Mexican-American War, the anxiously-awaited Pacific Mail steamers during the Gold Rush, the arrival of Teddy Roosevelt's Great White Fleet, the grimly unannounced ships bearing the dead and wounded and orphaned victims of Pearl Harbor, the last ride of the ferry *Eureka*, the first of the container ships that doomed the brawny waterfront that flourished for so long at the base of the hill.

Like the bear that went over the mountain, people have always climbed Telegraph Hill just to see what they could see. Even when Yerba Buena was just a handful of drunks and adventurers, it was one of the hamlet's favored sites for Sunday picnics, pleasure outings, and strolls. Despite its panoramic views, however, it was not considered a desirable place to live. Most of the early inhabitants of the hill were working-class Irish who favored the summit and the east side, which was known as the Twilight Side. Before 1900, large numbers of Italians began settling on the west side of the hill, called the Sunny Side. The two groups sometimes clashed. One Irish gang, aptly named the Rock Rollers, used their lofty position on the hill to hurl boulders down on their opponents. Many Spanish also settled on the hill. Eventually the Italians supplanted the Irish. They have themselves largely been supplanted by the Chinese, but Telegraph Hill will always feel like an Italian *quartiere*, a slice of Umbria magically transported to the city's oldest corner.

Artists and writers have always been drawn to Telegraph Hill. Actors Edwin and Junius Booth lived there, and Bret Harte, Mark Twain, Robert Louis Stevenson, and Frank Norris frequented it. The gentle bohemian writer Charles Warren Stoddard spent his childhood on the hill, leaving an elegiac description of it in his 1902 memoir *In the Footsteps of the Padres*. Stoddard described the cottages on the eastern side of the hill as "hanging gardens" approached by "airy bridges" and inhabited by "pleasant people who seemed to have drifted there and were living their lyrical if lonely lives in semi-solitude on islands in the air."

In a prescient 1897 piece in the *Wave* titled "Among the Cliff-Dwellers: A Peculiar Mixture of Races from the Four Corners of the Earth," Frank Norris led the reader on a tour of the top of Telegraph Hill, to a community he depicted as so isolated that it had become a world apart. Its Spanish, Italian, and Native American inhabitants had begun interbreeding, developing what Norris called "a new race." "Here on this wartlike protuberance above the city's roof, a great milling is going on, and a fusing of peoples, and in a few more generations the Celt and the Italian, the Mexican and the Chinaman, the Negro and the Portuguese . . . will be fused into one type. And what a type it will be."

The Hill remained a working-class, multi-ethnic neighborhood well into the 20th century. But the opening of Telegraph Hill Boulevard in 1923 doomed the steep-sided bohemia. Visitors poured into the new Julius's Castle restaurant, car traffic increased, and—the kiss of death—modern apartment buildings began to go up, replacing the drafty old cottages that had bad plumbing and single-burner stoves. In 1936, the *New York Times* ran a piece with the subtitle "San Francisco's Historic Bohemian Quarter Succumbs to the Forces of Economics and Modernism." Telegraph Hill became one of the most sought-after neighborhoods in San Francisco—and it still is. The city's financial elite may live in Pacific Heights or Seacliff, but the cognoscenti, those who are willing to trade garages and square footage and homogenous wealth for Napier Lane and boho neighbors and the innumerable ghosts of the city's past, prefer Telegraph Hill.

As with most of San Francisco, the wealth on Telegraph Hill doesn't show itself unless you try to buy real estate. In the mornings I regularly walk up from my office-apartment to the sunny lawn in front of Coit Tower, where I sit in a lawn chair, read the paper, drink my coffee, and look out at the finest view of the Bay Bridge in the city. Besides a flock of psychedelic parrots, the regulars are old Chinese men and women doing their morning exercises, who always greet me cheerfully. None of us have any money, and it doesn't matter. We're on top of the world.

Part of my routine is to circle Coit Tower. It takes about one minute. Starting from the southwest side and heading clockwise, in that one minute you see Chinatown, Nob Hill (a superb perspective that makes it look like a vast concave amphitheater, with the great brick chimney of the Cable Car Barn halfway up), Russian Hill, the Golden Gate Bridge, Alcatraz and Angel Islands, the North Bay, the hills of Napa and Sonoma, Richmond, the Embarcadero, Berkeley, the Bay Bridge and Oakland, Mount Diablo, the South Bay, the Ferry Building, and the entire Financial District, with a piece of Mount San Bruno and Bernal Heights in the distance. It's the best 60-second walk I know.

This quintessentially San Francisco hill was created, appropriately, by an earthquake. At the end of the memorable day we spent wandering around the city, geologist Doris Sloan and I drove to the base of Telegraph Hill. Her old favorite exposure at the foot of Lombard had been blocked off, but we looked from the car at its sheer yellowish face, exposed by 19th-century quarrying. Sloan explained the way the hill was created. When the Farallon Plate collided with the North American Plate more than 100 million years ago, sediments from the North American Plate were carried into a huge trench that formed at the edge of the subduction zone by enormous underwater landslides made up of water and sediment. These primordial landslides, known as turbidity currents, were probably triggered by powerful earthquakes. Over millions of years the sediments hardened into a sandstone called graywacke. The massive, nonlayered nature of the graywacke on Telegraph Hill, she said, indicated that it was probably formed by a single enormous landslide.

The fact that Telegraph Hill was created by one gigantic underwater landslide was mind-boggling enough. But then Sloan said something that I have never forgotten. "It took millions of years to form the rock, but the event that triggered the landslide only lasted for a few minutes."

As I stared up at the sheer face, for the first time I felt like someone had shone a spotlight into the dark backward and abysm of geological time. The idea that Telegraph Hill was created not just over millions of years but in a period of time no longer than a song on *Meet the Beatles*, made geology's inconceivably vast forces and time frames comprehensible. In *The Sense of an Ending: Studies in the Theory of Fiction*, Frank Kermode distinguished between what he called *kairos* time, or crisis time, and ordinary tick-tock time. In a universe measured in tedious tick-tock eons, the frozen waterfall that is Telegraph Hill is a permanent shrine to *kairos* time, a solid-stone reminder of the violent preciousness of every second.

And *kairos* time is matched by *kairos* space on Telegraph Hill. It is one of those compressed, dwarf-star-like places whose inches are as charged as its centuries. The hill's heavenly details, its steps and dirt trails and secret gardens, offer escape from the tiresome abstraction through which we customarily move. And the hill also offers literal escape. It is up the Filbert Steps that runaway con Humphrey Bogart stumbles in the most memorable of the many films shot on Telegraph Hill, *Dark Passage.* Last winter, there was a real-life sequel. I was at Varennes Street working when I heard a helicopter hovering over the east side of the hill. I went online and discovered that a burglar, cornered by the police, had climbed over the perpendicular cliff below Julius's Castle and was clinging to a tree growing out of the face. He clung to the tree all night. When the police finally got tired and left, he climbed down and got away. Even though I knew this meant a criminal was on the loose a few blocks away, I had to raise a figurative toast to the guy. Like Bogie, like everyone who has been lucky enough to live on Telegraph Hill, he had escaped.

But the greatest escape was pulled off by a retired house painter named George Yeomans. In 1943, Yeomans was wandering around the base of the hill when he discovered a 10-by-15-foot cabin hidden behind some thick underbrush. It was surrounded by landslides and made out of scrap lumber. Yeomans moved in, putting in a woodstove and borrowing water from a nearby warehouse. His house had no address: It was described as "west of Winthrop and 120 feet south of Chestnut." He lived there until 1956, when the city finally kicked him out and ordered the owner of the lot to dismantle the cabin.

That heavenly playhouse is sadly gone, but Telegraph Hill still has secret passages into other dimensions. Late one night in the early 1970s, a starry-eyed newcomer to the city, I fell into one of them. I had been roistering in the Grant and Green bar and had stumbled up to Filbert Street to get some fresh air. I walked uphill a few steps, sat down in a little doorway, and leaned back to contemplate the night. Suddenly the door opened and I fell backward into pitch darkness, sliding headfirst down a flight of stairs. I had no idea how long I was going to fall. After seven or eight steps, I crashed into something hard. Rubbing my head, I stood up and looked around. I was in a dingy storage room filled with garbage cans. Standing there in the darkness, I began to laugh. I felt like I had just fallen down a rabbit hole into Wonderland.

I still feel that way about Telegraph Hill. Maybe it's because from the midnight stillness of Grant and Edith you can see the lights of Chinatown shimmering to the south, then turn and see distant ships moving silently across the darkened waters to the north. Or because from the top of Coit Tower you can see the Pacific. Or because Kid Rambler, my beloved green straight-six with the bungee cord on the door, appears for a split-second in Phil Kaufman's remake of *Invasion of the Body Snatchers*, just before it was towed away forever from Union Street. Or because from Calhoun Terrace you can see the 1930s. Or because I burned so many years of my life, that three-minute underwater earthquake, in the bars on upper Grant. Or because the barking of the sea lions sometimes carries up from the water. I don't really know why. But Telegraph Hill will always be my lucky spot, my enchanted hill, my secret garden—the heart and soul of my city.

CHAPTER 48

DANCING
ON THE BRINK
OF THE WORLD

The small beach 600 yards southwest of Candlestick Park,
off Harney Way, site of the vanished Crocker Mound

During my endless wanderings through San Francisco, I often found myself thinking about the first people who lived here, the Yelamu. They intrigued me for several reasons. For one thing, we were both fascinated with the same little piece of turf. Like all California Indians, the Yelamu were passionately devoted to their home territory. They knew every inch of it. The 19th-century journalist and adventurer Stephen Powers wrote that mothers of the Mattole tribe of northwestern California taught their children their tribal boundaries by reciting its features "in a kind of sing-song," repeating the names of boulders, trees, canyons, and other landmarks until the children had learned every foot of their domain. Since this was an almost exact description of my own increasingly problematic behavior since I began to work on this book—I actually once forced my daughter to learn an inane sentence whose words were reminders of street names in our neighborhood—it was clear to me that the Yelamu were either kindred spirits or escapees from the same mental hospital. Either way, I wanted to know more about them.

Then there was my abiding interest in the city's primordial landscape, the city before the city. The Yelamu had moved naked through a naked world. I thought that by learning more about them, I might be able to imagine that harsh and innocent terrain.

The native people who lived in San Francisco, the Yelamu, were members of a larger group of Indians called the Ohlone, or, as the Spanish called them, the Costanoans. The Ohlone shared many cultural practices, but they were not a tribe and were not politically or ethnically unified; "Ohlone" refers to a language family consisting of either six or eight languages. Numbering between 10,000 and 17,000 at the time of Spanish contact, the Ohlone occupied the area from the San Francisco Bay south to Big Sur and east toward the Central Valley. They lived in about 50 politically autonomous communities or tribal groups, each with from 50 to 500 people and a number of villages, some permanent, some seasonal.

In trying to imagine San Francisco during the endless years that the Ohlone lived here, the first thing you have to get your head around is how *few* of them there were. About 1,500 Ohlone lived on the peninsula, with a proportional number inhabiting the 10 percent of the peninsula occupied by San Francisco. Randall Milliken, an expert on the Yelamu and author of an authoritative study of the destruction of Bay Area Indian culture, *A Time of Little Choice: The Disintegration of Tribal Culture in the San Francisco Bay Area, 1769–1810*, estimates that San Francisco's population was between 160 and 300 people at European contact—less than the number of people who live in some of the apartment buildings down the street from my house. For thousands of years, you could walk clear across San Francisco and barely see a soul.

The Yelamu were made up of one or two dozen related families, with each family averaging 15 members. They lived in a non-hierarchical way, but that did not mean they exalted individuality. For them, as for all California

Indians, the individual was nothing, the family and the group everything. "What is a man?" a Pomo Indian once asked. "A man is nothing. Without his family he is of less importance than a bug crossing the trail, of less importance than spit or dung."

The essence of Yelamu life, like that of all California Indians, was interdependence, respect for the natural world, and a cosmic order preserved by ritual, self-purification, and moderation. The Yelamu did not practice agriculture, but they were expert hunters and knew every edible and medicinal plant that grew within the boundaries of their little world. Their practices allowed them to survive for millennia, without doing major damage to the earth.

The center of social life, for men, was the *temescal*, the sweat lodge, where they gathered to socialize and hang out. Both sexes met at village centers where stories were recited, and traditional songs sung again and again, accompanied by endless dancing—another link with the frolicsome city to come. A persistent complaint among early Spanish settlers was that the Indians' endless singing prevented them from sleeping.

A few fragments of Ohlone songs have come down to us. One seems to be a form of sympathetic magic, like the ancient cave paintings at Lascaux and Altamira: "I dream of you, / I dream of you jumping. / Rabbit, / Jackrabbit, / Quail." There is an endearingly direct line from a love song: "Come! Come! I mean you with the brown hat." And last, and most haunting, a single line that could be the city's motto: "Dancing on the brink of the world."

I wanted to find the exact locations where these spiritual, conservative, deeply resourceful people had lived. In the back of my mind lurked memories of a trip I made many years ago to the Little Bighorn Battlefield National Monument in Montana. Scattered across the old battlefield were dozens of white marker stones, on the rolling hills and down in the ravines, each one marking the place where a soldier had fallen. In 1999, several red granite stones were added, commemorating the places where Indian warriors had died. The random specificity of these stones pierced me, brought that long-gone day alive. I wanted to put similar markers in the streets of San Francisco.

The first place to start was with shell mounds—the largest and most dramatic artifacts left by the local Indians. In 1909, a U.C. Berkeley graduate student named Nels Nelson cataloged 425 of them in the Bay Area, including 18 in San Francisco. At the most rudimentary level, these enigmatic, now-vanished mounds, some of which are as old as 3,500 years, bear witness to the vast quantities of shellfish consumed by the Ohlone. But archaeologists believe they were more than garbage dumps: They were also territorial landmarks, ceremonial sites, and burial grounds. And the Ohlone lived on top of them. For reasons that are unclear, the shell mounds were gradually abandoned after 700 C.E.

Including the shell mounds, there are about 50 places in San Francisco where Indian artifacts have been discovered. Most of them are in the city's deep south—near Islais Creek, at the Hunters Point shipyard, or in Visitacion Valley, with a few in the Bayview. There is a major site by Mission Creek and one by Mission Dolores. There are a half dozen sprinkled across the northern waterfront, including three found recently in Fort Mason, and a site off Merrie Way at Point Lobos, near a 19th-century workingman's fair called the Pleasure Grounds created by San Francisco's Santa Claus, Adolph Sutro. There are a few oddball outliers, including a skeleton unearthed in 1861 at Beach and Hyde, at the bottom of Russian Hill where the Buena Vista bar now stands. Some are in the western part of the city: a couple of sites by Lake Merced and the "sparse remains of bones" found on the S.F. State campus. Near the Civic Center BART is a site where the 5,000-year-old bones of a woman were found. Finally, there are several sites on or south of Market Street, including one at Third and Harrison, one at Ecker and Stevenson, and one at Fifth and Market.

To make sense of this mess, I called up Randall Milliken. He said the Yelamu were composed of three semi-sedentary groups, all related. One group moved seasonally along Mission Creek, from a winter village called Sitlintac on the shore of the bay just south of AT&T Park, to a summer village, Chutchui, near Mission Dolores three miles inland. The second group moved between Tubsinthe, a large winter village on a cove south of Candlestick Park, and the summer village, Amuctac, in nearby Visitacion Valley. The third cluster of families lived seasonally at Petlenuc, near the beach area facing the sea and the Golden Gate.

Milliken said that the usage of these sites was casual. "There were always five or six sites," he said. "San Francisco was like a great big campsite where you just move around and pick out the one you like the best. The two big ones were on the bay, at Visitacion and at Mission Creek. Suppose you're living down at Visitacion, you've got an aunt and uncle up by the Presidio [at Petlenuc], maybe you have some bad crops two or three years in a row, so you move up there. They used the whole peninsula."

I asked Milliken if he knew where all the sites were in San Francisco. "The sites don't matter that much," he replied. "They're all buried under stuff. You should just walk around San Francisco and look for the best places, where there's water and it's warm and protected from the wind, and visualize what it looked like before 1776." For someone determined to put a plaque on the site of every long-vanished bush where some Yelamu hunter once pissed, this answer was not encouraging.

I asked Paul Scolari, the American Indian liaison for the National Park Service in San Francisco, about the sites at Crissy Field, the historic aviation field on the northern waterfront, now a glorious urban promenade. "There's one located just east of the marsh near the beach, the other buried under the Sports Basement [a big retail store]," Scolari said. Archaeological evidence indicated they were food-processing camps, he explained, but beyond that little was known about them or how they were used. "No one really knows the life patterns," he said. "This is the coldest place on the peninsula, so these were presumably summer camps, but how much they moved about on the peninsula, how long they stayed in one place, is conjectural."

The experts had basically told me to get out there and use my imagination. It was time to hit the streets.

I decided to head first to the site of the largest shell mound found in San Francisco, the so-called Crocker Mound, or CA-SFR-7, in the poetic official nomenclature. The Crocker Mound was believed to be the site of Tubsinthe, the big winter village. It was probably the most important site in San Francisco. Information about archaeological sites is semi-classified, but in an environmental impact report for the proposed development in Hunters Point, I discovered that SFR-7 is located about a third of a mile southwest of Candlestick Park, on what was once a sheltered cove and lagoon off Harney Way near the Candlestick Point State Recreation Area.

I drove down Highway 101 and parked on the edge of the huge Candlestick parking lot. Traffic noise from the freeway hummed in the distance. The big stadium, where I once saw Willie Mays make a basket catch and Jerry Rice break the all-time touchdown record, stood empty. To the north, the derelict shipyard of Hunters Point loomed up, behind the gaunt Double Rock housing projects. There were Indian sites all over the place around here—13 or 14 within a half mile.

A funky scene was going down in the parking lot. A couple of black guys smoking a joint in a parked car looked warily at me as I went past. A Latino man in a City of San Francisco car was taking a nap, the seat back and his mouth open. A group of friendly older black men were firing up an enormous barbecue on wheels, which they had pulled behind a pickup truck. They had enough ribs, burgers, and sausages flaming away on it to feed an army. It wasn't clear who they were barbecuing for. Off the rocky point beyond them, a few windsurfers were riding in hard on the wind-chopped waves.

I wandered through the little-used recreation area. Except for the wind-surfers and a woman being dragged along by a huge, wolflike dog, it was deserted. A jackrabbit came bounding through the grass and disappeared. I wandered out to the end of a fishing pier, where two Chinese men were smoking cigarettes and rummaging through an ice chest. They said they had caught a shark. Off to the west, above the placid waters of the bay, a billowing cloud hung over Mount San Bruno.

I walked toward the north. The ranger station was boarded up. The Candlestick parking lot, where my father taught me how to drive, faded into vacant-lot squalor on the north side, with odd chained-off roads leading nowhere, their asphalt cracking. A rusty sign pointed toward a defunct boat-launching ramp, near a closed public bathroom and a row of broken light poles. Beyond it, I recognized the polluted beach of Double Rock, the most obscure and waste-strewn stretch of waterfront in San Francisco, which I had stumbled on a few months earlier after climbing through a gap in a cyclone fence behind a trucking company off Armstrong. Behind it, the old World War II plants at Hunters Point drowsed. The scene looked like a Futurist painting by Mario Sironi.

I walked over to the south side of the parking lot and headed southeast. In a few minutes I came upon a forlorn little beach, filled with broken-up bricks and pieces of stone. South of that beach was a longer, narrow strip of rocky shoreline, below a walkway. The city dump, located right on the county line, was across the nearby freeway. Nels Nelson had described the site as located on "the first cove north of the San Francisco and San Mateo

County Lines." An 1862 Coast Survey map showed that the shell mound was located on a small sandy terrace that faced both the bay and a lagoon, now long gone.

There was no sign of any shell mound, but this strange little beach was where Tubsinthe had once stood.

If you closed your eyes and made the freeway and the dump and the parking lot and the Executive Park development and the ambient industrial wasteland vibe go away, you could understand why people had chosen to live here, and kept living here in basically the same way longer than almost any people have ever lived anywhere on this planet. It was warm—by San Francisco standards, anyway. It was close to an old vanished branch of Islais Creek and to the groves of oak and buckeye trees that once grew here. It was steps away from the shellfish-rich mudflats. And it fronted a part of the bay calm enough to cross to the East Bay by tule-reed boat.

This was now a forgotten backwater of San Francisco, bordering some of its most blighted and crime-ridden neighborhoods, seven miles from downtown. But when Greece was in its archaic period, and for more than 1,000 years after that, this was a swankier San Francisco address than Pacific Heights or Seacliff.

Crossing Tubsinthe off my list, I decided to explore some of the sites closer to downtown. I visited a site known as the Market Street shell midden, SFR-113, buried under the southeast corner of Market and Fifth Streets. It was discovered during archaeological testing for excavations for the San Francisco Shopping Centre. Today this intersection is in the busiest part of the city, a half block from the Powell Street cable car turnaround. But before the city existed, this was a no-man's-land of parallel, east-west running sand ridges, some as high as 80 feet. There were no known streams in the area. The bay was more than 500 yards away to the east.

No one was quite sure what the Yelamu, or their ancestors, had been doing in these high sand hills. According to the field report on this site, it was occupied during two different periods—first around 120 B.C.E., then around 120 C.E. But beyond that, the authors of the report, Allen Pastron and Michael Walsh, admitted they were stumped. The artifacts were a "vague and confusing array." They concluded that it was probably a site where foragers would return, a "low bulk" procurement site where only limited quantities of food, in particular rabbits, were found. They speculated that the Indians had been drawn to it "because it represented high ground in close proximity to the salt marshes and tidal flats that lay immediately to the east and south." In conclusion, they called it "perhaps the most poorly understood region in the entire Bay Area."

Amen to that, I thought. I certainly understood nothing. I'd walked past this corner a thousand times. It was packed with people. Shoppers hurried past with Nordstrom bags. Well-disciplined European families walked purposefully along. Streetcars rolled past. There was absolutely nothing to evoke the people who had sat for unknown reasons atop high sand hills here a thousand years ago. I placed my figurative marker, but it was a purely mechanical operation.

Over the next few weeks I checked out several other sites, but none of them brought the Yelamu alive. The changes had been too great. I went on to other things.

A few months later I was standing at dusk on the little lawn at the top of Vallejo Street on Russian Hill, drinking a margarita in a red plastic cup and looking out at downtown and the Bay Bridge. I had walked up to this magical little square of public green via a circuitous and illogical route from North Beach. It struck me that if some deity with too much time on his hands had mapped my movements, the way Paul Auster recorded one of his characters' movements through Manhattan in *City of Glass*, the way I was trying to map the Yelamu, it would have looked like a meaningless Jackson Pollock squiggle. That thought led me to ponder what the Yelamu might have been doing in those high sand dunes on Market Street, "perhaps the most poorly understood region in the entire Bay Area." I took a sip of my drink. At some point in the past few thousand years, surely someone wandered up there with the Ohlone equivalent of a margarita, plunked herself down in the warm sand, and looked out over the bay, for no reason at all.

Stymied by the things that separated us, I had forgotten the things we had in common. I had been trying too hard. I didn't need to totally inhabit their minds and souls: All I needed was to find a few mundane things we shared. And one of them was the simple pleasure of being here, in this place we both called home.

It was a small place. But we both loved it precisely because it was small. In a Maidu myth, Earthmaker told the people he had just created, "Living in a country that is little, not big, you will be content." That contentment united the Yelamu not just with me, but every city dweller who loves her neighborhood. The Yelamu had arranged their lives so they could do almost all of their business within a short walk. A leisurely five-minute stroll down to the tidal flats to pick up some mussels, a two-mile jaunt to a grove of live oak trees to gather acorns—these were their routines. My errands are different, but the distances are the same. As I walk down Filbert Street to go to the hardware store in Chinatown, or amble across Russian Hill toward Crissy Field, I am following in the footsteps of the first San Franciscans.

We shared something else: love of the natural world. For the Yelamu, San Francisco was one big campsite, Milliken had said. From backpacking in the Sierra, I knew the mundane exaltation of domesticating a grand and alien landscape. I don't carry a backpack in San Francisco, and I can turn on a tap to get water, but even in a city, the world is still the world.

Standing on that hill, I knew I would never completely understand the Yelamu, any more than they would have understood me. But our shared passion for this place, for finding the universe in this place, was a human hand reaching across the centuries.

And so as I walk through San Francisco, as I have done for most of my life and will do until I die, I walk in the company of friendly ghosts. They and their world are gone now, their campsites and villages buried beneath skyscrapers, their trees cut down, their streams covered by concrete. But they look through my eyes. We walk together through this ordinary place in the sanctified world, this 46-square-mile piece of eternity.

CHAPTER 49

LANDS END

*Unnamed rise off Lands End Trail,
a half a mile west of Eagle's Point*

This is where it begins and ends. The city has no dominion here. There is only the land and the sea and the place where they come together, a seething encounter as old as the planet. This is where San Francisco keeps its secrets. This is the wild corner.

The Lands End trail starts off El Camino del Mar and 33rd Avenue and ends near the ruins of the old Sutro Baths. It takes about an hour to make the round-trip. Outside of a stroll through a Rio favela, it is the most spectacular walk in any city in the world.

The walk begins at the Eagle's Point lookout. The majestic span of the Golden Gate Bridge appears to the east, the gentle curve of Baker Beach ending at the jagged serpentinite rocks that protect the hidden pocket beaches near Fort Point. Once a happy hunting ground for gay men, that stretch of coast has been opened by a new system of trails and stairs, but it's still obscure. Once, on a rocky promontory jutting out from a cliff above one of those beaches, I found a big green seagull's egg in a little declivity. As I stood there looking at it, a seagull suddenly dropped out of the sky like a Stuka dive-bomber and buzzed me. I started to walk away, but the gull kept circling until I was out of sight.

On the near side of Baker Beach, as you look down from the trail, is little China Beach. There's another little rocky shore west of China, almost directly below you, but you can't get to it. The cliffs are too high and too sheer. In fact, you can't climb down anywhere until you come to Mile Rock Beach, another mile up the trail. The only way to get to the foot of these cliffs is by water. There is a little rocky spire between China Beach and the nameless shore on the near side of it. From a perch near Eagle's Point I once saw a surfer paddle through that gap, becoming for that moment the sole possessor of the key to a beautiful door.

The trail runs below the Lincoln Park golf course and then the V.A. Hospital. It is verdant and overgrown and smells of eucalyptus and nameless aromatic bushes. Little springs create muddy pools. It climbs up and down, through gentle sandy patches, then steeper sections where stairs have been cut into the rock. Endless azure vistas appear around each corner. It feels like coastal California, but also like the Mediterranean. You could be on the Via d'Amore in the Cinque Terre or a corniche road in Positano or walking up to the Chora in Folegandros. You could be on any majestic cliff-side trail over any ocean in the world. But you are in San Francisco, a 20-minute drive from downtown.

To the north, the great expanse of Pacific stretches, the reddish Marin Headlands towering on the far side. Up the coast you can see Stinson and Bolinas and, on a clear day, Point Reyes, where Sir Francis Drake and Sebastián Cermeño made their uncanny California appearances during the age of Shakespeare. As you pass Mile Rock Beach, if the tide is low you can see the rusty remains of shipwrecks. Dozens of ships have been lost here, lost in the fog or gone off course, their hulls ripped open by the jagged rocks. Once mighty, they have suffered a sea-change into oxidized shadows. A peculiar white patch on the side of the cliff next to the trail is a link with the days when navigation was a matter of life and death. Ship captains used that mark to align themselves properly in the center of the channel that goes through the Golden Gate strait.

The trail levels out as it approaches the end. Intricate mazes of trees adjoin the ocean side of the trail, offering little tangled bowers from which to observe the currents that drift across the waters. Up above stands the shell-riddled bridge of the U.S.S. *San Francisco*. The trail turns south and civilization comes into view: The Cliff House, where Mark Twain once went on a frozen early-morning excursion, and the Seal Rock Inn, where a distant disciple of Twain's named Hunter S. Thompson holed up to write *Fear and Loathing on the Campaign Trail '72*. Out on the horizon line you can see the Farallones, those dragon's teeth that kept mariners from discovering San Francisco Bay for hundreds of years.

There is only one significant place in San Francisco where I have never set foot: the rocky shoreline at the base of the cliffs at Lands End. For years, that unknown shoreline has called to me. It was the ultimate San Francisco mystery. What was down there? Would I find a secret beach at low tide? Were there caves? Loot from a forgotten shipwreck? The mysteriously preserved oar from Ayala's lost *cayuco*? An ongoing secret rave, accessible via a tunnel bored through the cliffs that emerged in a hole in someone's backyard at 46th and Clement?

Every time I walked on Lands End, I eyeballed the cliff. It was nasty—300 feet high and steep. But trees and bushes were growing out of its side, and I remembered what one of the Norwegian commandos who climbed up a vertical ravine to blow up Hitler's heavy water plant had said: "Where trees grow, a man can make his way."

I wanted to, but for one reason or another—not being a Norwegian commando foremost among them—I never climbed down. I still plan to make it down there someday. But if I don't, maybe it's just as well.

I fell in love with San Francisco when I was a kid growing up in the Berkeley Hills and looked across the bay to what I thought was the most miraculous city in the world, a shining Valhalla at the end of a rainbow bridge. The years have gone by, but I still find her as magnificent as ever—a soaring sand castle built where the tide comes in, a thousand white pennants waving from cathedral spires, the last place to have a drink before America stops and the endless ocean begins.

"The last time I saw Paris, her heart was warm and gay, / No matter how they change her, I'll remember her that way." Oscar Hammerstein wrote those lyrics to the song he wrote with Jerome Kern in 1940, when Paris had fallen to the Germans. The song became a hit because it reflected the universal human desire to preserve the places we love, to keep them sacred, even if only in memory. Paris might be crushed beneath the Nazi boot, but Paris would live on forever. Ernest Hemingway said the same thing when he called Paris "a moveable feast." It was a place you could take with you.

The place in the world I love most happens to be San Francisco. It could have been somewhere else, but it isn't. And the San Francisco that I keep in my heart, the San Francisco that I will take with me even if I never see her again, is the city that is a window open to the world. The city that is as inseparable from her magnificent setting as the lyrics of a song are from its music. The city that rises from the sea as gracefully as Botticelli's Venus. The city composed of an infinite number of accidental perfect arrangements with the earth and the sea and the sky. The city whose beauty, like Cleopatra's, is endless:

> *Age cannot wither her, nor custom stale*
> *Her infinite variety; other women cloy*
> *The appetites they feed, but she makes hungry*
> *Where most she satisfies . . .*

I have spent much of my life exploring San Francisco. But perhaps it is better not to see everything. To let a small mystery stand in for the great one. To know that somewhere far below, down there where the sea crashes endlessly into the land, is a rock that I will never climb.

ACKNOWLEDGMENTS

I would like to thank the following people for their help: Caroline Bins, Peter Brastow, Joan Chase, John Dell'Osso, Greg Gaar, Dylan Hayes, Sarah He, Karen Johnson, James Lockett, Randall Milliken, Carmen Mohr, Paul Scolari, Sandra Silvestri, Kirra Swenerton, Buck Tergis, Yoshio Takakuwa, and Cindy Wu.

Special thanks to Doris Sloan and Peter Field, who were extraordinarily generous with their time, expertise, and passion. Sloan is responsible for what little I know about geology, and Field for virtually everything printable I know about the Tenderloin.

The staff at the San Francisco History Center of the San Francisco Public Library were very helpful in tracking down obscure clippings and documents.

I also wish to thank the Lannan Foundation, which generously awarded me a monthlong residency in Marfa, Texas, while I was doing research for this book.

Thanks also to Jon Adams for his graceful and apt illustrations.

Thanks to my agent and friend Ellen Levine, an old-school agent who cares as much about the words on the page as she does about the zeros in the contract.

And finally, thanks to Kathy Belden and Rachel Mannheimer at Bloomsbury. I couldn't have asked for better editors.

Of the general histories of San Francisco, Oscar Lewis's *San Francisco: Mission to Metropolis*, the longtime standard, is still useful. Rand Richards's well-researched *Historic San Francisco: A Concise History and Guide* provides a helpful reference to specific historic sites. Of the many oversize illustrated histories of the city, T. H. Watkins and Roger R. Olmsted's elegantly written *Mirror of the Dream: An Illustrated History of San Francisco* stands out, as does James Beach Alexander and James Lee Heig's sumptuous *San Francisco: Building the Dream City.*

For the Spanish period, Simon Barton's *A History of Spain* and William Maltby's *The Rise and Fall of the Spanish Empire* provide solid background. C. H. Haring's *The Spanish Empire in America* and Charles Edward Chapman's *A History of California: The Spanish Period* remain informative. Harry Kelsey's *Juan Rodríguez Cabrillo* is eye-opening, while William Schurz's *The Manila Galleon* offers a fascinating look at that legendary trade route. Kirkpatrick Sales's *The Conquest of Paradise* is a polemical but powerful analysis of the Spanish colonial enterprise. *Lands of Promise and Despair: Chronicles of Early California, 1535–1846,* is a first-rate anthology of primary sources about early California, as is Peter Browning's *San Francisco/Yerba Buena: From the Beginning to the Gold Rush.* For early explorers, see Henry R. Wagner's *Spanish Voyages to the Northwest Coast of America in the 16th Century,* Theodore Treutlin's *San Francisco Bay: Discovery and Colonization,* Alan K. Brown's authoritative edition of Pedro Font's *With Anza to California, 1775–1776,* and the venerable volumes on Anza's explorations by Herbert Bolton (who wins the Shoe Leather Award for retracing every step of Anza's 10,000-mile explorations).

For the frontier period, Douglas Monroy's unsparing *Fallen Among Strangers: Making of Mexican Culture* is superb. *Contested Eden: California Before the Gold Rush,* published by the California Historical Society, is a strong collection of essays. Leonard Pitt's classic *The Decline of the Californios: A*

Social History of the Spanish-Speaking Californias, 1846–1890, is invaluable. *Juana Briones of 19th-Century California* by Jeanne Farr McDonnell sheds fascinating light on the enigmatic, inspiring "mother of San Francisco." *The Father of All: The de la Guerra Family, Power, and Patriarchy in Mexican California* by Louise Pubols is an excellent analysis of the Californios, especially during the secularizing period. Richard Henry Dana's *Two Years Before the Mast* is a literary masterpiece that evokes the hide-and-tallow days. Several works explore the history of the Presidio, including John Langelier and Daniel Rosen's *El Presidio de San Francisco: Spain and Mexico, 1776–1846*, and Barbara Voss's *The Archaeology of Ethnogenesis: Race and Sexuality in Colonial San Francisco*.

The charmed Yerba Buena years inspired a rich literature, including John Henry Brown's *Reminiscences and Incidents of the "Early Days" of San Francisco*, William Heath Davis's *Sixty Years in California*, and Joseph T. Downey's *Filings from an Old Saw: Reminiscences of San Francisco*. Important secondary material includes *Captain Richardson: Mariner, Ranchero, and Founder of San Francisco* by Robert Ryal Miller, the sentimental but informative *Spanish Arcadia* by Nellie Van de Grift Sanchez, and Zoeth Eldredge's musty and dusty but important two-volume *Beginnings of San Francisco: From the Expedition of Anza, 1774, to the City Charter of April 15, 1850*. *San Francisco Memoirs: 1835–1851*, edited by Malcolm Barker, is an excellent anthology of early writings about Yerba Buena/San Francisco, as is Oscar Lewis's *Sketches of Early California: A Collection of Personal Adventures*. Nor should one ignore the delightful little essay by Douglas S. Watson, bearing the wonderful title "An Hour's Walk Through Yerba Buena: The town That Existed for Eleven Years, Seven Months and Five Days, Then Became San Francisco."

The event that gave birth to San Francisco, the Gold Rush, also inspired perhaps the best single book ever written about the city, *The Annals of San Francisco* by Frank Soule, John H. Gihon, and James Nisbet. Other important contemporary works include Bayard Taylor's clear-eyed *El Dorado: Adventures in the Path of Empire*, Louise Clappe's classic *The Shirley Letters*, Frank Marryat's witty *Mountains and Molehills: Or, Recollections of a Burnt Journal*, and T. A. Barry and B. A. Patten's *Men and Memories of San Francisco: In the "Spring of '50."* First-rate modern histories include Rand Richards's *Mud, Blood, and Gold: San Francisco in 1849* and Charles Fracchia's *When the Water*

Came Up to Montgomery Street. The classic about the Gold Rush itself is J. S. Halliday's *The World Rushed In: The California Gold Rush Experience.* Ken Burns's PBS TV series *The West,* an excellent overall introduction to the saga of the American frontier, is strong on the Gold Rush.

Roger Lotchin's *San Francisco, 1846–1856: From Hamlet to City* is a brilliant analysis of the city's formative decade and one of the best books ever written about the city. *San Francisco 1865–1932: Politics, Power and Urban Development* by William Issel and Robert W. Cherny is another major study. Doris Muscatine's *Old San Francisco: The Biography of a City from Early Days to the Earthquake* is a detailed account of the city before the quake. Gray Brechin's *Imperial San Francisco: Urban Power, Earthly Ruin* provides a mordant interpretation of the city's mining origins. Mary Floyd Williams's *History of the San Francisco Committee of Vigilance of 1851* is an authoritative and sympathetic account of the first vigilance movement by a pioneering female scholar; later revisionist views include *Strain of Violence: Historical Studies of American Violence and Vigilantism* by Richard Maxwell Brown and Robert Senkewicz's *Vigilantes in Gold Rush San Francisco.* Philip J. Ethington's *The Public City: The Political Construction of Urban Life in San Francisco* is an important academic study that offers a trenchant defense of the Vigilance Committees as a manifestation of small-*r* republicanism. B. E. Lloyd's eccentric *Lights and Shades in San Francisco* offers a wide-ranging look at the city in the 1870s (its chapters on Chinatown are particularly interesting).

Good books on the Gilded Age include Oscar Lewis and Carroll D. Hall's *Bonanza Inn: American's First Luxury Hotel,* Lewis's *The Big Four: The Story of Huntington, Stanford, Hopkins, and Crocker, and the Building of the Central Pacific,* and Robert Rayner's *The Associates: Four Capitalists Who Created California.*

On the 1906 earthquake and fire, several books stand out: Dennis Smith's riveting *San Francisco Is Burning: The Untold Story of the 1906 Earthquake,* Gladys Hansen's groundbreaking *Denial of Disaster: The Untold Story and Photographs of the San Francisco Earthquake,* William Bronson's *The Earth Shook, the Sky Burned,* and Philip Fradkin's *The Great Earthquake and Firestorms of 1906: How San Francisco Nearly Destroyed Itself.* Simon Winchester's *A Crack in the Edge of the World: America and the Great California Earthquake of 1906* is good on the geology. The official *Report of the State Earthquake Investigation Commission,* by Andrew Lawson, has fascinatingly detailed accounts of damage throughout the city. The *1906 San Francisco Earthquake Centennial Field Guides*, edited by Carol S. Prentice, provides walking tours of Shipley and other sunken streets.

San Francisco in the 1930s is well described in Nancy Olmsted's *The Ferry Building*, as well as in the sparkling *San Francisco in the 1930s: The WPA Guide to the City by the Bay*. Kevin Starr's *Endangered Dreams: The Great Depression in California* is a solid history of the state during the Depression era.

The 1940s and 1950s are splendidly evoked by Mr. San Francisco, Herb Caen, in classics like *Baghdad by the Bay* and *Don't Call It Frisco*. *The World of Herb Caen: San Francisco, 1938–1997*, edited by Barnaby Conrad, offers a good selection of Caen's eclectic writings. The World War II era is explored in Roger Lotchin's *The Bad City in the Good War: San Francisco, Los Angeles, Oakland, and San Diego*, as well as a collection he edited, *The Way We Really Were: The Golden State in the Second World War*.

The hippie phenomenon is intelligently chronicled in Charles Perry's *The Haight Ashbury: A History*. Josh Sides's *Erotic City: Sexual Revolutions and the Making of Modern San Francisco* provides a solid overview of the city's gay history. The classic book about the AIDS crisis remains Randy Shilts's *And the Band Played On*, while David Weissman's film *We Were Here* is an extraordinarily powerful documentary. *Reclaiming San Francisco: History, Politics, Culture*, edited by James Brook, Chris Carlsson, and Nancy J. Peters, is a stimulating collection of essays with a progressive political slant. David Talbot's *Season of the Witch: Enchantment, Terror, and Deliverance in the City of Love*, one of the best recent books about San Francisco, offers a vivid, deeply reported history of the city's turbulent passage through the hippie era, the Jonestown massacre, the Moscone-Milk assassinations, and the AIDS crisis.

On natural San Francisco, E. Breck Parkman's "The California Serengeti: Two Hypotheses Regarding the Pleistocene Paleoecology of the San Francisco Bay Area" offers a vivid look at the age of megafauna. Harold Gilliam's *The Natural World of San Francisco* and *The Weather of the San Francisco Bay Region* are models of lyrical and informed prose. The transformation of the city's natural landscape is well described in Greg Gaar and Ryder W. Miller's *San Francisco: A Natural History*. Nancy Olmstead's *Vanished Waters* is a fine history of Mission Bay. *Geology of the San Francisco Bay*

Region by Doris Sloan and *Natural History of San Francisco Bay* by Ariel Rubissow Okamoto and Kathleen M. Wong offer first-rate introductions to their subjects. John McPhee's classic *Assembling California* is a deeper account of plate tectonics. *San Francisco Bay: Portrait of an Estuary* by John Hart, with photos by David Sanger, and *Bay Area Wild* by Galen Rowell with Michael Sewell feature beautiful photographs and stimulating texts. Laura Cunningham's *A State of Change: Forgotten Landscapes of California* offers evocative re-creations of vanished landscapes by a talented artist and researcher. The eclectic 1951 *Geologic Guidebook of the Bay Area Counties* is dated but irresistible. Clyde Wahrhaftig's *A Streetcar to Subduction* will subduct even the most rock-averse reader, as will Peter White's fascinating *The Farallon Islands: Sentinels of the Golden Gate*.

On the California Indians, the standard works are the *Handbook of North American Indians*, volume 8, edited by Robert Heizer, and *Handbook of the Indians of California* by Alfred Kroeber. *The Ohlone: Past and Present Native Americans of the San Francisco Bay Region*, edited by Lowell Bean, is a useful and wide-ranging anthology. Malcolm Margolin's classic *The Ohlone Way: Indian Life in the San Francisco–Monterey Bay Area* is a lovely and informed imagining of their culture. The most authoritative study of the Yelamu after European contact is *A Time of Little Choice: The Disintegration of Tribal Culture in the San Francisco Bay Area, 1769–1810*, by Randall Milliken. Also very useful is the National Park Service publication *Ohlone/Costanoan Indians of the San Francisco Peninsula and Their Neighbors, Yesterday and Today*, by Randall Milliken, Laurence H. Shoup, and Beverly R. Ortiz. The dreadful story of white California's destruction of the state's native peoples is well told in James J. Rawls's *Indians of California: The Changing Image*. Brian Fagan's *Before California: An Archaeologist Looks at Our Earliest Inhabitants* is a lively account of the archaeological record of the state's first people. Theodora Kroeber and Robert F. Heizer's *Almost Ancestors: The First Californians* combines a moving text with superb photographs of native people. Finally, Kroeber's *Ishi in Two Worlds* is a book one never forgets.

For the intellectual and cultural history of California until World War I, see Kevin Starr's magisterial *Americans and the California Dream, 1850–1915*, the first and finest volume in his indispensable multivolume history of the state. Starr's brief *California: A History* provides a good introduction to the Golden State. Josiah Royce's 1886 classic, *California: A Study of American Character*, offers a penetrating moral analysis of the Gold Rush and the vigilante movement. *California Heritage*, edited by John and Laree Caughey, is a first-rate anthology of primary sources.

The standard book about San Francisco's early literary scene is *San Francisco's Literary Frontier* by Franklin Walker. The city's riotous journalistic tradition is entertainingly recounted by John Bruce in *Gaudy Century, 1848–1948: San Francisco's 100 Years of Robust Journalism*. Mark Twain's San Francisco journalism is collected in *Clemens of the "Call": Mark Twain in San Francisco*, edited by Edgar Branch, and *Mark Twain's San Francisco*, edited by Bernard Taper. Oscar Lewis's *Bay Window Bohemia* covers the gaslit fin de siècle era. Lawrence Ferlinghetti and Nancy J. Peters provide a fine illustrated look at the literary scene through the 1970s in *Literary San Francisco: A Pictorial History from Its Beginnings to the Present Day*. The Beats are well covered in Steven Watson's *The Birth of the Beat Generation: Visionaries, Rebels, and Hipsters, 1944–1960*, and James Campbell's *This Is the Beat Generation: New York, San Francisco, Paris*. Don Herron's *The Literary World of San Francisco and Its Environs* is an outstanding guidebook.

On the city's sinful side, Herbert Asbury's *The Barbary Coast: An Informal History of the San Francisco Underworld* is riotously entertaining, if not entirely reliable. Curt Gentry's *The Madams of San Francisco* is a great read.

Philip Choy's *San Francisco Chinatown: A Guide to Its History and Architecture* provides a good short history of its subject; his *The Architecture of San Francisco Chinatown* is fascinating. Erica Y. Z. Pan's *The Impact of the 1906 Earthquake on San Francisco's Chinatown* is also informative. Bonnie Tsui's *American Chinatown: A People's History of Five Neighborhoods* is an affectionate reported look at five contemporary Chinatowns. *Genthe's Photographs of San Francisco's Old Chinatown* is one of the great photo essays ever taken of a neighborhood.

The standard work on the history of African Americans in San Francisco is Albert Broussard's admirably nuanced *Black San Francisco: The Struggle for Racial Equality in the West, 1900–1954*. The rollicking history of the Fillmore in its heyday is told in *Harlem of the West: The San Francisco Fillmore Jazz Era* by Elizabeth Pepin and Lewis Watts. On Japantown, a city planning document, *San Francisco Japantown: Historic Context Statement*, by Donna Graves and Page and Trumbull, Inc. is informative, as is Suzie Kobuchi Okazaki's *Nihonmachi: A Story of San Francisco's Japantown*. Reid Yoshio Yokoyama's undergraduate honors thesis, *Return, Rebuild and Redevelop: Japanese American Resettlement in San Francisco 1945–1958* explores that still-murky subject. Reginald Kearney's *African-American Views of the Japanese: Solidarity or Sedition?* is also interesting. An excellent short account of the Western Addition debacle is provided by Jordan Klein in his M.A. thesis, *A Community Lost*. That tragedy is also the subject of Peter Stein's fine PBS documentary *The Fillmore*. James Baldwin's documentary *Take This Hammer* remains powerful.

On architecture, Michael Corbett's excellent *Splendid Survivors: San Francisco's Downtown Architectural Heritage*, an important text in the nascent protectionist movement, assigns grades to every significant downtown building in an attempt to save them. *Here Today: San Francisco's Architectural Heritage*, by Roger R. Olmsted and T. H. Watkins, is a similarly engaged and informed book. Daniel Burnham's original *Report on a Plan for San Francisco* offers a fascinating look at the architect's utopian plan for the city. Kevin Starr's *Golden Gate: The Life and Times of America's Greatest Bridge* is an elegant short history of one of the world's most beautiful structures. *San Francisco Architecture: An Illustrated Guide to Over 1,000 of the Best Buildings, Parks, and Public Artworks in the Bay Area*, by Sally Byrne Woodbridge, John Marshall Woodbridge, and Chuck Byrne, is a comprehensive guide to important Bay Area buildings. In a more sociological vein, Paul Groth's *Living Downtown: The History of Residential Hotels in the United States* offers the definitive history of SROs in America.

For specific neighborhoods, Arcadia's photo-rich Images of America series is very useful. *San Francisco's Telegraph Hill* by David Myrick and William Kostura's *Russian Hill: The Summit 1853–1906* are fascinating histories of those fabled hills.

Of the many love letters to and sui generis books about San Francisco, some of the more noteworthy include: Harold Gilliam's *The Face of San Francisco*, a memorably glowing portrait with superb photographs by Phil Palmer; Herb Caen's *San Francisco: City on Golden Hills*, with charming illustrations by Dong Kingman; and *Infinite City: A San Francisco Atlas*, edited by Rebecca Solnit, a marvelously idiosyncratic look at the city from a wild range of perspectives.

INDEX

NOTE: Page numbers in *italics* indicate a sketch.

A NOTE ON THE AUTHOR

Gary Kamiya was born in Oakland, California, in 1953 and grew up in Berkeley. After dropping out of Yale and working at a shipyard at Newport News, Virginia, he drove a taxi for seven years in San Francisco while getting a B.A. and an M.A. in English at the University of California, Berkeley. After cofounding a short-lived city magazine called *Frisko*, he got his first real job at the age of 37 as an editor of the *San Francisco Examiner*'s Sunday magazine. After five years at the *Examiner*, where he was a culture critic and book editor, he left to cofound Salon.com, where he was executive editor for 12 years and then a columnist. His first book, *Shadow Knights: The Secret War Against Hitler*, was a critically acclaimed history of Britain's top-secret Special Operations Executive. He is married to the novelist Kate Moses. They have two children.